D1558822

BROOK TROUT

Also by Nick Karas

The Crow Shooter's Handbook
Score Better at Trap
Score Better at Skeet
America's Favorite Saltwater Fishing
The Guide to Fishing New York's Salt Water
The Striped Bass
Brook Trout

BROOK TROUT

Nick Karas

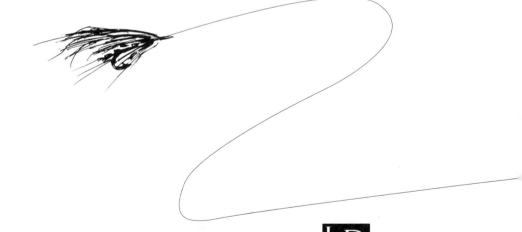

THE LYONS PRESS

This book is dedicated

"to the return of the native."

Copyright © 1997 by Nick Karas
All illustrations © 1997 by Nick Karas unless otherwise noted

Printed in the United States of America

10   9   8   7   6   5   4   3   2

Designed by Holly A. Block/*Fleuron & Associates*
Chapter-heading illustrations by Ed Sutton

Library of Congress Cataloging-in-Publication Data

Karas, Nick.
    Brook trout / Nick Karas.
        p. cm.
    Includes bibliographical references and index.
    ISBN 1-55821-479-8 (cloth)
    1. Brook trout.   2. Brook trout fishing.   I. Title.
SH689.3.K37   1997
597.5′54—dc21   96–51839
                                         CIP

CONTENTS

PART IV THE CURRENT STATE OF BROOK TROUT

APPENDICES

PREFACE

According to Indian legend, brook trout were not always the speckled beauties we know today. "Once long, long ago," said old Jesse Logan, of the Cornplanter Reservation in Warren County, Pennsylvania, the last (in 1928) of the Shikellemus tribe, "when Manitou visited the land of the Iroquois to lead His lost children back to the Happy Hunting Ground in the Far East, He grew weak with hunger and cold on his long quest. Toward night He stopped beside a pool in the Seneca country [New York] which was overshadowed by colossal white pines and hemlocks. Noticing that it was full of handsome trout, as black as ebony, He reached in His hand and easily caught the largest of the superb fish. Looking at it He was struck by its beauty and agile grace, and decided to control His hunger and let it live, so He dropped it back into the deep pool.

"The trout went its way, but instantly its sides took on a silvery hue where the fingers of the Great Spirit had held it, and all of its kind became marked with the same silvery sheen and many colored spots and halos, as a token of their having been handled by the kindly Manitou. For that reason, the Seneca Indians and others of the Six Nations would not eat brook trout. Brook trout were sacred to the highest instincts of their race. But what the redmen spared," said Logan, "white men destroyed by the millions."

So why write a book about such a dastardly deed?

Because the story of brook trout and of our own relations with this unique fish has never been fully documented and evaluated, laid bare for all to see. Perhaps in so doing we can help reverse the fish's decline. At the least we can learn to avoid making the same mistakes again.

I've tried to recount the indescribable fascination these fish create in anyone who has been exposed to them. This is especially true if the exposure occurs when one is young, because the fascination is intensified and carried throughout life. To a small but dedicated cadre of anglers, in both the United States and Canada, there's still only one trout: the native, the brook or speckled trout.

Most Americans find brook trout of less interest, however, especially when they're in the same pool with browns and rainbows, which grow larger, fight more savagely, jump more often, and are far more tolerant of today's higher water temperatures and pollution. One Minnesota biologist, who has a high esteem for brown trout, nevertheless described them as little better than "cold-water carp, because they have usurped brook trout in waters that have lost their pristine qualities."

Our typical domestic trout waters are no longer the realm of the true, wild brook trout of our forefathers. Most brook trout we encounter today are domesticated, the products of fish culturists whose goal was to provide as many brook trout as possible, as large as possible, in as short a time as possible, and with the least possible investment.

Small populations of wild or heritage brook trout still exist today in some states, but the fish are often stunted because of overcrowding and forced to eke out a living in less fertile habitats, often higher in elevation, in the dendritic beginnings of watersheds where they've been driven by the introduction of exotic trout, browns and rainbows.

Idyllic brook trout habitats still exist, but one must travel to fish them—the northern tiers of Manitoba, Ontario, Québec, and most of Labrador; the primordial-like waters of southern Argentina and Chile. All are worth the effort, and that's what part of this book is about.

Nick Karas
St. James, New York
Summer 1996

ACKNOWLEDGMENTS

Nancy Adams, Nova Scotia Dept. of Nat. Res.; Gaylord Alexander, Michigan Dept. of Nat. Res.; Lorne Allard; Ed Avery, Wisconsin Dept. of Nat. Res.; Gary Beisser, Georgia Dept. of Nat. Res.; Forrest Bonney, Maine Fisheries & Wildlife; James Borawa, North Carolina Wildlife Com.; Jim and Judith Bowman; Craig Burley, Washington Dept. of Wildlife; L. W. Coady, Fisheries and Oceans Canada; Lorraine and Jack Cooper, Minipi Camps; Kathy Crotty, Destination Labrador; Glenn Davis, Utah Div. of Wildlife Res.; Scott Decker, New Hampshire Fish and Game Dept.; Rene Demers; Thurston Doyston, Montana Fish and Wildlife; Donald Dufford, Illinois Dept. of Con.; Ray DuPuis; John Durbin, Saskatchewan Environ. and Res. Management; Mark Ebbers, Minnesota Dept. of Nat. Res.; Gord Ellis; Howard Eskin; Timothy Farley, Calif. Inland Fisheries Div.; Russell Fieldhouse, N.Y.S. Dept. of Environ. Con.

Siegfried Gagnon, Québec Ministry of Fishing and Hunting; Don Gapen Sr.; William Geddings, South Carolina Wildlife Res. Dept.; Alan Godfrey, Prince Edward Island Dept. of Environ.; Mary Grosso and Mary Schubert, Brookhaven (N.Y.) Free Library; John Hammar, Swedish Institute of Freshwater Research; Judy Hammond, Ont. Ministry of Culture, Tourism and Recreation; Robert Hanten, South Dakota Game and Fish; Michael Hatch, New Mexico Fish & Game; Rachel Hill, Ont. Ministry of Nat. Res.; William Hooper, New Brunswick Fish and Wildlife; Phil Hulbert, N.Y.S. Dept. of Environ. Con.; Jack G. Imhof, Aquatic Biologist, Ontario Ministry of Nat. Res.; Mark Jones, Colorado Div. of Wildlife; Walter Keller, N.Y.S. Dept. of Environ. Con.; David Kerkhof, Suffolk County (N.Y.) Historical Assoc.; Richard Kirn, Vermont Fish & Wildlife Dept.; Kaarlo Kjellman, Osprey Fishing Charters; Charles Krueger, Cornell Univ., Dept. of Nat. Res.; Vince LaConte, Ohio Dept. of Nat. Res.; Michel LeBlanc, Québec Ministry of Hunting and Fishing; Michel Legault, Québec Ministry of Hunting and Fishing.

Stephen E. Moore, Great Smoky Mountains National Park; Peter B. Mayle, Univ. of Calif., Davis; Peter Rafle Jr., Trout Unlimited; Pat Ryan, Fisheries and Oceans Canada; Yves Ste-Marie; Clark Shackleford, Idaho Fish & Game; Peter Simmons, Mus. of the City of New York; C. Lavett Smith, Curator Emeritus, Am. Mus. of Nat. History; Marguerite Smith, Connecticut Dept. of Environ. Protection; Robert Soldwedel, New Jersey Fish, Game and Wildlife; Joe Stefanski; Ed Sutton; Rob Swainson, Ont. Ministry of Nat. Res.; Ed Van Put, N.Y.S. Dept. of Environ. Con.; Joe White, Wyoming Game and Fish Dept.; Ed Woltmann, N.Y.S. Dept. of Environ. Con.; Gaige Wunder, Iowa Dept. of Nat. Res.

Why the Fascination
with Brook Trout?

"Catching a Trout," the famous Courier print drawn by William Tate in 1853 depicting the feat. Webster is alleged to have caught a 14½-pound

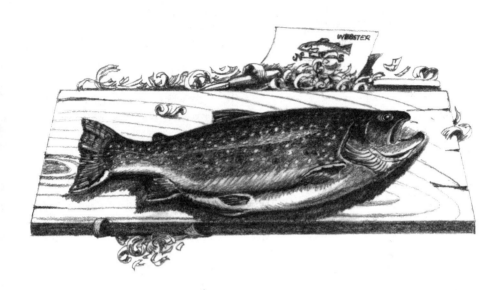

1 DANIEL WEBSTER AND HIS "DEVIL TROUT"

The village of Brookhaven, New York, is a quiet, reserved village tucked among small harbors, tidal creeks, and salt marshes on Long Island's South Shore. Its many old houses are hidden beneath remnants of majestic elms and copper beeches. It's much like many other small communities on Paumonok except for one of its Presbyterian churches, built in 1745. Age alone can often be enough to make a church noteworthy but this one has a special claim to celebrity. Over a century and a half ago its congregation witnessed Daniel Webster catch the world's largest brook trout just a long cast from its minister's pulpit.

All that remains today of this historic event are some obscure records and a diary; a "picture drawn of the fish shortly after it was caught" that must be languishing, long forgotten, in some Long Island attic; a weather vane carved on a cherry plank in the outline of the trout; a brass nameplate inscribed SUFFOLK CLUB tacked on a pew in the little church; and a Currier print that depicts Webster catching the trout. Its caption reads, "We hab you now, Sar!"

Webster, like others born in the mountains of New Hampshire in the late 1700s, fished for trout in his boyhood days. But with Webster, that infatuation intensified and continued throughout his life. He was a modern paladin whose card could have read: "Have rod, will travel." There were no noteworthy brook trout streams on Long Island to which he hadn't been invited. As early as 1820, the senator, now from Massachusetts, began visiting the famous Long Island trout streams. He was a regular patron of Sam Carman's tavern, gristmill, and general store at "the crossing-over place" at Fireplace Mills, later renamed South Haven. In Carman's custody, "Black Dan"—as many in Congress called him, because he always wore black—was able to slake his two greatest thirsts, trout and rum, often at the same time.

Come Sunday morning, however, in the acutely religious America of their time, both men could always be found across the road in the little white Presbyterian church, in a pew reserved for this unique fishing fraternity. Years later, after Webster's death, the anglers formed the Suffolk Club. They built a Federal clubhouse a few hundred yards north of Carman's house, on the edge of the pond created by the milldam. Often, they were joined by other famous anglers such as Martin Van Buren, president-to-be and later Webster's adversary; Philip Hone, mayor of New York City; and American inventor John Stevens and his brother Edward, both of Hoboken. The latter is said to have "never thrown a fly until he was 40 years old."

While a member of the Senate, Webster maintained a law practice with offices in Boston and New York City. In Manhattan, he lived at the Astor Hotel on Vesey Street. One of his closest fishing cronies was Philip Hone, in 1825 the city's mayor. Hone inflamed Webster with rumors of a monstrous trout, "bigger than any seen before," that had been spotted on Long Island. According to Hone's diary—which he didn't begin keeping until 1828 and might more appropriately be called his memoirs—one spring afternoon in 1823, he and Webster took the early ferry from Manhattan to Brooklyn. Catching the Friday stage, they arrived at Carman's inn well after dark. Later, they were joined by Walter Browne and Martin Van Buren, who two years earlier had been elected to the U.S. Senate from New York. The next day they fished the spring-fed East Connecticut River (renamed the Carmans River) from sunup to sunset without sight of the trout. Carman told them the huge fish had last been seen a few days ago.

The next day, their luck changed slightly. Webster saw for the first time the fish that was to plague him. But no matter how often he and his friends cast, they couldn't get it to take their flies. After that, Webster, who often fished Long Island's other famous trout ponds and streams, returned often to Fireplace Mills, trying to catch the big trout. It would be several years before he would see it again. Carman and his slaves did see it from time to time, relaying letters to Webster, and this helped feed his desire.

It wasn't until 1827 that both Webster and Hone were again at Carman's. By now the fish had become a full-blown obsession. "We left Broucklyn [sic] on Friday," according to Hone's diary, traveling by stage, and arrived after dark. In addition to the tavern, Carman operated a community gristmill where the present-day Montauk Highway crosses the river. The day before, records have it, Carman and his slaves had taken out the mill's huge waterwheel and "banked" it for repairs. The freedom to forage in the pool above where the wheel had stood would surely entice the behemoth to venture forth.

Webster and Hone fished Saturday without sighting the fish. That night, we're told, rum and mulled cider flowed freely at Carman's tavern—so freely that Webster had to be carried to bed by two men. The next morning, after the bell tolled, Webster, Hone,

Figure 1.1 The old South Haven Church, moved to the village of Brookhaven (known as Fireplace in Sam Carman's time).

and Carman dutifully went to church to do penance for their indulgences. Most people of the day considered fishing on Sundays morally suspect, but before they entered church, Carman solemnly ordered his slave Lige to sit guard at the pool and watch for the trout. If it should appear he was to call them immediately, even in church. They then made their way to a pew beneath the scowling eyes of preacher Ezra "Priest" King, also a devoted trout fisherman. Fortunately for the revelers it wasn't the front pew, because King, from the manse across the road, had heard them carrying on the night before.

Sermons in those days were short if they lasted two hours, and Priest was a notoriously long-winded speaker. His voice droned on and on about the eternal faults of man, the wickedness of his life, his succumbing to the evils of drink and other sins. It must have seemed to Webster that King would never end. At last, it was time for a hymn.

While the congregation joined in singing "Shall We Gather at the River?" the senator's eyes must have strained through the open window for a glimpse of the pool. The new red leaves of the swamp maples flooded the river's banks with color, mixing with the yellows of the willows and the greens of the alders. Shadbushes were at the height of their bloom, and the yellow flowers of a dying forsythia framed the window.

The hymn over, everyone started to sit and prepare themselves for another long harangue, but they were interrupted by the shuffling of Lige's feet. It caught the attention of Carman and Webster. Dan knew immediately what had happened: Nothing but the fear of a beating from Carman for not reporting a sighting of the trout could have induced the slave to enter church.

"He's heah, Mistah Carman. He's in de hole where de wheel was," said Lige. "Ephraim waitin' by de watah, lookin' at 'im."

No matter how one tries, there's no way to leave the middle pew of a church inconspicuously. Everyone's eyes were on the trio as they walked out. The congregants, too, knew what the intrusion into God's House meant: The Big Trout. One by one many of the men also found an excuse to slip out. Within a few minutes the church was almost empty. Even the Reverend King left the pulpit and continued to deliver his sermon from the aisle, slowly working his way to the rear. After a hasty benediction, he ran to the pool with the rest of the congregation.

From Currier's print of the event, made 27 years later, we know Webster was in a black Sunday suit like most churchgoers of his day. He fished from a punt, whipping a 15-foot fly rod back and forth across the pool. Lige was in the boat with a landing net, as was Philip Hone, but where was the fish? Had it returned with the tide to the bay?

The congregation lined the pool's western bank and watched while Webster cast. The distal of three red-colored wet flies settled gently onto the water. The others quickly followed. With small flicks of the willowy rod's tip, Webster made them dance in short steps just under the pool's surface. There was a bulge in the surface and one fly disappeared. Webster set the hook. A small trout broke the water. A dull, disappointed moan came in unison from the onlookers.

The advocate impatiently pulled in the little brook trout and quickly released it. Webster went through the motions of casting the flies again but disappointment must have been written vividly across his face. Had he missed the trout again? Why was he constantly being plagued by this prize fish, the biggest trout anyone had ever seen?

After a half hour of fruitless casting, bankside watchers were losing interest. A few began to leave. Webster made another long cast toward the bush where Lige said he had last seen the fish. As the flies landed, a massive swirl a few feet beyond broke the pool's placid surface. It was a big fish. Webster saw it. So did Hone and Lige. Webster snatched up the flies and again presented them, this time with a longer cast and renewed interest.

It was the most eloquent cast he could muster and the most important he would ever attempt; it was a trial of lives. The flies settled upon the water. For a moment surface tension kept them afloat. Nothing happened for what seemed like the longest time, as the three men watched. In a blink of an eye, the farthest fly sank first; the two others followed. The fish approached the distal fly with a savage, committed rush, the kind only brook trout make when they decide to strike. As the trout took the fly, its momentum carried its back clear of the water, creating a horrendous splash that startled the witnesses who lined the bank like a jury in its box.

What followed was a real trial in every sense—the trial of two combatants, the trout fighting for its life and Webster for peace of mind, which at times can be as dear as life itself. It was a trial that wasn't decided until the final appeal was made from both sides.

The trout gave up only after a long, drawn-out struggle. The congregation watched silent and spellbound. Finally, Lige slipped the long-handled net under the fish, pulling it into the boat. The behemoth's back had turned black from its long life in the river's acid tan-colored waters. But its underside flashed orange and red and the telltale white trim on its fins left no doubt as to its status as the biggest of all brook trout.

"We hab you now, Sar!" Lige is reported to have said.

Webster held up the fish for everyone to see. The somber, reserved onlookers broke out into unthinkable cheers—on the Sabbath. They jumped and shouted wildly along the banks of the river. Records have it that Squire Carman's surrey horses were alarmed by the noise and took off down the road without a driver.

Lige carried the huge fish to Carman's store as everyone tried to guess its weight. Sam deftly slid the weights on his flour scale until the arm gingerly balanced at 14 pounds, 8 ounces. Webster had caught the biggest brook trout in creation. A fish that large couldn't go unrecorded. Carman placed it against a wall and drew its outline. Philip Hone copied the outline and the next day transferred it to a cherry plank. Eventually, the carved trout served as the church weather vane. It's recorded that the wooden trout was increased in size by one-third before it was carved so that when viewed from the ground on the church spire it would look "more natural."

The fish, packed in ice and sawdust, accompanied Webster and Hone back to Manhattan. It's said that Martin Van Buren, Browne, and the Stevens brothers joined them at Delmonico's, a new restaurant on Beaver Street, where "there was more than enough trout for everyone."

That's one version of the capture of the world's first 14½-pound brook trout. There have been several others, all written by authoritative, qualified persons. One that closely parallels the above account came from Edna Valentine Trapnell, who was privy to more local information than anyone because most of the people involved, outside of the fishers, were her relatives. When I corresponded with her in 1965, she was quite elderly and living in Los Angeles. She was born in Brookhaven (Fireplace) and grew up there. Her ancestors had arrived in Plymouth in 1621. She was able to glean from those who had lived during Carman's time, and from their diaries, information about the great fish upon which her story, in the May 1933 issue of *Field & Stream* magazine, was based. The differences aren't great but her research indicated that the fish was caught the first time it was seen, "in the administration of James Madison and in the year of grace 1823." Webster, Hone, Browne, Van Buren, and John and Edward Stevens were all there.

According to Trapnell, the big trout was spotted just before church services and all of the men present tried to catch it. "Twenty pounds if it's an ounce!" Philip Hone was reported to have gasped at the sight of the brook trout. It really isn't certain whether Webster, Edward Stevens, or Martin Van Buren caught the big trout. But it was recorded that Sam Carman landed the fish with the net and not Lige, as pictured by artist Arthur Fitzwilliam Tait in the 1854 Currier lithograph. There is even some speculation that it wasn't a fly the brook trout took, but a garden worm.

Nor did the band of fishers consume the trout immediately or at Delmonico's Restaurant. There were several reports, possibly based on one initial account, that the big fish was kept alive for two weeks in a water pen specifically constructed to satisfy the curiosity and incredulity of the neighborhood. Many came from afar to see it, and it was pronounced by competent judges to be undoubtedly a "Long Island brook trout."

Frank Forester, this nation's first outdoors chronicler, commented on the trout-versus-salmon controversy after the fact, in the first edition, in 1849, of his book *Fish and Fishing*, printed in London (later editions were printed in New York). Forester agreed with the pro-salmon side but reversed his thinking in the U.S. edition, which appeared in 1850: "There is, I am aware, a tale that many years since a Trout of eleven pounds was taken at Fireplace; and a rough sketch of the fish is still to be seen on the wall of the tavern bar-room. I know, however, that this fish was considered at the time, by all the true sportsmen who saw it, to be a Salmon, and the sketch is said to bear out that opinion, though I do not myself understand how a mere outline, not filled up, can convey any very distinct idea of the species intended." Few agreed with Forester's identification of the big fish when, years later, he changed his mind and called it a brook trout.

"After it was killed," wrote Trapnell, "Uncle Sam Carman had it placed against the wall and an outline drawn. Philip Hone, copying this outline, had a weather vane made, one-third larger than the trout, so that it would appear natural when viewed from below; had it carved and gilded and set up on top of the church spire.

"On the back of the wooden fish is written: 14 ¼ pounds.

"And what a feast Uncle Sam got up for the fishermen when that giant trout was killed! The pantry, cellar, milk room and smoke house, and all the mighty culinary lore of Aunt Ellen, his wife—she who had been a Havens, of Moriches, a line long-known for its house-wife ability—were called into play. It is told how nine kinds of pickles alone graced that table, and as for the blue point oysters—and in those days they were blue points—and the smoked ham boiled in cider and the sillabubs [a wine or cider dessert drink] and the slip-and-go-downs [?] and—oh, what's the use? Those days are gone forever!

"That was a long time ago, but here you may still see the church today. And also a picture of that great trout as he looked in the day when Daniel Webster and Philip Hone and their friends helped catch and eat him."

Figure 1.2 The cherry weather vane carved from the "Great Trout's" profile, now located in the vestibule of the South Haven Presbyterian Church in the village of Brookhaven, N.Y.

According to Eugene V. Connett III, who reflected upon this catch in his book *Any Luck?* in 1933—the same year Trapnell's magazine piece appeared—"The Big Trout was quickly taken to the [Sam Carman's] shop and laid on a piece of board; its outline was traced and the fish weighed and returned to the water, in an inclosed pen that harbored Carman's live goose decoys. The board was then sawed out, later to be sent to a Bond Street woodcarver to be furnished up properly. A picture was painted of the trout by Miss Nellie Stone of Morristown [N.J.]. This picture is now in the possession of the Miller family in Brookhaven. The wooden effigy was later used as a weather vane on the South Haven Presbyterian Church, and years after was given to the oldest member of the congregation Ellen C. Miller. Today [1933] it hangs over the doorway of Clinton Miller of Brookhaven."

It rests now in the vestibule of the church, moved from South Haven to Brookhaven.

"A glance at the watercolor," Connett continued—both he and Trapnell must have seen it—"dispels the theory [that it was a salmon]."

Connett's version had a happier ending for the brook trout. "The trout, after being kept in the pen for some time at Carman's was sent to Macomb's Dam [on the Harlem River], above New York City, where we hope it lived happily ever afterwards."

The shipping of the fish to New York alive wasn't as preposterous a feat in 1827 as it might seem today. According to Connett, in the days before the Long Island Rail Road was built, market wagons fitted with large water tanks set out from New York and traveled along the route of the Sag Harbor Stage Coach—South Country Road. They stopped at each trout "pound," picking up trout offered for sale by proprietors, and returned to the city with their loads. It was thus possible for patrons of Delmonico's and other fashionable restaurants to enjoy what was considered "the finest tasting trout in the United States." Because of the horde of trout it was impossible to weigh them. Instead, owners netted the fish and placed them in tubs; then purchaser and seller estimated the weight, haggling until a satisfactory figure was reached. Constant practice made the matter less troublesome than might be imagined.

In 1829, a year after his first wife's death, Webster married Caroline LeRoy, daughter of wealthy Manhattan banker Herman LeRoy, who had a large country estate in Islip, just a few miles west of Fireplace Mills. Though Webster continued his fishing exploits on Long Island as well as the rest of the country, he never again caught a brook trout as large as the one from Sam Carman's mill pool. Nor did anyone else until a Canadian physician, fishing in the wilds of western Ontario in 1916, caught one that just equaled the size of the fish Webster had caught 89 years earlier.

Webster's fish predated the keeping of official records—not until 1895 would *Field & Stream* assume the custodial task of maintaining records of the largest freshwater fish caught by anglers. Despite this, the fish Webster (or another) caught was witnessed and authenticated by a member of the clergy and his congregation and entered into the church's records, as well as by a president-to-be and an ex-mayor of New York City. The fisherman was both attorney and senator, and later secretary of state. How much more honesty could one ask for? However, in no literature or personal writings of his own or of anyone else did Webster ever take credit for catching such a large brook trout. But someone did, as we'll soon discover.

Trapnell seems to have had greater access to the source materials than did Connett, but it's difficult to discern where the actual descriptions ended and her coloring began.

"The fish–weather vane remained on the church for many years until," as her story went, "a late summer thunderstorm, as big for a storm as that trout was for trout, came down on the little village of Fireplace Mills. There was a tremendous peal of thunder preceded by a blinding flash of sputtering, crackling, blue-green light which struck the church spire and knocked the wooden fish into the gutters. The lightning went down through the drain pipe and killed a mule that had taken shelter from the storm in the graveyard below . . . quite a proper place as it turned out to be."

The East Connecticut River, now known as Carmans River, still flows on Long Island. The big pool at the base of the mill yielded trout as late as 1958, when it was destroyed and the mill torn down to make way for a superhighway. If Daniel Webster had been alive, I wonder if he could have saved the pool—as he did in 1845, when he had the Long Island Rail

Figure 1.3 Part of the pool below the millrace remains on the East Connecticut (Carmans) River.

Road remove a stone bridge it had built over the river downstream of the pool; the bridge's opening was too small, and backed the river into the pool. Brook trout inhabit the remnant of the pool even today.

Carman's tavern and home stood until 1936, when it was torn down and replaced by a fuel oil company office. The historic little church also felt the hand of progress. Carmans, as the community first appeared on maps, was renamed Fireplace Mills, then South Haven. After the first bridge was built it no longer prospered at "the crossing-over place." Over the years the congregation dwindled to the point that the church was nearly abandoned. Those who needed religious guidance attended another Presbyterian church in Brookhaven (Fireplace). In 1961 it gave up its location and graveyard and was moved 2 miles away to Brookhaven village.

The heavy cherry weather vane has better stood the test of time and elements and, though suffering a little from weather and lightning, can still be seen in the church's vestibule. Today, as one walks down the aisle of the old church, one can almost hear Priest King delivering his sermon on that warm May Sunday, more than 150 years ago. And, in a center pew, one can see the spot, now marked by a brass plate, where Webster must have squirmed and fought with his conscience, and finally abandoned the word of God to do battle with a huge trout.

A somewhat abbreviated version of the above story appeared in a 1966 issue of *Sports Illustrated*, and a fuller version in the 1970 Summer issue of *Sports Afield*'s quarterly publication, *Rod & Gun*. Eleven years later, in 1981, in an issue of *The American Fly Fisher, The Journal of the American Museum of Fly Fishing*, Kenneth Shewmaker attempted to debunk the story as a fabrication. As a Webster scholar working on a doctorate at Dartmouth College, he had two major criticisms of the above accounts and those by several other authors.

The first was that they lacked citations for various statements and facts. One would hardly find citations in *Sports Illustrated* or *Sports Afield*. His approach to denouncing the story was to research all the publications, diaries, and biographies of the people involved, looking for some printed reference to the catching of the 14½-pound brook trout. I'm sure his search was scholarly and intensive, but after a lengthy period he came up without a single reference—and concluded that the event never occurred. Thus, his second criticism: Because he couldn't find documentation, it wasn't true.

Shewmaker was guilty of choosing documentary data that supported his personal thesis and disregarding other data that might have supported the catching of a 14½- or, as in some accounts, 14¼-pound brook trout. He was aware of Charles Eliot Goodspeed's *Angling in America*, a 1939 documentation of fishing in these United States, because he referred to it in his 1981 critique. However, he failed to add William O. Ayers's reference to a 15-pounder being taken on Long Island. Ayers wrote in the *Boston Journal of Natural History* for April 1843 that "eight or ten years since a trout was caught at Fireplace, which weighed fifteen pounds. It must, I suppose, have been this species *Salmo [Salvelinus] fontinalis*. It was called by many who saw it a salmon trout, on account of its great size or perhaps some peculiarity in the coloring, but the most experienced fisherman who was engaged in taking it (it was caught with a seine) considered it only a very large individual of the common brook trout. I must muse here, that on that stream, and possibly in other parts of the island, the name salmon trout is often applied to any specimen very strongly tinged with red on the abdomen, and it may have been so in this instance."

More appropriately, the term "salmon trout" was usually applied to large sea-run brook trout, whose normally gaudy coloration is obscured by a layer of guanine—caused by exposure to salt and, to some degree, brackish water. Then, they do look a lot like salmon. However, the vermiculations on the back and the red dots on the sides are never completely hidden. And Ayers's recollection of "eight or ten years" was not exact; some leeway would have put the catching of the trout within the time frame of Webster's alleged feat. As to it being taken in a seine, this is as open to conjecture as the determination that it was a salmon, or that it could have been another fish taken on another occasion.

This kind of literary research reminds me of a tale a teacher told me while I was in graduate school. It seems that two monks were walking down a dusty road somewhere in Italy during the Middle Ages. One spied a donkey tied to a post. For some reason, one monk asked the other, "How many teeth do you think there are in a donkey's mouth?" Being true scholars of that era they immediately returned to the monastery and spent days poring through the Bible looking for a reference that stated how many teeth were in a donkey's mouth. Though there were plenty of references to donkeys, they couldn't find one about the number of teeth. In frustration, they finally declared that "It isn't in the Bible, therefore we can never know how many teeth are in a donkey's mouth!"

Shewmaker's argument is weakened by his placing too much credence on the Currier print. Arthur Fitzwilliam Tait, an Englishman who had come to this country in 1850, drew the sketch in 1854, 27 years after the event, probably prompted by the death of Daniel Webster (of cirrhosis of the liver) on October 24, 1852. Currier had issued another lithograph of Webster, a portrait, just after his death. Tait, a freelance artist, saw this as an opportunity to sell yet another of his works to Nathaniel Currier.

When Currier published a lithograph in 1835 showing Planter's Hotel in New Orleans after it had been gutted by fire, he ushered in a new era in pictorial journalism. Currier began selling individual prints of historic events, and the more sensational the event, the better they sold—the precursor of the tabloid newspaper. Tait has been criticized as over-dramatizing his scenes and making them look implausible—probably with Currier's encouragement. But drama sold then as it does today. In the case of Webster and his great trout, Tait probably had no access to first-hand, contemporary knowledge of the tale; otherwise the trout would really have been big.

While Tait later became an outdoorsman and fell in love with Long Island and the Adirondacks, where he owned a home on Long Lake, his print reveals that he had no idea of the actual size of a 14½-pound brook trout, or with the events as documented by others who were there. He put Lige in the boat with Webster and had him landing the trout; Trapnell stated that it was Sam Carman who actually landed it. Nor is there any mention in any of the story versions of the anglers fishing from a punt. Tait may have taken it upon himself to put them in one, possibly influenced by contemporary English painter Henry Alken (1785–1841) and his watercolor *Fishing in a Punt*, or even more so by the 19th-century engraving *Punt Fishing* by W. Burraud. Both very closely resemble Tait's drawing of Webster and Hone.

Shewmaker wrote that the fish was taken from the mill pond, but it was actually taken from the pool below the spot where the wheel poured its water into the East Connecticut River. There was no need to use a boat to fish this small pool.

The only two accurate items in the Currier lithograph are Webster's likeness and the flat landscape in the background. The second man in the boat is most likely Philip Hone, because the figure is quite similar to portraits of the one-time mayor found now in the Museum of the City of New York. Hone was described as an "intimate" friend of Webster's and the two often fished together, a fact revealed in Hone's diary. While the scene includes Hone, though, it may well be that Edward Stevens also fished with Webster. There's even a reference stating that it was Stevens and not Webster who caught the big trout. And therein may be at least part of the reason that Shewmaker came up empty when investigating the fishing life of Webster.

One more fact might substantiate the size of the fish, if not its catcher. Shewmaker wrote, without citation or accreditation, that "Philip Hone transferred Carman's scratches onto a linen." Trapnell credited Uncle Sam Carman as having placed the fish against a wall and having an outline made of it. What happened to this outline? Connett, Trapnell, and others also said it was placed on a plank. The trout's effigy is indeed on a cherry plank, a valuable construction wood even in those days. The carving of the fish is neat, accurate, and crisp—obviously the work of an experienced wood sculptor. Connett's reference to "a Bond Street woodcarver" has real credence.

Trapnell's *Field & Stream* feature was illustrated with a photograph taken against the side of the church, under a shuttered window. Under the window was "a painting of the big trout" alongside the weather vane. Though it's difficult to see the trout in the painting, it's a big fish, almost as big as the weather vane next to it. When I asked Trapnell about it, she answered: "The painting of the fish used to hang in the hall of the Miller homestead. Geo. M. kindly took it outside for me to photograph. The Millers have sold [their house] and moved. I suppose the son has it but I don't know where he went."

Could this be the outline Carman or Hone made, or the linen Shewmaker referred to?

Shewmaker also erred by placing too much faith in the accuracy of publications of that period. After all, it had been only nine years earlier, in 1814, that the brook trout was first scientifically recognized as a species. Then it took 60 years more to get its first name right. Nor did newspapers of that day have the objectivity of today's press. One has but to read fishing reports in the New York *Sun* or *Evening Post* of the day to realize this.

To some degree, Shewmaker was correct in pointing out the discrepancies among the varied accounts of the big fish and just who did or didn't catch it. There's little doubt that some of the narration was constructed to meld available facts into a plausible story. However, there's just too much circumstantial evidence of a big trout being caught on the East Connecticut River at "the crossing-over place" to discard the whole story as fiction. I doubt that the question of who caught the fish will ever be satisfactorily answered. At this point, I too doubt it was Webster. Even so, it's a good story about our brook trout heritage, and about how thoroughly this species of fish was entwined with the lives of ordinary and extraordinary Americans.

2 Dr. John William Cook and his "Devil Trout"

Nearly 90 years later and almost 1,000 miles from Fireplace Mills, at the western edge of the brook trout's range, a Fort William, Ontario, physician took a breather from the day's efforts. From the river's bank he gazed at the cloud of insects hovering above the tailrace pool that formed below Rabbit Rapids, a mile below Virgin Rapids, near the spot where the Nipigon River escapes Lake Nipigon. At that time the Nipigon was still a powerful, massive, thunderous river, unfettered by hydroelectric dams in its race to meet Lake Superior, 30 or so miles away.

For several days, the physician and his companions had been slowly pushing their way upriver, camping and fishing along what was already a well-trodden Ontario wilderness. The sojourn had begun at Nipigon Station, just a few miles above the port of Red Rock, where the Nipigon meets the largest of the great lakes. They and their Indian guides, hired from the nearby settlement of Parmachenee, just above the European settlement of Nipigon, labored past rapids and portages, resting where the river turned into small lakes. Often these were no more than bulges, where the Nipigon had been temporarily backed up as it carved its way through Precambrian granite. Even though the Ojibway guides did most of the heavy work, this trek was still fatiguing.

As the story has been told and retold, it was late in the day, after six, on July 21, 1916, when Cook, through tired eyes, surveyed the pool. The guides had already set up camp,

WORLD'S RECORD BROOK TROUT!
WEIGHT—14½ lbs   LENGTH—2 FT. 10 IN   DEPTH—9 IN.
CAUGHT IN THE NIPIGON RIVER 1916, BY DR COOK OF FORT WILLIAM

Figure 2.1   The half-mount of Dr. Cook's 14½-pound brook trout, the world's record, caught in 1916 on the Nipigon River. The mount was destroyed in the Nipigon Museum fire in 1990. (Courtesy Gord Ellis.)

but Cook was thinking of fishing just a bit more before dark. This far north, days were long and nights short at this time of year. It wasn't the first time Cook had fished the Nipigon. The legendary river was only 75 miles from his home and now easily accessed by railroad. He knew it produced big brook trout, and the specter of 7-, 8-, and 9-pound speckled trout had often lured him from his medical practice.

The river had already garnered a worldwide reputation as having the continent's best brook trout fishing. In the 75 years since its lode had been discovered, big brook trout had become the norm. There were even reports of several 20-pounders. One was a fish taken about 1850 by a member of the provincial crew that first surveyed the area. But even with such largess, the quality of fishing was by Cook's time beginning to show signs of decline. Unregulated overfishing was one cause. But worse causes were soon to come.

On that day, the sun's warmth had triggered an unusually large hatch of big mayflies. The water was littered with their ephemeral bodies, and brook trout were glutting themselves on the easy meal. Cook tried but could not raise a trout to his flies. As the story unfolds, one of the guides, sensing Cook's frustration, began turning over stones near shore and caught a small sculpin, a *cockatouche* in the Ojibway language. It was a forage fish plentiful everywhere in the river and its lakes, and one of several reasons that brook trout here grew so large. Cook didn't resist as the guide threaded it onto his hook.

Figure 2.2 This is what the world's record brook trout might have looked like. The author holds a modern replica of Dr. Cook's record fish, constructed from the dimensions of the original fish. It hangs in the regional office of the Ontario Ministry of Natural Resources in Nipigon.

"Grudgingly," as the story goes, "the angler tied it to the line's tippet, then flipped the minnow into the pool."

The doctor was said to be using a 5-ounce fly rod, and the fish's strike was so strong that the rod doubled over. After an arduous hour-long tug-of-war, a great fish was brought to net. It's reported that at first Cook was disappointed, believing he had caught a lake trout. But the excited guides confirmed that this was no laker but "an enormous speckled trout." The fish weighed 14½ pounds and measured 31½ inches in length and 11½ inches in girth (really, half girth).

Many outside the Nipigon area who didn't see the fish didn't believe it was a brook trout and challenged its identification. The fish was split in two and half of it mounted on birch bark. One skin, the right-hand side, was sent to the Royal Ontario Museum in Toronto, where an ichthyologist confirmed that indeed it was a *Salvelinus fontinalis,* and the largest ever caught. He was unaware of Daniel Webster's brook trout.

Of course in Webster's time there were no outdoors magazines or columnists on newspapers. Only on rare occasions did fishing reports find their way into the nation's broadsheets. However, by 1916 there were weekly news tabloids, daily newspapers, and outdoors writers who appeared regularly in magazines and newspapers. There were even several magazines dedicated to hunting and fishing. Best of all, the record-keeping body for catches of superlative freshwater fishes was *Field & Stream* magazine. It began publication in 1895, in St. Paul, Minnesota, and almost immediately started the process of record keeping. Cook's fish found its way into the magazine's records only several years after it was caught, though. Today, it's one of the world's longest-standing fishing records.

Ironically, the only mention in the contemporary press was a 2-inch entry in the

monthly letters-to-the-editor section in the September 1916 issue of a competing publication, *Forest and Stream*. The "Fish and Fishing Editor" was someone who wrote under
the nom de plume "Seneca." Next to his was the camping column written by "Nessmuk,"
alias George Washington Sears.

BIG TROUT FROM NEPIGON

Editor Fish and Fishing:

Recently, Dr. W. J. [sic] Cook, of Fort Williams, landed a trout in the Nepigon
[sic] District that tipped the scales at at 14.5 pounds. The size of the fish was
so remarkable that its species was called into question. The trout was sent to
the Game and Fisheries Department to have the question settled. In order to
remove doubts, the Department sent the fish to Ottawa, so that Dr. Prince,
the fisheries expert, could decide the question. The Department has received
a report from Dr. Prince in which he states that it is a true speckled trout.
O.T.S. Toronto, Canada.

The Nepigon District during the past year or two has produced some exceptionally large brook trout, which is all, I believe, to the fact that the Game and
Fisheries Department has been protecting the fish [brook trout] from the pike.
Last year, special men were employed, I am told, in capturing the pike and this
year the Indians are being allowed in the district to fish for pike without the cus-
tomary license.

—**Forest and Stream**, *Sept. 1916, Vol. LXXXVI, No. 9, page 1154*

Controversy as to who really caught the 14½-pound Nipigon fish, and when, has sur-
faced periodically since the catch. In Cook's time, Nipigon was still just a whistle-stop on
the Canadian Pacific Railway, which had only the year before completed passenger service linking eastern and western Canada. Red Rock was the steamer port a few miles
downriver from Nipigon. Since 1840, anglers coming from the East—from Chicago,
Toronto, and New York—used Red Rock as a ship's landing and place to start fishing on
the Nipigon. By the time Cook got around to fishing the river, guided trips upriver were
old hat. They had been organized for more than 60 years, and well-established campsites
along the river had been in operation for several decades.

One of the top outfitters after the turn of the century was Jack McKirdy Sr. It was he who
had organized the trip for Cook and his party. The first night they stayed at a hotel next to the
Hudson's Bay Company store in Nepigon (sic) Station, which by then had become the village
of Nipigon. McKirdy customized trips upriver that lasted anywhere from three to five weeks,
depending on the sports' available time and money. Full-blown trips ran upriver from
Nipigon to Virgin Island on Lake Nipigon, just above where the river began, and, of course,
back down again.

In addition to brook trout, the river was filled with other fishes—lake trout, walleye, northern pike, whitefish, and sturgeon. But it was the brook trout, called speckled trout by most Canadians, that brought itinerant anglers here. Brook trout were everywhere along the river's actual 41-mile course, but congregated particularly at the base of every rapids and falls. There were several portages, some quite a few miles long. During the height of the tourist fishing season, entrepreneurial Ojibway usually waited at the bottom of these portages with oxen or horse and wagon. For a few dollars they would cart canoes (at that time still made from birch bark, by a local Indian named Joe Wadow), tents, food, and fishing gear; they could also repair damaged equiment. The service was appreciated by the guides even more than by the sports. On some portages the anglers could even ride.

McKirdy hired an Ojibway named Andrew Lexie from the Indian settlement of Parmachenee to head Dr. Cook's group. Lexie was assisted by five other Indians, according to Ray DuPuis, 63, of Nipigon. DuPuis, a dedicated speckled trout fisherman, had known the guides when he was young and interviewed them when they were old men. This outfitting arrangement was later confirmed in an interview of Cook by a wire-service reporter years after the event. Three canoes were used, including one only for gear, according to Dupuis's interview with Lexie. However, it's more likely that there were four or even five, because McKirdy also assigned a cook and all of his gear to the party. Due to the difficulty of navigating the fast river and the fact that half of the trip was up-current, two guides with one angler were always used in each canoe. And there were four anglers, according to Cook.

According to Lexie, Cook's party left Nipigon on August 24, 1915, not 1916. The first fishing stop upriver was at the slight run of rapids and pool above Parmachenee, where Clay Hill Creek enters from the west. From there they pushed on to Camp Alexander, at the base of Long Rapids, a 2½-mile portage. This was usually the end of the first day's travel, and the guides set up camp for the first night. At dawn the guides prepared for the day's journey. All of the equipment was carried to the top of the portage that ended just above Cameron Falls, the southern-end outlet of Jessie Lake.

From Camp Alexander, Cook and his party hiked the rugged trail to Cameron Falls. From here they paddled through Lakes Jessie and Maria, separated from each other by The Narrows. The lakes temporarily return to a riverlike stretch for a few hundred yards—to Cedar Portage and an excellent trout hole at Split Rock. The anglers ended their second day at Camp Cincinnati, just below Pine Portage. From here on, upriver travel was slowed by numerous rapids, fast water, short falls, and four portages.

According to DuPuis, Lexie and the other guides couldn't remember the exact date when the fish was caught, but they emphatically agreed that it wasn't in July, as is now the most widely accepted month. Instead, they recalled it being during the first week in September, and this would just about fit the time schedule if they did depart August 24. Actually, both months are in a way correct: Later research revealed that Cook twice fished the Nipigon that year, in July and again in September. The guides told DuPuis that brook trout fishing on the Nipigon in 1916 was a lot like it was at the time he interviewed them.

Very few fish of more than 8 pounds were caught; the largest were in the range of 4 to 5 pounds. On some days they even had a difficult time catching enough for dinner.

Dupuis's interview with Lexie revealed that the doctor and his friends—another physician as well as two dentists—were fishing with Parmachene Belle and Silver Doctor patterns. Cook used an 8-ounce bamboo fly rod. The fish was caught late in the evening at Rabbit Rapids, also known as McDonald Rapids. It was tough fishing because the shore was lined with big boulders and the water along shore was shallow—only 1 to 2 feet deep until one reached the big circulating pool.

One version of the guides' combined stories claimed that a guide, not Cook, caught the big trout. They said Cook liked to drink, and had that evening passed out in his tent. The guide took Cook's fly rod and switched the wet fly for a *cockatouche*, with which they traditionally caught brook trout. According to this version, Cook was awakened to see the trout. He then entered into a verbal agreement with the guide to let him claim the fish; the guide was to be compensated later. Because he never got his reward, the guide remained disgruntled for years. They never identified the guide.

Regardless of who the angler really was, after the fish was landed, according to Lexie, the guides had a great disagreement about its species. One claimed it was a lake trout— it was too big to be a speckled trout—and was going to cut it up and eat it. But Lexie said it was a speckled trout. Challenging Lexie's authority and knowledge, they all then agreed to go downriver, by foot, to the next camp to ask the opinion of the head guide there, an older Indian, whose name Lexie could not recall. Under lantern light, the other guide agreed with Lexie: It was a huge speckled trout, the biggest any had ever seen.

A somewhat different version of the catching of this big brook trout is recorded in a book entitled *Paddle, Pack and Speckled Trout* by Edwin Mills. Mills, a wire-service reporter, described what happened to the big trout after it was caught and added even more color to a story with an already vivid complexion. The account by Mills appeared in an issue of the magazine *Outdoors Canada*. It was written by Gord Ellis, a Canadian writer from Thunder Bay (the current name of Fort William, where Cook lived), who's probably the most knowledgeable person today about Dr. Cook's exploits.

According to Ellis, Mills was a unique individual—a fanatic brook trout fisher and an adventurer who spent much of the 1930s and '40s chasing speckled trout on the 21 major rapids that remained in the upper part of the Nipigon River before they, too, were silenced by a series of hydroelectric dams. Mills had apparently interviewed Dr. Cook on several occasions and gained information on the river and his catch directly from him.

According to Mills's version, Cook was fishing with three other anglers (possibly the physician and two dentists described in Dupuis's interview)—R. J. Byrnes, H. H. Neeland, and J. A. Fyfe, as well as cook Lafelle Boudain and guides Joe Hardy, Sam King, Michael Bouchard, John Ogama, Louis Musquash, Jim Shuse, and Lawrence Martin. "In the evening, a huge hatch of brown flies came off the surface of the pool, and Cook's artificial flies simply weren't fooling the trout." It would be another 21 years before Don

Gapen invented the Muddler Minnow, an imitation of the *cockatouche,* on the banks of the lower Nipigon River.

"Many fishermen still balk at the idea," wrote Mills in his book, "but the offering that finally fooled the monstrous 'speck' in the hole was a minnow—more specifically a *cockatouche.* Cook may have already known about the sculpin-like minnow's trout appeal, but it's likely that a guide actually caught the minnow in question and gave it to the doctor. Cook then impaled it on a hook and attached it to his rather light, five-weight fly line." (Weight lines are a modern gauge of a fly line's size, and the author probably was referring to the 5-ounce bamboo rod that Cook was supposed to have used.)

Cook then recalled what happened next, according to Ellis, in a piece written by Mills that appeared in a Canadian Press wire story on May 12, 1950. Mills also acted as a stringer for CP: "'I was fishing with a minnow,'" Mills quoted. "'When it settled below the surface, the big fish took the bait and was away.'"

Cook played the fish, according to Mills, and called friends to bring the net. He fought it for some time and netted it after a great struggle. When he opened the fish, he found it had a stomach full of brown flies. "It was greedy enough to take the minnow, too," said Cook. Mills reported that Cook said he thought he'd caught a lake trout but the excitement of the guides confirmed for him that it was a huge speckled trout. "The fish weighed 14.5 pounds and measured 31.5 inches in length and 11.5 inches from the top of the back to the belly." (This is an odd way to measure a fish's girth unless it's already split in half.) "The catch," wrote Mills, "sparked excitement and furor throughout the angling world, and Cook wisely sent the specimen [whole or split, but in either case, without the brown flies] to ichthyological authorities in Washington and Ottawa, as well as the Royal Ontario Museum. All pronounced it unquestionably a true brook trout.

"After the catch," according to Mills's account, "the fish was split down the middle and the two skins were mounted separately on birch bark paneling." Though this was a technique used in many wilderness camps at the time to preserve a skin, a fish that large, and that had traveled to so many esteemed scientists, should surely have been mounted in the round. There were good fish taxidermists in both countries in that period. Cook's reasoning for the type of mount is mysterious. The photo of the skin mount taken by Gord Ellis contradicts Mills's description of "the fish was split down the middle," because it illustrates more than half of the fish; because of this, there probably never was a second mount.

Over the next few decades, according to Ellis, the mounts (or mount) were bandied around northwestern Ontario. Finally, one of them found its way back to Nipigon. For many years, the blackened, wrinkled skin of this wondrous trout gathered dust in a case in the Nipigon Museum, under a sign that read OLD, DEAD FISH. In 1990, the museum burned, and with it went half of the physical evidence of Cook's catch. The other half, if there ever was one, is still out there, somewhere, maybe.

There's more to Mills's story. The interview with Cook didn't take place after he caught the fish, but after an incident that occurred 34 years later:

[*Toronto*], *Globe and Mail,* May 1949

HUGE SPECKLED TROUT CAUGHT, NEAR 12 POUNDS

Barry's Bay, Ont., May 11, (CP)

This backwoods settlement is still talking about Murray Daly's speckled trout—the monster, weighing nearly 12 pounds, he dragged from Spectacle Lakes Sunday. He caught it with worms and triple-hooked spinner while fishing in calm, shallow water, 50 feet off-shore. The trout took 20 minutes to land. It came close to the world record for speckled trout of 14½ pounds, set by Dr. J. W. Cook in 1916 with a fish caught on the Nipigon River, near Port Arthur. In New York, *Field and Stream* magazine said that prize-winning speckled trout in its contests for the last 10 years have averaged between five and eight pounds.

"It didn't put up as hard a fight as you'd imagine a fish that size would," Mr. Daly, a 39-year-old lumber mill operator, told the Canadian Press last night. "It was in pretty shallow water. Maybe in deep water it would have fought more."

Mr. Daly said he'd been fishing "since I was born" but he'd never seen a speckled trout like that.

HAVING IT MOUNTED

Neither had any other fishermen in this district 100 miles north-west of Ottawa. All day Sunday they flocked into his house to see the fish, lodged in the Daly refrigerator and later put in a cold storage locker. Mr. Daly is having it mounted.

The fish broke water constantly during the 2-minute battle, he said, but the shallow water kept it from diving. He was still-fishing with an 18-pound test line and an ordinary casting rod when the trout struck. Experts said it was too early in the season for flies.

Mrs. Daly, who does a lot of fishing herself, was like most of the anglers in the district. She, at first, didn't think it was a speckled trout. The average one caught in Canada runs at little more than three pounds.

Spectacle Lakes—10 miles from the border of Algonquin Park and renamed because they resemble spectacles—were restocked with thousands of fingerling trout within the last three years and fishing was permitted this year for the first time since restocking. Mr. Daly's fish was estimated to be between six and eight years old, one of the few left in the lakes before they were fished out.

RECORD HOLDER BELIEVES FISH STORY

Fort William, May 12, (CP)

Dr. J. W. Cook said yesterday he could quite believe that Murray J. Daly was almost speechless after hooking a speckled trout weighting 11 pounds, 13 ounces last Sunday in Spectacle Lake near Barry's Bay, Ont. It was Dr. Cook who, 34 years ago, caught the largest speckled trout on record, a monster topping the scales at 14 pounds, 8 ounces.

Dr. Cook's big fish was mounted and now hangs in the Fort William Tourist Bureau. He made his catch at Macdonald's Rapids, about a mile below Virgin Falls on the Nipigon River, in 1915 .

"The river that day was covered with brown flies," Dr. Cook recalled. "I was fishing with a minnow. When it had settled a little below the surface, the big fish took the bite and was away."

Dr. Cook played his fish and called friends to bring a net. He played it for some time and netted it after a great struggle.

Figure 2.3   A 13-pound brook trout? No! it's a 13-pound splake taken by Esko Kuokkanen of Thunder Bay in 1993. Most splake are man-made crosses between female lake trout and male brook trout; they are usually sterile and the progeny more closely resemble lake trout. However, Kuokkanen's splake was a natural cross between a male lake and a female brook trout; it more closely resembles the female and can reproduce.

"When he opened the fish, it was found to have a stomach full of brown flies," he said. "It was greedy enough to take the minnow, too." Dr. Cook first thought he had landed a lake trout. But as it lay on the shore, Indian guides began to gibber and gesture excitedly. They insisted he had caught an extremely big speckled trout. The fish was weighed and certified by fish experts at Ottawa.

That's not quite the full story of this half of the fish, according to Dan Gapen Sr.—Don Gapen's second son, who grew up on the banks of the Nipigon River. His father ran one of Canadian Pacific Railway's grand resort hotels at "Nepigon Station," located on a high bluff above the eastern side of the river, and the fish was displayed in the hotel for many years. When the hotel was sold and the family moved back to their original home in Minnesota, Gapen kept the fish. The birch-bark mount was pulled out of the basement from time to time and traveled with him and his father to various sportsmen's shows in the Midwest to help them promote Gapen's fly, the Muddler Minnow, and a line of fishing lures and equipment.

"It was pretty ratty-looking even when we first got it," Dan Gapen said, "and age didn't improve it any. After a while, most people forgot about the world's record brook trout and we stopped hauling it around." Gapen, who enjoys dual citizenship, encouraged the museum idea in Nipigon. When it was finally set up, he returned the fish to Canada.

Nor does the saga of the 14½-pound brook trout end with its loss in the fire or the whereabouts of the other half. W. B. Scott, in a 1973 *Fisheries Research Bulletin* (Canada), said that "Andrew Lexie mounted both sides of the fish on birch bark backgrounds."

"Whether there is another side to this mount is now a hot topic," Gord Ellis wrote in a personal communication in December 1994. "One Nipigon old-timer told me this year that there was no second side, that it is a modern myth. He said that it took more than half the fish to make a half-fish mount." Looking at the photograph Ellis took of the mount before it was destroyed in 1990, I tend to agree with the "old-timer."

From the beginning, there were doubts about both Daniel Webster's and Dr. John William Cook's fish being brook trout. Both were identified as being brook trout by experts at the times. However, were they brook trout only in outward appearance? Can a genetically pure brook trout, *Salvelinus fontinalis*, really grow to 14 or more pounds? This question has never been fully laid to rest. But it was again challenged by events that took place as recently as late May 1993, and not far from the Nipigon.

The environment on Long Island easily could have produced a 14½-pounder in 1827. The lower half of the Carmans River is tidal and flows into saline Great South Bay and the Atlantic Ocean. The river just below Fireplace Mills is fresh water, but is backed up by tides. A few hundred yards farther downstream it's all salt. Brook trout, like other charrs and salmon, are anadromous—that is, they're capable of living in either fresh or salt water. As brook trout grow, their diet changes from insects to small and then larger fish. The abundance of small fishes to feed upon is a real attraction to brook trout that have access to a marine environment. And access to the Atlantic was much more direct in 1827 than it is today. At that time, Smith Inlet, just 2 miles from the river's mouth, was open to the ocean. Food there was limitless, and an already big brook trout had little to fear from most predators as long as it avoided bluefish. It would thus have been able to reach its maximum growth potential.

There are big brook trout elsewhere in strictly freshwater environments, but only a few come close to challenging Cook's fish, an all-tackle International Game Fish Association record. The current world-record brook trout taken on a fly rod is a 10-pound, 7-ounce fish taken on the Assinica Branch of the Broadback River in Québec. On other gear it's a 12-pound, 2-ounce brook trout taken from a lake in Argentina that was stocked in 1908 and had no other salmonids. Ken Bohling Jr., who caught this fish, said that when it was first landed it probably weighed at least 13½ pounds. The fish wasn't brought to a scale until several days later. It took first place in IGFA's 1991 annual fishing contest, but didn't qualify for a line-class record because the 15-year-old sent it to the IGFA too late.

For a few weeks in 1993, Esko Kuokkanen shook the world of brook trout anglers. While fishing on a large, clear lake near his home in Thunder Bay, he hooked and landed a huge trout that had a square tail, red dots surrounded by a light blue halo, vermiculations over its back, and the telltale white piping on its fins with black backup strips—a brook trout's trademark. It weighed 13 pounds, 4.1 ounces, was 29½ inches long, and had a girth of 19 inches—all in proportion for a brook trout that large. Superficially it looked like a brook, and that's what Ministry of Natural Resources (MNR) biologist Jon George at first said it was. But then he decided that it didn't look quite right. Just to be sure, the fish was sent to Lakehead University, where Professor Walter Monmot did an internal examination. After counting the pyloric ceca, he said he thought it might be a splake. The number fell between those of a brook and of a lake trout.

To be absolutely sure, a sample of the fish was then sent to MNR's genetic assessment lab in Maple, in southern Ontario. "It is a true splake, 50 percent brook trout and 50 percent lake trout," said Bill Martin, the senior research technician who analyzed the sample of Kuokkanen's fish. "We would call this a first generation splake. The splake stocked by [MNR] hatcheries are usually a lake trout backcross, which means a female lake trout is bred with a male splake."

"Backcross" splake more closely resemble lake trout because they're genetically 75 percent lake trout and 25 percent brook trout, have a slightly forked tail, have a smaller lake trout–like head, and often lack the blue halos around the red dots. More than likely, Kuokkanen's fish was a natural hybrid, even though these are a rare occurrence. The genetic composition of all charr species is so similar that natural hybridization does occur from time to time. There's evidence that in northern Labrador, brook trout have hybridized in the wild with Arctic charr (Hammar).

Gord Ellis's comments in a Thunder Bay newspaper at the time of the catch make interesting speculation. "The fact that the Nipigon [River] system has had evidence of some lake trout–brook trout hybridization," he wrote, "opens an interesting can of worms. Is it even remotely possible that Dr. Cook's big 'spec' had a little lake trout blood in its veins? Perish the thought!

"Lake trout and brook trout have always lived quite closely together in the big river. A piece written in 1884 recounts a fishing trip on the Nipigon River and the writer, Henry Vail, mentions catching brook trout and lake trout side by side in the heavy water below Virgin Falls [now flooded by dams]. Located less than a mile below this spot, was Rabbit Rapids, home of the legendary 14½-pounder. More recently, a video tape was made of a lake trout and brook trout going through the spawning motions on the lower Nipigon River. And of course, the geneticists have already proven that these unions can bear fruit.

"Whether Cook's giant trout was really a hybrid will probably never be known. The old wrinkled mount of the world record went up in smoke along with the rest of the Nipigon Museum—ruling out the chance of DNA testing.

"Perhaps it's just as well. It sure would be a letdown to learn that Dr. Cook's storied old fish was—like Kuokkanen's dandy—just a really big splake."

3. WHAT'S IN A NAME?

How did this strictly North American charr get its name? Who named this bespeckled beauty? When? And why did they call it a brook trout when it wasn't a trout at all?

These are gnawing questions to many brook trout fishers. The attempt to answer them reveals some of the fish's chacteristics—its penchant for specific environments and its ability to cope with changes in its unique biosphere. It also reveals much about the kind of people who came in daily contact with brook trout and brings to light the role this species played in the development of America.

It seems likely that the first English-speaking people to see *Salvelinus fontinalis*, and add it to their diet and vocabulary, were settlers of Plymouth, Massachusetts, in 1620. More than 200 European boats were fishing for cod off Newfoundland as early as 1578, among them vessels from England, and although they may well have seen sea-run brook trout in the estuary at the mouth of the St. John's River, we have no record of anyone noting their existence. Though the English settlement of Jamestown in Virginia predated Plymouth by 13 years, there were no brook trout in the lower portions of the James River for them to discover.

In 1602, Bartholomew Gosnold, one of Sir Walter Raleigh's captains, was sent to Buzzards Bay to found a colony. He failed to do so, but a few years later returned to set up his own trading post on Cuttyhunk Island, on the extreme western end of the Elizabeth Islands, a chain that begins at the southwestern end of Cape Cod. There he

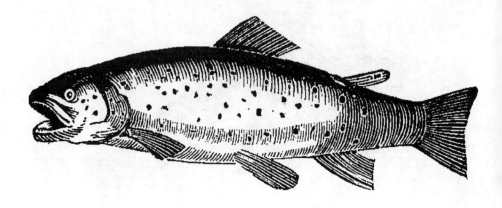

Figure 3.1   Fresh Water Trout. Dr. Jerome V. C. Smith's "Common Trout," the first illustration ever reproduced of the Eastern brook trout, *Salvelinus fontinalis*, from his 1833 book *Natural History of the Fishes of Massachusetts.*

passed several winters, and may have seen trout if he trekked east to the mainland or took a boat north from Cuttyhunk Island across Buzzards Bay. He surely found striped bass plentiful at Cuttyhunk and readily talked about it, but he never told anyone about seeing anything that looked like a trout.

The only Europeans of this period who may have been familiar with this fish were French fur traders and Jesuit priests who settled the North Shore of the St. Lawrence River. In 1599, they established the wilderness outpost of Tadoussac where the Saguenay River flows into the St. Lawrence. It's the oldest continuous French settlement on the continent. More than likely they saw brook trout, because the fish annually migrate up the Saguenay to spawn in nearby brooks, away from the saline St. Lawrence. However, they would have used the term *l'omble de mer* or *truite de mer* for those sea-run brook trout in the big river; *l'omble de fontaine* for those in the brooks. It's unlikely they were the first Europeans to see brook trout, however. French fur traders predated the Dutch on the lower end of Manhattan Island. They had established a transient village on the shores of a deep, freshwater pond on the lower part of the island that later became known as The Collect.

Back in what was later to become Massachusetts, and only 250 yards to the southeast of where 18-year-old Priscilla Mullins became the first European to tread on Plymouth Rock, on Monday morning, December 11, 1620, was a small stream that tumbled from the hills into Plymouth Harbor. The stream was one reason this band of wayward pilgrims chose this site over two others: It had "the best water that ever we drank." It also had brook trout.

The next day, as they rode at anchor aboard the *Mayflower* off Plymouth Beach, the

Table 3.1. Here's the ultimate list of common names for brook trout as used by Americans, English- and French-speaking Canadians, and various Indian and Inuit dialects. Small wonder that a trout known so intimately by so many people for such a long time evolved so many aliases.

Aana	*Masmakus (Mashmakus)*	Slob trout
American brook trout	*Masumek*	Speck
Atagwasu	*Matamekew*	Speckled charr (char)
Aurora trout	*Mouchetée*	Speckled trout
Breac	Mountain trout (in the	Spotted trout
Brook charr (char)	Carolinas)	Squaretail
Brook trout	Mud trout (in the Maritimes)	Square-tailed trout
Brookie	Native trout	*Truchas de arroyos* (Spanish)
Coaster	New York charr (char)	*Truite*
Common brook trout	*Nitilliq*	*Truite de lac*
Eastern brook trout	*Omble de fontaine*	*Truite de mer*
Eastern speckled trout	Omble mouchetée	*Truite ruisseau*
Fontinalis (Argentina)	Salmon trout	*Truite saumonée*
Hemlock trout	Salter	White sea trout
Iqalugaq	Sea trout	

settlers laid out a plan for New Plymouth, as they called it, and named the stream Town Brook—"brook" being the common term for small streams in their native East Anglia.

Brook comes from Old English, a language era arbitrarily designated as ending in A.D. 1150. Old English is only slightly modified Saxon, the Teutonic dialect those invaders brought with them from mainland Europe. The term has its root in the Saxon word *broc*, pronounced "bruk." When the Pilgrims finished naming the moving waters of the New World, there wasn't a creek, kill, or stream within miles of Plymouth. They were all brooks.

Nor were trout unfamiliar to these settlers. Trout were abundant in English streams— *true* trout, brown trout to be exact, a close relative and genealogical spinoff of Atlantic salmon. That the fish they saw in Town Brook were really charr made no difference to Priscilla Mullins or anyone else who went there to fetch a pail of water. They were shaped like brown trout and they had spots like brown trout, although colored a bit differently. The only real distinction was that they tasted a lot better than English trout. These had to be trout, and because they were found in brooks, henceforth they were called brook trout.

Of course, fish nomenclature wasn't important to the colonists, and they changed the fish's name to reflect where it lived. Thus, the trout found in the numerous ponds surrounding New Plymouth were called "pond" trout. *Pond* is another typically Old English word. And when they were caught from the waters of Plymouth Harbor or outside in Cape Cod Bay, they were called "sea" trout. Thus the same fish was called brook, pond, or sea trout, depending upon locale. Later, sea trout were also called "salters."

This practice continued for more than 200 years in New England in general and Massachusetts in particular. In 1833, a physician-turned-ichthyologist (also see "Mitchill" in the bibliography) produced this country's second attempt to classify its fishes. When it came to identifying brook trout, he could have been one of Scrooby village postmaster William Brewster's boys. The following is from his book: *A Natural History of the Fishes of Massachusetts,* by Jerome V. C. Smith, M.D., Boston, 1833:

> These are pond-trout, river or brook-trout, and sea-trout. The two former being such fish as live exclusively in fresh water, and the latter, such as live, a great part of the year, in that which is salt or brackish, ascending the streams as spring advances, and returning to their native element so soon as the spawning season is over. [Smith had it reversed.]
>
> There are but few natural ponds or lakes in this state which contain trout, for it is that which is found in natural ponds, which we denominate pond-trout, and not the more common fish which is generally found in artificial mill-ponds, and which closely resembles such as are found in the brooks and rivers, which being flooded, form the ponds.

"But what's in a name?" asked Shakespeare. To paraphrase the bard, would this fish by any other name smell, look, or taste the same?

The answer is yes, but maybe not when it comes to *Salvelinus fontinalis,* because answering the question What is this fish's name? may explain its game.

Its more popular alias in the United States is brook trout, more specifically eastern brook trout, but it's also known by its descriptive names: speckled trout in Canada, squaretail in Maine. While it does live in brooks, it also lives in streams, creeks, rivers, ponds, lakes, and even salt water. In the latter environs it's still referred to as sea trout or sometimes the salter, but mostly by old-time Long Islanders or Cape Codders. While the Great Lakes aren't saline and brook trout there could thus never be called salters, those that annually leave rivers and streams to wander about this vast freshwater sea are there called "coasters."

But isn't "eastern" in the name redundant? We know its natural range is restricted to eastern North America, in the Appalachians as far south as Georgia, as far north as Labrador and Ungava, and as far west as Minnesota. However, there was a good reason "eastern" was later tacked onto "brook trout," although it's no longer valid today.

When settlers, most of English descent or recent arrivals, first came down the western slopes of the Rocky Mountains, they too discovered that brooks there were filled with trout; ergo, these fish first became known as brook trout. For a time these western trout were called just brook trout. But because they looked considerably different from brook trout in the East, there was a compelling need to call them something else. To end this madness they were called California brook trout, and later just California trout.

These same trout also swam in brooks in Washington, Oregon, British Columbia, and even Alaska. People in these areas didn't take kindly to others calling their trout

"California trout." Even in California, and everywhere else for that matter, people who had been east at one time or another didn't think they looked much like brook trout. Even easterners were getting confused, so they and Californians agreed to call the fish from the East eastern brook trout, and those from the West western brook trout. About that time, westerners who still didn't like the handle hung on their trout made another change and began calling them rainbow trout, after the colors along their sides.

Well, that ended the confusion in the West, but brook trout were indelibly marked as eastern brook trout. The name "eastern brook trout," brookies for short, was universally accepted by biologists and lay fishers until fish culturists decided to get involved.

The ecologies of many rivers, streams, brooks, and creeks in the East were in a state of flux; waters were rapidly losing their brook trout populations because of the denudation of the eastern forests. Watersheds without their leafy mantles warmed above 69 or 70 degrees, and brookies couldn't tolerate the heat. They either moved upstream to cooler water or died.

Fish culturists hate a void. In the mid- to late 1800s they discovered so many trout streams within their aegis without trout that they began stocking exotic species. In 1883, Baron Lucius von Behr and Fred Mather stepped onto the scene. Behr shipped jars upon jars of fertilized trout eggs collected from fish on his Black Forest estate in Germany to Mather's newly completed fish hatchery in Cold Spring Harbor, on Long Island.

Their brown coloration and country of origin led American anglers to dub the new arrivals "German brown trout." However, about 1917, everything German in this country developed a negative connotation and fish managers dropped the "German." The fish were simply called brown trout. Since they could survive slightly higher temperatures they were stocked in streams that once held brook trout, and some that still did.

But what about our brookies?

Where both species appeared in the same stream, lay fishermen began calling brookies "natives," as opposed to foreigners or non-native imports such as brown trout. The fish didn't mind, and both species got along to a degree. However, natives tended to sulk in stream and pool bottoms or moved into smaller feeder streams, where temperatures were a degree or two cooler. And when bigger waters warmed in July and August, the natives went home and the browns settled deeper in the deepest pools.

Culturists thought there was room for more variety in eastern streams, and imported from California cans upon cans of California trout, alias rainbow trout. "Bows," as some anglers call them, like a habitat somewhere between those preferred by brown and by brook trout, perhaps favoring the brook trout's environment. The natives didn't have a chance. Rainbows are far more aggressive and grow bigger and faster than brookies. In a short time, the natives didn't dare set fin in the main stream. They were relegated to smaller, shallower, tree-covered feeder streams. Only when they were a few years older and big enough not to become rainbow fodder did they dare venture into the realm usurped by western brook trout.

While 'bows were great fighters and leapers and became immediate favorites with some anglers, others still demanded that their fish managers keep streams well stocked with natives as well as foreigners. To accomplish this, eastern hatcheries began turning out tons of small brookies for the streams. But the constant interbreeding produced a lackluster fish that preferred worms, liver, or pellet-shaped flies, that had little or no inclination to fight, and whose flesh paled in both color and taste to the salmon-colored meat of the original brook trout.

After years of complaint, in an attempt to revitalize their brood fish and return to something akin to the original fish, hatchery managers began to import foreign brookies—not really that foreign, maybe more like lost siblings. The managers went north to the Rivers Temiscamie and Assinica in Québec, where wild brook trout lived that were really big and even more gaudily colored. It was hoped that these wild strains would bolster the genetics of the pen-raised pets. It worked, to a degree, but many of these wild fish also became tamed in the process.

Today there's a trend, a very intelligent trend, that couldn't have taken place 100 years ago, because the ecology of the streams at that time had been so altered that they wouldn't sustain a wild population of brook trout. But now, thanks to vast natural and managed reforestation efforts, the return to a near-natural state of large numbers of failed hillside farms, and various stream reclamation efforts, the water quality in many trout streams has risen. By adopting the new method of selecting remnants of remaining wild strains of brook trout as hatchery stock—but only for a single unique watershed—managers have slowly been able to reestablish natives in some of their original habitat.

All of this may seem like a lot of effort to replace a trout that isn't even a trout. Actually, *Salvelinus fontinalis* is a charr. True, it's a close cousin to the trout, as close as cousins can get, but just calling it a trout doesn't make it one. *Salvelinus* is an old Germanic word for Arctic charr found in the Alps. The literature just says that it's an old name; no one has ever explained what it means. *Fontinalis* is easy: It's Latin (*fons*) and means "dweller near springs," which is just what brookies do. "Charr," sometimes wrongly spelled "char," is an adequate name for brook trout. It's derived from the Celtic word *cear*, which means "blood." The name is appropriate because the sides of all charrs—the only charr they saw in Europe was the Arctic charr—turn blood red during the fall spawning period.

Of course, brookies aren't the world's only misnamed charr. There are Dolly Varden trout, lake trout, bull trout, and kundascha (*leucomaenis*) in Asia—and all are charr. The only charr actually called "charr" is the circumpolar Arctic charr. The more nearly correct name for *Salvelinus fontinalis* (it's still off the mark) is the one used in Canada: the speckled trout. Of course, most Canadians call them "speckles" and nothing else. If I were to select a new name for this fish, I'd call it "speckled charr," which means what it says and nothing else. Some ichthyologists are even tossing around a new term for charrs wrongly called trout: brook charr—along with lake charr, Dolly Varden charr, bull charr, as well as Arctic charr. These sound very appropriate, but I still like speckled charr best.

BROOK TROUT AND THEIR UNIQUENESS

4 What Are Brook Trout and How Did They Get Here?

Order: *Salmoniformis (fish with soft-rayed fins)*
Family: *Salmonidae (trout, salmon, and whitefish)*
Genus: *Salvelinus (an old Germanic name for charr)*
Subgenus: *Baione (a suggested subgenus)*
Species: *Fontinalis (living in springs)*

Brook trout are members of an ancient order of fishes that had its beginnings more than 100 million years ago in the Oligocene Epoch—a geological time zone characterized by the development of higher forms of animals. The Salmonidae, today represented by the salmons, trouts, charrs, whitefishes, and ciscos, vary greatly in outward appearance, but are grouped together because they all have two features in common: adipose and pelvic fins. The adipose is a small, vestigial fin—fleshy, and lacking supportive fin rays—located on the back between the dorsal and beginning of the caudal (tail) fin. Its function is a mystery to ichthyologists. Oddly enough, it also appears on some species of catfish—a far cry from the salmonids.

Paleoichthyologists theorize that somewhere before the Oligocene Epoch of the Quaternary period on the geological clock, probably in the late Mesozoic era, all of these adipose-finned fish had a common ancestor; they all possess a double number of chromosomes, while other closely related orders in their class contain single sets of chromosome, as do most other animals. An examination of their fossilized remains and

35

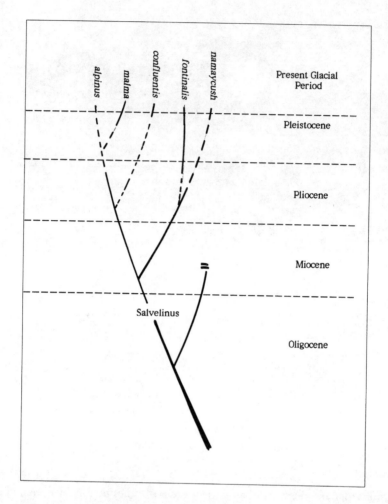

Figure 4.1 A suggested phylogeny of North American *Salvelini* (Smith and Stearley).

extrapolation of physical characteristics, usually from bony skeletal parts, indicates that a progressive reduction of bony skull parts had begun by the Oligocene Epoch; it would continue to modern examples. This indicates that charrs (*Salvelini*, plural) and another branch of the salmonlike fishes (e.g., smelts) had already divided into separate groups. Charr differ from true trout in that they have teeth only on the head of the chevron of the vomer, a boat-shaped bone in the back part of the mouth's roof, and these are often only feebly developed.

In the late Oligocene, the salmonlike group divided into *Salmo* and *Oncorhynchus*. Sometime during the Pliocene Epoch, *Salmo* had an offshoot, the brown trout; during the Miocene, *Oncorhynchus* divided into the six Pacific salmon species, along with another branch that today is represented by rainbow and cutthroat trout. These two later species, along with brown trout, are the world's only true trouts.

On the other side of the salmonid tree, the *Salvelini* also divided during the late Miocene. During the next epoch, Pliocene, one branch gave rise to *confluentus* (bull trout), *malma* (Dolly Varden), and *alpinus* (Arctic charr), and the other to *fontinalis* (brook trout), *namaycush* (lake trout), *leucomaenis* (kund-ascha), and a few other Asiatic forms whose taxonomy is still being evolved.

A unique feature developed in the brook/lake trout branch that may have its manifestations in today's examples of these two species. Unlike Arctic charr, Dolly Varden, and bull trout—whose taxonomy is still in a state of flux because of the great variety of strains and even subspecies of these circumpolar fishes that appear in the Northern Hemisphere—brook and lake trout physically appear quite similar to all other brook and lake trout throughout their ranges. Thus it seems likely that current forms of these two species have changed little since their parent stock broke away from other *Salvelini*; they, too, then separated in the Pliocene epoch.

The only recognized variation in lake trout is the *Siscowet*. It appears only in Lake Superior, and is regarded by some taxonomists as a subspecies: *Salvelinus namaycush siscowet*. This lake trout carries an exceptional amount of fat, probably as insulation, because it prefers deeper water than the other lake trout with which it cohabits; it even spawns at depths below 300 feet.

Different strains of brook trout do exist, but rarely in the same watershed, and this calls for a definition of *strain*. As an example, one population of brook trout may have initially colonized a single watershed. For this example, assume that the watershed was composed of two main branches. One drained a high, rugged, and hilly or mountainous terrain, while the second meandered at a lower elevation with less relief. As long as the lower branch remained in the same physical state with its flora intact, one strain filled both branches. But as the lower branch experienced forestry, farming, and the effects of civilization, only those brook trout with a different genetic (genotypic) makeup—one that gave them the ability to adapt to an elevated mean temperature, turbid waters, and fewer gravel beds upon which to spawn—survived. Today, the brook trout in both branches would appear the same (phenotypic), but differ genetically and hence are considered by some a different strain. In efforts to rehabilitate such streams, it's crucial to the success of the stocking effort that the stocked fish be of the same genotypic characteristics as the native. This may require a search to the very headwaters of that branch, and seeking out populations that have been isolated. The next step is to determine genetically the gene pool to which they belong (Krueger).

Different strains or even subspecies occur naturally and frequently in all fishes, but for some unexplained reason this phenomenon in brook trout seems suppressed. Here, the causative factor for strains is usually isolation from the species' main genetic pool. Only two examples of different strains, or subspecies, have been recorded as cohabiting with mainstream brook trout. One is the aurora trout, a nonspotted brook trout that appeared in three small lakes at the headwaters of the Montreal River in the Témiskaming district of Ontario. It was first described by biologists in 1925 as a distinct species, *Salvelinus timagamiensis*, and believed to be form of Arctic charr, because it lacked the typical vermiculates on the back characteristic of all brook trout. However, further scrutiny of the aurora trout in 1967 showed that it was too closely allied to *fontinalis* to be considered a separate species; it was then reclassified as *Salvelinus fontinalis timagamiensis*. Sadly, by this time the stock of aurora trout was so reduced that reproduction failed. Today it's doubtful that any examples remain alive. (See the discussion of the aurora trout, pages 84–86.)

The other brook trout that didn't outwardly look like a brook trout was the silver charr, which shared Monadnock Lake near Dublin, New Hampshire, with typical-looking brook trout. It was first described as a species, *Salvelinus agassizii*. Biologists of the day thought it more closely related to lake trout than brook trout because, like lake trout, it moved into shallow waters in October to spawn. However, in 1967 ichthyologist Dr. Robert J. Behnke, examining preserved examples, showed that it had evolved instead from brook trout. The silver trout is now believed to be extinct, its demise caused not by stock reduction but by assimilation with existent brook trout. Even though brook trout had long coexisted with silver, for some reason their presence eventually eliminated the strain. Only 13 examples, all preserved specimens, remain of the silver trout. That they crossed with brook trout was an indication of the closeness of their relation to *fontinalis* rather than *alpinus*. Later DNA testing of tissue from preserved examples of silver charr and aurora trout showed that both were closely linked to brook trout.

Early confusion as to the niche brook trout should occupy derived from the numerous early methods of naming a new plant or animal, usually done in the namer's native language. What was needed was an international way of naming species in a language all biologists could understand. This task finally was undertaken by Caroli A. von Linné (1701–78), a Swedish botanist. Among other things, in 1758 he devised the binominal nomenclature system of naming existing and new species. Linné decided to use Latin, the Italic language of Rome, not only because of its wide use in many different countries but because of its use in many universities that were often run by the Catholic church. The name of the first person to describe a species was added to the end of the two Latinized names (genus and species) and all three became that species' scientific name. He latinized his own name, too, and throughout literature was known as Linnaeus. With some modifications his became the system used by today's scientists.

In 1732, Linné explored Lapland in what today is northern Norway, Sweden, and Finland, and there first encountered Arctic charr. When it came to naming this fish, however, he relied on descriptions by predecessors and their vocabulary. He placed Arctic charr in a genus he called *Salvelinus*, which first appeared in his book *Systema naturae*, published in 1758. He never explained or defined the meaning of *Salvelinus*. No one today is quite sure of its meaning. Some believe it might have been the word Laplanders used for this red sustenance fish found in their lakes and rivers.

However, according to John Hammar (Hammer), a scientist with the Swedish Institute of Freshwater Research and an avid charr biologist since the 1970s, "*Salvelinus* has nothing to do with any Scandinavian, Finnish, or Sami words for charr." According to Hammar, Linné's original papers referred to earlier papers by others. Among them were Francis Willughby's two papers, *De Historia Piscium* and *Ichthyographia*, from 1686, with reference to the charr *Umbla altera* and including the German expression "*ein Salvelin.*"

The German word for Arctic charr is *See-Saibling* (also *Salbing* or *Sailbing*). Hammar and Peter B. Mayle (Mayle) of the Department of Wildlife and Fishes Biology, University of California at Davis, believe, as do many other ichthyologists (probably because of Arno Press's [New York Times Co.] 1978 reprinting of Willughby's papers), that the words *Salvelinus* and *Saibling* are derived from the German-related expression *Salvelin*. Further, according to Hammar, Artedi (1738), upon which Linné bases his charr descriptions, places the origin of the word *Salvelinus* with charr found in a watershed in Austria, outside of Linz. In all likelihood, Linné took the German reference *Salvelini* and latinized it to *Salvelinus*. The origin of the word *charr* is easy: it's Celtic and was discussed in chapter 3.

There were no brook trout in Europe at the time Linné was renaming his world, so the first scientific description of brook trout was done in North America by Dr. Samuel Latham Mitchill (1764–1831). Using Linné's system but not his intuitiveness, Mitchill wrongly placed brook trout in the genus *Salmo,* and it became *Salmo fontinalis* (Mitchill). The fault wasn't all his. In Mitchill's day there were no biologists as we know them today; most were physicians, who usually worked in more than one or two disciplines. Mitchill was the epitome of these men. While he was first a physician, he was also a man of many trades and at best master of none.

Born in North Hempstead on Long Island, New York, he served both in Albany and Washington at various times as a senator and congressman. He was also an academic who taught, but not all at once, natural history, agriculture, botany, and chemistry at Columbia College. He was an avid promoter of science as well as a practicing physician and a prolific writer. His most notable contribution was a paper on the fishes of New York State. At the time, the biological sciences as we know them were in their infancy. Many errors were made due to primitive procedural techniques and a general lack of knowledge, which allowed specimens to be placed in the wrong genera, orders, or even families based on incorrect morphological analysis. Mitchill was also a sloppy biologist and made errors in observation that later embarrassed even him.

He had foresight, however, and named the brook trout, in the first edition of *Report, In Part, of Samuel L. Mitchill, M.D., Professor of Natural History, & etc., on the Fishes of New York*. This was a vanity printing done January 1, 1814, by D. Carlisle, No. 31 Broadway. Later that same year it was republished, without mention of the first printing, and with some but not all needed corrections, in *Transactions of the Literary and Philosophical Society of New York* (I-355–492).

While the book was poor as a piece of biological literature, it was "one of the rarest contributions to ichthyology," according to Dr. Theodore Gill, professor of zoology at

Columbia University and this country's preeminent biologist at the turn of the century, in his 1898 introduction to an exact reprint of Mitchill's publication. Gill believed the book was valuable because it was the first attempt in the United States to begin scientifically classifying fish. Dedicated brook trout anglers might be interested in reading Mitchill's exact description of their fish:

Salmo S. *Fontinalis**—New York Trout

Mouth wide. Teeth sharp. Tongue distinct. Skin without scales. Back a mottled pale and brown. Sides dark brown with yellow and red spots; the yellow larger than the red. The latter appearing like scarlet dots. Lateral line straight. The yellow and red spots both above and below that line. Sides of the abdomen orange red. Lowest part of the belly whitetish, with a smutty tinge. First rays of the pectoral, ventral and anal fins white, the second black; the rest purplish red. Dorsal fin mottled, of yellowish and black. Tail rather concave, but not amounting to a fork, and of a reddish purple, with blackish spots above and below. Eye large, iris pale.

[13] Rays B.10; V.7: P. 12: D. 13-O: A.11: C. 23.

Its characters, as derived from the fins and colours, differs so much from the salmo fario of the books, that it may be deemed another species; or at any rate a wide variety.

Most of the 24 species Mitchill described came from fish markets, which lined lower Manhattan along Fulton Street. However, when it came to brook trout, he made his examination *in situ,* (on location). Being a native Long Islander, he was already familiar with this fish and its wide distribution, because at that time Long Island offered the best brook trout fishing in the country. The island was endowed with many spring-fed ponds and streams that were always cool, an ideal habitat for this species. In the second publication of that year, he added personal comment to the more reserved scientific description of a brook trout:

Is reckoned to be a most dainty fish. They travel to Hempstead and Islip, for the pleasure of catching and eating him. He is bought at the extravagant price of a quarter of a dollar for a single fish not more than 10 or 12 inches long. He lives in running water only, and not in stagnant ponds; and, therefore, the lively streams descending north and south from their sources on Long-Island, exactly suit the constitution of this fish. The heaviest Long-Island trout that I have heard of, weighed four and a half pounds.

I copy the following article from the news-papers: "Mr. Robbins, of the Philadelphia theatre, visited Long-Island (New York State) in the late summer of 1814; during his stay in that place, he caught *one hundred and ninety freshwater trout,* weighing as follows, viz.

Date	Trout, caught at	No. of Trout	lbs.	oz.
Sept. 6th	Nicol's	14	X	X
8th	Patchogue	9	7	8
9th	"	21	10	8
10th	"	78	26	0
12th	"	5	5	0
13th	"	4	5	0
15th	Fireplace Mill	1	3	0
16th	"	16	16	8
17th	"	9	3	0
19th	Patchogue	23	47	0
20th	"	6	7	0
21st	"	4	8	3
Days 12		Fish 190	139 lbs.	11 oz.

"The largest fish caught at Patchogue, weighed two pounds and 8 ounces; the largest at Fireplace, three pounds.

"Dr. Post, of New-York, caught one hundred and fifty trout weighing one hundred and five pounds, in the month of April 1811, in the waters of Long Island.

"Mr. Purvis, of New-York, caught a trout weighing four pounds eight ounces, measuring twenty-four inches in length. A drawing of the fish remains at Fireplace, near where it was caught."

Purvis's fish was caught at Sam Carman's tavern (Fireplace Mills) at the "crossing-over place." Daniel Webster's 14½-pound trout, caught 16 years and one month later, probably had its outline drawn under that of Mr. Purvis's brook trout. Drawing outlines of big brook trout on walls was the custom of the period, as it is today in many fishing camps.

It didn't take long for more exacting biologists of the day to begin correcting many of Mitchill's errors. Mitchill had grouped the brook trout with *Salmo* because it so closely resembled the brown trout. The genus designation was revised in 1836 by John Richardson, an English biologist who traveled across northern Canada in 1826 with Sir John Franklin, the English admiral and Arctic explorer. Richardson, in his book *Fauna Borieli Americain,* which resulted from the adventure, reclassified the brook trout as *Salvelinus fontinalis* (Mitchill). Mitchill's name was still attached to the scientific name but now appeared, as is the correct procedure, in parentheses because the Latin name had been modified. Richardson, who also called this fish "The New York Charr," was the first to classify the fish as a charr species, although he wasn't the first to use the generic name. In 1832, S. Nilsson (in *Prodromus ichthyologieae Scandinaviae*) reclassified the lake trout as a *Salvelini* (plural), which would have included the brook trout, although he didn't refer to it. In later literature (1893) it was described as genus *Salvelinis* (Nilsson) Richardson, meaning that Nilsson first used the name *Salvelinus* (not necessarily brook trout but for other charrs) and was then corrected by Sir John Richardson. This is the reason Richardson's name isn't in parentheses.

An early New York biologist, James E. DeKay, in *Zoölogy of New York,* 1842, believing that brook trout should be in a genus of their own, separate from lake trout and other charrs, replaced *Salvelinus* with *Bione.* However, few followed his name change. Even though the genus name *Salvelinus* was now correct, writers who followed—even some with science backgrounds, such as Thaddeus Norris, in his classic *The American Angler's Book* (1864)—either preferred to use *Salmo* rather than *Salvelinus* or were unaware of the change.

The first general publication to use *Salvelinus* was a revision of G. Brown Goode's massive species compendium *American Fishes.* The book was first published in 1887, but was revised and expanded in 1903 by Dr. Theodore Gill. It appeared a year after *American Food & Game Fishes* was published by David Starr Jordan and Barton W. Evermann. However, Jordan had already adopted *Salvelinus* (as did Ayres and Kirtland in the *Boston Journal of Natural History*) in 1878, in *Proceedings of the U.S. Natural History Museum.* However, it took someone of Jordan's stature to make the change from *Salmo* to *Salvelinus* official. In the 1878 publication, he removed the older genus designation, continued the species designation, and when writing *American Food & Games Fishes* in 1886 described it again as *Salvelinus.* Even though this publication is now over 100 years old, Jordan and Evermann's book is still the accepted authority for description and classification of many fish species. But *Salmo* didn't die easily:

> The Eastern Brook Trout must have been discovered by the first settlers of North America soon after their coming to the New World; yet, strange to say, the only allusion to it in colonial times is in the *"Remonstrance of New Netherland,"* addressed by that colony to the States General in 1649. It was first brought before the world of science in 1814, when Dr. Mitchill named it *Salmo fontinalis,* a name which has become almost classical. Our ichthyologists having recently decided that its technical name shall be *Salvelinus,* a wail has arisen from our anglers, and the ever witty Charles Hallock† has voiced the general discontent in his rhythmical protest, beginning: "I am Salmo fontinalis,"* which concludes as follows:
>
> > "No fulsome titles do I covet,
> > Science holds no bribe for me.
> > Slavery for those who love it.
> > From nomenclature leave me free,
> > Yet they call me Salvelinus.
> > Can you fancy sin more heinous."
>
> †*Editor of Forest and Stream*
> **American Angler II, 247*
>
> *From* American Fishes *by G. Browne Good, 1887*
> *Revised by Theodore Gill, 1903*

BAPTISM OF THE BROOK TROUT

I AM Salmo Fontinalis,
To the sparkling fountain born,
And my home is where oxalis,
Heather bell and rose adorn
The crystal basin in the dell,
(Undine the wood-nymph knows it well,)
That is where I love to dwell.
There was I baptized and christened,
'Neath the sombre aisles of oak,
Mute the cascade paused and listened,
Never a word the brooklet spoke;
Bobolink was witness then,
Likewise Ousel, Linnet, Wren,
And all the brownies joined "amen."
Noted oft in ancient story,
Erst from immemorial time,
Poets, anglers, hermits hoary
Confirm my vested rights sublime.
All along the mountain range,
'Tis writ in mystic symbols strange:
"Naught shall abrogate or change."
Thus as Salmo Fontinalis
Recognized the wide world o'er, *
In my limpid crystal palace,
Content withal, I ask no more;
Leaping through the rainbow spray,
Snatching flies the livelong day.
Naught to do but live and play.
**But scientists have changed this most appropriate*
designation to S. Salvelinus, more's the pity!

By Charles Hallock, in
The Speckled Brook Trout, Louis Rhead, Ed., 1902

The debate about the correct location of brook trout in the salmonid tree continues. More recently, in 1954, Canadian biologist Vadim D. Vladykov suggested a tentative rearrangement for charr in which *Salvelinis fontinalis* represents a distinct subgenus *Baione*, established in 1842 by DeKay. Vladykov reinstated the use of *Baione* as a subgeneric name to emphasize the distinction of *Salvelinus fontinalis* from other species in the genus. E. P. Slastenenko (1958) meanwhile used *Bione* as a generic designation for the brook trout. The subgeneric nomenclature was adopted by J. S. Nelson (1976) in *Fishes of the World* and Robert Behnke in 1980 (*Charrs*, ed. E. K. Balon), who also included the species *Salvelinus agassizii* (silver trout). However, S. U. Qadri dropped the use of the genus or subgenus *Baione* in his doctoral thesis in 1964, saying: "The genus or subgenus *Baione*, established because of the absence of basibranchial teeth, uninterrupted row of vomerine and palatine teeth, and square tail, is dropped because these features are also observed in various species of the genus *Salvelinus.*" While there is some division among ichthyologists today, most use *Salvelinus* as the generic name.

5 GLACIATION AND DISTRIBUTION OF BROOK TROUT

The world of the brook trout has never been one of stability. Instead, it has been one with land masses in a constant state of flux, either separating, clashing, rising, or falling, with hemispheric ice sheets marching back and forth like huge bulldozers, scouring and reshaping the land and its lakes and rivers—and pushing and pulling its flora and fauna.

During the Oligocene Epoch, 100 million or more years ago, something in the environment caused the main stem of the salmonids to separate from other bony fishes; soon thereafter the charrs separated from the salmon and true trout. This was in a geological period when the earliest glaciers—a phenomenon of which we have no real evidence but, when extrapolated back, explains events that followed—began to infringe upon the lives of fish and other animals in the Northern Hemisphere.

Salmonids that became charrs probably possessed a physiology slightly different from their contemporaries that allowed them to move into and successfully colonize waters colder than other fish could tolerate. The champion of this cold-water habitat is the Arctic charr, but the brook trout is a close second. Cold-water environments are its arena. In some northern waters, Atlantic salmon also share a habitat with charrs, but they never reach the growth potential exhibited by more southerly salmon populations. Early after separation from the main stem of charrs, the common ancestor from which brook and lake trout eventually evolved developed a body type and physiology better suited to the changing ambient environment; adaptation was not a barrier to it. This lack of specialization was thus its salvation during these constantly changing times.

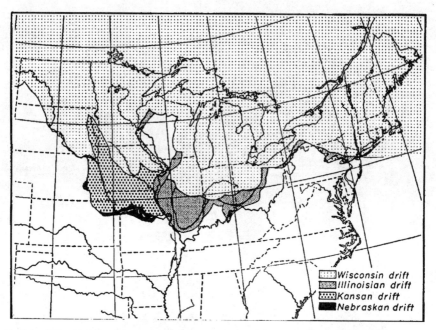

:::::	Wisconsin drift
	Illinoisian drift
	Kansan drift
■	Nebraskan drift

Figure 5.1 Map showing the southern limit of glacial drift in the United States. Some ice sheets extended farther south than the Wisconsin Ice Sheet, the youngest and uppermost. (After R. F. Flint.)

That it preferred cold water and had an unlimited supply of it across northern parts of the world was its key to survival. But in a very real way, this, too, was a specialization that doomed it when changes took place in the southern fringes of its range. Brook trout evolved an unspecialized body form that was unaffected by glacial movement. However, the fish's distribution across eastern North America was profoundly manipulated by glaciers.

There have been at least 10 separate ice ages within the last million years. There's bountiful evidence left upon the land by the Wisconsin Ice Sheet, the last great continental glacier of the late Pleistocene, today's epoch, that swept down from an epicenter near Hudson Bay. Glacial geologists have evidence that at least three earlier glaciers (Nebraskan, the oldest, and Kansan and Illinoisan) preceded it, and a few more probably date back to pre-Oligocene epochs. The last glacier, which began about 55,000 years ago, interests us most because it shaped the current distribution of brook trout.

Glaciers are the result of periodic changes in the shape of the earth's elliptical orbit around the sun and changes in the earth's angle of tilt toward the sun. It's not so much cold winters that start the formation of glaciers as it is cold summers. Continental ice sheets, as they grow in size because of unmelted winter snows, become increasingly self-perpetuating. As they enlarge in size and weight they depress the earth's land masses, which float on a core of molten magma. While one end of a continent is being depressed, the other end gains altitude, which further reduces that area's mean temperatures.

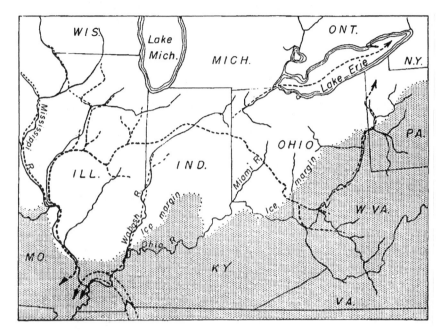

Figure 5.2 Drainage changes in the Ohio and Mississippi river basins due to glaciation. Preglacial drainage courses are shown in broken lines. (After R. F. Flint.)

Twenty thousand years is hardly a blink in geological or evolutionary time. But it's long enough for some fishes to evolve new strains or even species. In Salmonids, this occurred with Arctic charr but not brook or lake trout, with two possible exceptions. When the Wisconsin Glacier, about 20,000 years ago, sat more than 1,000 feet astride Manhattan, the isle wasn't an island but a hilltop. The edge of the continental shelf and ocean were more than 70 miles away and 600 feet lower than today.

At that time, the Arctic was on Manhattan and the temperate zone ranged as far south as today's northern rim of the Gulf of Mexico. Most of central North America south of Canada drains southward, toward the Gulf, and those fish in the lakes and marshes at the northern ends of these rivers and their watersheds began to move southward with the advance of the glaciers. At the same time another phenomenon occurred. Temperate fishes on the southern edge were now able to move into an environment that had been too warm for their survival but that was now cooling to their liking. But those on the northern end, if they couldn't link up with a southward-flowing watershed, faced extinction. If they couldn't find passage routes away from the extreme cold to which they couldn't adapt and waters too cold to hatch their eggs, then these trapped parts of populations were eradicated. All the fishes we today associate with the northern United States and Canada—northern pike, lake and brook trout, grayling, and even Arctic charr—were then common to the states that border the Gulf of Mexico.

When a glacier recedes, just the opposite happens. Meltwater from the southern terminus of the Wisconsin Glacier filled the vast inland depression that housed the Great Lakes
drainage and rose until it flowed out of the basin. At the southernmost end of this great
ice mass, temporary lakes or refugia began to form. At first these usually flooded across the
sources of several watersheds, such as the Mississippi and Ohio rivers, and gave the most
northerly of fishes that were able to live near them a route to move east and west as far as
a refugium extended. This freed some fish species restricted to eastern parts of the United
States to move a few degrees westward, and those in the center to move eastward.

The refugium at the southern end of the Great Lakes basin became the center of the
northward-expanding brook trout population. As its ice retreated northward, various
parts of the Great Lakes became ice-free and the water often rose above its present elevation, allowing brook trout to cross later physical barriers and to disperse and continuously
colonize new areas as each became available. However, it was not an even retreat. As climatic changes vacillated back and forth, glacial tongues reentered valleys and reengulfed
lakes, only to melt and move back again. Refugia glacial melt created slowly shifting habitats, and the ever-opportunistic brook trout continued to exist. Though local extinctions
probably took place, recolonizations were common occurrences.

One of the early unravelers of postglacial distribution of Great Lakes fish was Dr. H.
H. MacKay, of the Fish and Wildlife Branch of Ontario's Department of Lands and
Forests. He wrote the following in *Fishes of Ontario,* 1963:

> Because of early connections between the Alaska-Yukon route and the more
> southerly areas which were free of ice, it is believed that all the salmonids
> (except the brook trout), the northern pike, the fine-scale sucker *(Catostomus
> catostomus),* the burbot, the trout perch *(Percopsis omiscomaycus),* and certain
> sculpins *(Cottidae)* used this means of eventually entering the Great Lakes
> watershed. Northern pike, fine-scaled sucker and burbot may also have used
> the Mississippi refugium. The fallfish *(Semotilus corporalis)* probably came
> from the Atlantic coastal refugium.
>
> Carl Hubbs and Karl Lagler in *Fishes of the Great Lakes Refugium* have also
> suggested that brook trout, came from the eastern and western refugia.
>
> During the marine invasion in postglacial times, the waters of the St.
> Lawrence Valley, Lake Ontario and Lake Champlain were salt. At this time, many
> forms that exist now as freshwater forms entered from the ocean; for example,
> smelt, shad, and alewife, which may be considered relics of the marine invasion
> or marine derivatives.

It's probable that ancestors of Lake Ontario salmon entered this lake during the
marine invasion. Their descendants continued to live in the lake without returning to
the sea. A. A. Blair reported in a 1956 paper that he examined the scales of a salmon that
had been taken in Lake Ontario prior to 1870 and concluded that it had never been to
sea. MacKay further postulated on the barriers these fishes encountered:

The St. Lawrence River was at first very short but, as the land continued to rise following the recession of the ice, the river lengthened. During this time, it is probable that anadromous fishes adjusted their movements in a changing environment. With the exception of the St. Lawrence River, all natural drainage connections into the Mississippi and the Atlantic ocean have ceased.

After the recession of the ice, there remained extensive flooded areas, swamps, marshes and shallow lakes by means of which fish inhabiting these areas would spread out in many directions. This postglacial condition probably accounts for the widespread distribution of the mud minnow (Umbra). A good example of the effect of ecological factors in limiting the distribution of certain forms, is the 65°F. July isotherm which coincides approximately with the northern limit of the smallmouth and largemouth bass.

For brook trout this July isotherm is 48.2 degrees Fahrenheit and is a line drawn approximately from Nain on the Labrador coast, west near Povungnituk to near the Manitoba–Northwest Territories border on Hudson Bay.

Brook trout took advantage of high lake or refugia levels and colonized areas they could never reach today. One example is the brook trout population in the Nipigon River versus those in Nipigon Lake. The lake is 313 feet higher than Lake Superior and 32 miles to the north. Brook trout are great rapids runners, but unlike salmon, steelhead (rainbow) trout, and even Arctic charr, brook trout can jump and leap only small falls. The Nipigon River is filled with roaring chutes and falls with angular rather than straight drops. Most were eventually negotiable by brook trout. However, Virgin Falls, a mile from the mouth of Lake Nipigon, is a 20-foot vertical drop, and no brook trout could make it over. At one time the lake held one of the largest populations of big brook trout in the fish's entire range. So how did they get above the falls?

About 8,700 years ago, Lake Nipigon (known geologically then as Lake Kelvin) received most of its water from the northwest, through a short, temporary river from a huge glacial lake called Lake Agassiz. Lake Kelvin and its tremendous glacial flow carved some of the canyonlike features of today's Nipigon River Valley. Lake Agassiz, inhabited by brook trout, covered most of western Ontario and all of Manitoba and Saskatchewan. All of the meltwater on the western side of the glacier would eventually drain to the ocean and the lake would dry up, except for its last vestige, Lake Manitoba. Today, it survives by infusions of runoff and ground water.

One could say that brook trout rode the melt northward, and some rode it upward. Water temperature is crucial to this species' survival; its ideal range is between 35 and 55 degrees Fahrenheit. As the glaciers melted back, mean winter temperatures gradually rose. With the elevation of land after the heavy mantle of ice disappeared, temperatures at the southern zone of the fish's range, at one time near the Gulf of Mexico, became too warm in summer, and especially at spawning, for the fish to survive.

Brook trout never made real inroads into watersheds west of the Mississippi River.

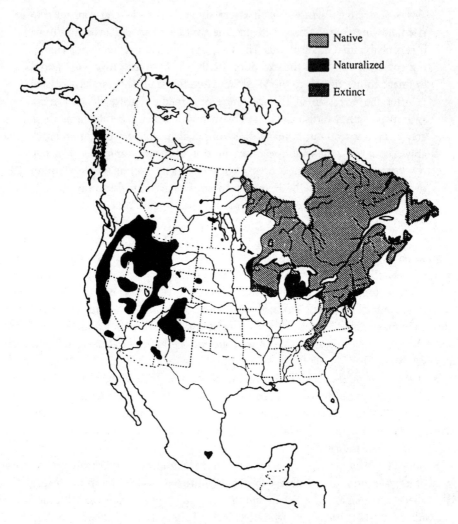

Figure 5.3   Distribution of *Salvelinus fontinalis* in North America.

Tributaries to the Mississippi's western drainage had little elevation except at their far distant headwaters. Populations that didn't move into northern parts of the watershed were eliminated. Eventually, all populations in the southern part of the Mississippi's drainage perished as the land and its waters warmed. When lowland temperatures became too warm, those fish in the Mississippi's eastern tributaries moved up and into the Appalachian Mountains. Populations that inhabited the Piedmont Plateau on the eastern side of the Appalachians and even the Atlantic Coastal Plain south of the Appalachians, except for those in Chesapeake Bay (Susquehanna River and Delaware Bay, Delaware River), had no north-flowing rivers in which brook trout could find a cooler habitat. However, they could move west and upstream, because water temperatures were cool in streams at higher elevations.

But there was a limit as to how far up they could go. Even the sources of many east-flowing watersheds weren't high enough to allow brook trout to survive during late spring and summer. Several did meet the fish's strict criteria, however. Today, small populations of wild brook trout still exist in parts of Georgia, North Carolina, Tennessee, and Kentucky, along the highest ridges of the Great Smoky Mountains.

Elsewhere, in places such as Michigan, Wisconsin, Pennsylvania, New Jersey, New York, and New England, as long as forests existed summer waters were cool enough to allow brook trout to survive without glaciers at their back doors.

DISTRIBUTION

Today, brook trout still exist over much of the terrain they inhabited when the first Europeans arrived. What has changed is the density and magnitude of their populations and the completeness of their dispersal in a watershed, or even of their branch-by-branch distribution. Overfishing contributed to reducing the population, but changed land uses—forestry, agriculture, industry, and municipal development—have accounted for the greatest losses.

Currently, the brook trout's range covers all of New York, New England, the Canadian Maritimes, Labrador, and Newfoundland. In Québec the brook trout is on Anticosti Island and in the Gulf of St. Lawrence, and also covers almost all of the province, including the offshore Belcher and Akamiski Islands in Hudson Bay and all except the northern tip of Ungava. Here, because of a low mean-temperature barricade, brook trout distribution appears to stop at the 60-degree latitude line. This is marked on the western side of Ungava Bay by the east-flowing Payne River (Rivière Arnaud) and on the western (Hudson Bay) side by the Inuit village of Povungnituk. It seems strange that dozens of what appear to be ideal brook trout rivers flowing seaward from the center of the peninsula along its 500-mile northern coast should not contain this species, especially when the waters flanking each side of this area have them. The temperature barrier is the only plausible explanation for this unique phenomenon.

Brook trout exist in all of the Québec and Ontario rivers and streams that enter Hudson and James bays. The exception is a vast watershed in Ontario composed of Attawapiskat Lake and its main drain, the Attawapiskat River. The watershed exists in the midst of, and is closely intertwined and flanked by, the Albany, Ekwan, and Winisk watersheds, which do contain brook trout. Only the lower 80 miles of the Attawapiskat, a slow, windy, meandering section—the least likely brook trout habitat—contains the occasional brook trout. While rapids and barriers might keep brook trout in this lower section from moving upstream, the upper drainages should have been colonized by this species, as were all of its neighbor streams, at its headwaters when it was part of the Lake Agassiz refugium. At that time, fish had the ability to move across headwater systems. Why they didn't is a mystery.

In Manitoba, early investigators found brook trout spread along all of the streams that enter James and Hudson bays, including the Hays, Nelson, Fawn, Severn, and Churchill rivers and as far north as Seal River. However, a biologist collecting fish samples in the upper Nelson River a few years ago couldn't find brook trout. Another unique phenomenon occurs in brook trout distribution in Manitoba and along its western limit of distribution. It's similar to that on the Ungava Peninsula, except that this is an east-west barrier. In all of Manitoba's east- and northeast-flowing rivers, brook trout either don't appear or aren't significant west of the 96th degree of longitude. It's as if the fish knew where this man-made line existed and refused to cross it. This same longitudinal line, where it crosses into Minnesota, is also the western limit of brook trout in the United States.

In Minnesota, brook trout are indigenous in the watershed streams that form the beginning of the Mississippi River, but below its junction with the Minnesota River they appear only in the waters east of the Mississippi as far south as its junction with the Wisconsin River. They're spread throughout Wisconsin, but not much farther south into Illinois. They appeared at one time in a part of Illinois north of a line drawn from the junction of the Mississippi and Wisconsin rivers in an east-southeast direction and ending on the western shores of Lake Michigan, above Evanston. The only area west of the Mississippi River where they once existed was in the very northeastern corner of Iowa, opposite the spot where the Wisconsin River flows into the Mississippi near Prairie du Chien, and probably in streams between the Upper Iowa and Yellow rivers in Iowa.

It's difficult to understand why—in a state that today has such a wide distribution of brook trout and is so intensively fished—when the first settlers arrived on Michigan's Lower Peninsula, it was almost devoid of the species. What's even more perplexing is that in the period between 13,200 and 14,000 years ago, when glacial Lake Chicago (the beginnings of Lake Michigan) was on the peninsula's western side and Lake Saginaw (Lake Huron) on its eastern, this part of the state was the crossroads for fish distribution and migration between the two temporary refugia.

Brook trout used as migration routes these flooded lake plains at the southern end of the melting continental glacier, which at its extreme reached as far south as the middle of Illinois, Indiana, and Ohio. The Upper Peninsula wasn't free of its icy mantle until about 11,500 years ago, when the glacier melted back far enough to form one big temporary lake, Lake Algonquin. The broad, elevated (400–600 feet above sea level today), hilly plateau that forms the northern half of the Lower Peninsula was the first to be exposed. Over its surface developed numerous idyllic streams that today flow in all directions and eventually into either Lake Michigan or Lake Huron.

But why were there no brook trout in them? As the glacier retreated, the Upper Peninsula was immediately colonized by brook trout from the lake-refugium, and so were rivers in Wisconsin and Ontario. The only watershed on the Lower Peninsula in which they appeared, according to early explorers, was the Muskegon River. This river begins on the southern side of the plateau and flows southwest into Lake Michigan at Muskegon.

Douglas Houghton, a scientist who surveyed a large part of the wilds of Michigan before 1840, while it was still a part of the Northwest Territories, then the Michigan Territory, wrote that upon personal observation and examination, the streams of the Lower Peninsula contained no brook trout. His associate, Bela Hubbard, later made the same statement. This was corroborated by early settlers, woodsmen, and sportsmen. However, 30 years later, by 1870, brook trout were recognized for the first time in a series of small, north-flowing streams that drained the very tip of the peninsula—above an imaginary line drawn from Traverse City, on the shore of Lake Michigan, northeast to Rogers City on Lake Huron.

How brook trout got to this area is also a mystery. Gaylord Alexander, a biologist with Michigan's Department of Natural Resource's Hunt Creek Fisheries Research Station, speculated, like earlier biologists, that these first brook trout were migrants that crossed the relatively shallow waters of the Straits of Mackinaw, just 5 miles at its narrowest, which separates the two peninsulas.

But why did they wait 12,000 years to make the trek? This phenomenon is still unexplained, even with sophisticated, modern-day capabilities; it's especially confusing in light of the fact that all of the other states and provinces in the Great Lakes Basin were well colonized by brook trout as the last glacier retreated beyond the basin's vast drainage. South of the line between Traverse and Rogers cities, brook trout were planted in an intensive stocking operation by both the state and private fishing clubs.

At one time, brook trout occurred naturally in northern Ohio, but only in a small strip of short watersheds along the southern shore of Lake Erie, where small streams flowed into the lake. Their natural range covered all of Pennsylvania, but here their numbers were greatest on the eastern slopes of the Appalachians (Alleghenies), in the northeastern part of the state, and particularly in Pike and Monroe counties. Farther south, they spread into the eastern half of West Virginia and extreme western parts of Virginia, along with North and South Carolina and the extreme northern part of Georgia. The most southerly remnant of the original brook trout distribution exists in the headwaters of the Chattahoochee River in Georgia.

In the South they inhabited headwaters of the Chattahoochee, the southern spurs of the Georgia Alleghenies, tributaries of the Catawba (Bucks Creek at Pleasant Garden), the North Fork of the Swannanoa River near Mt. Mitchell in North Carolina, the French Broad River, and extreme eastern parts of Tennessee and Kentucky.

Along the eastern slopes of the Alleghenies they're native to Maryland north and west of the Chesapeake Bay as well as part of the Susquehanna drainage and northeast to the coast. They were native to all western and northern counties in New Jersey, but today exist only in the very northwestern corner of the state.

TEMPERATURE AS A DISTRIBUTION CONTROL

Temperature is the single most important factor in determining distribution of brook trout over their range. Where they have retreated from their primordial range the cause is usually a warming of the ambient water temperatures. The optimal temperature range appears to be between 36 and 68 degrees Fahrenheit. But some populations have adapted to slightly warmer ranges, and others to slightly lower. Trout have been known to inhabit waters as warm as 75 degrees but only when this occurs in swift-moving streams or rivers. The immediate problem is one of sufficient oxygen. As temperatures rise, the ability of water to hold oxygen decreases. Swift-moving water can supply a greater volume of water and thus of oxygen over the gills with less effort from the fish.

"The area of distribution of the Eastern brook trout, which is delimited to the north and the east by the Arctic and Atlantic oceans, respectively, is just as decisively delimited in the west where the line marking the annual surplus precipitation becomes less than four inches, and in the south by the line where the mean temperature for the summer months rises about 70 degrees," wrote Bridges and Mullan in 1958.

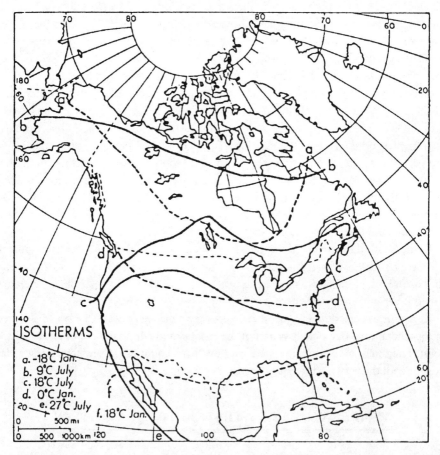

Figure 5.4 The northward distribution of brook trout is delimited by a mean low July temperature of 9°C. Low temperatures prolong the incubation period, hindering the fry's ability to store sufficient quantities of lipids needed to survive the long, non-feeding period under the ice.

Where brook trout have access to salt water, the adult fish also tend to move into a marine estuary in winter if water temperatures fall too low. A good example occurs on Long Island, where numerous spring-fed streams flow directly into tidal rivers and saline bays. Temperatures in these range from a few degrees above freezing during the most severe winters to 66 to 68 degrees during extremely warm summers. During normal summers, they range between 54 and 64 degrees. When water temperatures rise above 65 degrees, larger brook trout avoid it by moving into salt water to feed until temperatures drop below 50–52 degrees. This phenomenon allows trout to continue feeding on other foods when insect hatches in fresh water have slowed or ceased with winter weather.

As one travels farther north along the Atlantic Coast, to where ocean waters stay at 50 degrees or lower, brook trout remain in the marine environment for longer periods. North of the Bay of Fundy, where marine temperatures seldom rise above 50 degrees even in late summer, brook trout are found in salt water throughout the year, except during spawning migrations.

South of Long Island the converse is true. New Jersey's sandy coastal plain and scrublike flora are similar to those of Long Island. Its streams are also similar in nature to Long Island's, especially in acidity—caused by tannic acid leachates. They differ in that New Jersey's streams are long, with lengthy runs on the flats at a slow pace and with a lesser volume of spring-fed water. Together, these factors elevate temperatures too high for brook trout to establish themselves. The only New Jersey coastal streams successfully colonized by brook trout in historical times were those along the very northern part of the Jersey coast, south of New York Harbor, where streams are shorter and waters cooler. No brook trout today inhabit coastal streams south of the mid-Jersey coast.

Brook trout are still a very adaptable fish. Since 1835 they've been introduced to environments into which they could not have expanded naturally. Fish culturists moved them west with human migration to the Pacific. Today, self-sustaining populations occur in South Dakota, Montana, Wyoming, Colorado, New Mexico, Idaho, Washington, Oregon, California, Nevada, Utah, and Arizona as well as British Columbia, Alberta, and Saskatchewan. Abroad, brook trout were introduced in 19 countries in Eurasia, Central and South America, Africa, and New Zealand. They were introduced to England as early as 1865 and to the Continent in 1884.

The fish have readily adapted to living outside of their natural range wherever they find the correct temperatures as well as oxygen, carbon dioxide, and hydrogen ion concentrations (acidity) within tolerance limits for this species. Of course, the water must be free flowing, as in streams and rivers or over springs in lakes, and there must be suitable gravel on the spawning sites to protect the eggs from predation during incubation.

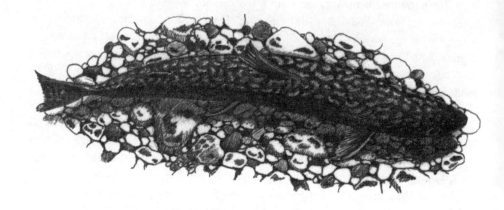

6   THE FISH

DESCRIPTION

Brook trout are the prettiest fish in the world, in both color and body form. The only close rivals they have are male Arctic charr, and then only when charr are decked out in their spawning colors. Brook trout, however, are gorgeous in either sex and at any time of the year. Their coloration and patterns are so unique that the fish are seldom confused with others; indeed, they hardly need description at all.

There are, however, five external features that allow immediate distinction of brook trout from either brown or rainbow trout or other charrs. White pipings on the outer edges of all but the caudal (tail) fin immediately identify a fish as a charr and not a trout. In some far northern populations, even the ventral portion of the caudal fin on charr has a slight white piping. Immediately interior of white leading edges on brook trout fins is a narrow black stripe. This, too, is found on some strains of male Arctic charr, but only when they don their spawning livery. Body spots on true trout are on a light background; they're reversed on all charr. Also, trout have large, easily visible scales, whereas charr have very small scales. Both are cycloid scales, characteristically thin, smooth, and partially embedded in the skin in an overlapping pattern, typical of fast-swimming fishes. Along the entire lateral line, brook trout average about 230 scales. The feature wholly unique to brook trout is the wormlike vermiculations on its back and head. These appear on the dorsal (back), adipose, and caudal fins like a series of tiger stripes.

Like all salmonids, brook trout sport a vestigial adipose fin on their back, located closer to the caudal than to the dorsal fin. Brook trout also have paired pectoral and pelvic fins and a singular anal fin, just posterior of the vent. The body is generally fusiform (torpedolike) in shape, laterally compressed slightly in young fish but becoming more noticeable in both sexes (though especially males) as fish age. Males also experience secondary sexual dimorphism as they grow older. Their pectoral and ventral fins elongate, and so does the maxillary (upper) jaw. Even to the untrained eye, sexual differentiation is not difficult when viewing both sexes at once.

Body shape also changes drastically (seasonal dimorphism) in males in preparation for spawning. Older males and some females develop a back hump under the dorsal fin, though this is nowhere near as pronounced as in Pacific salmon. With males, their body depth (girth) also increases, and not entirely as a result of enlarged milt sacs. Males also develop a hook (kype) in the lower jaw. All of these features quickly fade after spawning. By winter's end males again look normal. Females also undergo temporary body changes at spawning time, with genital papillae often extending beyond the anal vent.

In anadromous brook trout, as well as those that inhabit large inland lakes, the body also undergoes some modification. Most obvious is the head, which, while it does not actually become smaller, appears to do so because other body proportions increase more rapidly. This happens when fish are exposed to unlimited food and body growth progresses at a rate faster than head. Overall appearance is more salmonlike than charrlike. This led to confusion in the early classification of sea-run brook trout.

Depending upon the fish's environment, coloration can vary greatly, ranging from a light metallic blue in fish that enter salt water (salters) or fish that leave natal streams and spend part of the year in large, deep, clear lakes (coasters), to dark brown or yellowish in trout trapped behind beaver dams or in high mountain ponds whose streams drain leachates from surrounding conifer forests.

In general, back coloration is olive drab or greenish brown fading down the sides into a light brown and a yellowish color below the lateral line. On the abdomen, it merges into a pearly white that's replaced during spawning phases by roseate, then by red and orange hues with a black swath along the very bottom. Upon this palette, vermiculations are just a bit lighter green and phase into yellow, wormlike patterns, which—as they run down the sides—break into pale yellow, irregularly shaped dots, and eventually become blotches. Over this collage are dispersed small vermilion dots surrounded by powder blue halos. What could be prettier?

Unlike those of true trout, body dots don't appear on the head or the gill covers, but green vermiculations from the back run forward onto the head and snout. Ventral (bottom) fins are red and almost transparent, while dorsal and caudal fins are dark and patterned. The bottom of the caudal fin also sports the white piping with its trailing edge lined in black, but not with as distinct a stripe as on the ventral fins. Young brook trout have eight to twelve wide, vertical parr markings along the length of their body and usually a few red, yellow, and blue spots. Both male and female brook trout undergo color changes as spawning approaches. In both sexes, all of the colors intensify, but this is more pronounced in males, especially when they're in their full glory just before and during spawning. This spawning color change is unique among salmonids to charrs and Pacific salmon.

The brook trout's head is large compared with the rest of the body—nearly a quarter of its total length. Eyes are large and the snout is long compared with other charrs (except lake trout) and true trout. In other charrs, the maxillary jaw ends forward under the eye, but in brook trout it extends posteriorly for a longer distance, giving the appearance of a large mouth. The mouth is almost as long in lake trout, a charr more closely related to brook trout than are other charrs. The body shape of males and females is the same except for a bit larger maxillae in males.

Brook trout and other charrs are morphologically distinguished from salmon and true trout by differences in skeletal parts in the skull. Brook trout have teeth visible to the naked eye on the tongue and throat, but none on the roof of the mouth; there's an outer row on the lower jaw and an inner and outer row on the upper jaw.

HABITAT

Compared with all other charrs and even salmon and trout, brook trout are the least specialized in their habitat demands. This allows them to live in a great variety of environments with a wide range of tolerances. As their specific scientific name indicates, they "live in springs." But this is only the beginning. All springs eventually become a part of oceans, and brook trout follow these waters to the end. They inhabit small trickles, rivulets, creeks, and beaver ponds. They live in larger streams and lakes, from the Great Lakes, to little lakes and ponds, to small rivers, and to big rivers with tumbling falls and rapids. Because of a unique organ in their kidney (glomerulus), they're anadromous and can move downstream with the flow of water into riverine estuaries; they're equally at home in brackish streams that feel the surge of tides, in purely saline bays, or even in the oceans themselves.

Brook trout are the classic example of a cold-water species and thrive best in the northern half of the Northern Hemisphere. Only one other salmonid likes its water a bit colder, and that's why it's called the "Arctic" charr. The range of water temperatures in which brook trout can survive is wide, from 32 to 72 degrees Fahrenheit. These are the extremes, but within this range the more practical limits are 34 to 69 or 70 degrees. While brook trout can tolerate freezing temperatures, they do migrate downstream as winter progresses. In larger streams, colder, outside air lowers water temperatures less than in small, shallow creeks. Brook trout, especially younger fish, have been known to tolerate temperatures as high as 78 degrees for short periods or temperatures as high as 74 degrees for longer times—as long as the water is clean and fast moving. Their optimal temperature range for growth and survival is a lot narrower: 55 to 65 degrees Fahrenheit.

Brook trout exhibit a dichotomy of growth responses to water temperatures below 50 degrees. In streams and ponds at higher elevations in the southern part of their range, growth is recognizably slower. But in areas in northern parts of their range, such as northern portions of Labrador, Québec, Ontario, and Manitoba, where temperatures may stay below 50 degrees for most of the summer and warm above this only on the surface, brook trout growth is often better than that of trout at higher temperatures in the southern parts of their range. These are truly cold-water animals. Through myriad generations they've adapted to survive and even grow at low temperatures.

This demand for cooler temperatures caused wild brook trout strains to disappear from large portions of watersheds in their southern range. The cause was elevated temperatures that resulted from poor forestry practices, denudation of upper reaches of watersheds, overintensive agriculture, and even in some areas a change to greater municipal land use. Brook trout have been likened to canaries used in mines to detect deteriorating air quality. When brook trout disappear from a stream it's a sign that water quality has deteriorated and the stream is in trouble.

Because the environment brook trout colonized as they followed melting continental ice sheets north was covered primarily by coniferous forests, they developed the ability to cope with waters more acidic than other species can tolerate. Conifer leachates are high in tannic acid. Brook trout developed an ability to survive in these brown waters with high concentrations of dissolved hydrogen ions, or a low pH. Wild brook trout can survive a pH range of from 4.1 to 9.5. Uncontaminated rainwater usually has a pH value of 7.0. Brook trout can tolerate an acidity as low as 3.4 for a short time but don't fully function (reproduce) when the pH falls below 4.8. Brook trout in southern parts of their range, and in Michigan, Pennsylvania, New York, Maine, Ontario, and Québec, have suffered most in the last 40 years, because acid rain has lowered pH levels in brook trout waters that already had a low pH. On the other end of the pH spectrum, brook trout can tolerate a high pH and have been known to survive in waters with a 9.8 concentration.

The rate of water flow in a river or stream is also a factor in where one will find brook trout. Slow, sluggish streams, or streams with plenty of backwater and pockets of little or no movement, aren't brook trout waters; these fish are energy conscious, and don't expend more than is necessary to find food. They're primarily "drift" feeders and prefer to lie in wait for food to come to them. But too fast a flow has a negative effect. In such a flow, fish must exert more energy to stay in place than is provided by the amount of food the moving water brings them. They can't operate at a net loss for very long and seek out ambient environments where the food en route more than equals the energy they burn to stay behind a boulder, or even in midstream.

This is one reason that brook trout are usually found in the placid-appearing waters just above a set of rapids or in the tail end, where the river's speed slackens. In streams, brook trout are quite territorial and will defend their feeding stations against other brook trout or fish. They only give way to larger brook trout or bigger fish. Going hand-in-hand with food as an energy source is the oxygen in the water, especially critical during warmer months. There's always more oxygen at the end of a set of rapids than at the beginning, because water is aerated as it tumbles through the rapids and thus temporarily enriched above its normal carrying capacity at that particular temperature.

BEHAVIOR

Movements of brook trout in a stream are quite local and follow a relatively predictable activity cycle. Biologists have concluded that they're habitually quiescent (inactive) during the normal hours of darkness. During the day, they also avoid activity during full-noon sunlight. Their activities are controlled, too, by the length of day and even the time of day. Most wanderings in search of food take place in the early morning and again in the late afternoon.

To save energy, when they aren't hunting brook trout locate themselves out of main currents and find protected areas behind large rocks or under overhanging bushes or undercut banks. One biologist studying brook trout habits on a small New Hampshire stream found no distinct correlation between movements of wild brook trout and either water temperature or flow. In other words, when the rivers were up the fish maintained their general place in a stream. When temperatures rose or fell they still preferred their chosen place. They were affected, however, by seasonal changes. Spawning season saw an increase in activity, but upstream movement was partially balanced by downstream movement; in effect it was of a "seesawing" nature.

Another researcher found that movements of brook trout fluctuated between upstream and downstream in a transitory manner, with indications of a slight movement upstream—an average of 0.78 mile—to spawn. Also, the bulk of the population showed a downstream movement during colder, winter months. Tag returns indicated that most of the population occupied the same general area as in the previous year.

Stocked brook trout, however, exhibited an immediate downstream movement when water temperatures were less than 50 degrees Fahrenheit. When water temperatures were above 50 degrees at stocking, the trout showed little or no movement. Limited movement by wild brook trout demonstrated the species' tendency toward a degree of territoriality. This was lacking in stocked fish because they weren't born in the locale or environment.

The brook trout is a solitary fish, but if alarmed or frightened will exhibit schooling tendencies.

Lake or pond habitat offers brook trout another set of living challenges. Immature and small adult brook trout are likely to stay in a stream habitat even when access to a lake or pond is nearby. The reason is that stream habitats usually offer more protection from predators, especially larger brook trout. During most summer months, larger brook trout typically inhabit the lake and move to rivers or streams only to spawn. In some shallow lakes in Labrador known to produce big brook trout, these fish often stay in the rivers after spawning because shallow lakes there might freeze completely, or the fish might become stranded in deeper holes by ice that reaches bottom on the shoals. The danger here is oxygen depletion by winter's end, often before the lake's mantle of ice thaws.

Big brook trout are also more likely to inhabit lakes and ponds in the summer because these environments usually produce more foods, especially small fishes, both trout and other species upon which trout prefer to feed as their sizes increase. In a lake, brook trout are more prone to inhabit the periphery, between 20 feet of depth and the shore, and shoals in the lake where water depths are 30 feet or less. Two factors keep them in these areas: the greater food production, because less sunlight is absorbed here and plant photosynthesis is more productive, and the warmer temperature of these waters, especially when deep waters in a lake can remain below 40 degrees throughout the entire summer.

Brook trout are only found in deeper water in a lake when upper water levels rise above 65 degrees, or when they're forced there to escape larger predator fishes. During hot summers, brook trout are likely to be on the shoals only when they contain cool springs, or late in the day or in early evening when surface waters cool. During especially warm periods, they may not feed in shoal waters at all until late in the day or early the next morning.

In lake and pond habitats, brook trout cruise the water, feeding more as individuals or in loosely connected schools. Among younger adults, these schools are composed mostly of fish of the same size or year-class. But as trout mature and numbers of big fish are reduced, schools are composed of multiple year-classes with a range of two to three years. Really big brook trout, fish above 7 pounds, tend to fend on their own and congregate only at spawning times. The only time brook trout in a lake environment are found in more defined schools is when water temperatures are high and the fish find a spring or source of cooler water on the bottom.

REPRODUCTION

Brook trout migrate for several reasons: food, temperature, living space, and spawning. Some migrations are short, such as a movement a few yards upstream to a feeding site vacated by a larger brook trout; or intermediate, such as up a river in search of cooler rivulet water as larger, less shaded streams warm in late spring into summer (Cunjack). Spawning migrations, however, are the most spectacular. Like Atlantic salmon and brown trout, brook trout are fall spawners. When a fish migrates to spawn is determined by its genetic composition. The precise times, however, are affected by water temperature, water flow (precipitation), and the length of daylight. While the "gatherings" may not begin precisely on the same day each year, the variation is so small that fair predictions can be made.

At one time, biologists believed water temperature to be the ultimate trigger telling fish when to begin the spawning season. However, water temperatures can vary widely and would produce a great disparity in starting times each year. Researchers now believe that photoperiod, or length of day, is more important. Precipitation and water temper-

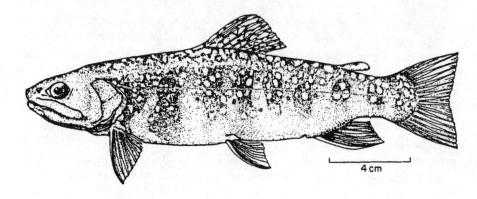

Figure 6.1   Brook trout, *Salvelinus fontinalis*, 19cm (7.6 inches) still showing lateral parr markings.

atures are secondary determining factors; duration of daylight is the initial motivator. Other factors only slightly change spawning time. However, not all brook trout are genetically keyed to spawn at the same time, so spawning can vary widely depending upon the latitude and altitude the fish occupy. For some fish living at high altitudes, spawning can occur as early as late September. But for most populations it begins in October. Brook trout are spawning at some locality in almost every month of the year, except during the summer.

During most summer months in Maine, Labrador, Québec, Ontario, and Manitoba, brook trout, especially larger adults, are found in lakes or large rivers, where food is abundant at this time of year. Come late August, they begin to migrate either toward the outlet and its moving water or out of the lake into small feeder streams. Their goal is to find a spot with sufficient gravel and a steady supply of oxygenated water—somewhere that won't later be damaged by ice. In large rivers, they usually migrate upstream or move into smaller streams with shallower, cooler, well-aerated water flowing over a mixture of coarse and fine gravel bottoms.

Brook trout consistently spawn in lakes, such as Lake Nipigon, where there are large springs welling out of the bottom in shoal (2 to 6 feet) water. In marine situations, where saline waters never rise much above 60 degrees, trout spend their summers there but migrate upstream to their natal waters in late August and September to spawn. Such streams usually contain two stocks of brook trout. One is anadromous and migrates from salt or brackish water; the other is initially nonmigratory. The stocks remain separated, not because they cannot interbreed but because they've developed the genetically coded penchant to spawn at slightly different times. There's some question as to whether coding of spawning times really exists and is the factor that makes sea-run fish move into fresh water to spawn.

Correct foods are also factors that can motivate a migration. As brook trout grow, their diets change. By the time they're about 12 inches long they become piscivorous (fish eating) in order to satiate an increased metabolism. In this case, nonmigratory groups may become migratory, as demonstrated in Massachusetts studies of salters searching for bigger food. They also change their affiliation and join other salters in the upstream migration when they decide to spawn.

In estuarine situations where summer waters are too warm and stream waters are cool, such as the spring-fed systems on Long Island or Cape Cod, fish are in the vicinity of spawning grounds throughout the summer. After spawning, however, they migrate to the estuaries to winter where food is more plentiful, returning in late May or even June when marine waters become too warm.

The female brook trout is the redd or nest builder. As such, she chooses where it will be constructed. She digs it in the gravel as the male guards her and drives off other males or paired fish looking for sites. The site is usually over gravel that ranges from pea to walnut in size. The site must also have an upwelling of current under the gravel, and if it isn't far from a fallen log over the stream, or is near an overhanging bank, so much the better. When an ideal site can't be found, the female will choose the best the stream has to offer, but suboptimal conditions reduce the chances that all of the eggs will mature. Despite this, the fish's great fecundity ensures that there are usually enough surviving eggs to maintain the species. This adaptability, coupled with their high fecundity, allows brook trout to maintain a presence in streams where other salmonids could not survive.

The redd or cavity is dug as the female lies on her side, close to the bottom. With strong, rapid undulations of her caudal fin, she creates a slight vacuum. This lifts sand, smaller gravel, and debris, which in turn are carried a short distance downstream by the current. This process goes on day and night until the female believes the redd is sufficiently deep. She tests it by lowering herself into the depression with her pelvic, anal, and caudal fins stiff and touching the gravel.

When the female is ready to spawn, the male, who has been making passes, nudges, and advances, comes alongside, and their bodies touch. The female drops her anal fin deeply into the depression and, at the same moment, sharply arches her back. Both fish open their mouths wide and tremble, with rapid undulations of the body, as eggs and milt are released at the same instant. The female doesn't drop all her eggs at once, instead laying only from 15 to 60 each time.

The coordinated release by both sexes is crucial to maximum fertilization of the released eggs. Under good habitat conditions, the fertilization rate of brook trout eggs is quite high, usually between 80 and 90 percent. Eggs are most vulnerable to fertilization the moment they're released. At this time, sperm must penetrate the translucent shell of the egg within three minutes and enter through the micropyle, a funnel-shaped opening in the egg's outer membrane. The surface of the egg is pocked with microscopic pores. From the moment the egg is released and even as the sperm is entering the micropyle, water begins to enter through these numerous pores, swelling the egg and causing the pores to constrict and the egg surface to harden. A brook trout egg is large, approximately ⅕ inch in diameter, and after release it rapidly increases in volume by 20 to 30 percent as it absorbs water. The micropyle is also being closed as the egg swells, quickly reducing the chance of fertilization. Eggs sink to the bottom as they absorb water and are slightly adhesive for a short period. They vary in color from pale lemon to orange-red. The average yield of a ½-pound female ranges from 400 to 600 eggs.

Immediately after the eggs are deposited, the female moves slightly upstream of the redd and begins a slow sweeping motion with her tail. In this "postnuptial dance," the female, using a sinuous, weaving motion of the ventral tips of the caudal and anal fins, gently moves gravel over the eggs without touching them. This dance isn't seen in rainbow or cutthroat trout, or Atlantic salmon; whether it occurs in other charrs has not been determined. The most likely candidates for a postnuptial dance would be Arctic charr, but these fish usually spawn under the ice or in open rivers during outside temperatures so low that accurate observations are difficult for humans.

At this time, the female brook trout viciously attacks any fish that may come near the redd, driving them off but returning before others can get near her eggs. In the meantime, her male partner may lose interest and move off, seeking another female digging a redd. The covering process takes but four or five minutes. As mentioned, not all eggs are deposited at one time. The female then moves a short distance ahead of the first redd and begins cutting a new depression. The total number of eggs deposited corresponds to the size of the fish, and can range from 100 in a female 6 inches long to 5,000 in one 22 inches. Peak spawning occurs in water temperatures between 39 and 49 degrees Fahrenheit, and continues both day and night.

Sexual maturity varies with the sexes. Some precocious males have ripe gonads and spawn during their first year (Age 0). Females, however, need at least 12 months to complete the ripening cycle of their eggs, and first spawn can occur as a yearling (Age I). Most, however, reach Age II, often still displaying parr markings. The farther north in their range, the longer it takes for either sex to reach sexual maturity. Some brook trout may be seven years old but still sexually immature. Flesh color is also a sign of sexual maturity. Flesh in immature brook trout ranges from gray to pink; in mature fish, it's red. This is caused by the accumulation of certain carotinoid substances in their flesh.

The duration of incubation depends upon the water temperatures throughout this period. Water temperatures can vary within a 24-hour day, and within a season as waters cool toward winter with shorter periods of daylight and conversely warm toward spring, and the duration of incubation is directly affected by these variables. Brook trout have adapted the incubation period of their eggs to the mean ambient temperatures in their environment. If they matured too early, before spring and warmer water could cause a proliferation of foods for the larvae and fry, they would starve. In 35-degree water the incubation period is about 144 days; at 40 degrees it's 103 days; at 45 degrees, 68 days; at 50 degrees, 44 days; and at 55 degrees, 35 days (Embody). However, a water temperature of above 53 degrees is lethal for developing eggs. The shortest incubation periods occur in rainbow trout, followed by brown trout. Lake trout incubation periods are 6 to 8 percent longer than those of brook trout.

GROWTH AND FEEDING

Hatched brook trout larvae remain in the protection of the redd's gravel from 23 to as many as 80 days, depending upon the latitude, until the yolk is absorbed; only after its absorption do the young fish begin to feed. They become free swimming at about 1½ inches, and scales begin forming when they're 2 inches long. As they grow they abandon the redd area and work their way to the edges of the stream or, in a lake, into shallow water where aquatic vegetation can afford them protection from predators (McNicol). The rate of growth will vary greatly over their range and is dependent upon local conditions—that is, food and competition with other larvae or fry, often of the same species. First-year growth is dependent upon several factors, the most immediate of which is the length of the growing season. Other factors include water temperature, population density, and availability of food.

There isn't much living in the brook trout's world upon which these fish won't feed (Ricker). They're predacious animals and need light to find their prey. During the day, they'll feed as long as there's sufficient light. During evenings when there's sufficient moonlight, they'll feed into the night. There's a recognizable feeding pattern in both juveniles and adults. They feed best in early morning and late afternoon when insect hatches are most likely to occur. They'll go "off their feed," however, when water temperatures become too warm—such as during midday and even midsummer.

Brook trout are omnivorous, carnivorous, piscivorous, and even cannibalistic, and will occasionally feed on plant material (Needham). Fry 0.8 to 1 inch long feed primarily on a macroscopic crustacean diet consisting of Entomostraca (ostracods, copepods, and cladocerans). At 1 to 1.5 inches in length, fry abandon crustacean foods for insect larvae, at first mainly chironomid diptera. They also begin taking their first terrestrial insects. At a length of 1.5 to 4 inches, their foods shift away from chironomids to *Ephemera* nymphs and Trichoptera larvae. Fish from 4 to 8 inches feed mainly on aquatic and terrestrial insects. Between 8 and 12 inches they begin feeding on small fish.

In a very thorough study of brook trout in Ontario, W. E. Ricker provided a review of the organisms eaten. The list is astonishing and suggests that a brook trout will eat any living creature it can get into its mouth: worms, leeches, crustaceans (cladocerans, amphipods, decopods), aquatic insects (over 80 genera eaten, but mayfly, caddis fly, midge, and blackfly larvae were most common), terrestrial insects (over 30 families, ants sometimes in abundance), spiders, mollusks (including clams and snails), a number of fish species, including young brook trout and brook trout eggs, minnows, sticklebacks, and cottids, frogs, salamanders, and a snake (in a 7-inch trout).

Although the fact was not mentioned by Ricker, an early researcher of this species noted that larger trout, particularly in northern waters during summer, are known to eat numbers of small mammals, mainly the field mouse, *Microtus*, but also the redback vole, *Cleithrionomys*, and shrews. A healthy diet of these, and even lemmings in their nightly migrations during a full moon across lakes in the Minipi River watershed in Labrador, has been credited as one reason brook trout there grow much larger than elsewhere. One reason brook trout with a nearby marine environment become anadromous as they get older is that sea-run trout eat invertebrates and fish found in marine and brackish waters. Ricker confirmed that brook trout engage in a limited amount of cannibalism, eating their own eggs at spawning time and their own young in spring.

In a study of food consumption, temperatures, and growth, brook trout weekly ate 50 percent of their own weight (in minnows) at 55.4 degrees Fahrenheit, but less than this amount at 48.2 and 62.6 degrees. While big brook trout, 4 pounds and heavier, are opportunistic feeders and will still consume large amounts of aquatic insect life, studies have shown that where small fish are available they prefer these, at times feeding upon fish almost exclusively.

Northern pike feed on brook trout in waters where both live. However, the most serious predators are fish-eating birds, such as kingfishers, loons, and mergansers. The recent expansion of cormorant populations summering in northern waters inhabited by brook trout indicates that these birds now are probably the fish's greatest threat.

HOW BIG IS THAT BROOK TROUT?

You don't have to be an ichthyologist to realize that brook trout look very much alike. While there are slight morphological differences in shape between widely separated populations or even between brook trout from watersheds in close proximity but geographically isolated, they pretty much conform to each other in shape. Brook trout, like most salmonids, seem to grow at a uniform proportion, especially between the weights of 1 and 5 pounds. Thereafter there's a tendency, especially in populations where sexual maturation is early and the life span doesn't extend much beyond three or four years, for fish to develop girth at a slightly greater rate than length during the latter half of their existence. Exceptions to this are Atlantic salmon and brook trout that spend a lot of time in marine or lacustrine environments.

Sensing this length-to-weight relation, several investigators at the turn of the century began gathering data to create a formula to determine the weight of a brook trout from the relationship of its length to girth. W. Hodgson Ellis of the School of Practical Science, Toronto, fished the north shore of Lake Superior in the late 1890s and was able to catch enough brook trout of 13 to 23 inches in a two-month period to devise a working formula. He based his formula on the assumption that weight of a brook trout in a well-fed population varies with the cube of its length. He drew two conclusions from his observations: that under similar conditions all brook trout have the same shape, and that they grow symmetrically. He did caution, however, that the formula he devised was only good for brook trout in the northern Lake Superior region.

Ellis used three dimensions in determining a brook trout's weight—length, breadth, and thickness. He didn't illustrate or describe what he meant by the latter two measurements, or where they were taken. I assume, and I hope correctly, that breadth was the side-to-side or lateral measurement of the fish, which could only be taken accurately with calipers, and that thickness was the measurement from dorsal to ventral surfaces at its greatest breadth. But it doesn't really matter because, he wrote, the two measurements, added together, are the girth. Girth is a measurement more easily taken with a tape.

Ellis believed that if one fish is twice as long as another, it will also be twice as thick and twice as deep. Ergo! It will be eight times as heavy. In other words, the weight varies as the cube of the length. He devised a table based on the weight of a 1-pound trout whose length was 13.17 inches, the cube of which is 2,286. The last number becomes the standard in the following formula devised by Ellis. The weight (W) is equal to the length (L) cubed, divided by 2,286.

Ellis graphed the length-to-weight relationship, and while a straight line would have been the ideal, the result was a slightly curved line that supported Ellis's theory and his formula as valid. However, when fish from the Rangeleys in Maine were used, the formula was off a bit and it was assumed that Lake Superior brook trout were "a bit stouter" than those from Maine. To correct for this difference in population characteristics the girth of a 2-pound Maine brook trout was used, and this led to a standard of 2,744. A second caveat was issued not to use the corrected formula for Maine fish of over 5 pounds, "because they do not grow symmetrically over 5 pounds but become obese."

A more workable formula for determining the approximate weight of brook trout was devised in recent times. It is length (L) times girth (G) squared and divided by 800. Simply measure the fish around its widest part with a string or tape measure, then multiply this number by itself, then multiply it again by the total length of the fish, then divide this number by 800. You get a figure that is close to the fish's actual weight.

LONGEVITY

Like most fish, brook trout can be aged by counting annual rings on their scales. They are not as long lived as Arctic charr or lake trout. In the wild, brook trout seldom live more than five years, with four the average lifespan. The exceptions are several populations in Québec and Labrador that regularly reach eight and even nine years. Brook trout introduced into California waters have been recorded as living to 20 years. Bunny Lake (Mono County, California) produced the oldest brook trout anywhere on record. Evidence suggests that slow-growing brook trout can live well beyond the four- to five-year average. Many trout in Bunny Lake were found to be at least 15 years old. Some were projected to be over 20, but accurate age analysis was difficult because annular rings in older fish are so close together that distinct separation is impossible.

BIGGEST BROOK TROUT

Factors that determine the size of a brook trout, or any other fish, are: genetic coding, available foods, duration of annual growing periods, rate of growth, sex, and individual age. The two prime factors are genetic coding and available foods. Given this, the largest brook trout would be a male, probably 9 or 10 years old, surrounded during its life by swarms of *Hexagenia*, tons of sculpin and little brook trout, and the occasional lemming or mouse; he would live in a shallow lake or a deep lake with a large, shallow shelf around its periphery, with a fair-sized river draining it; there would be no other salmonids or warm-water fish for competition; there would be long, temperate summers; and all of this would occur just north of the 50th parallel.

While brook trout may all appear alike or very similar externally they're not all the same internally, especially in chromosomal makeup—the programmed building blocks that determine all of their characteristics. Probably no more than 60 percent of a given population or even strain of brook trout is genetically exactly the same. The other 40 percent may look the same, but if the environment changes to favor other genetic factors in the fish's makeup, they'll have better chances for survival and will eventually dominate the population genetically.

Because of this, no matter how much food is available or what the state is of the other factors that determine a brook trout's size, it can only grow to a certain maximum size. The opposite is true only given an inexhaustible food supply. Regardless of a population's penchant for growth and possible maximum size, the fish won't attain this size if there isn't enough food. As an example, consider the big brook trout in the Rangeley Lakes in Maine. A portion of the lake's brook trout had probably developed a genetic penchant to reach weights of 10 pounds or more by the time the glacier cleared the state. Arctic charr were also trapped in the lake and its watershed as the last glacier receded. They selected deeper habitat than brook trout in the same waters, switched to feeding on a superabundant supply of macroscopic foods, proliferated to the maximum allowed by the food supply, and became stunted. Their appearance was so changed that they were labeled blueback trout.

Brook trout, with that unique gene-guided maximum size potential, fed on the inexhaustible supply of smaller bluebacks and grew to huge proportions. Another portion of the brook trout in the lake never grew larger than 4 or 5 pounds. Their presence was masked by the bigger fish, and they were thought to be the same fish that hadn't yet become behemoths. Over a few centuries, maybe less, the big fish prospered and dominated (only in size—not in numbers) the other, coexisting brook trout. Some grew to as large as 12 pounds, and a few undocumented reports even set the upper limit at 15 pounds.

Then the Oquossoc Fishing Club goofed. It brought landlocked salmon eggs to a hatchery it had built on Mooselookmeguntic Lake and released the fry into Rangeley Lake. The landlocks ate the bluebacks down to the last one and the charr became extinct. Smelt were then introduced as a forage-fish substitute—but they ate brook trout eggs. Within 20 years, the big brookies were history. Now the biggest fish annually taken from the Rangeleys is again between 4 and 5 pounds.

If one stands back and looks at the brook trout population as a whole and its distribution over eastern North America, one can pretty well determine the population's center, where fish on the average can grow to 7, 8, or 9 pounds with a great degree of regularity. This is a swath of Canadian terrain that starts in Manitoba and ends just short of the Labrador coast. It's bound on the north by the 55th parallel, and the south by the 50th. Included between the latitudes are Gods River; the northern half of Lake Nipigon; the Rupert, Broadback, Eastmain, and Témiscamie rivers; lakes Kaniapiskau, Mistassini, and Assinica in western Québec; the northern half of Laurentide Park and its rivers in eastern Québec; and all of the best brook trout waters of Labrador. There's naturally a bit of spillover of big trout populations in a few areas north and south of these imaginary lines. The Rangeleys in Maine, however, were a food-based anomaly.

One element that all of these places have in common is cold water, the same factor that separated brook trout from other salmonids. A second is that all of these fish are relatively slow growers and thus are able to live longer and increase in size. Another is an abundance of food, both insects and fish.

South of the 50th parallel, an abundant food supply, the high water quality demanded by brook trout, competition from warmer-water species, and a greater range of water temperatures, especially in summer months, all detract from the fish's ability to attain the 10-pound size possible farther north. North of the 55th parallel, shortened summer growing periods, colder waters that increase incubation times and thus shorten feeding and growth times, a reduction in some insect forms for food, and a reliance on cannibalism limit the maximum sizes to 5 and 6 pounds. While the populations north and south of the preferred zone are healthy, vigorous, and stabilized, the environment hinders these fish from reaching larger sizes even though the population might have the correct genetic coding.

A unique example of the relationship of food, growth, and population density in contained brook trout populations was vividly brought to light a few years ago in New York by Department of Environmental Conservation (DEC) biologist Bill Kelly and aide Ed Van Put. One of the sources of the Beaver Kill, a famous trout stream in the Catskill Mountains, is Balsam Lake. For more than 200 years the little pond produced an almost limitless quantity of wild or native brook trout. However, the fish were small—between 6 and 7 inches and seldom over 8, even though they were three-year-olds and sexually mature. About 1980, the DEC purchased nearby Crystal Lake, a small, 55-foot-deep body of water with no streams, which contained a few coarse fish species and a horde of crustaceans and aquatic insect forms. To reclaim it, the lake was treated with rotenone; the following April, fry from Balsam Lake were transferred to it.

By September, the progeny of the stunted parents were between 7 and 9 inches long. By the following spring, growing even throughout the winter, most were 10 inches; by September, they had reached 12 inches. They now average 15 to 16 inches, with some reaching 19. Because there are no streams flowing in or out, brook trout in the lake have adapted to spawning at the sites of springs within the lake. And, because these sites are limited in number and scope, they directly control the size of the total spawn and, ultimately, the population size. Since this factor keeps population numbers in check, it has allowed individual trout to maximize their growth potential.

The average maximum size to which most brook trout can grow with all factors in their favor is probably 7 or 8 pounds. A smaller portion will make it to 9 and even fewer to 10 pounds. Occasionally there will be unique individual fish that grow above 11 pounds. Brook trout outside of the preferred environment will have shortened life spans and rapid initial growth, mature sexually by Ages I and II, compete with exotic species and lose, find spawning sites less to their liking, have their genetic character changed by domesticated brook trout, die by Ages III or IV, and weigh less than a pound.

While this seems typical of today's scenario in the United States, this was probably what life was always like in the Lower 48 once glaciers freed all of the lands of Canada. The maximum size was probably 4 to 5 pounds, but only a small part of this population in the U.S. (Rangeleys excluded), even before Columbus arrived, ever attained it.

THE BIGGEST BROOK TROUT, ACCORDING TO THE IGFA

The International Game Fish Association (IGFA) has conducted an annual fishing contest since 1976, when it assumed from *Field & Stream* magazine the task of keeping track of the world's largest fish. The IGFA recognizes big fish that don't make it into the record book's line classes but are still noteworthy accomplishments. Its records serve as a source for determining where and when the bigger fish strike. However, they're not a complete list of all big brook trout that are caught annually, because not all fish meet IGFA tackle or technique requirements. And many big brook trout aren't entered because some anglers don't want recognition. An example of a big brook trout not entered in the competition is Gary Caputi's 9-pounder taken from Osprey Lake, Labrador, in June 1993.

From the following contest list, one can see years when brook trout weren't entered. To hold the number to a workable list, only those brook trout of 5 pounds, 7 ounces and larger are put forth here.

When	How Much	Where	By Whom
1978	9 lbs, 13 ozs	Minipi Lake, Lab.	Harvey Smith
1978	9 lbs, 7 ozs	Assinica Lake, Que.	Stephen Klopacz
1978	9 lbs, 4 ozs	Little Minipi L., Lab.	Judson Mariotti
1980	5 lbs, 9 ozs	Morgantown L., Ga.	Joe Rampley
1980	8 lbs, 4 ozs*	Menomin Inlet, Pa.	Harvey Smith
1981	9 lbs	Little Airy L., Lab.	Harvey Smith
8/29/81	7 lbs	Mistassini L., Que.	Victor Dragone

When	How Much	Where	By Whom
8/30/81	6 lbs, 9 ozs	South Knife R., Man.	Michael Grimshaw
8/3/82	8 lbs	Minipi Drainage. Lab.	F. Van Devender
8/10/82	8 lbs, 4 ozs	Ann Marie L., Lab.	James Reitnauer
9/1/82	7 lbs, 8 ozs	Mistassini L., Que.	Bill Atwood
9/5/82	10 lbs, 7 ozs	Broadback R., Que.†	James McGarry
7/24/83	8 lbs, 8 ozs	Minonipi L., Lab.	H. M. Golden
8/4/83	8 lbs, 4 ozs	Ann Marie L., Lab.	William E. Davis
7/13/84	8 lbs, 8 ozs	Ann Marie L., Lab.	Ken Washburn
8/10/84	8 lbs, 12 ozs	Ann Marie L., Lab.	Dave Brandt
6/26/85	6 lbs, 4 ozs	Lake Michigan, Wis.	Sharon E. Keas
8/10/86	8 lbs, 14 ozs	Ann Marie L., Lab.	Robert Ryan
8/19/86	9 lbs, 2 ozs	Minipi R., Lab.	Gregg Sevrinsen
9/2/86	9 lbs, 4 ozs	Broadback R., Que.†	Peter Baskin
6/29/87	10 lbs	Minonipi L., Lab	Sal Borelli
7/3/87	8 lbs, 4 ozs	Little Green L., Que.	Keith Whitham
8/11/87	9 lbs, 2 ozs	Minipi R., Lab.	Robert Ryan
7/17/88	6 lbs, 12 ozs	Green Bay, Mich.	Jeff Johnson
8/8/88	9 lbs, 7 ozs	Minipi R., Lab.	Robert B. Ryan
8/21/88	7 lbs, 12 ozs	Gull L., Calif.	Eric Petersen
8/15/89	8 lbs, 8 ozs	Minonipi L., Lab.	Robert B. Ryan
9/5/89	7 lbs, 4 ozs	Minipi R., Lab.	Harry Robertson
9/7/89	7 lbs, 8 ozs	Minipi R., Lab.	Harry Robertson
3/9/91	12 lbs, 2 ozs	L. Engano, Argentina	Kenneth Bohling
8/1/91	6 lbs, 4 ozs	Ann Marie L., Lab.	Greg Behrman
8/20/91	5 lbs, 7 ozs	Rupert R., Que.	Jack E. Morgan
5/4/93	7 lbs, 10 ozs	Round L., Sask.	Richard Meyers
7/28/94	7 lbs, 4 ozs	Emilie R., Lab.	Thomas B. Boyd
7/3/95	8 lbs, 9 ozs	Osprey Lake, Lab.	Andre Girard
7/11/95	8 lbs, 12 ozs	Minonipi Lake, Lab.	Dan S. Edgerton
8/29/95	6 lbs, 7 ozs	Minipi Lake, Lab.	Ronald L. Gougher

* fly-rod catch

†The South Fork Broadback River has since been renamed the Assinica River.

7 Wild, Domestic(ated), and Heritage Brook Trout

WHEN IS A BROOK TROUT NOT A BROOK TROUT?

That's not as easy to answer as it might appear. A brook trout, or any other fish, is viewed in two ways: one, by its outward or morphological (phenotypic) appearance, and the other, by its internal or genetic (genotypic) characteristics. In any given population—and a species is the average of all of its populations—all individuals may look much alike but genetically differ considerably. If every member of a population were genetically the same, then we'd have only one species of fish, flower, whatever.

Actually, in a population of fish, even down to a level as small as a group inhabiting a 100-yard stretch of a stream, no more than 60 to 70 percent are genetically (genotypically) exactly the same, although they may all appear (phenotypically) to be alike. It's genotypic variation that allows part of the population to survive should environmental conditions change in a way that favors brook trout with a slightly different genetic constitution.

Three factors can cause a population to change genetically: genetic drift, as just mentioned; migration, which allows the mixing of genes with other populations during mating; and mutation. To understand brook trout and why they can differ one must understand what constitutes a population. A population is made up of individuals of the same species living in close contact, so that any male or female in the group can mate at will with others in the group. If a physical barrier should suddenly divide this population, what's left is two parts of the same population. Given enough time after the

Figure 7.1   Seth Green, the father of fish culture in the United States.

separation, each group is likely to develop genetic differences unique to itself and slightly different from the other. Eventually, the barrier will have created two distinct populations. If the genetic differences continue to evolve over a longer period, the result can be different strains.

Changes that occur in a population are at first genetic and only later manifest themselves phenotypically. However, some quick changes in individual appearance can occur naturally, even within one generation, by hybridization between species. Although it's uncommon, closely related species can hybridize and produce progeny capable of reproduction. For this to occur, the two species must be evolutionarily close, as in the case of brook and lake trout. Both have the same number of chromosomes, 84. Lake trout, which occasionally cross naturally with brook trout (male lake trout and female brook trout) produce offspring that more closely resemble a brook trout. When male brook trout and female lake trout are crossed artificially (rare if not impossible in nature), they produce fish that look more like a lake trout and are called splake.

Another hybrid familiar to many anglers is the tiger trout, a cross between a male brook trout and a female brown trout. Since the introduction of the European brown trout to North America, examples of this hybrid have occurred in the wild. The progeny is infertile, however, because too many loci are in different positions on the gene and cannot match up when chromosome halves rejoin. Seth Green, America's first pisciculturist, successfully made the cross in 1878. New York had an active tiger trout program going in the late 1950s and early 1960s. First-generation splake are fertile, and in experiments this fertility has extended as far as four generations. Crosses between charr and trout (rainbow and brown) produce hybrids that cannot reproduce for the same reason as tiger trout.

FISH CULTURE AND PRESENT STOCKING PRACTICES

There's a fourth factor that can cause changes in the genetic makeup of fish populations: humanity. On no other fish species has our hand been felt more heavily than on brook trout. At one time, brook trout were distributed almost everywhere throughout the East. But the encroachment of humans reduced the brook trout's range by more than half, with only token populations existing today in out-of-the way places or in marginal-quality watersheds.

The brook trout's original range was in well-forested lands at all elevations. Many regions today considered too warm for brook trout during the height of summer were once much cooler because of the dense forest canopy. The destruction of brook trout habitat began as farmers cleared land for fields. Starting in the early 1800s, urban expansion created a demand for wooden building products. By 1825, the woodcutter's ax and later the saw were heard throughout the land. The complete denuding of forests began along the East Coast and swept unrelentingly westward to the Pacific, accelerating in the early 20th century as mechanization spread throughout the forest-products industry.

It was clear-cutting that did the irreversible damage. In just a few years, entire watersheds were stripped of trees. The destruction was compounded by erosion when logging roads funneled rainwater. Even worse were the splash dams—temporary log dams that blockaded a stream to create a pond. After the pond was filled with logs, the dam was dynamited and the torrent of water carried the logs downstream, destroying streambeds and -banks and leaving them boulder strewn and undercut. Then rain, which could no longer be held by the bare land and slowly absorbed into the groundwater, eroded the open fields and carried its products into the streams. Silt filled stream bottoms, smothering the gravel beds brook trout needed for spawning.

By the end of the Civil War, most eastern states were left with innumerable fishless streams. After a few decades, some of the habitat began to rebuild itself, and there arose a clamor to replace the trout. This period saw the formation of most state fish and game agencies. Naturally, their first thought was to restock brook trout. Attempts were made to transplant adult fish, but with minimal success. Adults from one system couldn't always adapt to a new, often warmer ecology. Transporting adults was also cumbersome and costly. Enter the fish culturists, who were at first seen as heroes but today have become the bane of fish management.

"They [brook trout] have always been the pets of fish-culturists; indeed, the experiments of Dr. Theodateus Garlick [1857—Cleveland], who inaugurated in 1853 the pisciculture practice in America, were made with these fish," said a 19th-century English observer. "They become thoroughly domesticated, and are as much under the control of their owners as horses and cattle. They've been acclimatized in England since 1868, and are on exhibition in the aquaria of the museum of fish-culture in South Kensington."

Our English observer was wrong. By 1853, Seth Green already had been raising brook trout for nearly 20 years. While Green wasn't the world's first pisciculturist—the Chinese had raised carp centuries before and the Roman Lucullus in the first century B.C. raised coarse fish in ponds—he was the first to raise trout in a hatchery. Undoubtedly the era's most successful fish culturist, Green was a Great Lakes commercial fisherman who, by 1837, had already been incubating brook trout. His motivation was to maintain a constant, year-round supply of fresh trout in his Rochester (N.Y.) fish store. Even then, brook trout were considered the best freshwater fish on the table.

Green told of how he first got the idea of raising trout while salmon fishing in Canada. For two days he watched salmon building redds then spawning, and figured he could duplicate the process with brook trout. By 1864 Green had built a series of brook trout rearing ponds between Mumford and Caledonia, southwest of Rochester, next to a gush of water created by Big Springs, which flows into Oatka Creek. He was fortuitous in choosing this site, not just because the water flow was good and temperatures varied only between 55 degrees in the summer and 43 degrees in the winter, but also because the water had a unique chemical composition and contained traces of lime and sulfur. He also developed the process for raising fertilized eggs inside his hatchery. New York State eventually assumed operation of the hatchery. Today, it's the oldest fish hatchery in the United States and is still in use.

Green was successful in raising astronomical numbers of brook trout, and eventually developed a technique for shipping brook trout eggs and fry to other hatcheries. Brook trout were stocked everywhere imaginable, and in some places that weren't. During the ensuing 50 years, brook trout, via stocking, spread across the West into new areas that had also suffered a loss of native trout species.

In 1868, Green was appointed one of three commissioners when New York established its State Fish Commission, predecessor to the DEC. He lasted one year, enough time to convince the legislature to appropriate $10,000 for a fish propagation program. When it did, he resigned to become its first superintendent of fish culture, a position he held until he died, at the age of 71, in 1888.

Even today, many state and federal hatcheries are still using stocks that originated in New York or Pennsylvania and are probably 50 generations old. Unfortunately, after a few generations the best hatchery fish weren't the best fishing fish. Hatchery personnel selected out fish whose genetic characteristics favored life in hatchery conditions: maximum production under crowded conditions in bell jars, concrete runs, and rearing ponds. They also provide the foods that produced maximum growth in the shortest time for fish in confined areas. Hatchery fish became too familiar with humans, especially at feeding time. And there was a price to pay for the fast initial growth: shorter life spans. Along the way, after generation upon generation, these fish gradually lost their wild characteristics. When stocked, they found it impossible to compete with wild brook trout or rainbow and brown trout. In a real sense they had become domesticated, and many biologists today refer to them as "domesticated" brook trout.

"Most New York ponds suitable for brook trout have been stocked with fish whose lineage is many generations removed from the wild. These fish, cultured and selected for hatchery performance traits, are commonly called domestic brook trout," wrote Walter T. Keller, a DEC biologist, in 1979.

Domesticated brook trout seldom lived more than a year or two. Worse, they often hybridized with wild brook trout, producing a fish unable to compete with non-native species. Wild brook trout also had difficulties competing with introduced non-native species. Those that escaped hybridization survived by retreating to less desirable upper-watershed habitats, where conditions generally did not allow brook trout populations to flourish. Because these populations have now been restricted to marginal habitats for many generations, it's doubtful just how well they could cope should downstream conditions improve. Domesticated brook trout compare unfavorably with the browns and rainbows often stocked in the same waters; this is why the species is held in such low regard by many anglers. But this is an erroneous concept: Domesticated brook trout only superficially resemble the brook trout that first inhabited our streams.

This loss of wildness didn't go unnoticed by anglers, fisheries managers, and hatchery personnel, especially as the number of ponds and streams with wild fish began to diminish. By 1975 there were only 11 ponds or lakes in New York that contained wild brook trout: Balsam Lake (26 acres); Dix Pond (14); Honnedaga (840), Horn (38), and Little Tupper Lakes (2,400); Nate (19), Stink (10), and Tamarack (13) ponds; Tunis Lake (28); and both Windfall Ponds (109 and 5 acres). Where wild fish occurred in streams, it was usually only in the beginnings of smaller headwater streams.

Walter Keller, the senior aquatic biologist for the DEC, out of Ray Brook, New York, from 1968 to 1976, fathered a plan to salvage the state's brook trout fishery. In his October 1979 report *Management of Wild and Hybrid Brook Trout in New York Lakes, Ponds, and Coastal Streams,* he outlined and justified the state's 15-year program; and in it he referred to brook trout in these various individual waters as strains, for instance, Balsam Lake Strain, Honnedaga Lake Strain, Dix Pond Strain, and so on. He defined *strain* as "a genetically distinct group of individuals of common origin and identified by the water(s) of origin of the parent stock(s)." While the definition is correct as far as it goes, his application of it to the individual populations in these various waters was too generous. He was really describing populations within a strain. Most ichthyogeneticists today believe that there are five or six strains of brook trout within the fish's entire distribution, and possibly two or three more populations that will need further investigation to determine their status. The brook trout mentioned above are really part of either the St. Lawrence, Hudson, or Delaware River Strains. For more on this, see Chapter 8: "Species, Subspecies, or Just a Strain?"

By the early 1950s, New York's brook trout were plagued with problems in addition to logging, the expansion of agriculture, and urbanization. Yellow perch were introduced to many Adirondack and Catskill ponds, usually by bait fishermen. These compete with young-of-the-year trout for available food in environments not overly abundant in that commodity. The return of beaver also had a negative effect on brook trout. After reintroduction the species' proliferation was extensive and rapid. Beaver ponds may produce a lot of brook trout fishing in Maine, but in New York they had the opposite effect. They prevented populations from reaching spawning grounds, elevated water temperatures in ponds to levels where brook trout couldn't survive, and increased acidity in water that was already on the edge of intolerability for brook trout.

Then came acid rain. By 1978, acidity had increased to the point that brook trout populations in 104 lakes and ponds disappeared. Liming was used in some acidic waters but proved too costly for general application. Today, liming is used only in a few ponds where endangered strains exist and several where fishing is still allowed.

New York's fisheries managers were becoming desperate. They had witnessed a steady decline in the wild characteristics of hatchery fish and had sought ways to change their hatchery program since the 1930s. There were three possible solutions to the problem of reestablishing quality brook trout fishing in state waters. One was to introduce a strain of brook trout from Canada—fish that grew larger and could cope with competition. The second was to develop a hybrid, a cross between these larger Canadian brook trout and domesticated (hatchery) trout. The third was to stop stocking waters with domesticated brook trout where wild brook trout still existed, or to stock only brook trout produced in the hatchery from wild stock that had originated in the same watershed. This choice also called for new hatchery techniques, rearing the fry in isolation in troughs, out of sight of hatchery personnel. These efforts weren't very successful until recent years.

Domesticated fish still had a role in urban and near-urban streams and ponds under heavy fishing pressure, where there was no expected holdover and where natural spawning was impossible. This put-and-take fishing does have its place. New York eventually elected to use all possible approaches.

Using original strains in the hatcheries for all of the state's hatchery stock was not practical because of the limited wild stock available. Thanks to Seth Green, New York had more experience with hatchery-reared brook trout than other states. For more than 100 years it had intensely studied their characteristics, both in and out the hatchery. In the mid-1970s, the state looked with great interest at the work of Dwight Webster, an ichthyologist at Cornell University (Ithaca, N.Y.) involved with hybridizing brook trout. Webster had developed a reputation a decade earlier by successfully enhancing natural production of wild brook trout by artificial means in several Adirondack ponds that suffered from limited natural spawning sites. Then, perhaps encouraged by the state, he began a series of experiments to bring new vitality to domestic trout.

The progeny of two different strains or even species exhibit features of growth greater than either parent. This is often called hybrid vigor. In most cases, it ends after the first generation. In the fall of 1959, Webster, accompanied by William Flick, also of Cornell, turned to a collection of rivers that rise on the central plateau in Québec and flow westward, all emptying into James Bay—the southern, thumblike extension of Hudson Bay. The men returned with brook trout eggs from two separate watersheds, closely located but with fish that were quite different in outward appearance: Assinica Lake (the

Broadback River) and the Témiscamie River. They were characteristically slow growers, lived almost twice as long as most brook trout—up to 10 years. Some grew to 9 pounds.

The eggs were hatched, raised to fry in several private ponds, and eventually crossed with domesticated brook trout to produce hybrids. Later, Webster and Flick gathered brook trout from the Minipi River system in Labrador. The end result was a hybrid cross between these and domesticated brook trout that produced fish that were wary and more difficult to catch, tolerated warmer water, had no trouble carrying over through the winter, and grew larger than their domesticated parents. When stocked, they sought refuge among rocks or under banks and chose the bottom of the water column in which to live—all characteristics opposite those of domesticated fingerlings.

But there was a problem. When wild and hybrid brook trout are raised in a hatchery environment, they become more susceptible to certain viral fish diseases, especially infectious pancreatic necrosis (IPN). This viral disease is deadly in a hatchery environment and easily spreads throughout all fish in a closed system. New York went into production first using both Canadian fish; then it abandoned several year-classes of Assinica fish, although they averaged larger than Témiscamie fish, because they developed IPN. This disease doesn't seem to bother brook trout in the wild, even though it's common in Assinica Lake fish and even seems to enhance their fecundity; Webster had to rotenone small portions of the fry population in his Brandon Park test waters to keep them from overpopulating the enclosed system. This stock was eliminated from the program, although some western states still use Assinica instead of Témiscamie stock. Today, almost all of New York's stocked fish are Témiscamie hybrids; the exceptions are a few waters that already contain wild brook trout, where original wild trout from Little Tupper Lake are used.

HERITAGE BROOK TROUT

To say that New York had an extensive brook trout fishery supported by domesticated fish would be a gross understatement. In 1978 the state managed 478 ponds with a combined surface area of 15,530 acres. However, the actors weren't playing their roles to the fullest and anglers began to complain about the poor quality of their fishing.

One of New York's options in trying to produce quality brook trout fishing was to turn the clock backward. In a sense, it would return to wild trout fishing by utilizing its heritage strain to reestablish or enhance the fishery where it existed or expand it into new areas lower in a watershed, or by reclaiming lakes and ponds and introducing brook trout as the sole species. It seemed appropriate that New York take such a step, because the fish was first scientifically described and named by Samuel Mitchill using a specimen from a Long Island stream that even today retains its wild status. And in 1975, New York named the brook trout the state fish. This heritage or wild fish approach is also being pursued in Pennsylvania, Vermont, New Hampshire, and Maine.

New York also chose to reestablish its heritage strains because its fisheries managers felt a moral obligation not to let a variation of a species become extinct due to indifference. There was also a scientific obligation: the need to maintain the large, varied gene pool so vital to the health and survival of a species. As environments change, the species and individuals within a species that survive are those with the greatest genetic ability to adapt to these changes. Brook trout are great survivors. For millions of years the environment has challenged this species with extremes. Brook trout responded and survived only because they've been able to maintain their relatively unspecialized body form and physiology.

The first step in developing a heritage trout program was to secure an environment where wild fish could survive without competition, where brook trout were the only predator species. Often, this meant the reclamation of a pond by using such chemicals as rotenone to kill its existing fish, then starting over from scratch. At the same time, it also meant locating and identifying remnant stocks that had never been contaminated by domesticated trout if they existed. Financed primarily by state monies, especially those generated by anglers who contributed through their state income tax returns by checking off donations to the "Return a Gift to Wildlife" program, this information was adroitly gathered in 1992 by the Perkins, Kreuger, and May team at Cornell University, who worked in cooperation with DEC biologists headed by Philip J. Hulbert of the Bureau of Fisheries.

They isolated 34 ponds or small streams that contained three unadulterated strains (Allegheny, Hudson/Delaware, and St. Lawrence) divided among the Allegheny, St. Lawrence, Susquehanna, Mohawk, Genesee, Hudson, and Delaware river basins. Their work should be continued because there may still be other waters with indigenous wild trout yet to be identified. These ponds and streams are located either on private land or in state parks where they can receive some degree of protection by stricter regulations or denial of entry. New York's DEC was given authority in 1977 by its legislature to set brook trout regulations aside from those for other trout species. Special regulations were immediately adopted—larger minimum lengths, reduced creel limits, and artificial lures only—to better protect both wild and hybrid brook trout in selected waters.

Keller's paper outlined his department's objectives, and the eventual goal was to establish or reestablish either wild (heritage) or hybrid populations of brook trout in 289 ponds or lakes encompassing 12,254 surface acres, as well as similar populations in Cayuga Lake with its nearly 42,500 acres and Lake Champlain's 91,508 acres of water.

THE FUTURE OF SALTER BROOK TROUT IN NEW YORK WATERS

Another way to return quality to New York's brook trout fishery is to reestablish sea-run brook trout in suitable waters. There are more than 100 independent watersheds on Long Island, ranging from mere trickles to fair-sized streams such as the Nissequogue,

Connetquot, Carmans, and Peconic rivers. At one time, almost every one had populations of native brook trout, alhough many were too small to be self-sustaining. Many streams entered brackish-water bays so closely together that they were more like tributaries than independent watersheds.

Most of the island's larger streams were dammed in colonial times to provide mill power or suitable habitat for raising cranberries. The latter activity (e.g., on the Peconic River) immediately elevated water temperatures, and those streams lost their brook trout. Before damming, brook trout populations near tidal portions of rivers had migrated seasonally to feed on forage fishes in the estuaries. Because most dams were located a bit above tidewater, some fish still had access to a portion of their spawning grounds. Today, there are a few undammed streams with a fair length of fresh water where the DEC is looking to reestablish salter populations. Unfortunately, reduced funding has put the project on hold. Instead, managers in Caleb Smith and Connetquot River State Parks have developed exceptional runs of brown trout, with some fish of up to 12 pounds in the Nissequogue River (Caleb Smith). In the Connetquot River, under the management of Connetquot River State Park, Gil Bergen, its superintendent and fish culturist, has developed a population of sea-run rainbow trout with some fish reaching 16 pounds.

According to Walter T. Keller, the DEC biologist who was in charge of the Heritage Strains Program in the late 1970s, "Characteristics of Canadian-strain brook trout suggest that they may offer a good opportunity for the use in establishment of 'salter' fisheries in some of Long Island's tributaries. The wanderlust common to the Témiscamie strain and its F1 hybrid, evident of their migration from ponds, indicates that they may be good candidates for this purpose."

Currently, there's hope among anglers that the DEC will develop a program to turn the Carmans River, where Daniel Webster took his 14 ½-pound brook trout, into a brook trout–only watershed. It had been stocked with brown and rainbow trout for more than a century. However, if the nonhybrid Témiscamie strain was used, the river might again produce a record brook trout. Isn't that an intriguing idea?

In 1995, New York's DEC inaugurated a two-year study of the tidal section of the Nissequogue River to determine the seasonal migration and movement patterns, growth rates, survival, and exploitation rates of salmonids in the river. Information gathered from this study will be used to better manage the salter populations in the state's tidal waters. Restrictive size (12 inches) and creel limits (three fish) have been placed on all tidal sections of trout streams in an attempt to allow brook trout, as well as browns and rainbows where they occur, to grow to their maximum trophy size.

MANAGING STREAMS FOR WILD BROOK TROUT

Upon discovering in 1991 that genetically unique populations of brook trout still existed in several Long Island streams, the DEC's regional fisheries management unit took steps to make protection and enhancement of these stocks a top priority. Over the years 1995–96, according to Ed Woltmann, the regional fisheries manager, his staff revisited all of the streams on Long Island that were historically classified as brook trout habitat. Their goal is to determine the status of the trout (browns and rainbows included) populations in each. Stream sections that now have trout or that have conditions suitable for trout survival will be considered critical habitats and afforded maximum protection through the state's regulatory programs. "No activities," said Woltmann, "that have the potential to disturb these streams or ponds shall be permitted."

Where necessary, regulations will be in force to protect brook trout populations at risk of exploitation. The DEC has already instituted a no-kill regulation on the upper Carmans River (within Southaven County Park) and a 10-inch size limit and three-fish creel limit on nearby Swan Lake, both of which, according to Woltmann, contain excellent brook trout populations. The goal of these regulations is to afford the slower-growing brook trout an opportunity to achieve their growth potential in these forage-rich waters. Stocking of DEC-reared brook trout (currently amounting to about 1,500 fish annually) shall cease on Long Island waters. Waters suitable for brook trout survival will be stocked only with "Long Island Heritage Strain" fish, preferably fish transferred from existing wild populations. The brook trout populations in two and possibly three streams have been DNA-tested at Cornell, and their genes show no indication of contamination by domesticated stock.

The plan also calls for some of Long Island's larger waters, such as the Carmans River, which contain brown as well as brook trout, to have stocking rates adjusted to ensure that the streams' carrying capacities aren't exceeded. Habitat improvement projects, too, are planned for the Carmans River and other trout waters on Long Island. Current plans call for efforts to reestablish brook trout as the main predator fish in the Carmans River, though brown and rainbow trout will still be stocked. Brown trout populations in the Carmans River are fairly compatible with brook trout. Both fish occupy similar habitats without detriment to the other. However, rainbow trout are more competitive with brook than with brown trout. To compensate, the plan calls for the use of rainbow trout in lower sections of the river below a dam. In this way, the lower stream will offer earlier-season anglers put-and-take rainbows—fish that seem unable to reproduce naturally in sufficient numbers to support a population.

There's also discussion of creating fishways in upper portions of the river to allow brook trout, especially those of Témiscamie heritage, and wild natives indigenous to the river to reach upstream spawning sites and contribute to natural reproduction. New York has taken a very active role in the return of the native!

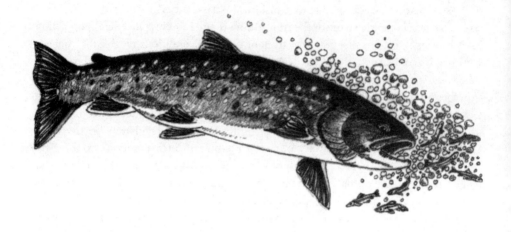

8 SPECIES, SUBSPECIES, OR JUST A STRAIN?

During the last 20 years, many cold-water fisheries managers have attempted to return to streams their original, wild occupants. This has also become the governing policy of the National Park Service. In the West, it has meant taking measures to reduce stocked populations of non-native brook trout where they compete with native species. In the East, it has meant the opposite. In Great Smoky Mountains National Park, populations of stocked rainbow and brown trout are being reduced in favor of brook trout. In areas outside of the federal park, state and sportsmen's groups are being discouraged from stocking these exotic species in higher elevations where stream conditions favor brook trout, and in upper watersheds where wild brook trout exist.

In the West, brook trout have often been relegated to areas where they don't grow large and thus offer little sport, and many anglers won't miss them. In the East, brown and rainbow trout have endeared themselves to anglers by occupying the lower, more productive parts of watersheds. As a result, they offer anglers better sportfishing than brook trout, which have been forced to inhabit less productive waters of the same watersheds. Still, there's enough momentum in the movement in the East to give brook trout a running start on their home court, especially in federal lands like Great Smoky Mountain National Park.

Some of this momentum has been created by Trout Unlimited in its quest for wild trout. This philosophy has filtered down to state fish and game agencies, and many have now made "wild" a part not only of their vocabulary but also of their brook trout fisheries. It has also sent many state biologists searching for remnants of original brook trout strains within their domain. And the buzzword today is *strain*. Until a decade or so ago, different brook trout populations were described as *races,* but most biologists who used the term felt it didn't quite describe a population that differed genetically only slightly from other populations—that it was too encompassing a word. Thus, *strain* today has become the more accepted and accurate name for such a portion of a population. Still, not everyone agrees about the exact definition of *species, subspecies*, and *strain.*

Species is the easiest to define: a population of fish that has a majority of physical characteristics in common but has so changed genetically from a part of the ancestral population that it can no longer produce fertile progeny when breeding with those populations. These changes may include time of spawning, age of maturation, spawning location, temperature preferences, and the like. Geneticists believe it takes a minimum of 50 adult or breeding males and 50 similar females to maintain the integrity of a gene pool and produce offspring resembling the general population.

In defining a *subspecies,* the lines are not drawn quite so clearly. The individuals in a species can often be divided into smaller groups or subspecies that differ from each other on a number of average rather than absolute characteristics. The prime characteristic distinguishing one group from another is usually the occupation of different ranges; great distances separate one end of the population spectrum from the other. Those individuals in the middle of the subspecies boundaries usually exhibit characteristics intermediately between the two extremes. This is especially true of brook trout, because they're so widely distributed. In such populations, individuals are still able to mate with members of other populations, but unlikely to do so given the physical separation. Thus distance becomes, in a way, a physical barrier. Personal interpretations of the factors affecting divergent characteristics create gray areas among biologists.

The most difficult definition for everyone to agree upon is that of a *strain*. Depending on who's doing the defining, a strain can be either a division among subspecies, thus one step further separated from the primordial stock, or a division within a species, but without a sufficient diversity of characteristics to be called a subspecies. This latter seems to be the most accepted definition. Too often, however, one biologist may be describing the characteristics of a subspecies that others would consider a strain.

With brook trout, the most accepted definition of a strain is also the latter, that is, various populations within the species that have too small a genetic diversity to give them subspecies status. In New York today, ichthyogeneticists recognize five different strains of brook trout: Allegheny, St. Lawrence, Susquehanna, Mohawk, and Delaware/Hudson (Perkins). If this wasn't a correct definition of strain, then we would have five subspecies, but we don't; the fish lack the genetic characteristics that would qualify them for subspecies or species distinction. There may have been more subspecies of *Salvelinus fontinalis* at one time, but so far only one has been recognized by a few taxonomists, *Salvelinus fontinalis timagamiensis.* Some biologists have proposed that Georgia or Southern Appalachian brook trout be regarded as a separate species, or at least a subspecies. Regardless of the definition, the truth is that some brook trout populations are genetically quite different from others.

To exhibit just how difficult it is to establish species or even true subspecies status, especially in the light of current attempts to reclassify populations of brook trout isolated in the upper elevations of the Southern Appalachians, it's interesting to follow the process used to place aurora trout *(S.f. timagamiensis)* in the scheme of things.

In 1923, a party of Pittsburgh anglers caught several brook trout in White Pine Lake, Gamble Township, Timagami Provincial Forest (MacKay), that were different from any they had ever seen. William H. Rinkenbach, one of the group, took one to the Carnegie Museum in Pittsburgh for identification. It wasn't until the following year, when additional specimens were obtained, that Arthur W. Henn of the museum decided it was a new species. The fish was known by a variety of names. Because of its resemblance to the shimmering and cascading splendor of the northern lights, Rinkenbach christened the fish "aurora trout." The origin of the specific name timagamiensis is obvious.

According to MacKay, aurora and brook trout had several morphological characteristics in common: size, blunt snout, shape of the maxillary, truncated caudal fin, 10 rays in the dorsal fin, 9 in the anal fin, numerous fine scales, similar numbers of pyloric caeca, vomer without a long, raised crest, vomerine teeth confined to the head of the bone, and strong teeth on the tongue and dentary; and the leading edges of the lower fins had a milk white border backed up with a thin, black stripe.

Aurora differed from brook trout in the absence of the wormlike vermiculations or marbled lines across the back, which, in brook trout, extend into the dorsal and caudal fins. The coloration also differed. The red spots with blue halos characteristic of brook trout were replaced by a blue or purplish sheen, more or less uniformly distributed over the body. Some exhibited one or two red spots with blue halos when in their spawning livery.

As to the aurora being a new species, MacKay speculated that if eggs were taken from a single female trout and fertilized, the resulting individuals would vary among themselves even if they were reared under similar conditions. Greater variation would be shown if different individuals were reared under widely differing conditions. Different sizes, forms, color, and markings are not sufficient to justify classifying a fish as a separate species if these changes are the result of the conditions under which the fish develop. But if differences in size, form, color, and markings are coupled with tendencies to occupy different habitats, choose different food, or breed in different places at different times, classification as a separate species is warranted.

In 1929, MacKay communicated with Dr. William C. Kendall, the dean of taxonomists at that time, and with the U.S. Department of Commerce's Bureau of Commercial Fisheries, Freeport, Maine, concerning the validity of classifying the charr described by Henn and Rinkenbach as a separate species. Kendall replied:

> In reference to your inquiry concerning the charr described and named by
> Henn and Rinkenbach, I cannot give any definite information concerning its

validity, not having seen a specimen. I have received the description to which you refer, and judge that the fish is similar to, if not identical with, the charr of Monadnock Lake (Dublin Pond), New Hampshire. [This was an error on Kendall's part. The Dublin Pond trout was described in 1885 as a new species of *Salvelinus* and given the specific name *S. agassizii* (Garman). Upon examining several specimens in 1967, Robert J. Behnke decided it had evolved from the brook trout. The silver trout, as it was popularly known, is now extinct.] This, I regard as a valid species. There is another which occurs or did occur in a small lake in Western New Hampshire which is very similar to it but differs in some small details. I have thought to describe it as a "new" species but have not yet done so. Again, there is one which occurs in a lake in Maine, also very similar in its characters.

These three resemble the *S. fontinalis* in some respects and the *S. alpinus* forms in others but, to me, seem to be neither one nor the other. I regard them as intermediate forms between the ancestral charr from which *S. fontinalis* diverged and *S. alpinus*. Therefore, not being derived from *S. fontinalis* and not integrating from it to some other form, they are not to be regarded as subspecies or varieties of *S. fontinalis*. If this is so, the question is, is each of these four "intermediates" a distinct species or are they all the same species? If the latter is the case, they should bear the name of *Salvelinus agassizii*. If they are distinct, then *S. timagamiensis* should stand. All depends upon what we consider as constituting a species.

I suspect that more of this style of fish have been caught in other places and regarded as variants of *S. fontinalis,* particularly in Canada.

W. R. Martin, in his master's thesis in 1939, showed that the aurora trout was identical with the brook trout in body proportions and distinct from the marine Arctic charr or any of its landlocked derivatives. The mean values for the relationships between head measurements and standard length corresponded almost exactly with the mean values of these measurements for brook trout. Divergence from the Arctic charr mean was large in all measurements and especially marked in the length of the maxillary.

Henn and Rinkenbach reported that all of the smaller specimens of aurora trout taken by them were infected by a parasitic copepod, *Salmincola edwardsii*. This parasite is widespread in trout waters of North America and Europe, including many trout waters in northern Ontario. It was common in northern brook trout hatcheries. The point here, in connection with the discussion of the validity of classifying aurora trout as a separate species, is the fact that the parasitic copepod, *edwardsii*, is specific to brook trout.

Everyone took a shot at identifying the aurora trout's lineage, even Vadim Vladykov, the eminent Canadian biologist, in his 1954 report on taxonomic studies of the North American charr (*Salvelinus* and *Cristivomer*). He came closest to the truth and regarded aurora trout *(Salvelinus timagamiensis)* as merely a color variety of the common brook trout.

Populations of these nonspeckled or nonspotted brook trout in a restricted portion of the Temiskaming District of Ontario were described by Henn and Rinkenbach in 1925 as a distinct species, *Salvelinus timagamiensis,* the aurora trout. But by 1967, there were far better ways of determining fish relationships. P. F. Sale (Sale) reexamined the aurora trout. By the use of electrophoresis of the trout's enzymes he demonstrated that it was closely allied to *Salvelinus fontinalis.* He suggested it be considered a subspecies, *S.f. timagamiensis.* Unfortunately, the stock was so decimated by the late 1950s that by 1973, when Scott and Crossman wrote their monumental work, *Freshwater Fishes of Canada,* it was considered extinct. Because of this, further work, unless from museum specimens, cannot be conducted.

Gaining subspecies, or even strain, status isn't easy.

A wild male brook trout in full spawning livery from the Dancelou River in northwest Ungava, Québec, at the very northern fringe of the brook trout's range.

Comparison of a male brook trout and male landlocked Arctic charr, both in spawning regalia and taken from the same pool on the Dancelou River in northern Québec in early September.

A Heritage-Strain male brook trout in spawning condition, taken from the upper section of the Connetquot River, Long Island, New York. Note the seasonal development of a "hump" on the back and exaggeration of the lower jaw. This is not a "beaver pond" fish from a leachate stream but the product of a cold, clear, spring-fed stream.

A 6-pound male brook trout from the Ashuanapi River, Labrador, illustrating all the morphological changes that take place as spawning nears: slight hook to lower jaw, exaggeration of the length of the lower jaw, build-up of musculature just ahead of the dorsal fin, and color changes. Most noteworthy is the black that covers the inside of the mouth along the lower gill covers and over the anterior portion of the belly.

Double-halo pattern on a brook trout from the Eagle River watershed in southern Labrador.

A wild brook trout, but from the Tunulic River in northeastern Ungava in Québec. Note the more fusiform body shape as compared to the Connetquot River form and more subdued lateral coloration.

Characteristic head of a female brook trout.

A 3½-inch male brook trout believed to be a wild or Heritage-Strain fish from South Branch Raritan River, New Jersey. The fish is about one and one half years old but still retains strong parr markings while developing exaggerated male sex coloration in late September.

(Courtesy Dickson Despommier)

Effective miniature spinning lures for brook trout. Left row, top to bottom: combo plug and spinner by Normark, parr-pattern brook trout by Rapala, and jointed minnow by Rebel. Right row, top to bottom: Anglia Mepps spinners in sizes from 2 to 0.

Traditional spoons used to take brook trout. Left row, top to bottom: CP Swing and three sizes of Kastmasters. Right row: three sizes of the Phoebe spoon.

All flies tied by Howard Eskin of Stony Brook, New York, unless otherwise noted.

Parmachene Belle.

Gray Fox.

Quill Gordon.

Light Hendrickson Dun (f.).

American March Brown Dun (f.).

Red Quill Dun (f.).

Light Cahill Dun (f.).

Royal Wulff.

The author's collection of fully dressed Mick Finns, from size 3/0 to 1, tied by Ron Jones of Chicotimi, Québec.

The Original Muddler Minnow tied by Don Gapen. *(Courtesy Dan Gapen)*

Gray Ghost.

Owens River Stone Fly.

Mickey Finn.

Supervisor.

Brookie Parr.

Magog Smelt.

Muddler Minnow.

Damselfly Nymph.

Mouse tied by Ron Jones.

9 THE FALL AND RISE OF BROOK TROUT IN SOUTHERN APPALACHIA

Unhampered by winter weather, 19th-century logging operations in the Southern Appalachian Mountains usually continued year-round, and the loss of of brook trout habitat proceeded at an accelerated rate over the Southern Appalachian's piedmont. The loss of the treetop canopy was devastating. Still, lower elevations of some watersheds offered marginal brook trout habitat as the forests began a slow recovery. By the late 1800s, many states denuded by logging operations had built hatcheries and developed stocking programs, but attempts to rear brook trout using indigenous stocks were a disaster; the wild stock did poorly in the hatcheries and were susceptible to hatchery diseases (Venters). In frustration, managers turned north for brook trout stock, to Michigan, Pennsylvania, New York, and Massachusetts (McCracken).

These imports fared better in the hatcheries, but as they were stocked into watersheds' lower reaches they bred with remaining wild trout, producing hybrids lacking the characteristics of native trout at higher elevations. This contamination of the gene pool began working upstream into headwaters that lacked impenetrable barriers. After the turn of the century, a massive restocking of southern brook trout waters began—which in some areas continues today. Some of the most active early stockers were the timber companies that had denuded the forests; perhaps this was a form of atonement. They stocked brook trout, but also brought in brown and rainbow trout for waters where changed and unfavorable environmental conditions meant brook trout no longer could take hold.

Local people soon noticed differences between the stocked brook trout and their native fish, populations of which still existed in the higher elevations (Venters). They considered their brook trout, which they called speckled trout, to be a different species, and came to look upon the northern brook trout as an inferior fish. In a way, it was. But it must be kept in mind that by the time the southern states began importing northern hatchery stocks, these domesticated fish had undergone many changes from the wild brook trout of northern waters.

For years, no one took the locals too seriously—until National Park Service biologist Robert E. Lennon began studying the morphological characteristics of southern (speckled) trout and comparing them with northern counterparts. In 1967 he suggested that the differences were great enough for them to be considered a separate species, or at least subspecies. He found that southern trout were usually smaller and had more speckles, which were colored a brighter red; their eyes, snout, and lower jaws were larger; and their pectoral fins were longer than those of northern brook trout. In addition, in streams where both stocks were mixed with brown and rainbow trout, northern brook trout did better.

Because of the ruggedness of the terrain in the higher elevations of the Southern Appalachians (Blue Ridge and Great Smoky mountains), logging operations there didn't get under way in full force until the late 1920s and early 1930s. At this time, upper-elevation streams still offered excellent brook trout fishing. "Mountaineer people exploited brook trout for food, profit and barter," according to a piece by James Yuskavitch in a 1991 issue of *Trout,* the Trout Unlimited magazine. "The Palmer Family," according to an interview he conducted with Great Smoky Mountains National Park historian Ed Trout, "had a lock on the fishing business on Catalooche Creek from the late teens to about 1934. They rented cabins for 50 cents a night, charged 50 cents for three meals, and 50 cents for the right to fish their hollow." Another story has it that an old-time mountaineer paid a local dentist for some dental work with 200 brook trout—caught that same day. Such was the species' former abundance in the lower elevations, down to perhaps 1,600 feet, where it was said that 14- to 18-inch fish were relatively common. Trout's statement brings up an interesting point. Were these lower-elevation trout part of the original southern brook trout strain? If they were, then they differed only morphologically from their upstream brethren, and the differences were probably caused by the environment and not genetics.

Great Smoky Mountains National Park, which straddles the mountainous border between Tennessee and North Carolina, became the last refuge of wild brook trout in the Southern Appalachians. Its history is closely entwined with the survival of brook trout in this region. English colonists quickly moved from the coast into these mountains. By the mid-1920s there were 1,200 farms and 7,300 people struggling to make a living on the marginal agricultural land that would eventually become the national park.

The park was started in 1924 but not formally established until 1934, after a 10-year period of gradual, almost acre-by-acre, land acquisition. When completed, it stretched for 70 miles and encompassed 517,000 acres of mountaintops. Only 30 percent of it is virgin forests; the rest is leftover clear-cut slashings of the timber industry. In 35 years of inten-

Figure 9.1   A wild Southern Appalachian brook trout from Great Smoky Mountain National Park, the extreme southern limit of the brook trout's range. (Courtesy Steve Moore.)

sive logging, nearly half of the brook trout's habitat had been destroyed. It was so thorough that state studies in the 1920s revealed that the brook trout fishery existed only where logging had not taken place. Most of the park land was purchased from timber companies after it was clear-cut. In 1937, Willis King, the park's first fisheries professional, wrote that "speckled trout today are largely confined to headwaters above 3,000 feet and have been exterminated from many streams."

So dire was the need to save brook trout that the first entry in the new park superintendent's ledger in March 1934 was the establishment of new fishing regulations. They included a 10-inch minimum limit on brook trout and a creel limit of 10 fish per day, and specified fly fishing only—the first such condition inaugurated in the United States. However, enforcing these rules in those days was impossible.

Even the park service was guilty of diluting the brook trout fishery. At lower elevations it began stocking rainbow trout from three hatcheries within the park's boundaries. These were shut down in the 1940s, but rainbow trout continued to be brought in from outside federal hatcheries. In a 19-year period ending in 1957, more than 1.5 million rainbows were stocked within the park's boundaries. The brook trout fishery was almost nonexistent. To remedy this, park personnel stocked more than 800,000 brook trout fingerlings, but they were of non-native stock because it was also too difficult to raise native strains.

Regardless of these well-intended efforts, the brook trout fishery continued to decline. When park personnel realized that brook trout had lost nearly 70 percent of their original habitat, they began to suspect that it might be because of rainbow trout and, in some cases, brown trout (Krueger). By 1975 the service halted all stocking in the park and closed all recreational fishing. Insidiously, the western import had been winning the trout wars by continually colonizing streams farther up the watershed. Only above natural barriers did brook trout survive. Unfortunately, park policy forbids construction of artificial barriers to upstream migration. By 1980, the U.S. Fish and Wildlife Service determined that brook trout were found in only 123 of the park's more than 1,000 miles of suitable trout waters. The alarm was sounded!

In 1983, Gary Larson and Steve Moore, biologists with the National Park Service's Uplands Field Research Laboratory in Gatlinberg, Tennessee, concluded their studies into the stream relationship of brook and rainbow trout. These studies supported the idea that rainbow trout were the current cause of the brook trout's shrinking range in Great Smoky Mountains National Park. Rainbows had initially driven brook trout from low-gradient sections of watersheds both inside and outside the park, and are even today working upstream. The problem remains of how to stop the decline and then, where possible, to reestablish brook trout in their original streams. Moore's options are limited, but he has continued to bolster brook trout populations above barriers with wild fish he catches below natural obstacles.

SOUTHERN-STRAIN BROOK TROUT

Between the late 1970s and early 1980s, brook trout in this Appalachian range were being considered for endangered species status. To achieve this, southern brook trout had to be elevated to species status, and this initiated a series of population-genetics studies. One side benefit of the search for primordial, uncontaminated brook trout was the discovery that a much larger number of streams, many outside the park, still had isolated populations of original stock. A number of streams even had no record of stocking—although such records were not always kept, or kept accurately. Then, too, there were a surfeit of individual stockings by sportsmen's clubs, private citizens, and timber companies. Geneticists were needed to unravel the can of worms and to determine the heritage of these "wild" fish in isolated mountain streams.

During the last 15 years, and especially the last 5, state agencies, often in cooperation with universities in Alabama, North Carolina, Georgia, Tennessee, Maryland, Pennsylvania, and New York, have addressed the task of identifying populations of wild or indigenous strains of brook trout in all of the Appalachians. Then they've conducted interstate comparisons to establish the degree of genetic diversity between these populations. Their primary technique is starch-gel electrophoresis, an important tool of taxonomists and ichthyogeneticists. Understanding how this technique works can help one better comprehend the external variations in brook trout from different locales.

To compare different populations of brook trout, eye, liver, and muscle tissue from each group are put into a blender to produce a brook trout puree. This is then put into a centrifuge, which separates the rough stock from a clear solution that includes the fish's protein. A paper wick is dipped into the protein-rich fish extract then sandwiched in a mold of potato-starch gel. The combination is placed on ice with electrodes attached to each end of the wick, and an electric current is run through it for several hours. The current causes enzymes (chemical catalysts) within the protein to move through the gel. Finally, the gel is stained to bring out the locations to which the various enzymes of this brook trout moved.

The location and relationship of the enzymes to each other produce what amounts to a fingerprint of this fish, which can then be compared to gel patterns from other trout. The presence of protein products from specific genes may be observed and compared among fish. The level of diversity is a measure of the separation among strains within populations.

The investigators began by using Lennon's suggestion—mentioned earlier—that these fish should be given species status. The first person to investigate the possibility on genetic grounds was John Harris, a Tennessee Technical University biologist. He began by looking at 35 brook trout populations along the Appalachian range from Georgia to New York, viewing them as a continuum of the population. Using two established methods—electrophoresis and meristics (the comparison of body characteristics)—he concluded that there were no differences at the subspecific level between northern and southern populations. These results didn't go over well with those promoting species status for this population of brook trout.

Bernie May and Mark Stoneking, in separate research papers published in 1980, criticized Harris's investigation, saying he had misinterpreted his data. In 1981, Stoneking undertook his own investigation, using only electrophoresis, and concluded that northern and southern populations were different; but he hedged, too, by stating that "probably two subspecies existed." He also discovered more genetic variation among northern populations than between wild southern and northern brook trout populations.

This variation was firmly established by further research in 1993 when May, along with David Perkins and Charles Krueger, all of Cornell University, were searching for remnants of New York's original wild strain. They found that, within the 10 major river drainages in the state that they sampled, there were 21 wild brook trout populations genetically different from each other and from hatchery stock samples. They were able to group the 21 samples into six separate watersheds and these into five populations, which were given strain status because of the degree of genetic diversity among them. They compared their findings to data from Gary McCracken's research on Southern Appalachian brook trout and determined that the southern population was a sixth strain. "The strain and subspecies is not [really that] important here," said Dr. Krueger. "What is important is that genetic differences exist."

This was significant because it mirrored the degree of diversity that investigators such as McCracken found among samples investigated in the Southern Appalachians. McCracken, a zoology professor at the University of Tennessee, also criticized the way Harris had interpreted his data. McCracken conducted his own investigations, which ended in 1993. He reached the same conclusion as Stoneking and offered the same probability. But while Stoneking had suggested subspecies status, McCracken suggested only strain status.

McCracken concluded that three possible brook trout strains existed in this southern part of the brook trout's range: "a speckled native fish, a Northern strain hatchery fish, and a hybrid fish with Northern and speckled genes." He confused the issue, though, by using the word *strain* to identify these three stocks. There's probably only one strain, the indigenous wild brook or speckled trout. When northern hatchery fish mate with speckled trout the progeny cannot be considered a natural strain but one that is manufactured or man-made.

However, McCracken believed that a definite physical boundary exists between northern and southern strains, which interrupts what would otherwise be a gradual continuum of slight genetic changes building one upon another as one travels from south to north sampling populations. The lack of such a barrier would preclude a separate species status but would enhance the definition of *strain*. However, he believed that a physical or geographic boundary does separate these two populations and that the southern strain can thus be considered a separate species or subspecies.

McCracken's boundary is the "billion-year-old" New River in Virginia. "The region of the New River drainage in southwestern Virginia," he wrote, "forms the boundary for several other floral and faunal groups, and we suspect that this region is the most likely boundary for the Northern versus Southern brook trout strains."

This is not a good example of a population boundary for a species that moves by water. The New River rises along the eastern side of the Blue Ridge Mountains and flows northeast, but doesn't drain to the Atlantic. Instead, its drainage has always been northwest, to the Ohio River. As the Appalachian folds rose the river was able to keep ahead of the pace; it continued to erode the folds as it passed through the much higher Continental Divide. It's not unique in this effort; several streams across the Appalachians accomplished the same feat without dividing faunal and floral populations. I suspect that climate, precipitation, temperature, and soil are the primary reasons for this change in plants and land animals. The New River is but another tributary to the Mississippi/Ohio/Allegheny River complex that rises in Pennsylvania and flows north into New York before turning south. After uniting with the Monongahela in Pittsburgh, the Allegheny River becomes the Ohio then joins with the Mississippi. Thus, the continuum is unbroken.

North Carolina's Wildlife Commission currently has under way a research project headed by biologist Jim Borawa, who began sampling brook trout for a genetics study in the summer of 1993. He and his associates have discovered an additional 158 streams, about 200 miles of which they believe contain unaltered brook trout populations.

The most recent investigation, which delved into the taxonomic status of southern brook trout in Georgia, was done in 1994 by Rex Dunham and his team from Auburn University (Alabama) and Jeff Durniak and Michael Spencer from Georgia's Department of Natural Resources. They examined 11 brook trout populations from 10 different streams and concluded that there appear to be two major forms of southern brook trout in Georgia, but they didn't explain what they meant by "forms." Their study suggested that "there is considerable sharing of genetic features between southern and northern brook trout," and added, "In general, Georgia populations appear to have allele [a group of genes that occur as alternative forms at a given site] frequencies which would classify them as southern brook trout. Though further analysis is needed, it is clear that Georgia populations are different from some North Carolina and Tennessee populations." The key is what they meant by "some" populations in these two states. If they're the same as wild stock, which I suspect they are, then they're part of the southern strain.

These probably reflect the two different refugia sources of brook trout populations that were available 20,000 and more years ago. The researchers hesitated, however, to make a definitive conclusion as to species or subspecies status. What they have identified correctly is a strain, because they described strain rather than subspecies or species characteristics in their samples.

It should have been a foregone conclusion to all of these researchers that they would have found genetic variances between brook trout at one end of a vast, widespread population and those at the other extreme, especially when so much distance was involved. But one must add another variable, that of time, which must accompany the three factors capable of causing genetic changes in a species. Brook trout from New York and those from Georgia have been separated by only 14,000 or so years in what has been a relatively stable environmental period. This is not a very long period when it comes to evolutionary change.

SOUTHERN BROOK TROUT AND NORTHERN GLACIERS

Those investigators trying to establish anything more than strain status in the classification of southern brook trout are suffering from what might be called scientific provincialism for not having considered the effects of glaciation on brook trout distribution. A 135,000-year span probably existed between the Wisconsin Glacier and the Illinoisan Glacier. In this interglacial period, brook trout inhabited great areas of Canada and the northern United States, much as they do today. As the last continental ice sheet, which had three centers of origin, began sweeping south, it pushed all life before it. Its most southerly advance in the eastern and central United States was from New York City northwestward across northern New Jersey, northeastern Pennsylvania, back into New York, around the northern base of the Allegheny Mountains, then southwest across the center of Ohio and Indiana and into southern Illinois. Here it reached its greatest southward advance at a line formed by the present towns of Carbondale, Marion, and Harrisburg, before turning westward through the middle of Iowa and then northwestward to Alaska.

The ice sheet is estimated to have been between 8,000 and 10,000 feet thick, but when it reached the relatively low northern terminus of the steeply folded Allegheny Mountains, from just north of the New York–Pennsylvania border, it did not override them. The northern end of this mountain group of the Appalachians seemed to have acted as a barrier to the massive advancing ice sheet even though it overrode all of the Appalachians north to their beginnings on the Gaspé Peninsula. Because of this action, the northern base of the Alleghenies became a pivotal point in salmonid retreat and their subsequent recolonization of the land once it was ice-free. The glacier's advance southward on both sides of the Appalachians forced brook trout, along with lake trout, Arctic charr, and Atlantic salmon, to occupy ranges south of the glacier's leading edge, over lands that in previous preglacial periods were far too warm for them to exist.

East-west waterborne movements were not possible among fish populations across the northern base of the Alleghenies because of the frozen state of the environment. At this time, both brook and lake trout populations became divided and were displaced east and west of the Appalachians. Arctic charr and Atlantic salmon populations were concentrated on the eastern side of the mountain range. Their anadromous capability and free use of the Atlantic Ocean enabled them to move south along the Atlantic seeking the estuaries of more hospitable river basins. The eastern portion of the now-divided brook trout population, along with these salmonids, adapted to waters on the piedmont, coastal terrace, and continental shelf as far south as Florida and the Gulf of Mexico. The only salmonid incapable of anadromy is the lake trout. The eastern population of this fish probably became extinct long before the glacier crossed the St. Lawrence Valley because it could not pass into salt water to migrate south in advance of the glacier. West of the new divisor, lake trout did escape into the Great Lakes Basin and used the headwaters of the Mississippi River to eventually survive the glacial epoch in the Mississippi refugium.

The displacement from and then recolonization of native waters by lake trout is not as certain or as clear as that by brook trout. While most biologists believe lake trout, *Salvelinus namaycush,* are incapable of anadromy, this does not explain how these fish populated some of the large offshore islands beyond the northern, Arctic coast of Canada. Two large freshwater lakes on the southern part of Baffin Island have sizable, well-establishd populations of lake trout. And I've caught lake trout in brackish, estuarine portions of several rivers that flow north in Ungava in northern Québec to enter saline Ungava Bay.

Preglacial brook trout population had now been divided by a physical barrier, the Appalachians, into two isolated populations, and had survived the 80,000-year glacial epoch in both Mississippi and Atlantic refugia. At this time, the major north-south communications and migration route for brook trout on the western side of the Appalachians was a river system that paralleled the southwest-northeast face of the glacier along its southern edge. This was the Allegheny River, which became the Ohio River in Pittsburgh and eventually the Mississippi River where, near the glacier's southernmost point in southern Illinois, it joined an abbreviated Father of Waters. During this period, all of the watersheds on the western side drained into these two rivers. Coincidentally, the other river that followed the glacier's western face entered the Mississippi slightly north of the Ohio. This was the Missouri River, which followed the glacier's northwestern edge almost to the Canadian border.

Though the tops of the Southern Appalachians weren't glaciated, they must not have been very hospitable places for brook trout. Their peaks and valleys were snow packed for extended periods, and if summers did occur at upper elevations, they must have been measured in weeks, especially in places such as Mount Mitchell, at 6,684 feet the highest of the Appalachians. Over the eastern piedmont, summers may have been only a month or two long, much as they are today in subarctic regions of Canada, which offer brook trout excellent habitat. This further strengthened the separation between western and eastern glacial populations of brook trout, because the few rivers that did flow west or east over the Continental Divide were probably locked in what seemed like perpetual ice.

Early in the postglacial period, as the vast ice sheet began melting, New York became the pivotal point for the brook trout's recolonization of its original ranges. This is supported by the recent work of Perkins, Krueger, and May in determining the heritage of New York State's brook trout. Their studies revealed five distinct brook trout groups within New York, based on genetic diversification. And they concluded that there was at least one more, a sixth group, different from New York's five, composed of fish from the Little Tennessee River (Tenn./N.C.) or southern strains and possibly two other groups: Patapsco/Potomac (Md.) and Monocacy (Ohio) rivers.

Genetic distances were calculated between their samples of New York and Pennsylvania brook trout and compared with those wild populations from Maryland (Morgan and Baker) and Great Smoky Mountains National Park (McCracken). The comparison revealed that all were significantly different. In the final analysis, the answer is yes, there is a unique strain of brook trout in the Southern Appalachians, but the characteristics that make it unique are no more so than those that separate the five other groups.

Perkins, Krueger, and May arrived at the strain or population separations using cluster analysis of the genetic distances they found with electrophoretic techniques. This included data from other investigators working outside of New York. They discovered that genetic variances between populations from different basins weren't based on the geographical separation of populations. In other words, one population could be separated from another by great geographic distances, but as long as they were able to make regular contact (mating), as in a situation where various drainages came together in a common lake, estuary, or ocean, the genetic difference between fish in the separate watersheds wasn't great.

However, in other examples where watersheds may have been in close proximity, such as where the end tips of tributaries from one watershed might be interlaced with those of another but forced by a height of land to drain in opposite directions, then genetic distance between populations was usually greater. It's interesting to note that slight genetic differences did occur within tributaries of the same watershed. However, the genetic distances were never as great as those between populations in separate watersheds. This indicated, according to Perkins, Krueger, and May, that little gene flow occurred among populations from different basins that evolved in isolation from each other.

The retreat of the glaciers was faster on the western than on the eastern side of the Appalachians. The Keewatin Ice Sheet retreated faster than the Labrador (really Québec) Ice Sheet. By 14,000 years ago, most of the Mississippi watershed was exposed, as was most of Michigan and all of Illinois, Indiana, Ohio, and Pennsylvania on the eastern side. In New York, however, only a strip of counties along the Pennsylvania border and the lower Mid-Hudson Valley were ice-free. Just prior to this, glacial Lakes Chicago (Lake Michigan) and Maumee, which was to become Lake Erie, were filled with glacial melt. Most of the glacial melt waters then flowed southwest along this front, into Lake Maumee, which was drained by the Allegheny/Ohio River complex.

It was brook trout from this population, from the Mississippi refugium, that spread upstream and eastward and began to populate small watersheds and casual glacial lakes north of the Alleghenies. Eight hundred years later parts of the Finger Lakes were exposed, and glacial melt then flowed south to the headwaters of the Susquehanna River. A bit later, meltwater from here flowed south, off the Adirondacks ice fields, and then west through the Mohawk River. Later it reversed its direction, as the Mississippi connection to the Great Lakes was severed by the rising land, and the water flowed east, filling glacial Lake Albany, which flowed down the Hudson Gorge, over the continental shelf, and into the Atlantic.

Before the connection with the Hudson watershed was made, brook trout from the Atlantic refugium were able to move north into central and southeastern New York. They migrated up the Susquehanna drainage, moved into the Finger Lakes and Mohawk River, and then traveled up the edge of what was to become Lake Ontario and populated the Salmon and Black rivers. When glacial melt finally began filling the Lake Ontario basin, it was the first time the divided populations—now differentiated in the north into three strains—had met since communications routes were first sealed by glaciers. Populations of Allegheny, Susquehanna/Mohawk, and Hudson/Delaware River strains were able to commingle.

While most of these routes are believed to be fairly accurate, they've been derived from de facto evidence. There's one area of confusion, however. It's difficult to dispute Perkins, Krueger, and May's evidence, based on electrophoretic work, that brook trout in the Susquehanna watershed came from the Atlantic refugium. However, there is evidence to suggest that they might not have. In 1935, John R. Greeley, New York's leading biologist with the then Conservation Department, compared various fish populations in the Susquehanna, Delaware, and Hudson rivers. If they were all of Atlantic refugium origin, the composition of fish populations in each watershed should be the same. They weren't.

Most of the 19 fish species in the Susquehanna also occurred in the Mississippi (Ohio/Allegheny rivers) basin. Twelve species that occurred in the Hudson watershed also occurred in Susquehanna and Mississippi drainages. However, none of these occurred in the Delaware drainage. The conclusions drawn by Dr. H. H. MacKay of the Ontario Fish and Wildlife Branch in 1963 were that these fish, along with brook trout, originated in the Mississippi refugium and that the Delaware watershed was populated by fish from the Atlantic refugium. They arrived in the Hudson, bypassing the Catskills and the Delaware River watershed, by way of the Finger Lakes; Lake Oneida, which was a swelling of the Mohawk River; and the upper Hudson watershed, which drained all of the Great Lakes into the Hudson before the St. Lawrence was free of glaciers. Thus, colonization—based on the total number of different fish species found in the Delaware River—would identify the Atlantic as the source of brook trout for this watershed.

The Labrador Ice Sheet was now melting at an accelerated rate. By 12,000 years ago, glacial Lake Bellville, centered on what would become Lake Ontario and the Champlain Valley and covering most of northern New York (except for the Adirondacks) including the still-blockaded St. Lawrence Valley, was connected to Lake Erie by the primordial Niagara River and a much larger Lake Algonquin, which still had icebergs calving along its northern rim. Brook trout from the west spread farther and farther east along this watery highway. Now the flow of the glacial melt switched directions. Instead of coursing down the Ohio River to the Mississippi, it flowed down the Champlain Valley as the Hudson River. The head of water was so great that it easily gouged its way through the old riverbed, creating a deep valley in the continental shelf that today still exists 600 feet below sea level as the Hudson Canyon.

Just 200 years later, the glacier blocking the western end of the St. Lawrence melted away. The weight of the glacier here was so heavy that it depressed the St. Lawrence and Champlain valleys below sea level. The Atlantic Ocean flooded as far inland as the base of today's Niagara Falls and down the Champlain Valley almost to where the now dried-up Hudson was just a small river. On the tide came brook trout, Arctic charr, Atlantic salmon, and even striped bass. When it came time to spawn the anadromous fish headed up all of the rivers, especially on the U.S. side, which were free of ice sooner than those to the north. But as the land mass responded to the loss of the glacial weight, the eastern end of glacial Lake Ontario rose above sea level. At first salt water ended near today's Thousand Islands. Lake Ontario eventually turned fresh, and for a while salmon and other anadromous fishes must have migrated up what was then a very short St. Lawrence River, to Lake Ontario and then to primordial spawning sites on such rivers as the Genesee, Oswego, Salmon, and Black. Brook trout of Atlantic origin used the now lengthening St. Lawrence River as a route to colonize rivers draining the northern Adirondacks and eventually those in Québec both north and south of the St. Lawrence.

Atlantic-origin brook trout in the St. Lawrence were now differentiated enough genetically from Susquehanna and Hudson River brook trout to be considered the newest brook trout population, the St. Lawrence Strain.

Brook trout recolonized the west-flowing Allegheny, Genesee (then flowing south), and Mohawk rivers; the latter was not yet a tributary to the Hudson but connected with rivers from the west, from the Mississippi (Great Lakes) refugium. Brook trout that populated the lower Hudson River basin came first from the south, from the Atlantic refugia. Those in the Adirondacks and eastern side of Lake Ontario were colonized from the Atlantic refugium, through the St. Lawrence Valley. Northern New York, Québec, Labrador, and the Canadian Atlantic provinces have brook trout of the same strain.

Looking back at the brook trout in the Southern Appalachians, it seems apparent that they were derived from one stock: the preglacial brook trout strain that inhabited watersheds on the western slope of the Appalachians and the upper elevations of the mountains. These brook trout were genetically the same strain as those trout that existed at lower elevations of the same watersheds when they were covered by dense virgin forests. All of these watersheds emptied into the Ohio/Allegheny River complex that existed, shaped maybe somewhat differently, in pre–Wisconsin Glacier times.

Much the same can be said of other watershed drainages on the southern and eastern sides of the Southern Appalachians. The Alabama River watershed drains the southern tip of these mountains, and the Chattahoochee (Appalachicola) watershed drains the southeastern edge and flows into the Gulf of Mexico. Over just a slight divide, the Savannah River watershed drains the rest of the Blue Ridge Mountains, along with other watersheds to the north, into the Atlantic. All of the brook trout in these rivers are of the same strain.

The continuing discovery of a much larger horde of wild brook trout in isolated, headwater streams at the southern end of the Appalachians means that endangered species status is no longer justified, but it also means that there's an increased stock for the future expansion of wild fish. Trout Unlimited (TU) has played an important role in the restoration of brook trout to as many streams as possible, both inside Great Smoky Mountains National Park, where hopes are that angling will eventually resume, and outside of it. The Appalachian Chapter (ACTU) applied for and received a financial grant from the FishAmerica Foundation to build a facility designed for rearing wild Southern Appalachian Strain brook trout near the Tennessee Wildlife Resources Agency's (TWRA) Tellico Hatchery.

It was completed in 1991 with a large volunteer force of TU members, both skilled and unskilled. Restoration of native brook trout is high on the agenda of the TWRA's trout-management objectives and forms a major part of the ACTU's conservation efforts. "The ultimate goal of the brook trout project," said Rick Bevans, a TWRA biologist, "is the reestablishment and stabilization of native brook trout populations."

In October 1991, the TWRA collected 45 wild northern-strain brook trout in the Meadow Branch, a tributary of the Tellico River watershed. Just under 5,000 eggs were taken from them. Most died because of the difficulty of raising wild trout in hatcheries; only 700 were reared. These were stocked into the Meadow Branch in March 1992. An October survey that year showed that 80 percent survived. In 1993 and 1994, respectively, 778 and 2,040 northern-strain brook trout were reared and stocked into the Meadow Branch, but the TWRA has since stopped rearing and stocking to evaluate the population over the next few years.

In 1993, the TRWA began a second renovation project, at Sycamore Creek, using southern-strain brook trout obtained from Smoky Mountains National Park. Sycamore Creek was historically a brook trout creek, but since the 1950s, rainbow trout had displaced brook trout. A barrier was constructed to restrict rainbows to the lower parts of the creek. In 1993, about 800 wild southern-strain brook trout were released into Sycamore Creek, and another 1,500 in 1995. With the modification of the existing hatchery dam near the mouth of Sycamore Creek and the removal of rainbow trout from about 5 miles of stream, the TRWA began one of the most ambitious renovation projects in Tennessee's history.

10   SALTERS AND COASTERS

The first Europeans to recognize brook trout that live part of their lives in a marine environment were French fur traders who, in 1596, set up an annual seasonal camp where the Saguenay River flows into the northern side of the St. Lawrence River—actually the Gulf of St. Lawrence. They chose this spot because it had long been a trading location for various Indian tribes in the area. In 1599, the French made it a permanent post when Jesuit and Récolett missionaries built a chapel there, a base from which to convert aborigines to their religion and for France's westward expansion into the continent's interior. It was named Tadoussac, after the Indians who inhabited the immediate area. It became the first permanent French settlement in North America.

At that time, sea-run brook trout, or salters as they became known along the New York and New England coasts, moved in large shoals in late summer along the shore on their way up the Saguenay to spawn in the Ste-Marguerite and other freshwater tributaries of the larger river. In late spring, these fish migrated back down the rivers and into the gulf to feed throughout the summer. The French recognized them as trout and similar to the seagoing brown trout of Europe, but they weren't bothered by nomenclature and simply called them *truite de mer*, or "trout of the sea." Later observers noted the differences in appearance and thought them a species separate from brook trout, and a rash of local and scientific names evolved. Today they're still called sea trout or, if one wants to be more specific when traveling in Québec, *l'omble de mer*.

The colonists who landed at Plymouth Rock named brook trout based on where they were found, accepting that they were all the same fish. Those brook trout in ponds were called pond trout, those in brooks brook trout, and those in Plymouth Bay or Cape Cod Bay sea trout.

DISTRIBUTION

When the first Europeans arrived in North America, sea-run brook trout could be found in almost every brook, creek, stream, or river to which they could return to spawn after a few months in salt water. The southernmost streams where brook trout exhibited these anadromous characteristics were in mid–New Jersey, of which the best known was the Manasquan River (Goodwin). From here northward, the sea-run brook trout's range included tributaries on both sides of the Hudson River as far north as the Mohawk River, all of the streams on both the South and North Shores of Long Island, the length of Connecticut, Rhode Island, and Massachusetts, and the streams on Block and Nantucket Islands and Martha's Vineyard. Streams on both sides of Cape Cod became famous for their salters, and the sea-run fish entered all of the streams along the coasts of New Hampshire and Maine.

Streams in all of the Canadian Maritime provinces were populated with sea-run brook trout, and at the mouth of the Gulf of St. Lawrence they were present on Prince Edward Island, Newfoundland, and Anticosti Island. Their range extended up the St. Lawrence River and into all of its tributaries on both shores to Québec City and probably as far as Montreal. They inhabited all of the streams along Labrador's Atlantic coast north as far as Hebron. They were unable to colonize streams beyond here, on the very northern part of the Labrador-Ungava peninsula, but reappeared as permanent populations in streams on the eastern side of Ungava Bay from the George River south, then west and north along the periphery of Ungava Bay to the Leaf River on the western side.

From the Leaf River north around the northern end of the Ungava Peninsula, brook trout encountered the same watershed colonization barriers as they did on the northern end of Labrador-Ungava. In Hudson Bay, their range began south of the Povungnituk River and included all of the rivers flowing into the the eastern side of the bay, including the offshore Belcher Islands, southward to James Bay. They inhabited all of the rivers entering the eastern side of James Bay but had only token populations in rivers along the bay's western side. This same light density of population held true in all rivers entering the western side of Hudson Bay in Ontario and Manitoba. Colonization is governed by the physical characteristics of the lower part of these rivers, which differ from those in Québec. The northern limit of their coastal colonization was the Seal River, though there may be sporadic populations utilizing the Caribou River, which enters Hudson Bay just 20 miles north of the Seal.

The northern limit of brook trout populations on the western side of Hudson Bay coincided closely with the location of the Povungnituk River on the western side and the Leaf

Figure 10.1   Some claim sea-run brook trout don't grow as large as non-migratory brook trout. Here is a 9-pound male taken by Michel LeBlanc on the first pool above tidewater on the Tunalic River in Northwest Ungava. The color change, which takes 10–14 days, is not yet complete. (Courtesy Jerry Gibbs.)

River on the western side of Ungava Bay, or the 60th parallel. The George River is located at approximately 58°45′ north latitude and the Hebron about 58°15′ north latitude.

Today, the distribution of sea-run brook trout has changed little. However, the region of the Atlantic Coast, between mid–New Jersey and mid–Maine has lost most of its salter fishes because of either dam construction or elevated stream temperatures. The only exclusions are a few streams on Cape Cod and Long Island where this hasn't occurred. What has changed in the Canadian Maritime provinces is the quantity of fish: It has been reduced by overfishing, introduction of exotic species, and regulations that favor Atlantic salmon over brook trout.

WHAT IS A SEA TROUT?

There was a great deal of confusion among anglers, writers, and observers of the early 1800s about whether sea trout were a form of brook trout, a subspecies, or even an altogether different species. Some tried to identify it as the North American variation of the European brown trout, which readily goes to sea. Ironically, this confusion stemmed from the abundance of sea trout in Canadian waters, in the St. Lawrence River and its associated gulf near Tadoussac.

Always a controversial figure, and not always an accurate or objective observer, was the preeminent outdoor writer of that day, Henry William Herbert, who wrote under the name Frank Forester from his nest at The Cedars, New Jersey. A chauvinistic and egocentric English émigré, Forester believed everything English was superior to anything American. He believed the trout that went to sea in waters along Long Island and Cape Cod were different fish from brook trout and took it upon himself to solve the question of the sea trout's proper classification.

> This beautiful fish [wrote Forester in 1847 in *Fish and Fishing*], which is the Salmon Trout of the Thames, the Sea Trout of Scotland, and the White Trout of Wales, Devonshire, and Ireland, is found nowhere on the continent of America except on the eastern side of the Province of New Brunswick and in the Gulf of St. Lawrence. It must on no account be confounded, as it has been by Dr. Smith in his "Fishes of Massachusetts," with the Brook Trout, Salmo Fontinalis, when they run down and remain permanently in salt-water, as they do, more or less, along the whole south side of Long Island, but especially at Fireplace [Mills], at Waquoit bay, on Cape Cod, and probably at many other points along the eastern coast; for the fish are totally distinct.
>
> Without farther comment I proceed to lay his observations before my readers, promising only, that while they fully prove the identity of the New Brunswick White Trout with the Salmon Trout of Yarrel's *Salmo trutta,* and distinguish it from the Brook Trout, whether English or American, *Salmo Fario,* or *Salmo Fontinalis,* they show remarkable differences in habit from the same fish in the British Islands.

Forester called upon a Mr. Perley, the emigration officer in Saint John, New Brunswick, for his opinion of sea trout:

> "You will perceive," says Mr. Perley, "that the White Trout [sea trout] of the Gulf of St. Lawrence, is precisely similar to the *Salmo Trutta* of Yarrel. In June, when in the finest condition, they are somewhat deeper, the shoulder is then exceedingly thick; the head, especially in the female, is very small. I never heard of any weighing more than seven ponds. I have never seen a White

Trout on this side of the province, or anywhere except within the gulf [St. Lawrence]. Many of the common Trout, *Salmo Fontinalis* also visit the mixed water of the estuaries, and very likely go out to sea. They then acquire a peculiar silvery brilliancy, and their condition becomes greatly improved; but they cannot be mistaken, even then, for the White Trout. They are a longer fish—their heads are larger—the color of the spots is more brilliant, and there are more of them; and the tri-colored fins leave no room for doubt, as the fins of the White Trout are very pale, and bluish white. When first lifted from sea, the backs of the White Trout are a bluish green, just the color of the wave; and the under part of the fish sparkles like molten silver."

In a report of the fly-fishing of the Province, which Mr. Perley was good enough to enclose, I find also the following pertinent remarks on this fish:

"It is to be understood," he [Perley] says, "that the whole Gulf of St. Lawrence abounds with White Trout [sea-run brook trout], from one to seven pounds in weight. They proceed up rivers as far as the head of the tide, but they never ascend into the purely fresh water. In saltwater they are caught only with the Prince Edward's Island fly."

This clear, able and sportsmanlike account [wrote Forester] of this fine fish perfectly establishes the fact of its existence as a distinct species, intermediate between the true Salmon, *Salmo Salar,* on the one hand, and the Brook Trout, *Salmo Fontinalis,* on the other. And it must on no account be confounded with the non-migratory Lake Trouts, and which are sometimes erroneously and absurdly called Salmon Trout. They never quit purely fresh-water.

The fish described as the *Salmo Trutta* in the [Brown's] *American-Angler's Guide* [1845] and in Smith's "Fishes of Massachusetts," is as I have already observed, nothing-resembling it, but the very Brook Trout described above, with the tri-colored fin, improved by a visit to salt-water.

I may here observe, *en-passant,* that my distinguished friend, Mr. Agassiz, was not aware, a few months since, of the existence of this fish as an American species.

Actually, Dr. Jerome V. C. Smith's and Mr. Perley's descriptions are quite similar. Dr. Smith, a physician who also practiced ichthyology, as did Dr. Samuel Mitchill of New York, accurately called the sea trout nothing more than a brook trout gone to sea and equated its habits with those of brown trout in Europe. Unfortunately, he inaccurately considered the Arctic charr of the Old Country the same species as the brown trout, and this gave Frank Forester a legitimate complaint, although not in the description of the fish nor of its actions in going to sea.

Aside from the question of classifying the fish, Smith is quite remarkable for his descriptions of sea-run brook trout in Massachusetts. He initially set about to catalog all of the fish of that state in his 1833 publication. But like many New Englanders, Smith still thought of Maine, which entered the Union in 1820, as part of the Bay Colony, and as such extended his description of fishes beyond Massachusetts to include Vermont, which had been a part of New York, and New Hampshire, as well as Maine.

Smith felt a special affinity for brook trout because it was his favorite fish as well as the dominant sporting fish in Massachusetts, especially in its larger and more numerous sea-run form. Because of this interest, Smith was a bit miffed at Mitchill, who in 1815 wrote his *Fishes of New York*. As the first to describe brook trout in scientific literature, the New York physician could add his own name to the latinized binominal scientific names. Smith compensated for being second by devoting almost a quarter of his book to brook trout and trout angling. And because sea-run trout were so popular, they received most of this space.

Smith's descriptions of sea-run brook trout fishing in the United States are invaluable in giving one a sense of the tremendous scope of this early fishery. The only other substantial sea-trout fishery in the U.S. was on Long Island, and its rural nature attracted writers from the metropolis to the west. The fish were mentioned by Smith, Forester, Roosevelt, Brown, Prime, Scott, and Hallock. The sea-run trout fishery here was quite extensive (Daniel Webster's big brook trout was a salter) and was at first fished more frequently than upstream brook trout populations.

Smith traveled and fished widely throughout his state and was impressed by the number of sea-run brook trout he found one November on Martha's Vineyard:

> In no place [he wrote of brook trout] have we seen them in such abundance as in Duke's county, upon Martha's Vineyard. It was here November last [1832], and of course in their spawning time, while returning home from a ramble among the heaths and hills of Chilmark and Tisbury, that crossing the principal brook of the island, our attraction [was] towards the agitated state of the waters, as its "being alive with fish."
>
> Proceeding with the order in which we arranged the three principal varieties of trout peculiar to this state and its vicinity we come now to the last, and by far the most esteemed, viz:—the *seatrout*. They are found, as may be inferred from the name, in salt and brackish waters of tide rivers, creeks and inland bays, in various parts of this and the adjoining states. But with the exception of "Fire-Place," on Long Island, we are not aware of their being known in the same plenty and perfection as in Waquoit Bay, upon Cape Cod; a well known resort.
>
> Waquoit Bay is a large expanse of shallow water upon the southern shore of Cape Cod. A number of small streams are discharged into it, which render its waters slightly brackish, and it has but one narrow outlet to the sea. There is another neighboring bay, called Popponesset upon the same shore, (scarcely less famous for the sea-trout than Waquoit,) into which the celebrated Marshpee [Mashpee is the correct spelling] river flows, perhaps the greatest resort of anglers in New England for the sea-trout, after they have begun to ascend the fresh water streams.

When taken from the salt water early in the spring, they are in high perfection, and nothing can exceed their piscatory symmetry. The general appearance of the skin is of a silvery brightness; the back being of a greenish and mackerel complexion; the spots of a vermilion color, mixed with others of a faint yellow, and sometimes slightly tinged with purple, extend the whole length on each side of the lateral line; the fins are light in color, firm in texture, and together with the tail are rather shorter and more rounded than in the common trout; the head and the mouth are very small, and the latter never black inside like the common or fresh water trout.

A fish of a pound weight, measures about eleven inches in length. Their average size is considerably larger than fresh water or brook trout—having been taken of nearly five pounds weight. Such instances, however, are rare. Three pounds being considered a very large fish. They are governed, by the operation of tide upon the bait, collecting in two well known rendezvous or sand spits which project into the bay, forming a favorable current.

To give some idea of the numbers which are occasionally taken, two persons took eighty sea-trout which, weighed fifty-nine pounds. This was on the flood tide, and the bait equally shrimp and minnow. There is another sandy point named Poponessett which forms one side of the channel called Sampson's Narrows, famous for the size and quality of the trout. A basket of twenty pounds capacity is often filled in this spot, at one tide.

The only trout which was taken at this outlet, confirms the fact that the nearer they are taken to the sea, and the salter the water, the more they possess the greenish color peculiar [to] the back of the mackerel, as well as a more dazzling and silvery brightness, compared to those living in waters at all brackish. For some idea of size we caught, a few years since, on the 24th of March [prior to 1833], three trout, which weighed eight and a quarter pounds—two of them approaching very nearly to three pounds each, besides many others at the same time, over a pound.

We now mention a well known and by far most frequented spot in all these waters, called Poket Point, in Waquoit Bay. It is a very remarkable place, and for many years, has been no less the resort of the angler, than the great abundance of fine sea-trout. In mid April 1829, two persons fishing from Poket Point, in five day's fishing, took 296 sea trout that weighed 191 pounds. The highest day was 82 trout and the largest was 2 pounds 11 ounces. It was on the 18th of May 1829, that two persons took 70 fine sea-trout, weighing 38 pounds. The largest weighed about a pound and a half, but none over. They were nearly all taken with the fly, and most of them with three or four varieties, the red and yellow palmer or hackle, the march brown, and grouse hackle.

The other stream which we proposed to notice, as being remarkable for its sea-trout, is called Marshpee Brook or River, and takes its rise from the

Marshpee or Wakeby pond, flowing through the plantation of the Marshpee tribe of Indians, adjoining the town of Falmouth and Sandwich, it empties into the Popponesset Bay. Like many other streams, it is called both a river and a brook, though it is well understood that when the former term is used, it applies to its lower waters, and vice versa.

We have little to say of its river part, except that being much deeper than the one last described, the trout are taken sometimes through the ice, in the winter and early spring in certain deep parts, known by the familiar names of the Crow's Nest, Amos's Landing, &c. From the peculiar nature of the stream, the fishing of Marshpee Brook may be considered as perfectly sui generis. It may be said, that the use of the fly in this stream, is out of the question [because of the dense growth of overhanging bushes along the stream].

There are a small species of trout in this stream which are called natives, and do not visit the lower parts of the river, they are easily distinguished from the sea-trout by their yellow sides, scarlet bellies and red fins. The latter [sea trout], however not only retain their silvery appearance, but grow brown on the back and black on the head, and in the mouth, according to the length of time they have been in the fresh water.

It is said that they come up with herrings, but the number taken by herring fishers in their hand nets is so few, as to establish the fact, not only that they run in the night, but of their continuing to ascend from the bay or mouth of the river, long after the herrings have passed into the Wakeby pond. Their bright, fresh-run appearance as well as their large size and numbers, may be mentioned in further confirmation of their running all summer long. For though the fishing may be tolerable by the middle of May, the greatest show of fish has always been taken in the middle of summer. At this time herring bait of course is not to be had, minnows, if possible, or worms, are then substituted.

The largest sea-trout in the State, have been taken in this brook; we believe nearly up to five pounds; two and three being by no means uncommon. The average size is much smaller than is generally admitted.

This [Mashpee Brook] is one brook that does not suffer a mill, that which is upon it, but now in decay, being so near the outlet from the pond as to be no impediment to the course of fish towards their cold-spring haunts, neither do they incline to penetrate into the still and warmer waters of the pond; but prefer invariably to spawn in the gravelly shallows of running water, for which it is so remarkably adapted. It has been renowned for the purity and coolness of the waters, the abundance of shelters, the size and plenty of fish, and indeed for every quality that constitutes a most perfect trout-stream, with the single exception of being, from its wild state, unfavorable to the use of the artificial fly.

In spring, before the sea-trout have begun to run, they will be to the narrows of Popponesset Bay, to Waquoit bay, to the lower waters of Marshpee river, and to Monument River, &c.; but if later in the spring, and in the early summer, though Marshpee brook will be the great dependence, the various other places where the sea-trout are found are almost innumerable; for there is not a rivulet that flows into the creeks of the salt marsh. Among the most celebrated, are two tidal rivers in Sandwich, Scusset and Scorton. The former has now suffered from the usual effects of a mill. As to the smaller streams, that which crosses the Barnstable road and enters the salt meadows, about four miles from Sandwich, near the Quaker Meeting-house, has, from our own experience, sometimes yielded great results; in fact, it may be said that the whole country is full of trout, and not confined, though peculiar to this town, for they abound in the neighboring towns of Falmouth, Barnstable, Wareham, Plymouth, and Marshfield.

There were really two major questions being posed at once in the mid-1800s: Was the sea-run brook trout a different species from the sea-run brown trout? If so, was it a separate species from the nonanadromous-acting brook trout that elected to stay all its life in fresh water, even when salt water was readily at hand—or fin?

The first serious attempt to distinguish between sea-run brown and sea-run brook trout was undertaken by Thaddeus Norris in his compendium *The American Angler's Book,* written in 1864 as a retort to Forester's statements in 1847. However, Norris did little to answer the question of whether sea-run brook trout are a separate species from other brook trout. In fact, he bolstered the misconception that they're two species.

> With a view of correcting an error which prevails in regard to this fish, I have adopted the specific name *Salmo canadensis.* It is improperly referred by Mr. Perley to *Salmo trutta,* an European species found in the rivers of Scotland and Ireland, and known there as the *Salmon Trout, Sea Trout,* or *White Trout.* As no scientific description of the Canadian Trout has yet been published, I have deemed it a matter of sufficient importance to give an account of its specific characteristics, comparing it with the European fish and the Brook Trout of America.
>
> Mr. Perley, in his letter to Frank Forester, gives none of the specific characteristics of this fish; even his account of its habits and general appearance would not warrant his referring it to the same species as the Sea Trout of Scotland, for he implies when comparing it with the Brook Trout *(S. fontinalis),* that the Canadian Trout has red spots, which *Salmo trutta* never has, but on the contrary dark irregular markings, somewhat resembling the letter X, which are the shape of those found also on the Salmon. Sir Humphrey Davy and Yarrell make no mention of red spots on Sea Trout of Scotland, and Irish and Scotch anglers, in whose company I have taken the Canadian fish, say, that the Sea Trout they caught in the "old country" is entirely a different fish, and has no red spots.

Mr. Perley says of the habits of the Canadian, or Sea Trout, as he calls them: "They proceed up the rivers as far as the head of tide in each, but never ascend into purely fresh water." Here he was no less at fault than in confounding it with the European fish, for it is an established fact, that all the Salmon Family seek fresh water for spawning, and of necessity spawning grounds with Brook Trout, or, as the Canadians call them, River Trout. This intimate association is one reason why they are so often confounded with the latter by careless observers; for a residence in fresh water gives them much the appearance of light-colored Brook Trout, and many persons can only distinguish them by laying an individual of each species side by side.

Norris, too, missed the significance of his last statement.

It was thus by imperfect observation, and too readily crediting stories of persons who were ignorant of the habits of this fish, that Mr. Perley not only referred it to an entirely different species and misled persons as to its habits, but has communicated the same errors to Frank Forester who entails them upon his readers.

Here, Norris himself made erroneous comparisons between the two populations of brook trout. "A Canadian Trout," he said, "fresh from the sea, compared with a Brook or River Trout, has larger and more distinct scales; the form is not so much compressed; the markings on the back are lighter, and not so vermiculated, but resemble more the broken segments of a circle; it has fewer red spots, which are also less distinct. It is more slender until it reaches two pounds, a fish of seventeen inches (including the caudal) after it has been some time in fresh water, weighing only a pound and three-quarters, while a Brook Trout of the same length, in good condition, would weigh three-quarters of a pound more."

Norris again missed the significance of his own statement: "If the number of rays in the fins indicate specific difference, this fish is more nearly allied to the Brook Trout than to the Sea Trout of Europe. There being only a difference of one ray in the pectorals, which may be accidental."

Ergo! They're the same fish.

Some years after Norris had written his book, and after a more familiar acquaintance with *Salvelinus canadensis,* he underwent an entire change of view and wrote that "*Salvelinus canadensis* is the *Salvelinus fontinalis* gone to sea."

His change was probably influenced by Genio C. Scott, who in 1875 published *Fishing in American Waters.* Scott had no illusions of being a scientific writer, just a good observer, and he made the following assertions:

This fish inhabits for nearly half the year the tidal waters of the streams in Canada, Nova Scotia, and Newfoundland. It is also taken in estuaries of rivers in Maine, Massachusetts, and Long Island. Being aware of the high authorities which assert this to be a distinct family of the Salmo genus, I must beg humbly to dissent; and from the following description I invite anglers to decide for themselves whether the sea trout is not the Salmo fontinalis or brook trout common to streams of the northern part of North America.

Sea trout are similar to brook trout in all facial peculiarities. It is shaped like brook trout; the vermiculate marks on the back and above the lateral line are like those of brook trout; its vermilion, white, and amber dots are like the brook trout's; its fins are like those of the brook trout, even to the square or slightly lunate end of tail. It has the amber back and silver sides of such brook trout as have access to estuary food. Owing to this food [wrong], it becomes whiter and brighter than those trout which inhabit swampy waters impregnated and discolored by decayed vegetable matter.

All the authorities agree that sea trout spawn at the heads of fresh-water streams, ascending from the estuary in August, and not returning until the following winter and spring [not so, either]. All brook trout visit the heads of streams in autumn, and return to the lower waters at the close of winter. Brook trout of mountainous streams are brighter than the black-mouthed trout of hemlock and tamarack swamps. The silver trout is indeed beautiful, with its sides glistening brightly with a satin sheen which sparkles with glowing lustre in the light. The only drawback that I experienced in taking silver trout arose from too many [small ones] offering for my flies at a time when I had seen larger ones coveting my flies.

By 1883, when A. R. Macdonough wrote his chapter, "Sea-Trout Fishing," in Alfred M. Mayer's voluminous hunting and fishing work *Sport With Rod & Gun*, the tide was already turning against those who considered sea trout a separate species. Macdonough, an experienced sea trout angler, had spent a month or so toward the end of four summers fishing for them in the same unidentified river. Located on the North Shore, it flowed into the St. Lawrence River just east of du Sault aux Cochons. He leased the river and wanted no competition, so he never identified it. On a later trip he was accompanied by Fitz James Fitch, who wrote his version of the same trip as a chapter on sea trout in the Orvis and Cheney book, *Fishing with the Fly* (1883). Judging from his description, this river was probably aux Outardes.

"What is a sea-trout?" Macdonough asked.

A problem, to begin with, though quite a minor one, since naturalists have for some time kept specimens waiting to decide whether he is a cadet of the noble salmon race or merely the chief of the familiar brook-trout tribe. Science inclines to the former view, upon certain slight but sure indications noted in fin-spines and gill-covers.

The witness of guides and gaffers leads the same way, and the Indians all say

BROOK TROUT AND THEIR UNIQUENESS

that the habits of the sea-trout and the brook-trout differ, and that the contrast between the markings of the two kinds of fish, taken from the same pool, forbids the idea of their identity. The testimony of many accomplished sportsmen affirms it.

The gradual change of color in the same fish, as he ascends the stream, from plain silvery gray to deepest dotted bronze; his haunts at the lower end of pools, behind rocks, and among roots; his action in taking the fly with an upward leap, not downward from above,—all these resemblances support the theory that the sea-trout is only an anadromous brook-trout. Indeed, the difference in color between the brook-trout and the sea-trout ranges within a far narrower scale than that between parr, grilse, and salmon.

SCIENCE FINALLY SOLVES THE RIDDLE

Not until the turn of the century did everyone finally agree that sea trout differ from other brook trout only in having a penchant for spending part of the year in salt water, where food is more readily found. The debate ended there, although fisheries biologists, whose scientific methods by now had become more sophisticated, still wondered why one part of a population of brook trout would head seaward and another, in the same environment, would not. Was it a question of genetic differences? An opportunistic migration for food? Or was it a natural part of maturation as trout grew and became more piscivorous?

The first challenge was to develop an understanding of the complete life cycle of sea trout. This was accepted by Canadian federal biologist H. C. White, who between 1928 and 1942 published four scientific papers (White) on the sea life of brook trout. Together, these became the definitive work on sea trout. His first laboratory was the streams and estuaries surrounding Prince Edward Island. Later, he shifted to numerous streams on Nova Scotia. Sometimes being first is enough to gain long-lasting fame. Not only was White first, but his work was thorough and enlightening, and subsequent investigators used his results as a place to start their own research into sea-run brook trout.

The most obvious distinction between pond or stream brook trout and sea trout is outward coloration, which has already been described extensively. However, early observers never knew the cause of sea trout coloration. The dorsal surface of a sea-run trout's body is a dark greenish blue color, sometimes more bluish than green; this gave rise to its early name, the white trout. This color is visible through a thin coat of silvery guanine crystals, a purine ($C_5H_5N_{50}$) that's a constituent of both ribonucleic (RNA) and dioxyribonucleic acid (DNA). The sides are very silvery, or have a pearl-like iridescence. Occasionally, a few pink spots are discernible through the guanine. Dorsal vermiculations still exist but are shrouded under the dark backing; they may show through as much lighter and often broken patterns.

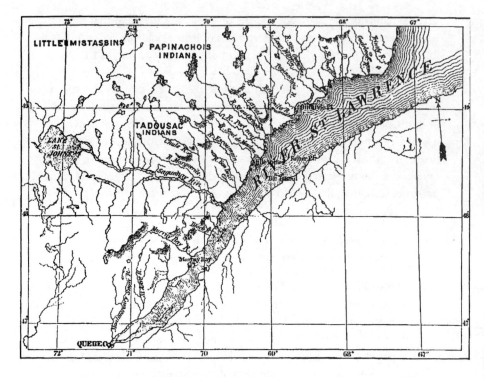

Figure 10.2   1883 Map of major sea-trout waters in the St. Lawrence River.

There are also differences in body proportions. While sea trout are more slender than other brook trout, their bodies are relatively thicker throughout. There are three causes of this. In some populations, sea trout are often three years old or more, and these changes in body shape are common to all maturing brook trout. To the casual observer they seem to stand out because streams with access to salt water hold few—if any—older, nonmigrant trout. The second cause of a change in body shape is a response to the change from a riverine to a less demanding lacustrine or, in this case, marine environment. Brook trout that are permanent residents of a fast-flowing stream have a constant need to maintain position in moving water, and are always leaner and often smaller than lacustrine fish. The third cause is rapid growth supported by an abundant supply of high-protein foods, including finfish, crustaceans, and marine worms.

Once brook trout enter a marine environment, they assume one of two habits, depending upon the physical characteristics of the environment. Where a stream enters salt water directly, without the aegis of a bay or estuary, fish will school according to year-class and will move from the river to feed along the coast. Their range is greater than that of fish whose natal streams have extensive estuaries. The extent of their movement varies more with the general physical characteristics of the ocean and immediate land.

Other populations of sea-run brook trout stay in the immediate area of a river or

Figure 10.3 A typical sea-run brook trout, male, taken in September on the Ste-Marguerite River, Québec, which flows into the Saguenay River, and then almost immediately into the St. Lawrence River.

stream's mouth, especially if the river has a lengthy tidal runout or ends in a partially enclosed bay, and don't always enter the ocean proper. Instead, they spend the main part of the year moving in and out with the tide. At times they may even ascend the parent stream when summer heat elevates the estuary's temperatures. These fish are referred to by some anglers in the Maritime provinces as "slob" trout.

Most brook trout populations within the proximity of salt water, from Long Island (N.Y.) north to Labrador, spawn from October through November. The urge to migrate back to fresh water to spawn begins almost universally, in all of these populations, near the end of August. White discovered an interesting phenomenon: Females on their first spawning run don't necessarily spawn that fall. They may remain in the river or accompany the spring migratory run to salt water and spawn on the subsequent fall migration. This is also a characteristic of another closely related salmonid, the Arctic charr.

Once in fresh water, a sea-run brook trout will within 10 to 14 days assume the same coloration as nonmigratory brook trout in the same stream. Once in the stream, the fish have at least two months to develop their full nuptial livery. During this period, they develop secondary sexual characteristics, which are more noticeable in males than females—kypes or hooked jaws, for example. There's also a separation of spawning stocks. Sea-run fish often spawn closer to tidewater, but also move upstream and build redds where nonmigratory brook trout spawn as well. White said he never witnessed sea-run and nonmigratory males or females spawning with each other.

WHEN DO SEA-RUN TROUT RUN TO SEA?

White was also the first biologist to equate the life stages of sea-run brook trout to those of Atlantic salmon. He was able to grasp an idea of the brook trout's overall adaptation to a saline life because of the large sea trout population he was able to observe during his investigations and the unique geography of his study site. In areas north or south of the Canadian Maritimes, he might not have been able to view the full range of the sea-run trout's relationship to both freshwater and saline enviornments. Because he was able to view a great number of sea trout, though, he could more completely understand their full life cycle in both environments. He posed a rather profound question in a 1940 paper that remains unanswered:

> In various species of salmonids which have access to the sea, some individuals descend to the sea where they spend a part of their life, whereas others complete their entire life cycle in fresh water. Whether fishes which behave so differently constitute separate populations with genetic differences, or whether the differences in behavior are mere manifestations of a wider range of behavior within a single species, has been a subject of speculation between ichthyologists.

Today's researchers would probably agree with his latter hypothesis: that it's inherent in the existing genetic makeup of all brook trout to live in a wider range of environments than just the typical, provincial freshwater scene.

The first seaward migration of the year begins in late April or early May and may continue until mid-June, depending upon the size of the population, the distance to salt water, and the fluctuation of temperatures. If temperatures at this time should suddenly fall, some fish may reverse their direction and momentarily work upstream. Brook trout heading seaward are composed of three groups, according to White: smolts, kelts, and nonmature large fish. All three retain the typical freshwater coloration throughout the winter, but as spring and their downstream trek approach, they begin a gradual color change, even while in fresh water.

Prior to White, the smolt state, which is intrinsic to salmon, was unrecognized in brook trout. These smaller spring-run fish closely resemble Atlantic salmon smolts, both in shape and in color. Of the brook trout smolt population, the greater percentage are two-year fish; a smaller percentage are three-year fish that didn't migrate in their second year.

As with salmon, brook trout kelts are mature fish that spawned the previous fall but wintered over in fresh water rather than making the fall return after spawning. Some of these are believed to be late spawners that were forced to stay upstream because of either low water, low temperatures, or ice entrapment. In salmon terminology, they're often referred to as black salmon or slinks, and some show few or no signs of guanine buildup. These fish are also referred to as mended-kelts, and are composed of brook trout that migrated to sea as two- and three-year-old smolts.

A third contingent of the downstream spring migration is made up of large brook trout that are still sexually immature and, of course, didn't spawn the previous fall. In some streams they comprise a rather large segment of a population that later ascends rivers in the summer. They're not distinguishable from kelts by either outward appearance or the condition of their scales. These nonmature large fish pose unanswered questions.

All three groups at first use the upper estuary as a staging area, as if developing school recognition, then drop to the area closer to the sea. By the time the seaward migration from fresh water stops, all of the trout in the estuary have abandoned it for open water. However, sea-run brook trout from Maine northward, and across and among the Maritime islands, don't move far. Their seaward range is confined to the waters of the outer estuary, its bays, and along the adjoining coasts for only a few miles. Sea trout in the Gulf of St. Lawrence, however, seem to move away from their natal streams in well-defined schools and disappear into the gulf, unseen except when taken in nets. This might be related to the lack of extensive estuarine environments in this region. Most streams, especially along the North Shore, empty directly into the gulf or ocean.

It seems that almost as soon as the last migrant has gone to sea, the first returning fish begin to appear. Some have been recorded as entering fresh water as early as the middle of June; however, most fish, where warming river waters are not a problem, return to maritime streams during the last two weeks of July. In the St. Lawrence River, this return may be two to four weeks later. Brook trout remain at sea from 40 to 85 days; most, however, are at sea for about 60. Those that migrated first to salt water also remain there longest. Life at sea must be hazardous for male brook trout, Smith discovered, because most of the returning population in the fall migration are females.

Brook trout are not as faithful in returning to the exact site where they hatched, matured, and developed site recognition as are salmon. They do return to the same river, but not necessarily to the exact tributary or natal location.

In the early 1950s another Canadian biologist, D. G. Wilder (Wilder) did an extensive investigation of sea-run versus sedentary brook trout populations to determine if a hereditary difference in the two populations caused the sea-run fish to migrate. He concluded that there was no heredity difference, which further supported White's idea that the ability to migrate, in this case to sea, exists in all brook trout.

GROWTH

If brook trout stayed at sea as long as Atlantic salmon, the current world record of 14½ pounds would easily be shattered. Actually, brook trout do remarkably well for spending just two months in their saline "stockyards." After all, it was a unique and abundant supply of sculpin and other piscivorous foods that made Dr. John William Cook's Nipigon trout grow so large. And it was the readily available shoals of blueback trout in the Rangeley lakes that allowed 10- and 12-pound brook trout to develop Maine's early reputation for having big-trout water. And it was the "slob" characteristic of Daniel Webster's 14½-pounder that created the piscean devil for America's most famous lawyer-legislator.

Because brook trout that go to sea have the opportunity to feed unabated on large and abundant foods, even for a time as brief as two months, they can in the same life span grow larger than brook trout that remain entirely in fresh water. There are reports of sea trout of 7 pounds from Alexander Bay (Newfoundland), and 8 and 9 pounds from Deer Harbor, Newfoundland. Record sea trout, according to one report, were landed in 1908 when fish of 10¾, 12, and 15 pounds were taken from the Fox River and Romaines Brook. The largest, from Romaines Brook, was 31 inches long and 8 inches deep. From their size, it was believed that these fish might have been sea-run brown trout. However, there's no record of brown trout in this area at that time. The locale had a history of producing large sea-run brook trout. Newfoundland's Department of Fisheries' records show that in 1941, Chief Protection Officer H. V. E. Smith took from the Serpentine River 23 sea trout, none of less than 2 pounds and one of slightly over 7 pounds.

The time brook trout spend in fresh and salt water is variable, as is the age of their first seaward migration. These two factors probably determine the ultimate size of sea trout in any population.

SALTERS

The only extensive research in the United States on sea-run brook trout was done by a Massachusetts Division of Fisheries biologist, who completed a six-year investigation of the Mashpee River and four other small brooks in Barnstable County on Cape Cod. An early study in 1925 by Henry B. Bigelow had contended that sea trout, or salters as they were called on the Cape, migrated upstream in May and June, spent the summer in the cooler, spring-fed waters of these streams, stayed there until fall, spawned, and then returned to the sea to winter.

In 1949, when the larger study was conducted by James Mullan (Mullan), the Mashpee River was believed to be the last source of these fish. Mashpee eggs were often collected by the state and used in its hatchery program because it was believed the sea-run fish, which by then had a 100-year-old reputation for robustness, fared better in interior streams than other stocks. The Mashpee was also unique in that it had been in private hands for so long, was undeveloped, and was still considered a pristine watershed. It did have a small dam on it, which had already rotted away by Dr. J. V. C. Smith's time, 1833, and there was some slight cranberry-bog development near its source pond.

Mullan and his aides dispelled one of the first myths by taking several silver salters and confining them immediately in pens in upper freshwater sections of the 4-mile stream. The salters lost their sea-run characteristics within 10 to 14 days. Mullan then reversed the project and took several normally colored brook trout from upper sections of the stream and placed them in salt water; within the same period they acquired the salter's dress. In subsequent projects he also demonstrated that hatchery-raised brook trout from another stock eventually assumed the migratory habits of sea-run trout on the Mashpee River.

Because the salter fishery had declined so drastically by 1949 in all Massachusetts streams, one project goal was to create fish with a seaward penchant. Biologists believed that if they overloaded the river with hatchery fish, some would head downstream to avoid the crowding that would occur and to search for food. Instead, researchers discovered that the trout wouldn't leave the stream for salt water until after the fish had spawned for the first time. They did go to sea, but the picture was complicated by a large upstream migration of salters in December.

The factor motivating brook trout, and probably all sea-run populations from Cape Cod southward, are not just spawning and food but also a third factor, temperature. Brook trout may migrate downstream in October and November after spawning for two reasons: a search for food and a search for more suitable ambient water temperatures. But when temperatures in the marine environment become too cool, the fish ascend the rivers and winter in springs where it can be as warm as 40 degrees.

The reverse is also true. When spring stream temperatures become warm, brook trout will migrate to the marine environment; the larger body of water remains cooler into spring than do inland waters. Once the sea becomes too warm, as in June and July, the fish migrate back into the relatively cooler stream waters. Salters also migrate upstream in early spring, not so much because of water temperatures but for food; they follow other anadromous fishes on spawning migrations. Brook trout are opportunistic feeders and are very responsive to environmental temperatures.

There are no big salters produced in these waters today, as there were in Smith's time; a 15-inch brook trout is an eye opener. The overall size of sea-run trout in almost all of their ranges has been reduced. In many areas from Cape Cod southward, the majority are under 10 inches, and these have helped feed the concept that sea-run trout never grow large. They don't—today.

COASTERS

A coaster is like every other brook trout in genetic composition. It's neither a subspecies nor a separate, unique strain unto itself. In habits and appearance, coasters are like sea-run brook trout. They differ from salters in that they adopt large bodies of fresh water as their secondary habitat, specifically the Great Lakes, and treat them as sea-run brook trout treat the ocean. Unlike sea trout, coasters spend most of their lives in the lake, except when they migrate into the rivers of their birth to spawn. After the act they return to the sanctuary of the lake, leaving their progeny to the whims of nature and humanity.

Every coaster's life has a riverine period: Eggs hatch, larvae develop through the fry and fingerling stages, and then comes the descent to the lake. This whole process can take from one to three years.

Coasters are littoral fish, seldom venturing over the pelagic realms of these vast inland freshwater seas. Nor are they found in depths greater than 20 or 30 feet unless driven there by temperatures or temporarily following food. Instead, they prefer to follow the shorelines in larger schools when they're little and in smaller numbers as they age (Scott). These schools are usually made up only of fish from the same year-class. It's this affinity for a shoreside life that spawned the name *coasters*.

Coasters moved north during the postglacial period, following the retreat of the ice sheet that covered the upper portion of the Mississippi watershed and the Mississippi refugium, which developed as meltwater flooded the land. These brook trout, probably a temporary union of existing strains, began the recolonization of lower levels of the numerous tributaries that entered the Great Lakes, and in some cases the entire watersheds. Today, descendants of these same fish form the populations still cruising the shores of the Great Lakes. All of the Great Lakes had and still have populations of coasters. However, in Lakes Erie and Ontario their numbers are drastically reduced. In Lake Michigan they sustain a Wisconsin sportfishery that annually allows anglers to harvest between 5,000 and 10,000 fish.

In Lake Superior, coasters may be a bit less transient and tend to spend summers on the shoals, especially among the island groups on the lake's North Shore. There, they provide the bulk of today's big fish—brook trout of 6 and 7 pounds or more in the lower Nipigon River fishery. In spring, as soon as the ice is off Lake Superior, they're found again on the shore and shoals of Nipigon Bay. Even during summer, when most coasters seem to have disappeared, there's the occasional catch. Their prime time ashore is late August and September, when they move into the lakelike estuary of the lower river and eventually spawn at the first series of rapids. Even before the first hydroelectric dam was built at Alexander's Landing, nearby Cameron Falls was too high for brook trout to jump, so the coasters never contributed to the population of huge fish in the upper river.

Accounts of early fishing at Isle Royale, and among Ste-Ignace and the islands in the chain that forms the lower periphery of Nipigon Bay, revealed catches of tremendous numbers of brook trout, and some that were even close to 20 pounds. The Nipigon watershed was not unique in producing big brook trout. A series of rivers along the eastern edge of the North Shore, which included the Chippewa, Montreal, Batchawana, and Agwa, also produced brook trout of 7 to 10 pounds and its share of coasters. These rivers differed from the Nipigon only in the depth of their fisheries. Because of this their stocks were depleted much faster—primarily by overfishing. Even the rapids at Sault Ste-Marie, the narrow restriction (St. Marie River) with riverlike characteristics that divides Lake Superior from Lake Huron, saw the spawning of untold numbers of coaster brook trout. And they were easily caught. Today, these areas of Lake Superior, like those in Lakes Michigan and Huron, have all seen their coaster numbers drastically reduced.

While overfishing must have played a part in the decline, the greatest causes were dams on spawning rivers, municipal and industrial pollution, the thoughtless, widespread use of DDT, and the heavy use of chemicals in agriculture. There are efforts afoot today to restore the coaster fishery. A "Coaster Brook Trout Workshop" (Bent), chaired by Lee Newman from the U.S. Fish and Wildlife Service, was held in Grand Portage in 1992 and involved federal, state, and provincial interagency personnel. Their goals were to identify both the reasons for the loss and the solutions that would halt the decline. We may yet see a return to better times for coasters—and anglers.

THE ORIGINS OF
SPORTFISHING FOR TROUT

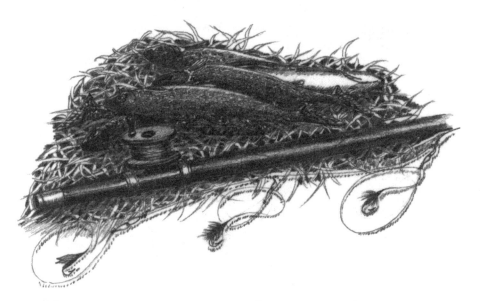

11 Manhattan: The Cradle of American Trout Fishing

Manhattan didn't always look the way it does now. It's impossible today to comprehend, especially as one dodges traffic and the crowds of hurrying people on the streets of lower Manhattan, that this world of concrete, steel, plastic, and glass was at one time a verdant place of trees, grasses, fields, sparkling streams, and ponds. Or—even more far-fetched—that brook trout fishing as an American sport had its start under these very asphalt roads and cement sidewalks.

Manhattan is a rocky island roughly 13 miles long and 2 miles wide that sits in the mouth of the Hudson River. Its basalt-and-granite base was shaped and sculpted by several south-flowing glaciers whose tracks and scars can still be seen upon the rocks' polished surfaces. Manhattan once was covered by conifer forests and inundated by swamps, ponds, springs, and numerous small brooks. The largest brook was Haarlem Creek. It started on the west side of Manhattan, near Amsterdam Avenue and 125th Street, on the northern end of what once was Morningside Park, and flowed east, between 106th and 110th streets, into the East River. Half of the creek was a tidal estuary, a favorite domain of sea-run brook trout. New Amsterdam was concentrated on the very southern tip of the island, most of it below present-day Wall Street, and its fishers favored streams on the island's southern end. Even in the 1700s, Haarlem Creek was still too far "into the country" to attract urban anglers from New York City.

On the lower end, two fair-sized streams drained the interior. One rose from a series of springs that poured forth from hillocks around today's 20th Street and Fifth Avenue. The Saponickan band living there called it Ishpetenga. It flowed southwest into the Hudson

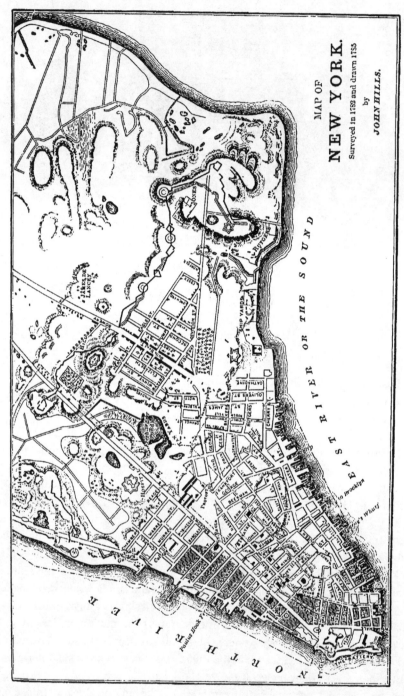

Figure 11.1   A map of New York in 1782 showing The Collect and the slow, northward expansion and encroachment of suburbia on lower Manhattan. Note the location of Fresh Pond, or The Collect. (From a collection in the Museum of the City of New York.)

near the mouth of another trout stream. This one had its origins in a deep, fair-sized pond where Worth and Centre streets now cross. It flowed northwesterly, almost in a straight line, and became the course for today's Canal Street. The pond was known as The Collect. The Dutch name for this trout pond was derived from one of its beaches, which they called Kalk Hoek—Chalk Point or Chalk Hook. It was given the name because the early Dutch settlers came here to collect the shells of freshwater mussels, which were ground and added to the mortar used to build their homes. When the English took over management of Manhattan in 1664 they assumed many of the Dutch words already in use for geographic features. Their inelegant pronunciation of Dutch turned the monosyllabic word "Kalk" (or "Chalk") into the dissyllable "Kal-leck"—hence, "Collect." The pond's name had nothing to do with collecting water in the area, as some writers have suggested, although it did have two small feeder streams. For decades, in the 1600s and 1700s, it was the source of drinking water for all of lower Manhattan's residents. The Collect and its associated streams contained brook trout as late as 1740.

Fishing for fun didn't become recognized even in England until the early 17th century. Izaak Walton's publication of *The Compleat Angler* in 1653 served to establish fishing as a sport worthy of gentlemen. He laid down sportfishing's rules with descriptions of the behavior, attitude, and manners anglers should possess. This fishing etiquette was lost on the English who emigrated to the New World. Their efforts to carve a life from the wilderness left them little time to fish for fun. However, after New Amsterdam became New York and its population of urban merchants grew in size and wealth, a small segment found enough time on their hands to pursue their own entertainment. This was happening in other colonial urban centers, as well.

In 1732 the first angling club in the United States was formed—The Schuylkill Club in Philadelphia; in 1734 New York City passed the first law to regulate recreational fishing; and in 1743 the first "book" on fishing, a 22-page pamphlet, was published in Boston.

The law passed by the Common Council of the City of New York on May 28, 1734, was unique among laws concerning fish, because it didn't deal with seasons or limits but rather with the manner in which fish could be taken. The law affected only The Collect, or Fresh Water Pond, as it was also known, and restricted fishing to "angle-rod, hook and line." The pond and its outlet stream had been a fishing ground since the first French fur traders established a temporary village on its shores in 1540, next to the bark houses of the Warpoes band. By the early 1700s, the depletion of its brook trout by both recreational and commercial fishermen had become so great that the city council felt compelled to prohibit commercial fishing to ensure future recreational fishing for the city's residents. However, The Collect (as well as Little Collect Pond, which drained into the bigger body of water) was abandoned as a source of drinking water because of pollution and filled in by 1803. To drain it, they had to deepen the outlet creek, which became known as The Canal and finally Canal Street. The fill came from nearby hills on Broadway and Chatham Square. These were first denuded, then "the land was planed down on their sides, and the earth cast into the suffering, and once thought unfath-

City of *New-York*, ſs.

A LAW

FOR

Preſerving the Fiſh in *Freſh-water Pond*.

BE IT ORDAINED by the Mayor, Recorder, Aldermen and Aſſiſtants of the City of *New-York*, convened in Common-Council, and it is hereby Ordained by the Authority of the ſame, That if any Perſon or Perſons whatſoever do, from henceforth, preſume to put, place or caſt into the Pond commonly called *Freſh-water Pond*, belonging to this Corporation, any Hoop-net, Draw-net, Purſe-net, Caſting-net, Cod-net, Bley-net, or any other Net or Nets whatſoever, and ſhall take and catch any of the Fiſh within the ſaid Pond therewith, or by any other Engine, Machine, Arts, Ways or Means whatſoever other than by Angling, with Angle-Rod, Hook and Line only: Every Perſon ſo offending againſt the Tenour of this Law, ſhall for every ſuch Offence forfeit and pay the Sum of *Twenty Shillings* of current Money of this Colony, to be recovered before the Mayor, Recorder or any one or more of the Aldermen of the ſaid City, by the Oath of one or more credible Witneſſes, and to be levyed, by Diſtreſs and Sale of the Goods and Chattles of ſuch Offender, the one Half thereof to the Informer, and the other Half to the Treaſurer of this City, for the Uſe of this Corporation, with reaſonable Coſts and Charges to be expended, for the Recovery of ſuch Forfeiture againſt the Offender or Offenders; and for want of ſufficient Diſtreſs, the Offender or Offenders to be committed into the Cuſtody of one of the Marſhals of the ſaid City, until ſuch Offender ſhall pay ſuch Forfeiture with reaſonable Charges of Proſecution, as aforeſaid: Dated at the City-Hall of the ſaid City the Twenty eighth Day of *May*, in the Seventh Year of His Majeſty's Reign, *Anno Domini* 1734.

By Order of Common-Council,

Will. Sharpas, Clerk

Figure 11.2 While The Collect was still a trip from lower Manhattan, the City of New York passed the first law in the United States restricting its fish to recreational anglers.

Figure 11.3   The Collect, the site of the first European (French) settlements on Manhattan in the 16th century, was still surrounded by farms in the early 1700s. (From *The Documentary History of the State of New York*, by E.B. O'Callaghan, M.D., 1849.)

omable, waters of the Pond, and it and its brook trout were no more forever."

Though Ishpetenga and The Collect were popular with trout fishers, they weren't the only brook trout waters on Manhattan. The drain from The Collect was also a favorite with fishers in the 1600s and 1700s. The lower portion, near the Hudson River, had a short tidal section that produced salters. Most freshwater brook trout were taken between the outlet of the pond and the spot where Stone Bridge was constructed to allow passage over the stream on Broadway. Canal Street paralleled the stream's southern side and intersected Broadway at the bridge. Anglers fished off the bridge as well as the streambanks, which were about 20 feet apart.

The name "Gramercy" is the only reminder today of "a crooked little stream that ran through Mayor Duane's farm," where the park now stands. Minetta Lane and Street are other reminders of brook trout streams on old Manhattan. "The Minetta was a famous stream for brook trout," said Felix Oldboy, who was quoted in Leslie's *History of Greater New York* in 1898 by Daniel Van Pelt. "It was a branch [actually two branches, East and West, were so called] of Bestevaer Kill [Dutch for "Grandfather's Creek"], which fell into the North [Hudson] River at the foot of Hammersley [Houston] Street. It had its source on the corner of today's 17th and 18th streets and 6th Avenue. At about 11th Street, near 5th Avenue, the Minetta's eastern branch separated from Grandfather's Creek and ran to the corner of Broadway and 20th Street."

In Harlem there was Haarlem Creek (mentioned earlier), which ran east along 96th

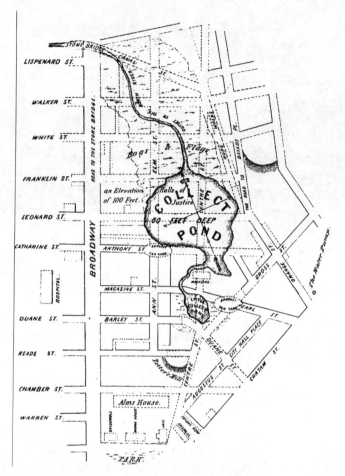

Figure 11.4 By 1789 city streets were already working their expansion toward The Collect; future streets were planned and laid out for when the water would be drained.

Street into the Harlem or East River. Part of this stream was used as a reservoir that included a series of small ponds, cascades, and "murmuring" brooks, into The Ramble, ending in Harlem Lake at the northeastern corner of what became Central Park. The lake was later renamed Harlem Mere.

Between the early 1700s and the early 1800s, Manhattan underwent a rapid transformation from a forested islet to a bucolic countryside, then to suburban and, finally, urban sprawl. Of course, the first fishes to disappear were the demanding brook trout as their habitat either dried up, was filled, or was turned into natural sewage conduits. Fishers, however, didn't seem to miss the loss of trouting opportunities immediately adjacent to their homes. After all, Long Island was just a few minutes by ferry to the east, and its brook-trout streams were boundless, weren't they?

Figure 11.5   The "Stone Bridge" at Broadway and Canal Street in 1811 showing the canal or outlet to The Collect. The natural stream was dug deeper in hopes of draining the pond. The bridge was a favorite place for city anglers who still were able to catch brook trout from its waters.

THE BE-SPECKLED TROUT

I don't that believe that Craig Béros, a dedicated ex-Wisconsin trout fisherman, had any idea that the site of his new restaurant–cum–brook-trout shrine at 420 Hudson Street was once just a long cast from one of Manhattan's best trout streams. Of course, the trout in the stream were native brook trout.

Ishpetenga's main source was a spring that rose from a granitic cleft among low-lying hillocks, where Fifth Avenue now crosses 20th Street. It flowed south, meeting a rivulet from the west that erupted as a spring now under Sixth Avenue, just a bit north of 14th Street. They joined at 11th Street, doubling Ishpetenga's width as it was turned southwest by a row of hillocks now capped by West Broadway.

Where Hudson Street now runs the stream bifurcated, forming an island the size of a city block that now would be bound by Hudson, Charlton, West Houston, and (on the west) Greenwich Street. The branches joined and flowed 100 yards before emptying into Muhheakun'nuk, as the Saponickan Clan of the Man-nah-tin tribe called the Hudson River. In those days, 1609, before Manhattan was enlarged, the Hudson's eastern shore was at the edge of Washington Street.

Béros's Anglers and Writers Restaurant, on Hudson and Leroy (St. Luke's Place) streets, is on what was a small rise on the eastern bank of the stream. James J. Walker (Mayor Jimmy Walker) Park, on the southern side of the block opposite the restaurant, would have been on the stream's western bank. To this day, when it rains heavily on Manhattan the land on the park's southern side gets wet, soggy, swamp-like. Maybe it's the stream trying to reclaim its birthright and unfetter its chains.

"I wanted to build a restaurant that reflected me and the things I like to do," Béros said, as I pored over his unbelievable collection of brook trout memorabilia, which forms the theme of his restaurant. It was immediately obvious that fishing for brook trout vies with his love of cooking. He once wrote a fishing column—hence the restaurant's name—for a small newspaper in Algoma, on the edge of Lake Michigan, where he grew up fishing for coaster brook trout. He brought a lot of Wisconsin with him to Manhattan, including milled Wisconsin white ash lumber for the restaurant's floors, an oak bar from a fishing lodge in Nicolet National Forest, where he and his extended family fished, and a tin ceiling from his uncle's hardware-and-tackle store. He should have brought the potbellied stove. As business grew, so did his jaunts for antique trout-fishing gear, until he began to run short of room to display it.

That was easily solved. He opened another shop next door, the Be-Speckled Trout, an extension of the shrine and a cross between an exquisite candy shop, like the sweet shop his uncle had in Wisconsin, and an old-fashioned fly-fishing shop. After his father died, his mother, Charlotte, came to live with him and now makes candies and desserts for their two restaurants.

Béros scours estate auctions, buying old fly boxes, rods, reels, and all of the trappings that make brook trout fishing unique. His lust for collecting fishing memorabilia knows few bounds. To display his bamboo fly rods, fishing prints, paintings, and brook trout carvings, he opened a second restaurant on the northern end of the same block, the Village Atelier ("artist's studio"). Here, served with a French flair, he features brook trout and even Wisconsin jack perch, flown in during the winter when they're at their very best. And if you don't feel bound by tradition to sip white wine with fish, his red wine collection will make your palate quiver.

If you happen to be near Walker Park in early spring, especially after a heavy rain, and see someone in hip boots toting a long, willowy bamboo rod, it's likely Craig Béros looking for enough water to float a Royal Coachman.

12   LONG ISLAND

F or nearly 250 years after the Pilgrims landed, whenever someone in the East or Canada said he was going trout fishing it was for but one species: brook trout. Brook trout became an integral part of life along the Atlantic seaboard as the colonists pushed the frontiers ever westward. For these people, eating brook trout became a part of everyday living. For all but the last 50 years of this monopoly, fishing for brook trout seldom involved a rod, reel, line, lures, or flies. Brook trout were looked upon primarily as an adjunct to frontier and then rural foods, and later as a gourmet delight. They often found their way to city markets. In 1815 at Fulton Street, a 12-inch brook trout sold for 25 cents, a small fortune in those days.

Fishing as a leisure activity was not part of the Puritan ethic that moved the people who came to this land. Those who fished because they liked to were considered idlers, woods bums, irresponsible people shirking their responsibilities of clearing land, establishing homesteads, or doing the business of industry. Most fishing, until the turn of the 19th century, was done with nets, seines, traps, or whatever would catch as many fish as possible, in the shortest possible time, with the least amount of effort.

In this period—from 1620 to about 1800—there was little or no middle class in the United States, especially not during the first 150 years, even though one was beginning to develop in England. When the Pilgrims landed on their famous rock, Izaak Walton was but a 27-year-old drapier in London. It would be 40 years before he would publish *The Compleat Angler*.

Until the Revolution, and probably for another 50 or so years thereafter, Americans still looked to England for their fishing rods, reels, lines, hooks, flies, and even literature. There was little such industry here, and it was the English who had planted the seeds of fishing for sport among American anglers, especially those in New York and on Long Island.

From 1776 to 1783, during the seven-year Revolutionary War occupation of New York City and Long Island, the British officers accustomed to field sports in England realized Long Island was an ideal place for their off-hours. To the chagrin of both the Whigs and their Tory supporters, the British even fished and hunted on Sundays. This exposure to the methods and equipment of trout fishing, and the recreational value the English placed on it, had a residual effect on the watching Americans.

There's little record of fishing for fun in American literature of the late 1700s.

Figure 12.1   A Long Island "salter" angler and his catch.

Sportfishing for brook trout predated the British occupation forces but had only a few practitioners, such as Boston merchant John Rowe. He kept a diary of his fishing exploits from 1764 to 1774, and in it recorded not only the species he caught but also their weight and numbers, the names and locations of brooks and ponds he fished, and the weather. He also mentioned that his rods were imported from England. Fishing for sport on a recognizable scale probably began independently at about the same time in freshwater streams outside Philadelphia, the largest colonial city until after the Revolution, and in Boston and New York. All three were occupied during the war by the British.

Of the three colonial metropolitan areas, none offered as much opportunity to catch trout as did the environs of New York, especially Long Island. Manhattan had at least a dozen fishable brook trout streams which drained the island in all directions. By the time The Collect was filled, brook trout populations in Ishpetenga and its sister stream just north of Wall Street had been depleted. Even Turtle Creek—at 3½ miles Manhattan's longest brook trout stream—held only a few trout. Beginning at about Snake Hill and flowing south into the East River at Turtle Bay, Turtle Creek's banks were a favorite for Sunday picnickers, and its brook trout populations suffered from overfishing.

By now, serious recreational anglers were turning eastward and were well aware of the numerous brook trout streams on Long Island. On Paumonok, there are 252 rivers, streams, creeks, brooks, and trickles that drain both the North and South Shores as well as the eastern and western ends of this huge terminal glacial moraine, which juts 120 miles into the Atlantic from the eastern side of Manhattan. While Newtown and Bushwick creeks held trout, the fishing was easier on Garritsens Creek, because S. I. Garritsen had constructed a milldam on the stream and his Mill Pond had "a goodly supply of brook trout." He even rented boats and established the first fishing station on Long Island.

The secret to the great brook trout productivity of Long Island lies in its soil and water. This huge sandbar—the gleanings of Québec and New England carried onto the continental shelf by the last glacier, which ended 20,000 years ago—acts as a big percolator and filter. Water that forms the beginnings of its streams rises from numerous springs on either side of the high, spinelike ridge that longitudinally follows the island's axis. Rain that fell 400 to 600 years before finally wells back to the surface, pouring forth clear and cool. The streams are continually cooled by springs along their way to the ocean, so that seldom does the water rise above 65 degrees or freeze in any but exceptionally cold winters. The voluminous and constant flow of these springs is the basis for a perfect cold-water environment, producing aquatic foods for brook trout throughout most of the year. When insect production slows, larger trout wend their way into brackish and saline estuaries, where a constant supply of fish food is available.

At one time, every stream on Long Island had a resident trout population. But not all streams were equal. Some are called "rivers," the remainder "creeks" or "brooks"; even the largest is but a good "stream" at best. The settlers who inhabited most of the eastern half of the island were English and had a peculiar habit of calling every stream a "river" in its tidal section and a "brook" in its freshwater part. Today's Connetquot River was called Great River or Connetquot River in tidewater sections, but Connetquot Brook in its freshwater.

Of the island's great number of streams, only about 40 were fishable. The larger were more popular because they held more fish and thus drew more anglers. Other than the Nissequogue River on the North Shore and the Peconic River on the eastern end, most larger and better trout streams known to postcolonial anglers were along the island's South Shore. From west to east they included Valley Stream, Massapequa Creek, Champlain Creek, and the Connetquot, Patchogue, Swan, and Carmans rivers.

During the first quarter of the 19th century, most of Long Island's streams were open to anyone who wanted to fish them. They were usually owned by farmers who didn't see a few anglers working their waters as a hazard to their livestock. In this period, pressure on brook trout was light, controlled more by poor access to the streams and ponds over primitive country roads than by a philosophy of private ownership. Long Island was bucolic, rustic beyond description, and totally rural. Because of its island aspect, it remained in this state as late as World War II.

In that same first quarter century, transportation was still primarily by sailing vessel. Land-based travel by horseback, buckboard, wagon, or stage was slow and difficult, over poorly kept dirt roads. For gentlemen anglers from The City, a trip to the trout streams began with a ferry ride across the East River and continued on a stagecoach. The trip from Greenpoint to Greenport, a distance of less than 100 miles, often took as long as three days. By 1825 roads had begun to improve, and the island was served by three

Figure 12.2   Long Island mill.

growing west-east routes: North Country, Middle Country, and South Country roads.

Because of the slowness of travel, country inns, taverns, and hostelries sprang up along the early stage routes. Most began as strategically located farmhouses with an extra room or two. Among the most popular were those located on or near famous shooting and fishing grounds, especially where the main west-east roads crossed streams. The site of Sam Carman's inn was at "the crossing-over place," on the East Connecticut River, known today as the Carmans River. Many were at the sites of mills, such as Carman's and Snedecor's on West Connetquot Brook. The millponds became trout ponds. It didn't take long for a few entrepreneurs to see the value of having a tavern and rooms for transient passengers and fishermen. Such businesses sprang up along South Country Road—the Montauk or Merrick Highway (depending upon your orientation)—the main stagecoach route from Greenpoint on the East River to Sag Harbor and, eventually, Amagansett. This road was to become the Main Street of many future towns and villages. As railroads developed (the Long Island Rail Road was started in 1834 and reached Greenport in 1844), they replaced stage lines and, by 1850, supplanted them.

MASSAPEQUA CREEK

South Country Road closely followed solid ground along the bay's shores and salt marshes. Where it forded streams, tidewater was usually found only on the southern side, but brook trout were found on both sides. In his classic book *Fish and Fishing* (1849), Frank Forester,

Figure 12.3 Fly-Fishing on Massapiqua [*sic*] Lake. From Genio C. Scott's *Fishing American Waters*, 1873.

the best fishing chronicler of the period, took the reader on an imaginary coach ride along South Country Road and described trout fishing at that time on Long Island:

> The natural formation of Long Island is not indeed such, that we should look to it, if strangers to its qualities in this respect, with any high degree of expectation as a mother of trout streams; and yet it is probably surpassed in this particular by no region of the world.

Forester has been criticized by modern-day writer Paul Schullery (*American Fly Fishing: A History*, Lyons & Burford, 1987) for the inaccuracy of some of his statements. However, when one considers the extent of the world of the brook trout known to Forester when he wrote his books, his statements don't seem quite as outlandish. True, there are faults with Forester's writing and reporting, but they should be viewed in relation to the state of writing and reporting of the times.

> On the right hand [when heading east], the salt meadows stretch away, a wide, waste, desolate expanse, to the bays, which glitter afar off under the declining sun, whence you can hear at times the bellowing roar of a heavy gun, telling of decimated flocks of brant and broadbill. Now we pass by a larger pond than any we have yet seen, with a mill at its outlet, and in a mile farther, pull up at the door of Jem Smith's tavern. And there we will halt to-night, although it be a better station for fowling than for fishing, for we are sure of neat though

homely accommodation, and of a kindly welcome; and here it is that the first essay is to be made of Long Island waters.

On this stream there are two ponds [Wantagh or Jackson Creek and its two ponds], both of which were formerly private property, and closed against all persons except those who were furnished with a permit; they are now open to all persons indiscriminately, and I believe without restriction as to the number [of fish] that may be taken by each individual. The consequence of this is, that these ponds have deteriorated very rapidly, and that, although they are well-stocked with small fish of fair flavor and quality, Trout are rarely taken of such a size as to remunerate the exertions of a good fisherman. Half a pound may be taken as a good average of the fish killed here. In the creek below, where the tide makes, there are, of course, fish, but I never have heard of much work being done in it; and, in truth, except that this is the first southern pond of any note, I would hardly advise the angler to pause here.

The first major trout stream traveling anglers encountered on this southerly route was Massapequa Creek. The land around it was given to Major Thomas Jones by his father-in-law, probably as his wife's dowry. Jones, an Irishman in the British forces, arrived in Oyster Bay in 1692 and soon after married Freelove Townsend. They were the first settlers just east of the village of Seaford. Their homestead became the focal point of the village of South Oyster Bay, as Massapequa was first called. Their tract encompassed 20,000 acres of land, marsh, and bay bottom south to the barrier beach against the Atlantic Ocean, which became known as Jones Beach. The dry land amounted only to about 6,000 acres. Jones became the high sheriff of Queens County and was made ranger general of Nassau (as Long Island was also known at that time), the head of a colonial militia that supported the Crown's troops. He also operated a whaling plant at Jones Beach.

The lake—really a millpond, at best—was created in 1832 when Judge David Richard Floyd-Jones built a milldam where Merrick Road (South Country Road) crossed the stream. At first, Massapequa Lake was a regular stop for any Manhattan or Brooklyn angler trekking the stage route on South Country Road. (Later, about the middle of the 19th century, descendent William Floyd-Jones decided to save the trout in the stream for himself and his fishing friends.) Daniel Webster, who must have been a lot like George Washington in his travels, was a frequent overnight guest of the judge. In the town of Babylon's history in 1938, Chauncy L. C. Ditmars wrote that he "owned some ancient wine glasses from which Webster and other celebrities sipped some of the choice nectar of the gods as they partook of choice viands of the [Jones's] table."

When staying in the area, Webster would contact Lawrence Verity of nearby Seaford. Verity was a bayman and veteran guide who was almost 100 years old when he died in 1919. He was in his late teens when he first met Webster. Verity often accompanied the older man when he went trout fishing and even deep-sea fishing out of Jones Inlet. Webster also stayed at Van De Water's Hotel in South Oyster Bay (Massapequa) and the American House in Babylon, as well as at Judge Jones's manor. He and Verity often fished other lakes and streams in the area before continuing east to Sam Carman's inn.

About 1850, Jones sold his Massapequa house and it became Obediah Snedecor's Hotel (the man should not be confused with Liff Snedecor's son, Obediah). Anglers stayed here and dined at Timothy Carman's, next door. Snedecor, Carman, and Jones were common Long Island names of this period. The Snedecors all seemed to be hostlers. The first Snedigar came from Holland about 1635 and settled in New Amsterdam. As the family enlarged, they quickly spread eastward, and the name came to be spelled, or misspelled, nine different ways. One Snediker established a hunting and fishing inn on Old Plank Road in Jamaica, another Snedeker's Hotel on Coney Island; Currier & Ives did a lithograph of the latter hotel next to the racetrack. The most famous establishment was Liff Snedecor's Connetquot Hotel, just east of Islip.

After the Civil War, public fishing in Long Island's streams, lakes, and ponds was greatly reduced, as individuals or sportsmen's clubs bought up the lands and waters. Massapequa Lake was visited often by fishing writer Genio C. Scott, who described it in his book *Fishing in American Waters*: "Lake Massapiqua [sic], at South Oyster Bay, on Long Island, is probably the best trout preserve in the United States," wrote Scott in 1875. Scott really didn't say much about the brook trout fishing but lauded Jones, probably because he was one of Jones's "invited guests." "It is owned by William Floyd Jones, Esq., who is one of the finest examples of an American gentleman. The preserve covers eighty acres, and is fed by a spring-brook [Massapequa and Massatayun creeks] which is seven miles in length, and all of it on Mr. Jones' estate. This gentleman maintains the preserve for his exclusive use and that of his invited guests. Not only for his fish-preserve and his system of fish culture is Mr. Jones preeminent, but as a farmer and horticulturist, a sportsman of first-class."

Scott's accuracy here is in question. While his descriptions are fine, his dating seems off by about 25 years. We know he was writing about Massapequa Lake, but what he wrote was only valid prior to 1850 and not as late as 1875. The lake had already changed ownership by then, according to others and to Frank Forester, who wrote in 1849, as he continued on his tour:

> About a mile and a half farther eastward, is a large pond [Massapequa Lake], and a fine house, both recently constructed at a great expense by Judge Jones—the former exclusively designed as a fish-pond. The place has, however, passed out of his hands, and the house is now kept as a hotel by one of the Snedecors. The pond has hitherto been private, but is now open, though with a limitation. It is well-stocked with fish of a fair size. When I was last there, a fortnight since, a gentleman had taken eight fish, weighing as many pounds, with the fly that morning. The largest did not exceed a pound and a half, but they were handsome, clean, well-fed fish, and, as the day was anything but propitious—easterly wind, and very raw and cold, I considered it fair sport. He had not been fishing above a couple of hours. I understand, however, that there are many Pike [pickerel] in this pond, and in the stream that supplies it; and I much fear that this must ultimately prove destructive to

all the fish in the water, although those resident on the spot assert that the Pike never grows in that region to above half a pound, and rarely to that weight, and that little, if any, detriment is observed to arise from his presence.

The original homestead was an unusual house because it was built of brick, a rarity in 1696, the year when it was supposedly constructed. However, Nathaniel Currier (pre–Currier & Ives) produced a print of it prior to 1857 entitled *The Old Stone House on L.I., 1699*. Large numerals, 1699, dating the house appear on its right side. In a seeming contradiction of its construction material, the bricks are either exceptionally large or the stones rather small. The print does, however, show a pond or reservoir on its western side.

As mentioned earlier, the house was built by Major Thomas Jones and his wife, Freelove Townsend. The "Old Brick House" stood on the eastern side of Massapequa Creek, before it was damned for mill power, and remained there until 1837, when William Floyd-Jones tore it down and built his grand manor a few hundred yards north. Over the next century—until 1850 or thereafter—Jones's estate was broken up piecemeal, and none exists intact today. In recent years the lake has been taken over by largemouth bass and white perch, though Massapequa Creek and Reservoir are still stocked annually by New York's Department of Environmental Conservation with brown, rainbow, and brook trout. For years the DEC stocked only brook trout in Massatayun Creek, which empties into Massapequa Creek above Massapequa Reservoir (not the lake). But warming waters have caused it to stock more browns and rainbows than natives.

Forester continued his tour:

> Some miles beyond this, still keeping the south-side road, we come to Babylon, where there is an excellent house, under the management of Mr. Concklin, of whom all accommodation may be obtained, both as regards fowl-shooting in the bays and Trout-fishing in the neighborhood. There are several ponds and streams [Carlls River; Argyle, Hawley, and Elda lakes; and Belmont Pond] more or less well-stocked in this vicinity, but none of any particular note, either for the size or flavor of the fish.

CONNETQUOT RIVER

Two other trout streams along South Country Road also rose in prominence at the end of the first quarter of the 19th century, not only because of the large natural stocks of brook trout in their watersheds but also because of their taverns or inns. The next stream down the road is Connetquot Brook, and on it was Eliphalet "Liff" Snedecor's Connetquot Hotel. Farther east along South Country Road, on the East Connecticut River, was Carman's inn, a tavern much frequented by Daniel Webster. After about 1860, all of these better streams were locked up in "preservers," really private clubs.

The Connetquot River rises just south of the height of land that forms Long Island's

THE CLUB HOUSE ABOUT 1870

Figure 12.4   The original photograph from which Goodspeed's line drawing was made. (From The Vanderbilt Collection, Dowling College, Oakdale, NY.)

hilly, backbonelike, east-west moraine. Here, two small, in-line ponds, Ackerly Pond, and along with numerous springs come together just south of Exit 58 of the L.I. Expressway to form the river's beginnings. The Connetquot River is similar to all other Long Island streams in that almost no waters from runoff, rain, or snow contribute directly to its flow, owing to the sandy, porous nature of the island's soil. The river's watershed covers about 1,600 acres. The main branch is relatively straight. As it flows southward it's continually augmented by more springs along its 5-mile trek toward saline Great South Bay.

The tidal section, known as the Great River, encompasses another 3 miles. Several small tributaries—one from the west in its upper reaches; a larger one, West Brook and West Brook Pond; and three from the east (West, Middle, and Rattlesnake brooks, the latter including Slade and East ponds)—all enter the tidal portion of the Connetquot River near the head of tide. Because these tributaries and springs promise a steady source of water and are cold even in August, trout survival is especially good, and natural production alone supported an extensive fishery as late as 1865.

Liff Snedecor's hotel and fishing grounds, near Oakdale in the town of Islip, some 45 miles east of Greenpoint, had, since 1825, been a favorite resort for sportsmen. Born in Huntington, Snedecor (1788–1861) moved to Islip Grange in 1820, where he rented the house next to the mill (not the miller's house) on the Connetquot River, and a 200-acre farm from William Nicoll, a descendent of the original patentee. His intent was to be a farmer, like his father, Lewis. But his children—four sons and two daughters—were then too young to help with farming. Obediah, his youngest and the one who eventually took over the inn, was only a year old when they moved into the house. Fortunately, the front steps of the house were on the main road between Manhattan and Montauk and on a good brook trout river. This location offered Snedecor the unexpected chance to house and feed itinerant anglers and established his future as a tavern keeper. Even a modest fee provided more profit than farming would have.

"On the 26th Sept. 1828, I left New York for Islip, 50 miles, and the next morning left Snedecor's Tavern at 7 AM (an excellent house, by the way) to take my stand by a man from the House who was in the upper stand," wrote Mr. X, in a letter published in the New York *Sun*, "Snedecor having driven to the west with the dogs."

Snedecor's Hotel, as it was called, was ideally situated for deer hunters as well as trout fishermen. The hunters were transported by water to blinds—Mr. X's "stands"—while packs of dogs drove the deer down to the river.

While Liff ran the deer hunts, his daughters did their share around the farm and inn. According to a writer for *The Mirror*, a daily New York newspaper (Mirror), in December 1837: "The morning broke tardily, and the house was silent long after I raised my window, looked forth at the weather, and returned again to my bed. At length, the creaking of beds, and murmuring of female voices in the next room, which was separated from mine only by a thin partition, told me that old Liffy's daughters were leaving their nests, and soon afterward there was a general stir throughout the bedrooms. We found a famous breakfast ready for us when we descended, and a singular display of shooting dresses."

The original three-story wooden-frame hotel was built before 1820 on the western side of the river, not far from the 10-foot-high dam and mill. The mill was built by 1751, possibly as early as 1701, by William Nicoll. The dam backed up the river for about three-quarters of a mile and prevented any salters, sea-run brook trout, from reaching their original spawning grounds on the main river. The river still had a few hundred yards of nontidal water before it became brackish. The brackish portion was long, and the river and its tidal marsh still supported a good salter fishery. The trout did spawn in the main river to a lesser degree, but continued to enter the rivulet tributaries on the eastern and western sides of the main stream, especially Rattlesnake Creek.

By 1820, the river had already become famous for producing big salters. Unfortunately, dam building ended the run on the main branch by 1875. In 1991, however, a 7½-pound salter was reportedly taken in one tributary, Rattlesnake Creek. This stream is unique today because it still runs freely to the sea, with no obstructions to limit migration of brook trout into and out of fresh water. The 7½-pound salter was larger by several pounds than any breeders used in the state hatchery on the river. Even though Gil Bergen, the park's superintendent, has a policy of releasing breeders into the river after they reach a certain age, this had to have been a sea-run fish because of its size, if the report is accurate.

The earliest account of the Connetquot as a fishery in a Manhattan publication appeared from an unidentified reporter in the August 5, 1837, edition of *Spirit of the Times:*

After spending a few days very pleasantly at Jackson's [another hotel in Islip], as you certainly may, have your carriage brought to the door, and drive down about three miles and a half, to the never-to-be-sufficiently praised Connequot Hotel opposite Fire Island, of Liff Snedeker's—an out and outer [your guess is as good as mine] at a mint julep, a deer hunt, or a good story. You can almost throw a fly from his door into his pond, and a famous one it is. Last season, as nearly as he could ascertain by a careful record 3,300 trout were taken from it by his boarders and friends. [This was a wild brook trout fishery; artificial propagation was still a few years away.] When we saw him, early in July last, above two thousand had been taken this year, and the fishing was still excellent. The stream running from it is a large one, and you may fish from a boat—if you hit upon a fine day, you may half fill it with trout. With a single exception, this is the only brook on the Island [not so] in which you can fish from a boat.

Connetquot Brook produced exceptional catches of brook trout for wealthy metropolitan anglers who took the stage to Snedecor's to fish and stay overnight. As its popularity grew and more anglers frequented the resort, catches were regularly reported in Manhattan and Brooklyn newspapers. In 1845, N. S. Prime wrote that "the sport or profit of fishing, hunting and fowling, probably induces more foreigners to visit the [Long Island] island, than all other motives put together; always excepting the abomination of horse-racing."

I wonder who he meant by "foreigners."

Because Snedecor's was close to the city, and a few days' fishing could be had without an extensive journey to Pennsylvania or upstate New York, it was popular with those who could afford the accommodations and transportation. Snedecor's was also a popular place with Frank Forester, who had a lot to say about it in his tour of the fishing establishments along South County Road:

Such, however, is not the case with the next station at which we arrive, Liff Snedecor's—in whose pond [Main Pond] the fish run to a larger size than in any water we have yet noted. The Trout here, both in the pond and in the stream below, are noted for their great beauty, both of form and color; and although there is some debate among connoisseurs as to the comparative flavor of Snedecor's fish and those taken at Carman's, eighteen miles further east, the judgment of the best sportsmen inclines to the former.

The pond is of the same character with those which I have described heretofore, and can be fished only from boats. It is open to all anglers [this was 1849], but the number of fish to be basketed by each person in one day is limited to a dozen. [First indication of limits on a brook trout catch.] In the stream there is no limit, nor indeed can there be, as the tide-waters cannot be preserved, or the free right of fishing them prohibited. The Trout here are not only very numerous and of the first quality of excellence—their flesh being

Figure 12.5   A sketch of the mill with the South Side Sportsmen's clubhouse in the background. (Courtesy The Vanderbilt Collection.)

redder than that of the Salmon—but very large; the average probably exceeds a pound, and fish of two and two and a half pounds weight are taken so frequently as to be no rarity.

The outlet of this pond, after running a few hundred yards, opens upon the salt meadows [Great River], where there is no obstacle whatever to throwing a long line. It is broader and longer than any stream we have hitherto encountered, and is incomparably the best, containing fish even larger than those of the pond above, and, in my opinion, of a finer flavor. I believe it, indeed, to be an indisputable fact, that Trout, which have access to salt water, are more highly colored and flavored than those which are confined to fresh streams by natural or artificial obstacles.

There is no distinction, of which I am aware, in favor of pond or stream, for the use of the fly, the fish taking it readily in either, although as a general rule they will rise to it earlier in the fresh, than in the tide-water.

At some distance down this stream there is a range of willows on the bank, nearly opposite to a place owned by Mrs. Ludlow; and under the trees are some holes famous for being the resorts of the largest fish, which affect here the deepest water and the principle channel. Here, as in the pond, fish of two and a half pounds are no rarity, and, in fact, such are taken here more frequently than above. I should say that one would rarely hook a Trout in this stream under one and a half pounds; and the true angler well knows that a well conditioned fresh-run fish, from this size to a pound larger, on the finest and most delicate tackle, will give him nothing of which to complain in the way of exercise or excitement.

Snedecor's Connetquot Hotel was a favored place to stay for Daniel Webster, even though his new father-in-law's estate was nearby in Islip. Webster habitually stopped here to fish for a few days before going farther east to Sam Carman's tavern. Snedecor's was also a stop for another avid brook trout fisherman, Philip Hone, who was a regular fishing companion of Webster's and mayor of New York City for one year, 1825. In his diary in 1843, Hone noted that he planned to stop here for the evening before going to Sam Carman's at Fireplace, but found it filled with guests. It's likely that the Snedecor Hone referred to was Obediah (not the son of Liff), who turned Judge Jones's house on Massapequa Lake into a hotel.

Forester continued his tour of Long Island:

> At a short distance from Snedecor's is another stream, known as Green's [Eggie's] Creek, which contains a peculiar and distinct variety of Trout, which is called in that district the Silver Trout. I have not seen this fish, but learn from good sportsmen that it is of a much lighter and more pearly hue than the common Trout, the bright and silvery lustre of the scales prevailing over the back and shoulders. It is crimson spotted, but the fins are less strongly yellow, and it is perhaps a slenderer fish in form. The flesh is said to be firm and well-flavored. The Silver Trout is rarely taken over or much under a pound in weight, and rises to the fly or takes the bait indiscriminately.
>
> At Patchogue, yet a few miles further [east], there is a very large pond [Canaan Lake on the Patchogue River], which was formerly perhaps the most famous on the island, both for the abundance and the size of the fish which it contained. They have, however, become latterly so scarce, that few persons from a distance think it worth their while to pause there, but proceed at once to Sam Carman's at Fireplace, eighteen miles eastward from Liff Snedecor's; these two being in fact the par excellence fishing grounds of the Island, and the difference between the two rather a matter of individual prejudice and fancy, than of any real or well-grounded opinion.

Like Philip Hone, a number of Manhattan sportsmen frequently found no room at the inn, any of these inns, and so formed a group to purchase Snedecor's Hotel, its immediate grounds, and enough of the surrounding pine and scrub oak barrens to keep the watershed intact. Liff's son Obediah had taken over management of the hotel by 1850 (Liff died in 1861) and was in command in 1866, when the anglers bought the hotel and environs. But the hotel changed hands three times in three years before the anglers finally took possession of it.

The first purchaser was Robert Maitland, who in 1864 bought the holdings on both sides of the river from William Nicoll VIII, heir of the original patentee. In 1865, Maitland sold the property to James B. Johnson of Manhattan, who, in turn, on January 9, 1866, sold it to William Barrett, Jones Rogers, and Shepard Knapp, all also of New York. The trio formed the South Side Sportsmen's Club, of which they were the initial nucleus, and sold the property to the club that same year. Throughout all of these sales Obediah stayed on, but he eventually moved out of the hotel to the nearby village of Babylon. He was kept on as the club's superintendent until 1871 and was an honorary member until 1878.

The South Side Sportsmen's Club (later the Southside Sportsmen's Club of Long Island), incorporated April 3, 1866, limited its membership to 100, charged each member a $100 initiation fee, and immediately began a massive expansion of the hotel and surrounding buildings. Eventually, the club possessed 3,475 acres and leased an adjoining 2,300 for more hunting grounds.

The last sale of the property was to the state of New York in 1963. While the general public was excluded from fishing the Connetquot River for 97 years, the hiatus was eventually to their benefit. Only a private club, with its wealth, could afford to maintain the river and its surrounding land in as pristine a state as when it had been purchased. Otherwise, it would have been swallowed up by the housing developments that began replacing a once-bucolic Long Island in 1950.

Among the original purchasers were corporation lawyer Samuel Barlow, Scottish industrialist Andrew Carnegie, restaurateur Lorenzo Delmonico, August Belmont, James Gordon Bennett Jr. of the New York *Herald,* journalist A. Oakey Hall, New York City mayor Abram Hewitt, George M. Robeson of the Bureau of Fisheries, and the nation's foremost naturalist-scientist, George Bird Grinnell. Buying in to the water and ponds around the Connetquot River seemed like such a good deal that in 1872, Robert Barnwell Roosevelt (Roosevelt), a club member, T.R.'s uncle, and at that time New York's fish commissioner, purchased 150 acres of land with a trout pond in nearby Sayville. In the club's guest register one can find the signatures of Ulysses S. Grant (1871) and General William T. Sherman (1872).

The club's membership roster was a veritable Who's Who in American Politics—state and federal senators and New York City and Long Island politicians. They were so powerful that when they deemed the highway, which for 200 years ran immediately in front of the clubhouse door, "too close," the county moved it. In 1868 members even had the Long Island Rail Road build a special "Club" stop on the Montauk Line, just opposite the clubhouse, for their exclusive use. It was closed in 1882. The club allowed the old mill to be operated for a while; today, rebuilt and maintained, it's in perfect condition. The remnant old highway still runs past the clubhouse door, over the milldam then eastward into the woods and oblivion.

The club expanded the hotel in stages, first incorporating the original three-story structure into a larger building to accommodate more members. Several more support buildings were added to the grounds. To ensure a goodly supply of trout, the first fish hatchery was built in 1868 on Lower Pond, at the base of the dam and gristmill. The water

Figure 12.6   A sketch of the club's first hatchery on Slade Pond, a widening of Rattlesnake Creek, a Connetquot River tributary. (Courtesy The Vanderbilt Collection.)

from Main Pond, behind the dam, was too warm in summer, however. Two years later the club built a hatchery on Slade Pond, a widening of Rattlesnake Creek and tributary to the river, but discovered the water supply there insufficient. The main river had the only flow guaranteed during summer, and in 1897 the club built a state-of-the-art hatchery about a mile upriver of the gristmill, above Main Pond. It still produces large numbers of trout.

Rainbows and browns as well as brook trout were raised; even Pacific salmon were introduced to the lower river in hopes of establishing a salmon run. Some members complained that these efforts came at the expense of brook trout. Because of the cold nature of the river, brook trout were able to hold their own, but stocking continues even today to augment natural reproduction. The original wild brook trout strain is confined to the cooler upper-headwater reaches of the main stream and some smaller tributaries. Salters still appear today at the base of the dam that forms Lower Pond, where enough is left of the river's freshwater portion for spawning.

The club remained private until 1963. As the old membership died off, property taxes became so exorbitant on this vast acreage, now surrounded by suburbs, that it was sold to the state, then leased back for 10 years. In 1973 it was opened as Connetquot River State Park, with limited public access. In 1987 the state legislature designated it the state's first park-preserve; it's maintained as a wilderness park. The hatchery is still in operation and provides exceptional amounts of fish for this and the Nissequogue River in Caleb Smith State Park on Long Island's North Shore. The land and river are still in their near-pristine state. Fishing is by permit. As in the English river system, an angler rents a beat for four hours and is the only fisher on that section. In addition to salters, sea-run brown and rainbow trout have been developed and 16- to 18-pound fish are not rare. Today, the Connetquot is a world-class stream.

CARMANS RIVER

If, in the early 1800s, you continued another 13 miles east along South Country Road, you'd pass through the village of Fireplace. Two miles later you'd come to Fireplace Mills, or the "crossing-over place," as it was more commonly known, and Sam Carman's tavern on the East Connecticut River. *Connecticut* is a generic Alqonquin-Lenape word that describes any freshwater river with a long, brackish, tidal runout. The original word is *quonne-tukq-u*. The English changed the syllabic construction and pronounced it "kon-net-tu-kut," or sometimes "kon-net-quot."

The river near Islip and Snedecor's Hotel was called West Connecticut, or Connetquot, Brook, and the river near Fireplace was East Connecticut, or just Connecticut, until as late as 1873, when it was changed to Carmans River. Even without Daniel Webster's catch of a 14½-pound salter from its waters, this was probably the most famous and popular brook trout stream on Long Island. Its early fame was based on the size and number of sea-run brook trout it produced and not the voluminous catches made on the ponds and nontidal streams. While the Connetquot's fame was built on the same basis as Carmans River's, the fishing itself was overshadowed by the the number of renowned people who preferred to fish there. Maybe some of its popularity was due to Sam Carman's versus Liff Snedecor's hospitality.

Forester had a difficult time trying to decide whether he preferred to fish the ponds on Liff Snedecor's place or the tidal waters at Sam Carman's. He didn't seem to let the dilemma bother him and fished both with great regularity:

> The character of the fishing at Fireplace is nearly similar to that at Islip; the stream flowing from the pond is larger, and contains much larger fish, the most beautiful, both in shape and brightness of color, of any on the island. The course of Carman's stream lies chiefly through open salt meadows, and the banks are entirely destitute of cover, so that very careful and delicate fishing is necessary in order to fill a basket. Even with ground bait it is desirable to keep out of sight, walking as far from the bank as possible, and to avoid jarring the water, so wary and shy are the larger fish. It is also advisable to fish down wind. Trolling is very successful in this water, the same precautions being taken, and the bait-fish being dropped as lightly on the surface, as if it were a fly, so as to create neither splash nor sound. The pond above is likewise deservedly celebrated, the fish averaging at least a pound in weight, and equal in all respects to any pond Trout in this or any other region. The fly-fishing

here in season is probably the best on Long Island, although of late, here, as everywhere else, Trout are becoming comparatively few in numbers; so that it has been found necessary to impose a limit on sportsmen.

Not many years ago, a celebrated English shot and angler who . . . I believe, was among the first, if not the very first, to use the fly on Long Island waters, took between forty and fifty good fish in this pond before dinner, and in the afternoon basketed above a dozen of yet larger size in the stream below.

This feat, the like of which will not, I fear, be soon heard of again, was performed with a fly, the body of which was composed of hare's-ear fur, and the hackle of a woodcock's wings—a very killing fly, be it observed, for all waters, especially early in the season.

Here's where Forester's credibility again comes into question. He wrote this about 1848, when fly fishing was already well established on Long Island and elsewhere in the United States. It's difficult to determine what he meant by "not many years ago." It's also interesting to note that he had begun to sound the alarm about overfishing the island's brook trout populations, because some stream owners had already set limits on daily catches. The decline in the fishery was one reason why so many well-heeled anglers formed clubs, purchased the streams and buildings, and took their fish out of the public domain.

On the same stream with Carman's pond, and at but a short distance above it, is another called Middle Island Pond [Lower Yaphank Lake or Lower Mill Pond], with a saw and flour-mill at the outlet, which contains a great number of fish, of very large and very uniform size, running from one and a half to two pounds weight. It is remarkable, however, that the Trout in the lower pond [Carman's Pond or, now, Hards Lake] being esteemed the best, those in the upper should be the worst of any taken on the south side of the island.

"In Carman's River the largest fish in America are [did he know of Webster's catch 25 years earlier?], I think it will be allowed, mostly caught, running often quite up to five lbs. weight, and I fully believe that if it were fished patiently and resolutely, especially at the gray twilight, or in the shimmering moon-shine quite down to the bay, through the salt meadows, with a small Trout on good spinning-tackle with three swivels, or with a very large gaudy fly, sunk by means of shot to several inches below the surface, fish might be taken of seven or eight pounds weight.

It was the superb waterfowling on the tidal marshes around Bellport Bay and the mouth of the East Connecticut River that first drew sportsmen to Fireplace (renamed Brookhaven about 1870). Numerous baymen acted as guides when the "birds were down," and itinerant sportsmen found Carman's hostelry to their liking. Waterfowlers are also often fishermen, and they quickly realized the largesse of brook trout in fresh and tidal portions of the river. If you've never fished an open, tidal river for brook trout,

Charles Hallock's account of doing so on the Carmans River, from his 1873 book *The Fishing Tourist*, is a vivid description and as valid today as it was then:

> Starting out betimes [early], when the tide serves right, we anglers follow a narrow lane that leads to the marshes beyond, and leaping an old rail-fence stride forth upon the flats. Before us stretched a wide expanse sere [withered] and brown, bounded in the distance by the blue ocean on which a single white sail is making an offing. There is nothing else to break the dreary monotony save the distant masts of a couple of large fishing-smacks which are high and dry upon the banks of the creek in which we are to fish. The cold [April] wind blows in our faces sharply, and whistles through our delicate fishing tackle now rigged and ready for use, and each heavy tramp falls with a squelch and a splash on the marsh, and the short, crisp, salt grass whisks up the blue ooze high on our boots.
>
> Ah! here is the creek at last. Whew! How the wind drives through its broad, deep channel, and throws up the waves against its muddy banks with a cold goblin chuckle! What a cast of the fly! Away it whisks, clear over the creek, and lodges upon the opposite bank. Foot by foot we cover the creek as we make our frequent casts, but yet no rise. At length we take one trout at the bend— a small one; after a while another; and another, a little larger.
>
> But, bless me if I like this sport!

Carmans River is one of four large, spring-fed streams on Long Island, three of which provide excellent brook-trout fishing. The fourth, Peconic River, is the largest and longest, but it was heavily modified in the mid-1700s by large dams on its lower portion and small dams on its upper reaches to create cranberry bogs. Unlike the Nissequogue River, which is composed of several large branches, Carmans River is a single stream, and is almost straight through most of its 12-mile length. It originally arose in small, shallow Pfeiffer Pond (recently filled), on the northern side of Middle Country Road, and flows south into Bellport Bay. Just above South Country Road (Montauk Highway), its spring-fed waters mix with tidal waters. Its last 3 miles are brackish and justify its being called a connecticut.

Only one small tributary enters the freshwater portion of the river, a trickle on the western side that enters the millpond and never had a name, until Suffolk County bought the river from Ken Hard; it's now Hards Lake. In the the river's tidal portion, where most trout fishing occurred in the 1800s, Little and Big Fish creeks flow in from the eastern side, and Little Neck Run and Yaphank (Yamphanke) Creek enter from the western side. All four creeks are small, with minute flows of fresh water.

On April 10, 1745, nearly all of the land on which the present hamlet of South Haven (Fireplace Mills) is located was sold to John Havens of Shelter Island for "720 pounds, lawful New York money." Three dams straddle the river, all built about the mid-1700s. Mordecai Homan built the original dam, just above the "crossing-over place" at the head of tidewater, where South Country Road crossed the river. He used the power to run a saw-, grist-, and fulling mill. During the next 50 years, the mill changed hands several times, eventually returning to the descendants of Mordecai Homan. Sam Carman Sr. married Theodosia Homan near the beginning of the 19th century and gained control of the mill. He died in 1821. It was Sam Carman Jr. who later turned part of his large house into a tavern and inn, which, during the early years of the 19th century, was also a stagecoach stop on the route from Brooklyn to Sag Harbor.

Sam Carman Jr. fathered a dozen children. When he died in 1869, at 80 years of age, the house was bequeathed to his son Henry and the mill to son Robert. The house stood on the northern side of Old Country Road (Montauk Highway), well in front of the mill, and existed until June 1936. Then it and the surrounding lands were purchased by Charles E. Johnson for use as a duck farm. He tore down the older, original part of the house and used its wooden sashes for duck houses, retaining the newer part, on the eastern side, as his home. This, too, was torn down, in December 1958, to make way for a new four-lane superhighway.

Carman's mill was in operation until 1910, then stood inactive until 1958. That year, the current dam was built north of the old dam to make way for the four-lane extension of Sunrise Highway. The Presbyterian church, which played a part in Webster's catching of the big trout, was moved to the hamlet of Brookhaven (alias Fireplace) to make way for the highway. The tavern, store, and mill were also torn down to make way for the road. Only the lower half of the famous pool exists now, between Montauk Highway and the four-laner.

Two other dams upstream were also built for mill power. The next one, 3 miles upstream from Carman's mill, forms Lower Yaphank Lake, or Lower Mill Pond, as it was first called. A mile farther upstream is the third dam, which forms Upper Yaphank Lake. All entrapped brook trout in Sam Carman's day and still hold fish today.

As on the Connetquot River, anglers who once freely fished the East Connecticut River in the mid-1800s began finding no room at the inn, and the wealthier of Carman's clientele formed their own group. Among them was Daniel Webster, who had heard of the big trout of the East Connecticut River and fished it for several years before he caught the 14½-pounder in 1827. Webster was so taken by the fishing that he sent Carman $100 that year as rent for land above the milldam and for exclusive fishing and shooting rights for himself and friends Philip Hone, John and Edward Stevens (who designed the schooner *America*), Walter Brown, and Martin Van Buren, who later became president. Webster built a small cottage, where he and his friends stayed when the inn was full.

These men were the forerunners of the club organized by August Belmont in New York City in 1858. This group included John Van Buren, the president's son, Peleg Hall, W. Butler Duncan, Watt Sherman, and Joseph Grafton. Webster was never a member of the club; he died in 1852. The Suffolk Club, as they were called, bought piecemeal, from 20 owners, a total of 1,500 acres around the pond and the old mill, but left the homestead to Carman. Opposite Carman's tavern, on a site several hundred yards north of Carman's inn on the western edge of the millpond, they erected their own three-story clubhouse, establishing their own shooting and fishing preserve and even building a trout hatchery. They main-tained a pew in the Presbyterian church on the southern side of South Country Road. Their membership was limited to 15, and, for its size, it was considered the wealthiest fish-ing club in the country. The Suffolk Club had many prominent anglers as its guests, the most famous being Theodore Roosevelt, who fished at the club on May 14, 1915. As did all members and guests, he had to list his catch. On that day he caught seven trout and released one, and entered his name in the club's Fishing Register No. 3.

After the turn of the century, the club's aging members became less active and the club was on the verge of disbanding. In 1923, Anson W. Hard, the club's 62nd and last member, and his wife, Florence Bourne-Hard, bought all of the members' shares and the 600 acres—all that remained of the original purchase—and the club was dissolved. Hard bought another 700 acres, and for several years kept the club as a private preserve for his family and friends. After his death in 1936, his son Kenneth took over the property and leased part of the upper river to a fishing club. Beginning in 1950, he operated it as a commercial fish-ing and shooting preserve. But here, too, escalating costs and high taxes, fueled by a feud with personalities in the county's administration, forced him in the 1960s to sell it to Suffolk County. Since 1964 it has been open as a county park, with controlled access to the fishery, the waters managed by New York's DEC.

Before his death, Anson Hard built for his family a spacious Georgian-style country manor, using parts of the old clubhouse. The manor became headquarters for Southaven Park, which is hoping to use it as a bed-and-breakfast facility. In 1991, the DEC realized that the brook trout in the river's upper reaches were part of the original strain, unadul-terated by domesticated hatchery trout. Under the state's program to reestablish original strains of brook trout in their indigenous waters, it hopes to restore the Carmans River as a brook trout fishery by expanding the population with stock obtained by breeding only the original strain.

NISSEQUOGUE RIVER

This last of Long Island's fishing troika, the Nissequogue River, little resembles the island's two other brook trout streams. It's the only one that flows north, but that's only the first of many differences. Angling literature of the 1800s only lightly heralded the river, but the Nissequogue's trout ponds were well described by every writer of that day, quite the opposite of today's river fishery. Prominent anglers of that era fished its ponds as well as those on Long Island's southern side. One was renamed Webster Pond because Daniel Webster fished it so often.

Under the Southside Sportsmen's Club's husbandry, the Connetquot River has often been likened to an English chalkstream, with its well-manicured banks, trimmed trees, man-made pools, and slow, steady flow of water with rafts of aquatic vegetation. In stark contrast, the Nissequogue River has in places ill-defined banks that lens into adjacent spring-fed swamps; in others its waters are forced to rush wildly, squeezed between banks of glacially sorted gravel. The river ranges greatly in character, from broad outflows of ankle-deep water, to alternate rushes of fast water, to deep, dark, sullen pools. After 1888 its caretaker was the Wyandanch Club, which seemed more interested in pond fishing, developing a system of impoundments and leaving the river close to its original state.

The Nissequogue is really three fisheries in one, made up of a series of ponds, three branches, and a large tidal section with a dependable sea-run trout population. The source of the Northeast Branch, the main branch, is 4 miles above tidewater in a series of springs and marshy areas on the northern slope of the island's longitudinal ridge, just north of Exit 58 of the L.I. Expressway. Coincidentally, this is just over a slight divide, whose waters flow south on the other side to form the Connetquot River.

Several small tributaries and impoundments form the southern branch and feed their waters into New Millpond, alias Stump or Blydenburgh Pond. The western branch is formed by two small tributaries, Bridge Branch and Whitman streams, which are dammed on their lower ends and form North Willow Pond and South Willow Pond (renamed Webster Pond after Daniel Webster). All three branches flow into the main branch of the river, which is eventually dammed to form Phillips Mill Pond. Below Phillips Mill Pond Dam is the head of tidewater. Willow, Webster (alias South Willow Pond), and Vail ponds and their connecting streams form the much shorter West Branch Nissequogue River.

There were no natural ponds on any of the river's three branches. All were built for either mill power or as trout-rearing ponds. The first dam was built at the head of tidewater for a gristmill at the present site of Phillips Mill Dam, sometime between 1700 and 1725. It was built on land given by Richard "Bull" Smythe to Richard and Amos Willet and Daniel and Richard Smith II. The land around the gristmill, and where Middle Country Road now crosses the Nissequogue River, became the original site of Smithtown. The spot where the road crosses the river is still a favorite of trout fishermen, especially on opening day, even though these tidal waters are always open to fishing. Tidewater rises less than 2 feet at the base of the dam, and before the dam's construction probably never extended more than a few hundred feet farther upstream. The millpond is now known as Phillips Mill Pond, after the last miller to operate it. White's Pool, at the dam's base, is still a popular fishing area. Sea-run brown, rainbow, and brook trout gather at its base after a 5-mile swim up the tidal portion of the meandering river from Long Island Sound. The millrace is still open and acts as a fish ladder. Jumpers like browns and rainbows need wait only for the top of the tide, when they can easily surmount the dam's lowered boards to return to fresh water to spawn.

The literature of the period had many references to fishing Stump Pond, but very few of Phillips Mill Pond. However, Robert Barnwell Roosevelt, an accomplished angler and writer, in his 1862 book *Game Fish of the North* did describe an incident there:

> One afternoon of a very boisterous day, I struck a large fish at the deep hole
> in the centre of Phillipse's Pond, on Long Island. He came out fiercely, and
> taking my fly as he went down, darted at once for the bottom, which is

absolutely covered with long, thick weeds. The moment he found he was struck he took refuge among them, and tangled himself so effectually that I could not feel him, and supposed he had escaped. By carefully exerting sufficient force, however, the weeds were loosened from the bottom, and the electric thrill of his renewed motion was again perceptible. He was allowed to draw the line through the weeds and play below them, as by so doing they would give a little, while if confined in them he would have a leverage against them, and could tear out the hook.

When he was somewhat exhausted, the question as to the better mode of landing him arose. The wind was blowing so hard as to raise quite a sea, which washed the weeds before it in spite of any strain that could be exerted by the rod, and drifted the boat as well, rendering the latter almost unmanageable, while the fish was still so vigorous as to threaten every moment to escape. I besought the boatman, who was an old hand at this business, to drop the boat down to the weeds and let me try and land my fish with one hand while holding the rod with the other.

He knew the dangers of such a course, and insisted upon rowing slowly and carefully for shore at a shallow place sheltered from the wind, although I greatly feared the hook would tear out or the rod snap under the strain of towing both weeds and fish; once near shore, he deliberately forced an oar into the mud and made the boat fast to it, and then taking up the net watched for a favorable chance. He waited for some time, carefully putting the weeds aside until a gleaming line of silver glanced for a moment beneath the water, when darting the net down he as suddenly brought it up, revealing within its folds the glorious colors of a splendid trout. That was the way to land a trout under difficulties, although I still think I could have done it successfully by myself.

Caleb Smith (1724–1800) was a farmer, Yale graduate, state legislator, judge, Revolutionary War patriot, and great-grandson of Richard "Bull" Smythe. Smythe bought the 10-square-mile township from Lyon Gardiner of Gardiners Island in 1663. Caleb's father, Daniel Smith II, gave him the land around most of the West Branch and built him a house in 1758 (Bramble). The building was believed built between 1751 and 1753, but during the foundation excavations for a new wing of the Wyandanch Club about 1895, certain old bricks were removed that bore the date "1758" and the initials "C. S." Smith's father had in 1718 leased a part of the land he later gave to Caleb to James Chipman, who farmed it. Chipman's house, built in 1736, probably by Daniel Smith, still stands on the southern side of Willow Pond and is the park superintendent's residence.

Except for Phillips Mill Pond at the head of tidewater, there were no ponds on the Nissequogue River when Caleb Smith and his bride moved into their new house. Even though the river was unfettered and pond fishing was de rigueur, there was quite an interest in stream fishing for brook trout during the early 1800s. In 1750, where Middle

Figure 12.7   On the path down to Vail's Pond, near Stump Pond, on Long Island in 1884. (Courtesy The Vanderbilt Collection.)

County Road and Willets Path meet, schoolmaster Moses Brush and his wife, Abigail, built a lovely small house (still existing) within a long cast from the confluence of Whitman and Bridge Branch streams, just a tad away from the main river. The house is located south of Middle Country Road (Jericho Turnpike) and just west of where Caleb Smith's house was to be built 28 years later.

Sometime between 1820 and 1825, Aaron Vail acquired the property as "a house of entertainment for trout fishermen" as well as a stop on the stagecoach line. According to Colonel Verne La Salle Rockwell (Ganz), a Smithtown historian, "Aaron Vail always knew some quiet nook from which the wary fish could be decoyed when the wind or weather was unfavorable for fishing the open ponds." Vail's house was reputed to be "homelike and many noted men frequented it during the trout season." South Willow Pond was created in 1785 when Caleb Smith dammed Bridge Branch Stream, where it crossed Willets Path almost at Brush's (Vail's) back door, and created more pond fishing for brook trout. North Willow Pond was created a few years later, in 1795, by Smith's son Paul Theodore Smith, when he dammed Whitman Stream. Smith then built a saw- and gristmill on the pond, and the Chipman House became the miller's home.

Daniel Webster was a regular at Vail's establishment between 1823 and 1850, staying there when he fished Willow, Phillips, and Stump ponds. Perhaps because it was so close

Figure 12.8 Daniel Webster frequented Vail's hostelry so often that the house became known as Webster House and South Willow Pond became Webster Pond. Here is the house today, a part of the Caleb Smith State Park.

to Vail's house, Webster fished South Willow Pond so often it was renamed Webster Pond. He stayed at Vail's house so frequently that today it is more commonly known as Webster House rather than Vail House. In addition to Webster Pond and Webster House, there's even a Webster's Bridge, seen in a 1903 photograph of Ed Thompson, a member of the Wyandanch Club. Thompson has on a big trout; another angler, almost under what looks like a footbridge, is ready with a landing net. At Thompson's feet is another large trout lying on the steep, brushy bank. It's probably a 5- or 6-pound brown trout, most likely produced at the club's new hatchery. Eighty-four-year-old Nelly Mosely, who grew up in Webster House and lived there until 1933, when her father was the Wyandanch Club's head gardener, recognized the bridge as the one on Willets Path, which separated their back door from the outlet of Webster Pond.

The dam that formed Stump Pond was built in 1798, when cousins Caleb Smith II, Joshua Smith II, and Isaac Blydenburgh formed a business venture. In 1811, Joshua sold his share to his partners. Caleb II willed his shares to his son Caleb III, who turned around and sold it to Isaac Blydenburgh's sons Richard and Isaac Watt Blydenburgh. The descendants of the Blydenburghs operated the mill until 1924. Pond names changed regularly on the Nissequogue, often reflecting first the original builder, then new millers who bought the business or property. This pond was first known as New Mill Pond, as

Figure 12.9 The Wyandanch Clubhouse today, a part of the Caleb Smith State Park. The Center part of the clubhouse shows the facade of the original Smith farmhouse.

opposed to the first Mill Pond built farther downriver before 1725. Because the Blydenburghs operated the mill for many years, the pond was referred to as Blydenburgh's Pond.

The 12-foot-high dam created the river's biggest impoundment, backing up water into its three branches to form a large but shallow reservoir. The builders probably hadn't anticipated that the dam would back the river as far into the woods as it did. This caused it to be called "Stump Pond," especially by anglers. Subsequently it was known as New Mill Pond then as (David) Welds Pond, after its last owner before it was taken over by the Suffolk County Parks Department in the early 1960s and officially renamed Blydenburgh Pond.

Fish populations trapped behind dams of new impoundments usually explode, owing to the release of a great amount of land-originating nutrients into the water, which fosters an expansion of aquatic life beginning at the bottom of the food chain. It probably took a dozen years before the new pond established a stable population of brook trout. By the 1830s, Stump Pond had developed a reputation with many anglers and writers and was a regular stop on the Long Island brook trout circuit. The Smiths and Blydenburgh built the pond to make money both from the mill and from a growing number of city anglers who wanted to fish its waters. Numerous ponds on both the North and South shores never had mills; they were built primarily as trout-rearing ponds, both for fee-based recreational angling and to supply trout to the traveling fish wagons that circled

Long Island, transporting live trout back to Brooklyn and Manhattan restaurants.

The *Spirit of the Times* ran a piece (August 5, 1837) praising the proprietor of Stump Pond (Major Blydenburgh, War of 1812), saying that it was "one of the largest [man-made] ponds on the Island, and quite the best for trout fishing probably in the Union." But in the same publication a few years later (April 8, 1843), the editor didn't think too highly of the major's conservation measures. He answered a reader who was asking for the best place to fish for trout thus:

> On the southside of Long Island, one can hardly go amiss, while at Smithtown there are three fine ponds and two creeks, in all of which we have had capital sport. Stump Pond was ever a favorite place of resort for us, but we hear that our old friend Maj. Blydenburgh has determined to intermit fishing in it this season save with the fly. Instead, if "any dear friend of Caesar's" will give a call to Conklin, at Babylon, Jesse "is bound to put him through." [Sounds as though they already had telephones.] There are half a dozen ponds in the immediate vicinity, but Jesse's and Capt. Dodds are the best two. Six or seven miles farther on you will find Crandall, at Islip; he has a good pond, and one of the finest creeks on the island; it's worth going ten times as far just to spend a day or two at his hotel. Then an hour's ride will take you to Liff Snedacor's—where there happens to be a large party of friends just now—and two hours more—if you sit behind a fast team—will land you at Uncle Sam Carman's at Fire Place.

Blydenburgh had witnessed the gradual depletion of trout fishing in Long Island's unregulated waters and was determined not to see it occur on his pond. He created the most rigid rules for fishing in that era. The editor of the *Spirit of the Times,* in a piece that appeared March 30, 1844, seemed to have undergone an attitude change and published the rules just before trout season opened.

> Trout Fishing at Stump Pond, L.I.—We have received a copy of the "rules and regulations" which are to govern the fishing at Mr. Blydenburgh's [he lost his rank] celebrated pond this season. It has not been leased, as we were informed lately, but in order to promote and perpetuate the sport, some pretty stringent rules have been determined upon. No one will be allowed to engage a boat for more than three days at any one time, and Mr. B. will send a person out with each, who will see that ten trout only are taken by each person. (Provided they are not seriously injured, small trout may be thrown in again.) A fee of one dollar per day to the proprietors of the pond, and one dollar for the person accompanying the boat, must be paid by each gentleman. A register will be kept of the names of visitors and the weight of the trout taken. As heretofore no fishing will be allowed on Sundays, and any infringement of the rules will subject the offender to a summary expulsion from the premises. The season will commence on Monday next. We know that the run of fish this Spring are

of unusually fine size. On all accounts we are glad that Mr. Blydenburgh has "laid down the law," for people who can only frighten the trout will now keep away, and a man who knows how to handle a fly-rod will be almost certain to take half a dozen sockdollagers in the course of an hour or two.

Even with the new regulations, catches in Stump Pond were deteriorating due to siltation and an overgrowth of aquatic vegetation. Here's what Frank Forester thought of Stump Pond four years later, in 1848:

> There are also many streams to the north side [of Long Island] containing Trout, but none, with a single exception, which can show size or numbers against the southern waters. That exception is Stump Pond, near Smithtown, now rented to a company of gentlemen, and of course shut to the public in general. The lakelet, known as Stump-pond [New Mill Pond], on the northern side of Long Island, which, as its name indicates, is filled with the butts of dead trees, and saturated with vegetable matter, has been for many years famous, or I should rather say infamous, for the ugliness, want of brilliancy, and indifferent quality in a culinary point of view, of its Trout. The fish in this large sheet of water are very numerous, and very large, but are for the most part ill-shaped, ill-conditioned, and inferior in flavor—long, lank fish, with very large black mouths. I have been informed that in latter years the fish in this water have been gradually improving.
>
> On Long Island, there are some half-dozen instances on record, within three times as many years, of fish, varying in weight from four to six pounds, taken with the rod and line. Two of these instances occurred at Stump-pond, on the north side; one in the pond itself, the other in the mill-pool, at the outlet.
>
> A gentleman from New York, who never threw a line, or taken a Trout in his life, and who had come out equipped with a complete outfit of Conroy's best and strongest tackle, all new. On throwing his hook, baited with a common lob-worm, into the water, was greeted with an immediate bite, and bob of the float, which instantly disappeared beneath the surface. The novice, ignorant of all the soft and shrewd seductions of the angler's art, hauled in his prize, by force, without the aid of gaff or landing-net, and brought to basket a five-pounder!
>
> The other instance, in all respects, is the very opposite of the former. The success of the fortunate fisherman is due as much to superior science in his craft, as is, in the former, attributable to blind and unmerited good luck. The hero of this anecdote is a gentleman, known by the nom de guerre of Commodore Limbrick, a character in which he has figured many a day in the columns of the [New York City] *Spirit of the Times,* and who is allowed to be one of the best and most experienced, as well as oldest fisherman of that city.
>
> After having fished all the morning, with various success in the pond, he

ascertained that in the pool below the mill [Forester assumed it was Stump Pond, but this one was Phillips Pond, and the pool below the mill was Whites Pool. There is no pool below Stump Pond.] there was a fish of extraordinary size, which had been observed repeatedly, and fished for constantly, at all hours of the day and evening, with every different variety of bait, to no purpose. Hearing this, he betook himself to the miller, and verified the information, and satisfied himself that neither fly nor minnow, nor redworm would attract the great Trout, he procured a mouse from the miller's trap. At the first cast of that inordinate dainty, [he caught] a fish that weighed four pounds and three-quarters!

Another fish or two of the like dimensions have been taken in Liff Snedecor's. In Carman's streams, it is on record, that at Fireplace, many years since, a Trout was taken of 11 pounds. A rough drawing of this fish is still to be seen on the wall of the tavern bar-room.

The reference to being rented to "a company of gentlemen" is interesting. The Wyandanch Club had a history of changing its name almost as often as pond names were changed on the Nissequogue River. In 1872, a group composed of wealthy hunters and fishermen from Brooklyn formed the Dexter Gun Club. In 1885, they reorganized and changed their name to Brooklyn Gun Club. Three years later, in 1888, Robert R. Hamilton of the B.G.C. negotiated the purchase of the Smith farm at Willow Pond. In 1893, they again changed their name, this time to the Wyandanch Club. The company of gentlemen Forester referred to in 1849 were predecessors of the Dexter Gun Club, a core of city anglers already familiar with these waters, who probably first gathered at Vail House.

After Caleb Smith's death in 1800, the estate continued in his descendants' hands until 1888, when Martha Smith-Prime, the last Smith to live there, sold it to the Brooklyn Gun Club. The club was not like those on the Connetquot and East Connecticut rivers. It had leased or rented parts of the 140-acre farm and its buildings before eventually buying Smith's holdings, and even occupied the Caleb Smith house for several years before finally buying it. Years before the club purchased the house, three Brooklyn men, Gustave Walter and Drs. Henry F. Allen and W. Wynn, used to visit Smithtown to shoot and fish and stayed at a "snug little inn," the Riverside Hotel, then kept by Benjamin B. Newton, who turned it into a hotel in 1859. It was more commodious than the nearby Vail (Webster) House. Newton's son William became the club's gamekeeper. It was these Brooklynites who first "hired" Caleb Smith's house. The Riverside Hotel eventually became Frank Friede's Riverside Inn, an expansive restaurant in the 1920s and '30s that served as a midway stop for the city's Gatsby-type people on their way to the Hamptons. It was reputed that the Prohibition law never was in effect there. The inn burned down in the 1970s, and its land is now a park used primarily by trout fishermen.

After the Brooklyn Gun Club purchased Smith's farm, it built in stages a spacious, three-story Victorian clubhouse that engulfed and towered over the original building, with

Figure 12.10 An angler with two big trout taken in 1903 from Willets Path Bridge. A corner of the Webster house shows along the photograph's left edge.

spacious dining and lounging facilities and 50 small apartments for its members on the top floor. The building still dominates the eastern side of Willow Pond. To expand its domain the club acquired several peripheral estates, including Aaron Vail's house. In 1893 it built Vail Pond, on the southern side of Middle Country Road, by creating a circular earthen dike then diverting into it outflow water from Webster Pond. Next to it, using copious springwater, it built an extensive series of hatchery ponds. In that same year it changed its name to the Wyandanch Club, in honor of the Long Island Indian sachem. It held title to the land until 1963, when its 543 acres were bought by the state of New York. The land was then leased back to the club for 10 years before the state took over its operation. All of its buildings still stand, and the clubhouse is a trout-fishing museum as well as headquarters for Caleb Smith State Park. Though a fair amount of natural brook trout reproduction takes place in the river, the fishery in both river and ponds is maintained today by periodic stockings from the Connetquot River State Park hatchery. It, too, is maintained as a wilderness park, and fishing is controlled by beats and permits.

Though Charles Hallock (1834–1917) was born and worked in Manhattan during this era (first as founder and editor of *Forest and Stream* and then as editor of *Field & Stream*, when it moved to New York in 1896), he was always a Long Islander at heart and often returned to his roots. His paternal ancestor Peter Hallock was one of a dozen English settlers who crossed the Long Island Sound from New Haven in 1640 and founded the village of Southold on Long Island's North Fork. By Hallock's time, the greatest period of brook trout fishing on Long Island was over and the days of free access to its waters were history. He didn't have to worry about that, however. His position, and his fishing prowess and knowledge, made him a sought-after guest at all of these clubs and private estates. An interesting account of "camp life" at the Wyandanch Club appeared in his book *The Fishing Tourist,* in 1873. It gave readers an intimate look into the lives of privileged trout fishermen on Long Island more than 100 years ago. It also lent support to other references that the Primes, who owned Caleb Smith's house, may have moved from it long before they sold it to the Brooklyn Gun Club, and may have rented or leased it to a group before the club was organized in 1873, or bought it in 1888, because Hallock's account appeared in print before any of these events occurred.

> The unusual facilities and attractions which these waters afford to sportsmen were recognized a century ago. The best localities were quickly appropriated by private individuals, who improved and [later] stocked them at considerable expense, and leased fishing privileges to city sportsmen at a fixed rate per diem, or $1 per pound for all fish taken. Several were subsequently secured by clubs, who laid out ornamental grounds, built spacious club-houses, and added largely to the original stock of fish. The principal of these is the South Side Club, near Islip, which comprises a hundred or more members. But there is a coterie of fifteen gentlemen, who enjoy at Smithtown, the use of angling privileges equal to those of private preserves.
>
> They have four ponds, of which the chief are Phillip's Pond and Stump Pond. The former is noted for its big fish. Their domain is an old-fashioned farm [Caleb Smith's], which literally flows with milk and honey. There are orchards that bend with fruit in its season, and with congregated turkeys always in the still watches of the night. Great willow trees environ the house, and through their loosely swaying branches the silvery moon may be seen glistening on the ponds.
>
> Through a wicket-gate and under overarching grape-vines a path leads to the "Lodge," within whose smoke-grimed precincts none but the elect may come. Its walls are hung with coats and old felt hats, and suits of water-proof, with creels and rods, and all the paraphernalia and complex gear of a sportsman's repertoire. Cosy lounges invite the weary; there are pipes and glasses for those who wish them; and in the centre of the room a huge square stove [Webster's stove from the Astor Hotel] emits a radiant glow. In the cool of April evenings, when the negro boy has crammed it full of wood, and the smoke from reeking pipes ascends in clouds, this room resounds with song and story, and many a stirring experience of camp and field. No striplings gather here. Some who stretch their legs around that stove are battle scarred.

Others have grown gray since they learned the rudiments of the "gentle art." Might I with propriety mention names I could introduce a royal party. To-morrow they will whip the ponds, and wade the connecting streams; and when their brief campaign is ended, you will see them wending cityward with hampers filled with trout nicely packed in ice and moss.

In the late 1800s other clubs from Brooklyn formed and bought tidal sections of this river, which meanders, so consistently forming oxbows that it was easy to dam their ends and form ponds. One group, the Nissequogue Club, with only 12 members, built a pond 1,800 feet long along the eastern side of the tidal portion of the Nissequogue River, just downstream of The Landing. These ponds paralleled the river's banks, and the copious flow of numerous springs, and a few man-made artesian wells, that came off the hillsides encasing the river provided water for them. The club members, desiring their brook trout to be more like the sea-run variety, built unique floodgates that allowed tidewater to enter but drain only to a certain level, maintaining a nearly full pond. This may have been the design of their most prominent member and president, architect Stanford White, whose untimely demise cut short his trout-fishing career. Most club members were wealthy New Yorkers who maintained lavish summer and year-round homes in the village of Nissequogue. The ponds were stocked with brook trout and members fished from platforms, de rigueur for this era.

The Stump Pond stumps that Forester described are long gone, and there's little or no trout fishing there today. It was never really good brook trout habitat, because its 12-foot-high dam didn't create sufficient depth. The impoundment continued to silt, and the dark bottom vegetation allowed the pond to warm too much for brook trout. Black bass were stocked in it years ago, and today it supports a fairly good warm-water fishery. The river, however, is today managed as Long Island's other world-class trout stream. Like the Connetquot, it has been preserved in a near-pristine state, and its waters receive continued and heavy stockings of brown, brook, and rainbow trout.

13   THE CATSKILLS

After establishing themselves on Manhattan, the Dutch quickly spread their patronal manors up both sides of the Hudson River and west across the mountains into what was to become Pennsylvania. Although they named almost every stream a *viskill* ("fish creek"), they never really developed an interest in an activity so unproductive as fishing for fun. They did have a grand penchant for exploring the interior and expanding their feudal-like powers over new lands, as well as one for naming every geographic feature they encountered.

The big river west of the Hudson they named The Great Fish Kill, but after the English assumed control of Manhattan in 1664 it was renamed the Delaware River, after Lord de La Warr, who governed the English colony at Jamestown. The Kaater's Kill, which flows into the Hudson below Albany and was the first route used by Dutch settlers to enter the mountains from the east, retained its Dutch name for a while, although the spelling was anglicized to Catts Kill and, eventually, Catskill Creek (a bit redundant). The river and its surrounding mountains have been known ever since as the Catskills.

On Long Island, good brook trout fishing was still available after 1850, but only to those who belonged to one of the elite clubs that purchased the best waters and restricted angling to members only. Even the smaller streams were often out of bounds, because by this time many had been dammed to create trout-rearing ponds. The owners of these early fish farms found a ready market for brook trout in Manhattan's restaurants. Thereafter, only a few ponds were open to anglers, for a fee. The tidal portions of some streams still had fair fisheries, although this, too, gradually waned because of dam building.

Even before the Civil War ended, frustrated anglers had begun turning elsewhere for their sport. There was fishing in nearby New Jersey, Connecticut, and Pennsylvania, but those states had enough of their own devotees of the willowy rod to fill their trout waters. The largest untapped brook trout population close to New York City lay northwest of Manhattan, in the Catskills. These rugged mountains lacked large, navigable rivers, and had thus far remained sparsely settled, their streams relatively unfished because of the difficulty of access.

The Catskill Mountains, a carved plateau that's considered an entity separate from the Allegheny Mountains, which end in Pennsylvania, are geologically unique because they were formed differently; this affects the organization of the watershed. A half-dozen peaks approach the 4,000-foot level. (Slide Mountain is the highest at 4,204 feet.) A score of lesser "mountains" are jammed between two major rivers, the Hudson River on the east (and its tributary the Mohawk River on the north) and the Delaware River on the southwest. While the peaks are not as high as those in the West, they do start almost at sea level, and this created a formidable barrier for travel into the interior. These numerous peaks and high-altitude valleys harbor some of the best trout fishing in the East, even today. Most of the Catskills' quarter-million acres are now protected in a preserve and park.

The Catskills' major watershed is the Delaware River. The Indians and early colonists considered the Delaware as starting at the Forks of the Delaware, as Hancock was first called. At that time, no one was sure which of the numerous branches was the longest and thus the Delaware proper, so they were all given different names. Its many headwaters, composed of several large streams and a plethora of brooks and creeks, all flow west into the main river. The farthest north is the West Branch Delaware (Mohawk Branch) River, which makes a sharp turn at the village of Deposit then flows southeast. In Hancock, on the main branch, it's joined by the East Branch Delaware (Papotunk or Popachton) River (Fadden). Upstream, the East Branch bifurcates at the hamlet of East Branch into the East Branch and (Great) Beaver Kill. In Roscoe, the Willowemoc separates from the Beaver Kill. In the village of Livingston Manor, the Little Beaver Kill, a small tributary, enters the Willowemoc from the south.

The main branch of the Delaware River flows southeast until it reaches the city of Port Jervis (Mohockomack Fork), where it turns sharply southwest, forming the border between New Jersey and Pennsylvania and eventually flowing into Delaware Bay. One large stream and a horde of smaller streams drain the southern and eastern slopes of the Catskill Mountains into the Delaware River. The other stream creating the fork is the Mahackamack or Never Sink. The Neversink River, whose watershed streams (Rondout and Basker or Bashe Kill) start on the southern side of Slide Mountain, flows southerly to meet the Delaware at Port Jervis. Upriver from Port Jervis, smaller streams include Mongaup and Ten-Mile rivers and Callicoon Creek. Schoharie Creek is the only major trout stream originating in the northeastern corner of the Catskills that flows north into the Mohawk River. Although 150 years ago almost all east-flowing streams from these mountains contained brook trout, today but one major trout stream remains, Esopus Creek, which flows to the Hudson.

The Delaware, West Branch, East Branch, and Beaver Kill were unique in that they were big rivers containing great numbers of brook trout. Big waters with brook trout were rare even in precolonial times, occurring only here and in a few rivers in Maine. Today, big rivers with brook trout occur only in Manitoba, Ontario, Québec, and Labrador. Today it's difficult to imagine the Delaware River—for example, the stretch from Hancock downstream to Port Jervis—as prime brook trout water. But it didn't look at all then like it does today.

The Delaware and Beaver Kill were reported to have "copious amounts of trout." Richard Jones, who operated a "fishware" on the West Branch "near the Forks of the Shehawken (Hancock)," wrote that in the late 1700s he caught "quantities of Eils and Trout, but no Bass, not so much as one." But Jones and others who operated fisheries below the Forks and up the East Branch did catch bass, "sea Bass," as they called them. These were striped bass, which today again inhabit the main river and even its watershed branches.

Before the incursions of Europeans, the Delaware was narrower and the water a bit faster, but probably not as deep. The forests and their deep duff, with topsoil intact, covered surrounding mountains like a huge sponge. Even the heaviest rains seldom raised the river's level appreciably or even clouded its waters. Flash floods were practically unknown. If they did occur, it was only in late winter or very early spring, with the breakup of river ice or when frozen ground couldn't absorb snowmelt. The river was narrower because the banks were squared and closer together, not eroded by floods. They were well defined, sharp, and steep, not lensing gradually up the valley's sides. The Delaware was a classic freestone river, its bottom filled with glacial boulders, graded stones, and gravel. Spawning sites, even in the main river, were innumerable. Silt was unheard of. The water was cooler. Dense conifer forests interspersed with hardwoods kept tributary streams cool and helped keep water temperatures low in the main stream. Even the main river was better sheltered, because trees grew down to the banks and overhung the river. Brook trout prospered.

Fishermen, searching for trout, began trickling into the Catskills during the early 1830s. Many were also hunters who came into these woods searching for deer in fall and winter. They fished the Esopus in the east and the Delaware, Beaver Kill, Willowemoc, and Saw Kill in the south. For accommodations, they usually lodged overnight with farmers or, when deeper into the woods, with local hunters in their "woods cabins."

Some farmers became innkeepers as well. A few, such as Merchant Lawrence, who had favorable locations in the larger valleys and outgoing personalities, emphasized the innkeeper part. Their hostelries became well known to anglers from New York City, Albany, and other urban centers. By the 1830s, according to Alf Evers's compendium *The Catskills* (1972), Milo Barber's inn, close to the Esopus in Shandaken, was a favorite with trout fishermen. By the 1840s, a writer for the *Catskill Democrat* wrote that "any quantity of trout may be taken by those skilled in that delightful recreation in the Esopus Creek near Barber's." Of course, these were brook trout, the only trout.

By the late 1830s, the streams and lakes of Sullivan County were well known to a small

Figure 13.1 "Brook-trout fishing in Sullivan County." The illustration was used to complement the poem "Callikoon" in Genio C. Scott's *Fishing in American Waters*, 1875.

but dedicated cadre of trout fishermen. Spreading the word of the area's fabulous brook trout fishing was Charles Fenno Hoffman. In 1832 he was beginning "a brief but notable career" as a poet, editor, and novelist, and wrote of a 6-pound trout being taken from Sullivan County's White Lake.

Artists and writers attracted to the Catskills also spread the word. One in particular was Thomas Cole, who was reported to have traveled through the Catskills with a paintbrush in one hand and a trout rod in the other. Landscape painter Asker B. Durand was fishing and painting from bases in local inns and farmhouses in the 1840s, according to Evers. "No painter-fisherman was more enthusiastic about the Catskills than Henry Inman, the fashionable portrait painter who delighted in working on Sullivan County fishing scenes. Upon Inman's death [1846], it was written 'in trout fishing especially he excelled. . . . A more ardent, accomplished or delightful disciple old Isaac Walton never had.'"

Thus ended the first era of fishing the Catskills—of fishing in its near-virgin state. Beginning about 1840, the Delaware River and its watershed underwent rapid and drastic water- and land-use changes that almost destroyed their ability to maintain a fishery. The change was so rapid that few anglers had the opportunity to sample the original fishing before it was gone. It literally disappeared before their eyes, before it could be documented to provide a realistic picture of what it once was. We have only hints of its greatness. The culprit? Woods-oriented industries.

The Catskills were pristine until 1765, when a Connecticut entrepreneur, Daniel

Skinner (Skinner's Falls), moved into the area. Skinner lashed together several huge, full-length white pine logs, added a makeshift rudder, and floated them from Cochecton down the Delaware to Philadelphia, where he sold them as ship's masts. What water traffic existed on the lower Delaware River moved only one way, downstream, and it was usually logging rafts. The river was not navigable above Port Jervis, at it was hazardous to that point even for shallow-draft craft. This lack of navigable waters preserved the Catskills long after more westerly parts of the nation were well settled.

The Catskills were heavily covered by an ancient climax forest of white pines and hemlocks. When the tall pines suitable for masts were gone, Skinner and other rafters who followed switched to any-sized pines, and for the next 50 years rafted them to lumber mills and fuel depots. By the early 1800s there came a lull in the river's activity, as the pine stands lay bare. However, about this same time the leather-tanning industry began to expand rapidly, as did the demand for tannic acid, heavily concentrated in hemlock bark. And so the remaining conifers of the Catskills were felled, their bark peeled and the logs left to rot. Huge rafts of hemlock bark went to the tanneries, and some wood to the sawmills. Rafting the bark and logs was a seasonal effort, however, and winter lulls slowed tannery production. Consequently, these raw materials were naturals for rail transportation. The Erie Railroad responded and built its first line along the eastern bank of the Delaware River, completing it in 1851. It hauled to the tanneries both cattle skins from Argentina, shipped via New York, and bark. As trees were stripped of their bark along the main rivers, the tanneries moved up numerous smaller valleys to reduce hauling distances. By 1856 there were 157 tanneries in the Catskills, 39 in Sullivan County alone.

The effect on the rivers and brook-trout fishing was devastating, and an account of it appeared in the July 1859 issue of the *New Harper's Monthly Magazine*:

> The banks of the Beaverkill and the Willowhemack, tributaries to the Delaware River, twenty years ago were famous for brook trout, and once were favorite places for the lovers of piscatorial sports. These haunts, where genius once found leisure from the toils of city life, with thousands of others which a few years ago abounded in game are now deserted, and fret their way to the ocean, stained by tan and thickened by the refuse wood that tumbles from the teeth of the grating saw.

The conifers were now gone. But after the barkers came the acid men, who scoured the hills for every hardwood tree they could find, even down to saplings. They cut them into "four-footers" and floated them down the streams for the furnaces at the distilleries, which produced wood alcohol, acetate, and charcoal. These chemical plants needed large amounts of water to flush the distillation retorts, and the corrosive effluent was disastrous to plant, animal, and insect life in the river. The last acid factory closed in 1955, at Horton, on the Beaver Kill. One charcoal plant is still in operation today at Deposit, on the West Branch Delaware River.

The practice was berated by the Forest, Fish & Game Commission of New York report in 1900: "Acid factories in Sullivan County were running acids into the trout streams in quantities injurious to fish. The foreman at Beaver Kill Hatchery was sent to the Spring Brook and investigated. He dipped out some of the water, placed in it a six-inch trout, and the fish died in four minutes." The commission did nothing about it.

The Erie Railroad not only carried freight but also handled passengers. It had active programs targeting fishermen, who were told they could board trains in Hoboken and in a few hours arrive in the "country's best trout fishing." A few hours was stretching it, however, because at midcentury the Erie's trains managed only about 15 miles per hour, especially after entering the hills of New York. Although the railroad gave anglers access to smaller streams along the Delaware, such as the Neversink, Mongaup, Ten-Mile, and Callicoon, getting into the interior and the headwaters of the watershed was still difficult.

Most trout-fishing forays into the center of the mountains started in Manhattan, with a boat ride up the Hudson to towns along the river. The earliest road west started at Kingston, once the state capital, and paralleled the course of Rondout Creek to near its source. A valuable look into what it took to fish these interior waters is found in the diary of a member of an active fishing club known as The Fishicians, a group of New York doctors who traveled far and wide to catch brook trout, often to the Catskills or Maine. The diarist was Dr. Walter DeForest Day (see "Day"), and his account vividly described the trip of four club members and two friends. They had planned a trip to Maine, probably the Rangeleys, but it fell through. Instead, they decided to fish the Neversink River above Claryville. Here are excerpts from Dr. Day's diary:

> As the spring of 1865 approached those members of the Club of Fishicians, who were located in New York, had several informal meetings all looking towards the streams of Maine as the ground for the next Campaign. [The Civil War had just ended and they used military jargon in jest.] About this time a letter came from the Judge, proposing that we should try the Neversink again. This was not altogether unfamiliar ground, for the club had tried it the preceding spring and found it wanting; it began to be, however, "there or nowhere," and as we recalled the scenes of our former "bout," its dark pools and bright shallows, framed in hemlock and laurel, together with the substantial comforts of bed and board, won us over.
>
> On Monday, May 22, 1865. Maj. Gen. Fitch and Brig. Gen. Day [the ranks were temporary and among themselves] broke camp at Catskill at 5 A.M. and took the H.R.R.R. [Hudson River Rail Road] without the loss of a man, as far as Rhinebeck. A pontoon bridge was thrown across the river [Rondout Creek, next to Kingston] by a fat Dutchman whose name our reporter has been unable to learn, and hurrying through the ruins of [the town of Rondout], they made a junction with Adams at about 8 A.M. of the same day.
>
> After a few informal remarks from the Admiral, upon the hat of Gen. Day which he then saw for the first time, the *impedimenta* were very carefully stowed upon the stage as nearly as possible, in the same manner as they had

been for the last twenty years, and outside seats having been secured the party started for Ellenville [now Route 209, 43 miles away].

For several weeks preceding, the clouds have "brought fresh showers to thirsting flowers" almost every day and the country was in full dress. The Secretary believes that this drive is unsurpassed for freshness and a certain kind of beauty. It runs through a highly-cultivated country, rich in nodding crops, studded in May with flowering orchards; over roving hills and across valleys which stretch down to the river [Rondout Creek] beyond which rise the not undignified ranges of the Shawangunk Mountains.

There were few incidents worthy of record at this part of the journey. A capital dinner was enjoyed . . . and there were no drawbacks on the drive excepting the bad state of the roads. There were a good many cigars smoked on the top of that stage before we reached Nappanock [just 3 miles outside Ellenville], which, owing to the driver's extreme humanity towards his cattle [property], was at the late hour of 3:30 P.M. (There is a great difference in drivers. Because "money makes the mare go," it's no sign that whisky and cigars will.)

Here we found a large body of yeomanry assembled, who informed us that the road was hard and suggested that "now the fish had got to suffer" but they did not mention anything concerning the "permanent bridge." Yenviniqu's two-horse team met us there, and having transferred our goods to it, with that decorum, and attention to detail for which the club is so justly famous, under the guidance of a youthful Jehu, we struck off into the regions of trout streams and bark peelers. [They headed north from Napanoch, following the course of Rondout Creek on what is now Route 55A, paralleling the northeast side of Rondout Reservoir.]

It was now approaching the hours of evening and the air was cooler, the roads better and our driver far more reticent. Our spirits rose with the occasion and for several hours we howled along, beguiling the time by recalling the many familiar scenes along the route, 'till the prevailing evening shades found us at the foot of the mountain, beyond which lies Claryville.

A horrendous spring thunderstorm stopped them from arriving at Claryville, and they were forced to spend the night in an old, leaky barn just 2½ miles short of their goal. The next morning they arrived at the Lament & Snyder Inn, run by a man named Lament, his wife, and her brother Captain Charles Snyder. Both innkeepers were active anglers, and during the next 10 days often fished with the physicians and at times guided them. The doctors would depart daily, fishing in pairs or individually and working the waters of both the East and West branches of the Neversink River.

The Grand total was 1,535 brook trout [for just seven days of actual fishing, and when stream conditions were high and muddy because of recent rains]. This does not include Otis, Draper, and Charley. The Judge being lame was not able to do as much as the others. No fish were brought to basket heavier than a pound, but the finest creelful was that of Adams, on his return from the first trial of the East Branch [of the Neversink].

The next afternoon [Friday, May 30, 1865] we rode to Ellenville and taking stage from there on the morrow we reached Rondout in the evening, in time for both boat and train. We shook hands sorrowfully with the Judge, and taking passage on the *Thomas Cornell* we moved smoothly and swiftly down the river between the banks of June foliage. It was a beautiful evening and we stayed on deck till the evening shades shut out the landscape and contracted our view of the smaller circle of our own individual comfort and so we went below.

It's interesting to note Dr. Day's mention of the bark peelers who were then active in both valleys of this famed river. Within the next decade, the forest cover surrounding the Neversink was completely denuded, first by the barkers removing conifers, then by the acid makers removing the hardwoods.

By the 1880s, the valley lay abandoned and ruined. It's impossible for anyone familiar with the Catskills today to imagine the extent of the devastation. Covered only with scrap, broken trees, slashings, and exposed boulders, the landscape looked as if an atomic bomb had been dropped, leveling everything.

And now a unique event began to unfold. Lumber companies, along with the farmers who grew produce for the army of woodchoppers and grain and hay for their horses and oxen, literally abandoned their land holdings, heading west to skin still more virgin forests and, in the process, defaulting on their land taxes. The lands were then offered for taxes owed to anyone who could come up with the money. In many cases, however, they couldn't be sold even for this, and New York State ended up taking large sections in the interior of the Catskills for back taxes. These lands in Ulster County became, in 1885, the core of the Catskill Preserve and State Park.

Prior to this, wealthy New York merchants and industrialists had paid pennies an acre for huge tracts of tax-defaulted land, as had groups of anglers—who formed clubs and bought out abandoned or dying rooming houses and workmen's hotels—setting the lands aside as private trout-fishing tracts. They were responding to the rush of city anglers who were now invading the Catskills. On the few remaining trout streams, competition became keen.

Salmo Fontinalis, formed in 1873, was the first Catskill stream club. The Balsam Lake Club was formed in 1883; the Fly Fisher's Club of Brooklyn was incorporated in 1895; the Beaver Kill Fishing Association in 1900; the Tuscarora Club in 1901; and in 1913 the Whirling Dan Club, which in 1955 became the Quill Gordon Associates. George J. Gould, son of railroad magnate Jay Gould, started acquiring land in 1890 and eventually amassed 3,000 acres on the headwaters of the East Branch Delaware River. On the Neversink, even the wealthiest clubs were too late. All of the small farms and timberlands had been bought up by a few wealthy men, each acquiring thousands of acres. These included Clarence Roof and his West Branch purchase in 1882, and Ralph Govin, in 1889, on the East Branch.

Today, for miles along the West Branch Neversink River and at the upper reaches of the East Branch, posted signs reflect only a half-dozen names. The few homes built here look like baronial estates. These large holdings could never have been amassed given today's land values, even by the wealthiest members of our society.

Private ownership of lands and streams directly benefited their recovery. Both clubs and private owners practiced real conservation and managed their lands with trout fishing as their ultimate goal. The forests eventually returned, but siltation and spring runoff forever changed the character of the rivers. On lower parts of the East Branch Neversink, where numerous small farms and homes stand side by side, the water quality and fishing are still marginal.

Accounts of fishing the Catskills before the Civil War are relatively rare compared with fishing reports of Long Island's more accessible waters. Sporting journalism was itself relatively new. The first real chronicler of fishing was John Skinner who, with the first issue of *The American Turf Register and Sporting Magazine,* in September 1829, began sporadically recording fishing and fishing trips between accounts of horse racing. The publication became a monthly and continued until 1844. Even in these early days of sportfishing, Skinner sensed a growing interest in brook trout fishing in the Catskills, and in the August 1838 issue published the following piece on fishing in the area:

> Notwithstanding the present month is emphatically the shooting season in this section, we doubt if the proportion of anglers is not greater by twenty to one. There are hundreds upon hundreds of our citizens scattered about the country within 200 miles of us, and probably there is not a brook, river, or pond, within that circle in which they have not wet a line. The largest proportion [of anglers] are whipping their flies over the placid ponds of Long Island, where the run of trout this season is of unusually fine size. Two or three parties, made up principally of "old hands," have lately made a descent upon the rivers of Sullivan and Montgomery counties, in this state, with immense success.
>
> The Williewemauk, Calikoon, and Beaver-kill, are three of the finest trout streams in this country; they are comparatively unknown to city anglers and are less fished than others of like pretensions within our knowledge. The brook trout are large, very numerous, and of the most delicious flavour. The rivers referred to lie between 30 and 60 miles back of Newburgh. To reach them from town, take any of the North [Hudson] River steamers to Newburgh, and the stage to Monticello, where you will find some good trouting. Five miles farther on, at Liberty, you will reach Big Beaver-kill. [Little Beaver Kill is a tributary of the Willowemoc.] Make your headquarters at Mrs. Darby's [not a name unfamiliar even today], and you will be sure to find excellent accommodations, and capital fishing. You will reach the Williewemauk, seven miles further on, where Mrs. Purvis will take very good care of you.

Figure 13.2 "Headwaters of the Delaware River," also from Scott.

A half-dozen writers of fishing books in this same period provided coverage more consistent and in greater depth. The first was John J. Brown and *The American Angler's Guide*, first printed in 1845. Brown had no compunction about borrowing verbatim the writings of Drs. Samuel Mitchill and Jerome V. C. Smith, De Witt Clinton, and even Izaak Walton, Charles Cotton, and other English writers, and adding them to his book with just a tad of credit. Brown wrote:

> The silver trout, or common trout, is found in almost all our clear, swift-running northern streams, and weigh from one to 15 pounds. A splendid specimen of this species of trout is taken in Bashe's Kill [Baskerkill], Sullivan County, New-York, said to surpass anything of the kind in the world. The stream winds along the western side of the Shawangunk mountain, through the beautiful and well-cultivated valley of Memekating, has a smooth gravelly bottom and so remarkably clear and transparent is it, that the smallest insect is perceptible in its bed.

The following is a poem opposite the title page of Brown's book, under the heading "Trout Fishing in Sullivan County":

> *We break from the tree group, a glade deep with grass;*
> *The white clover's breath loads the senses as we pass.*

A sparkle—a streak—a broad glitter is seen,
The bright Callikoon, through its thickets of green!
We rush to the banks—its sweet music we hear;
Its gush, dash and gurgle, all blent to the ear.
No shadows are drawn by the cloud-covered sun,
We plunge into the crystal, our sport is begun.
Our line, where the ripple shoots onward, we throw,
It sweeps to the foam-spangled eddy below;
A tremor—a pull—the Trout upward is thrown.
He swings to our basket—the prize is our own!

—Street

In 1849, Frank Forester, with his classic *Fish and Fishing*, was the next writer to be published, first in a London edition and subsequently in the United States. Forester devoted only passing references and generalizations to fishing in the Catskills, however, probably because of his lack of knowledge of the area. A displaced Englishman who was active in the field sports in Great Britain, Forester had a tremendous ego and considered himself the dean of fishing and hunting writers in the U.S. He was particularly upset that an American, especially a tackle-shop dealer he held in low esteem, had beaten him to the publication of the first general book on fishing in North America. He flattered Brown's work by assuming a similar format in covering the field, especially when it came to brook trout fishing, while at the same time he was criticizing it. I suspect Forester deliberately misinterpreted Brown's writings in order to have a point of argument—that Brown had meant "silver trout" only as a synonym for "common trout," and not as an indication that he was describing two separate species.

> Independently of DeKay's Salmo *Erythrogaster*, I find mention made in the "American Angler's Guide," . . . of the Silver Trout, the common Trout, although to none is any scientific name attached.
>
> I beg, however, to assure my readers, that there are no such distinction exist-ing in nature. The Silver Trout, which is stated to be found in almost all of our clear, swift-running northern streams, and to weigh from one to fifteen pounds, is in no respect a different fish from the common trout of Long Island; nor does that fish differ from the Trout in any other place in the United States, where the Trout exists at all.
>
> I wish greatly, that the author of the "American Angler's Guide" had given some authority for his statements that this fish is taken in this country up to fifteen pounds, or even up to half that weight. I have myself seen a Trout, taken in the winter through the ice, in Orange County, New York, which lacked but a few ounces of six pounds.
>
> The Bashe's Kill, in Sullivan county, to which the Silver Trout is assigned, is a pretty Trout stream, but no wise superior to a thousand other in this coun-

try; and, like all mountainous streams, is far more celebrated for the number, than for the size of its fish.

In all the streams of the south-west counties [of New York], which find their way southwardly into the Delaware, the Susquehannah and the Alleghany, brook trout are found in vast numbers.

Brown owned Angling, Sporting & Hardware, a store at 103 Fulton Street, near the fish markets of lower Manhattan, where he obviously developed some of his fishing lore. He rubbed elbows with everyday anglers who were as interested in catching trout as the well-educated, elite men of letters who often fished under the guise of "gentlemen." Brown was not university educated, for which Forester and other writers later attacked him. One described him as being "a poor tackle maker without classical education or social position." He may have meant that Brown made poor tackle. I don't think Forester meant that Brown was financially poor, because his store profited well from his writings, but that he was a tackle dealer to the poor, because his equipment was not always English nor the most expensive.

To Forester's apparent chagrin, Brown's first book was a great success and went through several editions. In 1851 Brown came out with a second book, *Angler's Almanac,* and didn't even bother to respond to Forester's criticisms in print. Brown felt fly fishing was not difficult to learn and that anyone was capable of it. In his store he sold fishing equipment to the Delaware River's raftsmen, "who were buying tackle and flies before they walked home, toting lines, oars and their fishing kits."

There's a problem. As they say in Maine, You can't get there from here. That is, Brown's shop was on the Hudson, the wrong river for Delaware raftsmen "to walk home along," unless they crossed overland somewhere to Port Jervis. It was from them that Brown alleged he learned firsthand what brook trout fishing was like in the Catskills. Again, Brown wrote:

In the months of April and May the raftmen and lumbermen from the Delaware are seen in the fishing tackle stores of New York selecting, with the eyes of professors of the art, the red, black, and gray hackle flies, which they use with astonishing effect on the wooded rivers of Pennsylvania. Those brothers of the angle who have never cast a fly are advised to pluck up courage and at once do so; it will add greatly to their enjoyment. Take our word for it, less skill is necessary to success than is generally imagined and pretended by fly fishers.

By the 1860s, anglers, aided now by a railroad, were regularly fishing trout streams in counties bordering the Delaware River, both in New York and Pennsylvania. In his 1862 book *Game Fish of the North,* Robert Barnwell Roosevelt gave the first account of the fishery's impending demise, especially in the outer rim area of the Catskills:

The brooks of Long Island, especially on the southern shore, abound with trout. But they are few in comparison with the hordes that once swarmed in the streams of Sullivan and Orange counties, and in fact all the lower tier of counties in this State, before 1851 when the Erie Railroad was built, and opened the land to the crowd of market men. I am proud to say I have travelled that country when it took the stage coach twelve hours to go twenty-four miles, and when, if we were in a hurry, we walked, and sent our baggage by the coach. Now you are jerked along high above our favorite meadows, directly through our wildest hills, and often under our best streams, at the rate of forty miles an hour, and yet people call that an improvement. As well might you lug a man out of bed at night, drag him a dozen times round his room, and fling him back into bed, and say he was improved by the operation. No one wants to be lugged out of bed, precisely as no one wanted to travel beyond Sullivan County; the best shooting and fishing in the world was to be found there.

When the railroad was first opened, the county was literally overrun, and Bashe's Kill, Pine Kill, the Sandberg, the Mon Gaup and Callicoon, and even Beaver Kill, which we thought were inexhaustible, were fished out. For many years trout had almost ceased from out of the waters, but the horrible public, having their attention drawn to the Adirondacks, gave it a little rest, and now the fishing is good.

The crash of brook trout fishing within less than a decade, sometime between 1855 and 1865, because of the rivers' misuse by lumbering and associated industries, was mirrored in later writings. Thaddeus Norris, in his enormous *American Angler's Book* (1864), dealt more with Long Island trout and almost ignored the Catskills. His only references to the area were comments on Frank Forester's retort to Brown's book. He also took Brown to task, but other than "the trout of Sullivan and adjoining counties seldom exceeds four or five ounces," he said little.

Even Genio C. Scott, whose 1869 book, *Fishing American Waters,* was so thorough in covering fish as far north as the Gaspé and south to Florida, hardly mentioned the rivers of the Catskills. He openly admitted that "I love Long Island and venerate its trout streams." He wouldn't have felt so affectionate toward Long Island streams if his status as a writer didn't give him carte blanche entry to the clubs. He did comment on stream degradation, however, especially on the Delaware, where it was prevalent and closest to New York. The period from about 1865 to 1910 was the lowest ebb in trout fishing in the Catskills.

Streams in New Jersey and Connecticut, and those west of the Hudson to the Delaware Rivers, and far beyond in both this state and Pennsylvania, contain trout, and many of them are well stocked. Indeed, it would be difficult to find a stream within a radius of a hundred miles from the city of New York which has not more or less trout in it. The paper-mills, railroads, bleaching-fields, chemicals of acids and gases, lime, manures, and numerous kinds of manufactories which cast their choking and poisonous debris and filtrations into the streams, have not [yet] proved sufficient to depopulate them of their speckled beauties.

JOHN BURROUGHS (1837–1921)

One of the Catskill's best-known brook trout fishermen, though little heralded today, was John Burroughs. Born in Roxbury, Delaware County, New York, he was a natural-science writer and poet and heir to Henry Thoreau's legacy. He was a teacher, journalist, farmer, and close friend of Walt Whitman, who discovered his writing genius. He was also friend to John Muir and Theodore Roosevelt, and may have contributed to Roosevelt's love of the outdoors. In 1873 he settled onto a farm on the Esopus River, when it was still an excellent brook trout stream, and called it "Slabsides." From then on he wrote mostly about nature, and his later works took on strong philosophical themes. His writings are today a storehouse of knowledge about these mountains and their brook trout.

He traveled widely throughout the Catskills, usually on foot and cross-country, or perhaps more accurately cross-mountain, and was a consummate "camper-out," as he called sleeping in the woods. I doubt there was a Catskill stream he didn't fish. Among his favorites were the Delaware, Esopus, Beaver Kill, and, of course, Neversink.

He wrote frequently for magazines and was popular with readers of the *Atlantic Monthly*. During the spring of 1869, he traveled to the headwaters of the Delaware River and in the July issue wrote "Birch Browsings." The following summer he returned and made an extensive crossing through the high peaks of the Catskills, from east to west. Part of the trip appeared in the October 1870 issue of the *Atlantic Monthly,* as a 12-page piece called "Speckled Trout." This was an excellent account of angling near the end of the second era of trout fishing in the Catskills, just before the hemlock barkers denuded the mountains and ruined the fishing. Eventually, exotic fish species would be introduced, producing the present era of Catskills trout fishing.

"It was three o'clock in the afternoon," Burroughs wrote, "when the stage set us down at a little country store and post-office [Big Indian] amid the mountains of Shandaken, where the Esopus emerges from Big Ingin [Indian] Hollow, and takes an eastward course for the Hudson."

Burroughs and two friends met several others who had approached the Big Indian crossroads from another direction in the mountains. After they arrived, they climbed the valley of the Esopus River on foot, up Big Indian Hollow, to its headwaters in Winnisook Lake, just a few hundred yards over the height of land, a talon of Slide Mountain.

On the way in they met two groups of barkers who were coming out of the mountains for the summer to find jobs haying on farms in the valleys and bottomlands. Their entire fishing excursion was plagued by showers and rain, and they didn't make the watershed divide until the next day. They were also hampered by black flies and "no-see-ums" (gnats).

"We struck the Neversink [West Branch] quite unexpectedly about mid-afternoon, at a point where it is a good-sized trout-stream," Burroughs wrote. "Aaron and I went upstream and the others downstream."

The description here is a bit puzzling, because the West Branch Neversink is just a trickle on the other side of the same hollow in which the Esopus also rises, in Winnisook Lake, which is at best just a pond.

It has a gamy look, and with boyish eagerness [he was 33 at this time] I undid my fishing-tackle and wet my first fly in its waters. But the trees were too thick and their branches too near for fly-fishing, so I took in the line and tried a worm, and found the trout small, but plenty and eager.

It was one of those black, small brooks born of innumerable ice-cold springs, nourished in the shade and shod, as it were, with thick-matted moss, that every camper-out remembers. The fish are as black as the stream and very wild.

After an hour or so, the trout became less abundant [no wonder], and with nearly a hundred of the black sprites in our basket we turned back.

That night they again slept in the rain without shelter. The next day they moved farther down the West Branch Neversink, where they found an abandoned shed used by barkers to house the horses and oxen that dragged sleds filled with hemlock bark to the main river. The stable was filled with manure but the loft still held hay; it was the first night they didn't have to sleep in the rain. This was dedicated fishing. The river was swollen from the rain, but the next day the sun shone and the river was almost back to normal. Then they trekked farther down the Neversink.

The clearing was quite a recent one, made mostly by the bark-peelers who followed their calling in the mountains round about in summer, and worked in their shops making shingle in winter. Biscuit Brook came in here from the west [really north]—a fine, rapid trout-stream six or eight miles [just under 5 miles] in length, with plenty of deer in the mountains about its head. On its banks we found the house of an old woodsman, to whom we directed for information about the section we proposed to traverse.

"Is the way very difficult," said I, "across from the Neversink into the head of the Beaverkill?"

"Not to me; I could go it the darkest night ever was. And I can direct so you can find the way without any trouble. You go down the Neversink about a mile, when you come to Highfall Brook [High Falls Brook], the first stream that comes in from the right. Follow up it to Jim Reed's shanty, about three miles. Then cross the stream, and on the left bank, pretty well up on the side of the mountain, you will find a wood road. When the road begins to tilt over the mountain, strike down to your left and you can reach the Beaverkill before sundown."

Burroughs and his entourage felt they needed the full day for the trip and didn't get started until the following morning. He had little faith in woodsmen's or hunter's miles.

Besides, I was glad of another and final opportunity to pay my respects to the finny tribes of the Neversink. At this point [where Biscuit Brook enters], it was the finest trout stream I had ever beheld. I have seen many clear, cold streams, but none so absolutely transparent as that. It was so sparkling, its bed so free from sediment or impurities of any kind, that it had a new look, as if it had just come from the hand of its Creator.

This is a unique description of a primordial Catskill stream. Never again would the Neversink or other streams in these mountains be without sedimentation, the single most devastating factor in the elimination of brook trout spawning grounds.

Declining the hospitality offers of the settlers [the woodsman], we spread our blankets that night in the dilapidated shingle shop on the banks of the Biscuit Brook.

The next day they found Reed's shanty, a temporary structure erected by the bark job-ber, or buyer, to lodge and board his "hands" near their work. Reed wasn't at home so they pushed up the creek, noticing the barkers' recent handiwork—hemlocks peeled of their bark and left to rot. By 4 P.M. they reached the Beaver Kill, at the southwestern base of Doubletop Mountain, and pushed downstream along its banks toward the outlet stream from Balsam Lake. En route they passed almost within casting distance of Tunis Lake (both are really ponds of less than a half mile at their longest), which today, like Balsam, still boasts pure strains of wild brook trout.

The trout were plenty, and rose to the hook; but we held on our way, design-ing to go into camp about six o'clock. Many inviting places [on the Beaver Kill], first on one bank, then on the other, made us linger, till finally we reached a spot, a smooth, dry place overshadowed by balsam and hemlock, where the creek bent around a little flat, which was so entirely to our fancy that we unslung our knapsacks at once.

The trout were quite black, like all wood trout, and took the bait eagerly. That night we had out first fair and square camping out,—that is, sleeping on the ground with no shelter over us but the trees,—and it was in many respects the pleasantest night we spent in the woods.

Even the bugs were missing that night.

While a devoted wet-fly fisher, Burroughs had no reservations about using bait. Worms were the easiest to use, he believed, but darters, small bottom-dwelling minnows, were best for catching big brook trout. If you had neither, the next best was a trout's eye, followed by the anal fin.

The following day they followed the right or northern bank of the Beaver Kill for about 6 miles, looking to "strike" the outlet creek from Balsam Lake. It was another 2 miles to Balsam Lake, where they found a "cow-house in good repair along with a dug-out and pad-dle. Late that afternoon, the lake was alive with brook trout jumping and feeding."

While Burroughs was an excellent naturalist, botanist, and ornithologist, as an ichthy-ologist he was wanting, and his knowledge of brook trout, while excellent in many respects, was lacking in others. He wrote:

> The trout jumped most within a foot or two of shore, where the water was
> only a few inches deep. The shallowness of the water perhaps accounted for
> the inability of the fish to do more than lift their heads above the surface. They
> came up with mouth wide open, and dropped back again in the most impo-
> tent manner. Where there is depth of water, a trout will jump several feet into
> the air [he's talking about brook trout because there were no other trout
> species in those waters then, or even today]; and where there is a solid, unbro-
> ken sheet or column, they will scale falls and dams fifteen feet high.

Also interesting is his description of the brook trout in Balsam Lake in 1870.

> There were two varieties of trout in the lake,—what it seems proper to call sil-
> ver trout and golden trout; the former were the slimmer and seemed to keep
> apart from the latter. Starting from the outlet and working round on the east-
> ern side to the head, we invariably caught these at first. They glanced in the sun
> like bars of silver. Their sides and bellies were indeed as white as new silver. As
> we neared the head, and especially as we came near a space occupied by some
> kind of watergrass that grew in the deeper part of the lake, the other variety
> would begin to take the hook, which became a deep orange on their fins; and
> as we returned to the space of departure with the bottom of the boat strewn
> with these bright forms intermingled, it was a sight not soon to be forgotten.

The fish were all about the same size, between 8 and 10 inches long, and their flesh
was deep salmon in color. Burroughs said that the flesh of most other brook trout was
generally much lighter. As Burroughs fished Balsam Lake, it again started to rain, but that
didn't seem to harm the fishing. In fact, it improved it.

> For nearly an hour, amid the pouring rain and rattling thunder, the sport
> went on. I had on two flies and usually both were snapped at the moment they
> touched the water. But the sport did not degenerate into wanton slaughter [I
> guess it's all relative to the times], for many were missed and many merely
> slapped the hook with their tails; and when we [Burroughs and Aaron] were
> a few short of a hundred, the blue sky shone out, and, drenched to the skin,
> we rowed leisurely back to camp.
>
> I have thus run over some of the features of an ordinary trouting excursion
> to the woods.

Today, trout fishermen are drawn to the Catskills more by the romance surrounding
the development of fly fishing there and the colorful characters associated with it than
by the quality of the fishing. New York's DEC has been waging a battle of containment,
but has been unable to redevelop the fishery. This has been the case since the early 1900s.
Stream quality, even with the reforestation of many open lands, is still slowly degrading.

The DEC cannot properly manage the area's streams until the surrounding lands are returned to a condition that will allow them to retain runoff water. Flash floods throughout the year continue to erode streambanks. In many areas, suitable spawning sites are subjected to continuous siltation. A surprisingly large contributor to this problem is road development, especially that of access roads to the private woodlots still being harvested. Poor farming practices also contribute to the streams' degradation in the forms of barnyard runoff and of the heavy use of chemical fertilizers, pesticides, and herbicides, all of which find their way into the streams.

Elevated temperatures in the larger rivers and streams make them unsuitable as trout habitat in crucial summer periods. Droughts in the last two decades have also taken their toll on trout populations, and at times have been so severe that it was almost impossible to find the rivers. The effects of acid rain in an already acidic environment have been especially harsh on brook trout in the smaller feeder streams at the heads of the watersheds. Brook trout at midrange elevations have suffered from the slow upstream advance of exotic species, brown and rainbow trout. At lower elevations and in the main rivers, even these exotic fishes are suffering from the introduction years ago of large- and smallmouth bass.

The misuse of land remains the biggest problem, however. In 1994, Trout Unlimited initiated a two-year research study of the Beaver Kill and its tributaries, looking into past use and management and the economic value of the rivers and their sportfisheries to the surrounding communities. TU hired Jim Imhoff, a biologist whose specialty is stream reclamation, to head the project. When completed, it should help the DEC develop both short-term and long-range plans for these classic Catskill streams.

In the meantime, the DEC continues slowly to acquire fishing rights to many of the Catskills' waters. A large portion of the famous streams, however, mostly in the upper levels, are still locked up by private ownership and unlikely ever to be reopened. At most they're lightly fished, and as such function as reservoirs for the fisheries. In lower reaches, many stream sections now are artificial-lure fishing only. In other spots, especially those open throughout the year, catch-and-release regulations mandate that barbless hooks be used. In those areas where fish may be kept, special creel limits are in place.

The center of trout fishing, if there is such a place in the Catskills today, is the village of Roscoe, which touts itself as "Trout Town, U.S.A." With its typically cool, damp upcountry summers, angler activity here remains high throughout the season, and the town is fairly alive with anglers. But come September, the last month of the season, especially when the fall has come early and the engulfing green mountains have become speckled with color—a lot like a brook trout—fishing fever reaches its highest pitch. If it's just too miserable weatherwise to fish, even after one has driven a long way, one can spend a few pleasant hours among a half-dozen fly shops or delving into fly fishing's past in the nearby Catskill Fly Fishing Museum.

14   THE ADIRONDACKS

F ew places in North America are as synonymous with brook trout fishing as the Adirondacks. To fully understand the role they've played, however, one must know something of the history of this part of New York State. It wasn't fishing for brook trout that brought civilization to this region, but land development and the economic exploitation of its mineral, timber, water, hydroelectric, and, finally, tourism resources. It was money that drove the wheels and money that destroyed the fishery, and it's money today, through the use of cheaper high-sulfur fossil fuels and the resultant acid rain, that threatens the very existence of the fish and forests.

These time-worn mountains in northern New York exemplify the ideal that surrounds the brook trout in the minds of so many people. The brook trout's environment is one of cool, clear freestone mountain streams tumbling relentlessly seaward, dashing among huge glacial-relic boulders, then gliding into sullen, rock-lined pools sheltered from the noonday sun by towering, ancient hemlocks. These speckled beauties also inhabit numerous small, placid, coffee-stained ponds, tucked temporarily atop shallow alpine-like meadows, their surfaces rippled only by gentle winds that curl the rims of lily pads. The ponds' edges are marked by isolated, erratic glacial boulders and struggling stands of cattail and sweet flag. The only sounds are those of a light summer wind moving through leaves of spruce and white pine, the berating chatter of a kingfisher as it swoops to the surface to skewer a troutling, or the incessant hum of dragonflies. It is, in one's mind, a place of countless bright, sunny Sundays.

For more than two centuries these mountains were known only as the "North Woods"—a term that took on added meaning as the industrial revolution swept across America in the mid-1800s. To many of those who left the farms and forests to labor in the cities, the North Woods reminded them of their heritage, a place they could always return to, though few ever did. The North Woods were idealized in verse and prose by some of this nation's most talented and scholarly writers. Even as a youngster in the 1940s, I remember my uncles and their friends referring to trips to the North Woods—in spring to catch brook trout and in fall to hunt ruffed grouse and white-tailed deer. The North Woods were always somewhere just beyond the rim of my imagination until I was finally old enough to join them. Ironically, the Adirondacks are not an ideal habitat for either brook trout or deer, nor were they ever. Their fascination lies in their being one of the last areas in the eastern United States to be explored and exploited.

Unlike other areas in the realm of brook trout, the Adirondacks are a readily definable entity, now conveniently surrounded by the imaginary "Blue Line." They rest atop an elevated plateau, the remnants of the oldest mountains on earth. Mount Marcy, the highest, has been worn to a 5,344-foot nubbin by time and countless glaciers. From the size of its granitic Precambrian base, geologists believe it may have once been the highest mountain in the world. Today, the Adirondack Preserve and Park is the largest such reserve established in the Lower 48. Containing 5,300,000 acres, it's roughly elliptical in shape, 125 miles wide and 160 miles from north to south. After its forests were stripped and rivers harnessed for electricity, an enlightened New York legislature drew a blue line on a map around the remnant wilderness and by constitutional amendment proclaimed that, as of January 1, 1895, it should henceforth be "forever wild."

Mountains have valleys, and in the East these are usually filled with streams. At times these streams stop temporarily to become lakes, then again turn into rivers, all to the delight of fishes and fishers. Where the mountains are relatively high and located far enough north these lakes and rivers are often filled with brook trout—as is the case with the Adirondacks. There are 58 peaks of 2,000 feet or more. Of these, 46 are higher than 4,000 feet. Only three reach above 5,000 feet, but six come within 10 feet of that figure. Most of the "High Peaks" are concentrated in Essex County, in the east-central part of the group. The remaining peaks are classified somewhere between big hills and low mountains, but it's among these that most of the better brook trout waters are found.

Two dozen rivers drain the Adirondacks in all directions, eventually flowing into either the St. Lawrence or the Mohawk/Hudson river system. The major rivers include the Black, Oswegatchie, Grass, Raquette, St. Regis, Saranac, Ausable, Chateaugay, Chazy, Hudson, and Sacandaga. Of these, the Raquette River, the state's second longest (after the Hudson), has the greatest watershed in the Adirondacks and offered brook trout their best environment. Because of the surrounding area's basic Precambrian granite-gneiss-basalt composition, the mountain's waters are highly acidic and are further acidified by leachings from coniferous forest bogs. The result is a soil-poor, glacier-scarred terrain with rivers, deep-water lakes, and ponds that were never especially fertile. Because of this and the resultant dearth of aquatic insect life, brook trout rarely grew large here, although they were everywhere plentiful.

Some big brook trout must have been taken by early trappers and the Indians who first inhabited these mountains, but the fish were seen solely as food, an alternative to a steady diet of venison and not trophies to be recorded. There are no records of 6-pound or larger Adirondack brook trout, though I believe they may once have existed in limited numbers. There are only a few records of brook trout reaching 5 pounds, although there were many 3- to 4-pound fish. To anglers of the mid-1850s, who were being dispossessed of home waters on Long Island and in New Jersey, Pennsylvania, and southern New England, a land with a horde of such brook trout must have looked like an angler's Valhalla. This is one reason that George Page had such a difficult time, in 1863, convincing a group of New York City newspaper and magazine editors that the 6- to nearly 9-pound brook trout he brought back to Manhattan from Maine's Rangeley Lakes were really brook trout. Until then, everyone had believed that the standard for brook trout was established in the Adirondacks: 5 pounds at most, even though sea-run brook trout of up to 10 pounds had been taken on Long Island.

If the Catskills had been a difficult barrier for explorers and anglers bent on reaching their interior, the Adirondacks—with higher peaks and a larger land mass—were impassable. Early explorers and trappers did penetrate the region, but always on foot or by canoes laboriously poled and lined upstream. Most of the rivers were navigable only on their lower, flatland reaches. Once a traveler reached the plateau, the streams were marked by numerous falls and impassable cataracts. Thus the region remained relatively unexplored until after the Civil War, depicted on most maps by a large blank space.

The Adirondacks were always hostile and devoid of year-round inhabitants. Originally, the northern edges were the realm of the Hurons, but they made the fatal mistake of asking Samuel de Champlain to help them make war on their rivals the Mohawks, who were part of the Iroquois Confederacy. The Iroquois returned with a vengeance and almost annihilated the Hurons. As a result, no tribes from Canada or New England dared set foot in the Adirondack region. Even the Mohawks avoided it in winter, because deer were never plentiful and winters were too cold and too long.

In 1760, the British took control of French Canada and began surveying their new North American domain. Ten years later, one of Sir William Johnson's (British Superintendent of Indian Affairs for North America) surveyors drew an interesting map of what later became the North Woods. Unlike most maps, which are traditionally oriented with north at the top, this one was drawn looking southeast, with Ottawa at the bottom, New Hampshire and Vermont at the top, and the settlement of Katskill Landing on the right margin. Only a few years after it was published, this was the direction from which the English had to view their lost colonies.

It was basically a property map, showing territories and the names of landholders. The Adirondacks were a large blank area across which was written: "*COUGHSAGRAGE*, or the *Beaver Hunting Country of the Six Nations* [Iroquois]. Through this tract of Land, runs a Chain of Mountains, which from Lake Champlain on one side, and the River St. Lawrence on the other side, shew their tops always white with snow but altho this one unfavorable circumstance has hitherto secured it from claws of the Happy Land Jobbers yet no one doubts it is as fertile as the Land on the East side of the Lake and will in future furnish a comfortable retreat for many industrious Families."

The closest civilization was shown along the northern side of the Mohawk River. The names of British officers appeared on most of the land plots, a king's perk for those who served in the colonies. There was even one for Colonel Sir William Johnson, a dedicated trout fisherman who had learned the sport in England and was typical of many visiting British officer-sportsmen of the time. The British officers' interest in trout fishing, especially with the fly, their stature as gentlemen, and their rules of conduct and class separation had a subtle but profound influence on the Americans who knew them. Trout fishing in early America was a "gentlemen's sport."

By the early 1760s Johnson had secured his "lot," several thousand acres of wilderness extending north from the banks of the Mohawk River to the foothills on the southern edge of the Adirondacks. In 1769 he supposedly built a lodge on Sacandaga Lake at the head of the Sacandaga River. Sacandaga is 2 miles long, 5 miles north of Piseco Lake— another lake that loomed large in the early openings of the Adirondacks—and 37 miles north of Little Falls on the Mohawk River. This was quite an incursion into a wilderness controlled by the Iroquois, even though they were English allies. The "lodge" was a summer place, and Johnson fished the waters thereabouts. "He was without question an enthusiastic fisherman," wrote Paul Schullery in *American Fly Fishing: A History*, "and it takes little imagination, given his background, to assume he used flies, but no record survives that he did. Austin Hogan [first curator, in 1970, of the American Museum of Fly Fishing and founder of the museum's journal, *The American Fly Fisher*] attempted to establish Johnson as our first fly fisher, including a claim that he was fly fishing as early as 1761 . . . but there is no proof."

In reality, Johnson never got the opportunity to fish his newfound domain extensively: He died in 1774. His son, John Johnson, an active loyalist, lost his father's holdings after the Revolutionary War and fled to Canada. Who took over the lodge in their absence is unknown, but one of the first fishing clubs in the Adirondacks was formed about 1840 on Piseco Lake, not far away. In just a decade or two, such clubs would become legion.

In 1847, 83 years after Johnson's lodge was built, a group of anglers heading deeper into the Adirondacks, supposedly looking for unfished (or even slightly fished) waters, passed the mouth of the Sacandaga River, where it leaves Sacandaga Lake. One man wrote an account of what he saw in an 1852 diary, which appeared in the *Spirit of the Times*, March 4, 1854: "As we go North it becomes more mountainous. We pass the 'fish house,' so called from its being a sporting retreat of Sir William Johnson's in the olden times. It is on the banks of Sacandaga river. There are a few trout here and the deer have gone long ago." Even at this early date, brook trout populations were in decline along the outer periphery of the Adirondacks, compelling anglers to go farther inland in search of trout.

George Washington Bethune, one of the era's most knowledgeable trout fishermen, was an accomplished writer and editor of the first American edition of Izaak Walton's *Compleat Angler* (1847). Bethune, who was reputed to have fly fished on Piseco Lake as early as 1836, was a regular on the lake and one of the founders of the celebrated Piseco Lake Trout Club. The club gained notoriety in books, magazines, and newspapers, especially in *The American Turf Register and Sporting Magazine*, which began to popularize Adirondack brook trout fishing, and in the *Spirit of the Times*, edited in the 1840s and 1850s by William Trotter Porter. The first promoter to describe fishing in the North Woods in books was John J. Brown, in his 1845 *American Angler's Guide:*

> At Peseco Lake, Lake Louie [Lewey], and Lake Pleasant, in Hamilton County, N.Y., and other northern lakes, much sport is had by boat trolling with the rod and reel [for lake trout], and parties are made up from the cities of New York, Albany, Troy, Rochester, and places in the vicinity of the lakes, for a two-week's tour in that beautiful wilderness of exuberant nature.
>
> New Yorkers who would visit the sporting lakes of Hamilton County, will reach them most speedily and economically by leaving the city by the Monday night's boat for Albany, and taking the cars [train] for the west at 7 o'clock next morning, about 10 you reach Amsterdam, where you take the stage for Northville. Here stay till morning, when the regular mail conveyance, which leaves but once a week, carries you to Lake Pleasant, the first of the series.
>
> Salmon trout [lake trout] are there taken as the ice breaks up, and even in winter through the ice. But if you value comfort and have no fancy for the keen air of those elevated regions (where the season is two months later than on Long Island), the four weeks from and after the middle of May are infinitely preferable, even if you regard the quantity and quality of the fish. The speckled brook trout do not bite until the end of the month.

It's surprising how little Frank Forester had to say about the North Woods in his 1848 classic *Fish and Fishing*. To him and his contemporaries, most trout fishing north of Long Island or the Catskills was restricted to Hamilton County, on the southern edge of the Adirondacks, where the prey was lake trout, not brook trout.

> I am not aware that Salmon [Atlantic land-locked] are ever taken in the Black river, the Rackett river, or any other of the fine streams, all abounding with the finest Brook Trout, which make their way from the romantic region of the Adirondack lakes and highlands, to the northward, into the basin of the St. Lawrence.
>
> Upon Rackett Lake, Long Lake, Lake Piseco, and other large waters, this mode of fishing [trolling] would afford great amusement; and the only objection to it is, that it is a deadly way of capturing fish. But it is not half so bad, and is in fact honorable and legitimate.

There is an advantage in trolling which I have omitted. You can lay the trolling-rod on the stem of the boat, and use the fly-rod for casting, and thus "kill two birds with one stone"—troll with one rod, and cast your fly with the other. In this way, I raised and killed with my light Trout-rod many of my best and bravest Brook Trout.

I will close this subject by stating, that from the 15th of May to the 15th of June, and from the 1st to the 30th of September, are the best seasons for trolling on the lakes in Hamilton county.

JOHN BROWN AND FAMILY

After the Revolutionary War and the destruction of the Iroquois Confederacy, New York settlers began moving north from Utica (Fort Schuyler), following the valley of the Black River to Watertown and north to the St. Lawrence River. Communities such as Boonville, Lyons Falls, Lowville, and Carthage formed along the river's course and became jumping-off places to enter the mountains. The most accessible of these routes was the Moose River and its three branches, which penetrated far into the interior and drained a score of lakes in the central Adirondacks. This was also the Iroquois route to Canada. The eight (Fulton Chain) lakes of the Middle Branch Moose River were connected by a short portage to Raquette Lake. The Raquette River, its outlet, flowed north to the St. Lawrence River.

Although trappers had known the area since the mid-1700s, the first real economic thrust into these mountains came about as an attempt by John Brown, a Providence, Rhode Island, merchant, to salvage a $210,000 land deal foisted off on his inept son-in-law, John Francis, by Aaron Burr and company in 1796. The reluctant land baron found himself possessed of 210,000 acres of Adirondack wilderness along the Moose River, which subsequently became known as Brown's Tract.

Brown had made his new son-in-law a junior partner a year earlier, but neither had any idea what he'd bought; neither had ever been in upstate New York. Brown, resigned to the deal, figured the only way he could sell this unwanted land and get his money back was to make one parcel agriculturally successful as an example, then sell off the rest to potential settlers. He built a 25-mile road, Remsen Road, from Forestport to First Lake on the Fulton Chain. In 1799, at what later was to become Old Forge, he constructed a dam, which backed up the Middle Branch Moose River, and built a grist- and sawmill. He offered free land to would-be settlers, and even subsidized their getting started.

By 1800, 20 families had built crude wooden cabins, cleared the land, and begun farming. The land was poor, the winters horrible, and the summers too short. One by one they left. When Brown died in 1803 in a coach accident, the colony was all but abandoned. His heirs determined that the futile attempt to regain $210,000 had cost him $300,000.

In 1811 Robert Fulton (of steamboat fame), as chairman of a state commission to find a way to connect the Hudson River with the Great Lakes, canoed and surveyed the chain of eight lakes on the Middle Branch Moose River. He told the legislature to look elsewhere for a link, but described the lakes' beauty so enthusiastically that they were later named for him.

In that same year, another of Brown's sons-in-law tried to do what John Brown and all his capital couldn't. Sarah Brown, who had inherited an entire Adirondack township after her father's death, married German immigrant Charles F. Herreshoff. Herreshoff and his wife lived on a palatial estate on the coast of Rhode Island. Their sons and grandsons would later become renowned boat designers and builders.

Herreshoff moved by himself to the abandoned site, had workers rebuild the dam, mills, and settlers' houses, and tried in vain to get people to farm the land. He even built a new road, Brown's Tract Road, to replace the abandoned Remsen Road. Farming was again a failure, but a vein of iron ore was discovered behind the Herreshoff "Manor," a six-room, two-story house with a wraparound veranda that overlooked the Moose River. Herreshoff, a poor money manager, soon depleted his wife's inheritance, but the iron ore seemed to have possibilities. He invested more money, mostly borrowed from other Brown family members, and built an iron-smelting forge. The mine never produced ore of a sufficiently high grade to make money, and its sudden flooding by an underground spring put an end to it. He committed suicide on December 19, 1819. The community was again abandoned and the road fell prey to the engulfing woods.

Herreshoff's nephew and John Brown's grandson, John Brown Francis, next inherited the tract of land. He too tried to get settlers to return, but no one answered his call. In 1830 he leased it to Caleb Lyon of Lyonsdale (near where the Moose River joins the Black) for fishing and hunting. Lyon acted as agent for Township 7, as it was known, but eventually bought the land himself.

In 1832, at age 65, Nathaniel Foster, a famous early Adirondack trapper and guide, leased the area from Lyons and moved into Herreshoff's manor, the least dilapidated of the abandoned buildings at Thendara, as the site was called. Failing health soon caused him to move to Oneida County with his daughter, however. He died in 1840.

OTIS ARNOLD, THE CHAIN'S FIRST OUTFITTER

In 1837, a farmer named Otis Arnold, who had for years struggled to make a living on the red sands near Boonville, tramped east for 20 miles over the abandoned and unused Brown's Tract Road looking for somewhere to start a new farm. He made it to the clearing near First Lake. The manor and nearby buildings were still standing, and Arnold saw his future. A few weeks later he returned with his wife, Amy, his son, Edwin, and his five daughters. The trek took them three days over a poorly built road much damaged by the elements. More than 300 acres of land had been cleared around the abandoned manor, but the forest was reclaiming it. Arnold settled in as a squatter, but that didn't seem to bother Lyon, who never challenged him. In the next 30 years, Arnold carved an empire,

Figure 14.1 Arnold's Inn offered the first sportsman's lodging and guides in the Adirondacks and opened the mountain's wilderness to anglers.

or at least a squire's realm, from the wilderness. By 1846, his children numbered an even dozen: two boys and 10 girls.

As the story goes, a few years after Arnold took over the mansion, a trout fisherman knocked on the door looking for food and lodging. "He was received with hospitality and accommodated with pancakes, venison and a bed. In the morning he paid a modest reckoning, complimented the hostess on her cookery and then departed—a satisfied patron." That was the beginning of the hotel business in the Adirondacks. Arnold fed and housed any hungry wayfarer "at reasonable rates." The building, though termed a mansion, was almost primitive at first. It stood in the middle of a cleared field a half mile west of where the road crossed Moose River. Word-of-mouth passes quickly in the mountains, and the manor became known as Arnold's Inn. It was also a tavern; Arnold kept a stock of liquors for those whose thirst went beyond springwater.

Arnold left the farming to his wife and their 10 daughters, while he and Edwin trapped, hunted, and fished. Both had an insatiable appetite for brook trout. According to Joseph Grady, in *The Adirondacks* (1933), "A former guide once declared that Ed had devoured enough brook trout during his life to re-stock the entire Adirondacks with mature fish." When Ed died in 1906, he weighed nearly 300 pounds.

As more anglers and hunters appeared at their door, Arnold and his son developed great reputations as guides, and their hotel for its good food and rustic comfort. Supplies were carried in from Boonville by packhorses, or by sled in winter. Horses were also provided for anglers arriving at Boonville who couldn't walk the 20 miles. In the span of just a dozen years, the Arnolds opened the mountain's brook trout fishing to untold numbers of anglers. By 1850, their business had grown so large that they could no longer handle it alone, and they hired area trappers whose reputations exceeded even the Arnolds', including such Adirondack legends as Sam Dunakin and Jack Sheppard.

Otis Arnold's 31-year career in the Adirondacks came to an abrupt and tragic end. In 1868, he committed suicide after killing visiting guide Jim Short in a quarrel over a dog. Amy Arnold died the following spring. Ed Arnold, declaring he could no longer live in the mansion, moved to Old Forge, where he took over managing Forge House, a new kind of resort hotel. The mansion at Thendara was again abandoned, this time for good. It was razed in 1898, having become a hazard to children in the growing village of Old Forge.

THE ADIRONDACKS' FIRST BROOK TROUT FISHERMEN

Anglers searching for sport began trekking into the Adirondacks as soon as Remsen Road was opened, but more came with the opening of Brown's Tract Road. Most fished for brook trout on Moose River, its three branches, and the numerous lakes they drain during the Arnolds' reign.

It was in the early 1840s that a few widely scattered anglers penetrated the interior of the Adirondacks. They followed closely on the heels of lumbermen looking for hemlocks, a source of tannic acid for the thirsty tanning industry, and miners looking for iron and other minerals to feed the industrial revolution. These first anglers left little record of their exploits in the Adirondacks, other than our knowledge that they were there and that the fishing was good. Unfortunately, the scant records left us no clear idea of the maximum size of the brook trout they caught from the then-virgin waters.

These first anglers came from towns and villages along the Mohawk River, on the southern edge of the Adirondacks—Herkimer, Little Falls, Dolgeville, Utica, Rome, and Gloversville. If they had been "gentleman" anglers from New York City, Albany, or Boston, and not simply fishermen in search of brook trout, their adventures would surely have been recorded in the press. And these fishermen didn't travel into the wilderness solely for brook trout. For the first time, lake trout were available to traveling anglers. While these fish's larger size was often the main attraction, their followers were somewhat less dedicated, and fishing for them usually required a boat. Few went exploring into the mountains toting heavy boats on their backs. The advent of the lightweight cedar Adirondack guide boat was still a few years away, and serious lake trout fishing would have to wait.

The desecration of Catskill streams had already begun, although there was still plenty of good fishing there for traveling anglers. For Manhattan anglers, however, it was almost as easy to get to the Adirondacks as to the Catskills. River and railroad transportation to Albany and, eventually, to Montréal were widely available well before they made it to Callicoon in the Catskills. Consequently, the recreational brook trout fishery in some areas of the

Adirondacks predated that in the Catskills. Like its premier period in the Catskills, however, quality brook trout fishing in the Adirondacks was short lived. The pathfinders who discovered these waters dominated the first period, roughly from 1835 to 1850. The height of Adirondacks brook trout fishing was the period between 1850 and 1862, and it was dominated by gentlemen anglers from the cities who could afford guides and all the trappings needed to spend a week or two in a real wilderness.

As on Long Island and, later, in the Catskills, anglers first concentrated at stagecoach stops. Inns and hotels sprang up to serve travelers—prospectors, miners, lumbermen, and, finally, fishermen. It wasn't until the next decade, 1860 to 1870, that resort hotels began appearing around the lakes. By 1865, there were more than 50 such way stations and overnight inns at the periphery of the mountains. Within the next 10 years their numbers would quadruple. In the more remote areas, quality fishing extended into the late 1870s before it was overwhelmed by the tourists for whom fishing was only another item to check off on their hotel's daytime activities list.

The road to Piseco Lake was the first pathway opened to the Adirondacks by serious trout fishermen. The long stagecoach trek began at Little Falls on the Mohawk River, following the valley of East Canada Creek northeast and, eventually, to the lakes. At first, the fishing on lakes and nearby streams was excellent, but without regulations or limits it quickly deteriorated. Easy fishing and big catches of both brook and lake trout were history by the time of the Civil War. And for many, the war interfered with trout-fishing plans. A historian for Herkimer County, adjacent to the western side of Hamilton County, lamented as late as 1856 that the only visitors to the Fulton Chain of Lakes (just 22 miles north of Piseco and Sacandaga lakes) "were a few amateur [sports] fishermen."

The North Woods Walton Club was the precursor of the numerous anglers' clubs that eventually gained control of large sections of the mountain's watersheds, either by purchasing the land or by leasing fishing and hunting rights from lumber and paper companies, some of which abandoned the Adirondacks after stripping the trees. This club was formed in 1857 in Utica, with 51 members dedicated to angling who came from as far away as Binghamton, Rome, Amsterdam, and Albany. Some members were already familiar with the North Woods, having been part of a fishing club established 15 years earlier on Lake Piseco.

At first the club was known as the Brown's Tract Association, after the vast 210,000-acre patent known as John Brown's Tract that surrounded it. Its members were some of the state's most prominent and active legislators. One of its presidents was General Richard U. Sherman of Utica, later state fish and game protector of New York. His son, James S. Sherman, became vice-president of the United States (1909–13). George Dawson, editor and angling writer (*Pleasures of Rod and Reel for Trout and Salmon*, 1876), and Alfred B. Street, nature poet and for many years state librarian, brought a different character to the club. Dawson confirmed that there were no brook trout of over 5 pounds in the Adirondacks. His fishing experience spanned more than two decades on the Fulton Chain, Raquette, and Saranac lakes. His goal, to catch a brook trout of over 5

Figure 14.2 A fishing and hunting party, using Arnold's "Road" to penetrate the Raquette River watershed. Note the Adirondack guideboat being carried by one sportsman, probably the guide. From Verplank Colvin's 1874 Report.

pounds, was finally realized in June 1874 when he caught a 7-pounder. However, he had to travel to Maine's Rangeley Lake to do it.

Joseph F. Grady, in a chapter on the North Woods Club in his book *The Adirondacks, Fulton Chain—Big Moose Region* (1933), tells us that out of this early fishermen's organization came the Bisby Club, or First Bisby Lake Club, an outgrowth of the North Woods Waltonians organized by General Sherman in 1878, several years after the Walton Club disbanded. In 1893, the Bisby Club merged with the Adirondack League Club, an organization established in 1890 that today owns nearly 2,000 acres in that area. Grady said of the North Woods Walton Club, "Their invasion introduced a distinct outing innovation—organized group recreation in the Adirondacks."

RAILROADS OPEN THE MOUNTAINS

What really changed the character of wilderness brook trout fishing in the Adirondacks and opened the floodgates to resort anglers were railroads. At first, peripheral lines skirted the mountains; later, spurs were built to haul out minerals, timber, and hemlock bark and return with cattle hides to feed the growing number of tanneries. Railroads were built first on the less rugged western side of the Adirondacks. The Utica and Black River Railroad left Utica, and after Trenton picked up the valley of the Black River. From Boonville to Port Lydon it paralleled and competed with the expanding canal system, then continued northwest through Lowville and Carthage. A spur ran off to Watertown, while the main line connected to the Watertown and Potsdam Railroad, then the Ogdensburgh & Northern, which ended at the Canadian border at Rouses Point. Stops at Boonville and Port Lydon connected with stagecoach lines that drove into the heart of the mountains. These lines then connected with steamers on the larger lakes, making the trips to the hotels even easier.

In time, numerous routes into the interior developed on all sides of the Adirondacks. The Boonville route from the west opened before railroads reached Boonville. The bulk of the Adirondacks' lakes and ponds lie in a swath 40 miles wide and 100 miles long, which trends southwest to northeast from Boonville to Lyon Mountain.

When the U&BR line arrived in the early 1840s, Boonville continued to be the best "jumping-off" spot along the rail route for trout fishermen and deer hunters headed for Arnold's Inn. By 1855, Brown's Tract Road, the packhorse trail that led from Boonville to the hotel, just before First Lake, had gradually been upgraded to a wagon, then a stage-coach road. The First Lake settlement had grown into the village of Old Forge, and was the gateway to the seven other interconnected lakes that became known as the Fulton Chain. From Eighth Lake, the easternmost, it was just a short portage to Brown's Tract Pond Outlet, which flowed into Raquette Lake. From here, Raquette River's vast watershed allowed travelers into the heart of the Adirondacks. The remaining lakes and ponds were interconnected by short portages. By 1886, the need to portage was eliminated by the construction of a road from First to Raquette lakes that paralleled their routes. Eventually, a larger dam than Herreshoff's was built on the Middle Branch Moose River, just below First Lake, that backed up the water to Fourth Lake.

TRAVEL WRITERS AND RESORT HOTELS

Reverend William H. H. Murray, in his 1869 book, *Adventures in the Wilderness, or, Camp Life in the Adirondacks*, alluded to the Arnolds: "The Arnolds, I understand, of the Brown Tract district, owing to an unfortunate occurrence last fall, have all deserted that section of the country. The house their father kept is now unoccupied, and whether it will be open this spring, I know not." By 1879, Arnold's no longer appeared on maps of the area. Murray was one of the few writers of that era who knew Arnold and the pristine nature of the Adirondacks. His readers came in droves, swelling the steamships and crowding stagecoaches and hotels. New resort hotels couldn't be built fast enough, and the Adirondacks would never again be the same. Branded in cartoons of the day as Murray's Fools, they weren't really looking for a real wilderness to rough it, but rather for a place to spend two or three weeks away from the cities. In the process they created a legion of

Figure 14.3   A cartoon comment in *Harper's New Monthly Magazine* (1870) entitled "Murray's Fools." Murray's guidebook promised all its readers a "comfortable wilderness" that had all but disappeared by the time his book was published in 1869.

resort hotels whose owners changed the wilderness to suit their clients and in so doing altered the brook trout fishery.

Even though Arnold's hotel was no more, Murray and other travel writers continued to use its location as a way point. The stagecoach route that paralleled the Moose River from Boonville to Arnold's abandoned hotel, 23¾ miles away, was well used and deeply rutted by the time E. R. Wallace's *Descriptive Guide to the Adirondacks and Handbook of Travel* appeared in 1872. A flood of guidebooks to the Adirondacks began to appear in the late 1860s and throughout the 1870s, but Wallace's seems to have been the least promotion oriented. Later guidebooks were little more than hotel directories. Such publications were needed because by 1875 some 200 hotels were scattered throughout the Adirondacks, in areas outside of the Blue Line, and on the roads that led to the mountains. In his book, Wallace also described the Boonville-First Lake route into the interior:

> "BOONVILLE," says a correspondent of the Utica *Herald* whom we frequently
> have occasion to quote, "has long been the common point of entrance to the
> Hunter's Paradise. The people of that village unite in making welcome and aid-
> ing pleasure parties. There, men can be found who have passed the greater part
> of their lives in the woods, who know exactly what the tourist needs and what
> he should leave behind. There guides, horses and conveyances are to be
> obtained. There is located the Hulburt House [in Boonville, built in 1812],

which for the last 30 or 40 years, has been the rallying point of pilgrims to the Wilderness. They have planned their trips, and where they have returned to celebrate their success with rod and rifle. The flavor of trout and venison is as natural to the place as fragrance to a rose."

At Mile 12.5, the Boonville stage made its first stop, where Brown's Tract Road first crossed the Moose River. This was the site of Abner Lawrence's Hunter's Inn, established in 1859; within a year he, too, was guiding fishing and hunting parties. Opposite his inn was Lyons' tannery (built in 1866) and a settlement of about six houses. By 1875, Lyons' barkers had stripped the surrounding forests of hemlocks, fishing and hunting ended, and Lawrence moved back to Boonville. When Brown's Tract Road first opened, the community was known as Fording Place, because Herreshoff hadn't built a bridge to cross the river. Later it was known as Moose River Settlement, and the site was the first chance anglers had at wilderness brook trout fishing.

> Several miles from Boonville, the road enters the woods, and when the traveler arrives at Lawrence's, with an appetite sharpened to a razor-like keenness, by the joltings he has received while passing over the several patches of corduroy occurring on the way, he is ready to dispose of the excellent dinner that awaits his coming at this Hunter's Inn. It is truthfully remarked that "no steam whistle or driver's call, will give unwelcome warning that the train or stage is about to start, before the appetite is dulled."
>
> The houses of the small settlement here, now called Moose River Village, are mostly occupied by the families of the employes engaged in the mammoth Moose River Tannery of Caleb J. Lyons, located at this place. Moose River at this point, is twice as large as W. Canada Creek, and is very rapid. From its principal sources, the North and South Branch and the Eight Lakes, it flows from Hamilton Co., S.W. across Herkimer, into Lewis where it empties into Black River, just above Lyons Falls. Those familiar with this particular route, will be pleased to learn, that a bridge now spans the river here, obviating a fording.

From here, Brown's Tract Road bumped past the northern side of Bare Mountain, then along two excellent (at that time) brook trout ponds. The road existed as late as 1947 as a Jeep trail, preferably someone else's Jeep. It was said that if the coach was ahead of schedule and no one objected, one could always try for a few trout at Hellgate Ponds (now Okara Lakes). The distance from Lawrence's to Arnold's, before again crossing the Moose River, was 11¼ miles. At the end of Brown's Tract Road was Forest House, on the southern side of the road and the banks of the Middle Branch Moose River, a long cast from the edge of First Lake.

According to Wallace:

> The road from Lawrence's to Arnold's is not as smooth as Nicholson [asphalt]

pavement, though greatly improved of late; so much so, that ladies now [1872] ride the entire distance on a spring board. Some, however, still prefer pack-horses. When within 2½ miles of Arnold's, by turning right from the road and proceeding 20 or 30 rods, the Hell Gate Lakes, two secluded little ponds, 30 or 40 rods apart, may be visited. One mile N. W. of them lies another small lake [Grass Pond].

"Arnold's," says our spicy correspondent, "is dear to the hearts of the members of the old Walton Club [disbanded circa 1870], and of the hundreds of others, who have enjoyed the shelter of the house." North and east of it the country is as wild, as on the day when Christopher Columbus shipped his baggage for America. From Arnold's the tourist may either follow the smooth and pleasant road to the Forge (2.5 miles), or proceed 50 or 60 rods east to Moose River, and gain the same point by boat (4 miles).

From the bridge where the road crosses the river, ½ mile beyond Arnold's, a good portage extends 1 mile southeast to Nick's Lake, one of the prettiest sheets in these woods. It is only about 1 mile long, but its shores are so serrated with bays and promontories, that it is some 6 miles around it. Trout are plentiful in its waters, which empty into [South Branch] Moose River. It's east inlet flows from a sweet little pond hardly three boat-lengths distant. Two and a half miles southeast of Nick's Lake is another beautiful little pond, well supplied with speckled trout.

Another well-known writer and editor of the era was Charles Hallock, whose guidebook, *The Fishing Tourist,* was oriented more toward anglers than sightseeing tourists. It appeared in 1873, just a year after Wallace's first edition. Hallock was influenced by Wallace's description of a trip to Arnold's, but the two excerpts provide today's angler with a better picture of what it was like to pursue brook trout in that period. Said Hallock:

From the southwest the approach is via Boonville, on the Utica and Black River R.R. A wagon-road (so called) leads directly to the Fulton chain of lakes, into the heart of what is known as "John Brown's Tract"; but it is practicable for wheels only for about 14 miles, or a little beyond Moose River. Thence to Arnold's old sporting-house, 8 miles. The success of the journey must depend upon one's ingenuity in surmounting obstacles. The difficulties of the way are graphically portrayed by the pen and pencil of T. B. Thorpe, in the 19th volume of *Harper's Magazine;* though the road has been considerably improved since the article was published. Some few boulders have sunk into the mud, and trunks of trees that then crossed the road have rotted away, so that it is no longer necessary to go around them. Consequently the distance is somewhat shortened, and the road made more level.

From Arnold's there is a navigable water-course all the way to Raquette Lake, a distance of 30 miles, broken by three portages or "carries," whose aggregate length is 2¾ miles. This "John Brown's Tract" is about 20 miles square and contains 210,000 acres. It is one of the finest fishing and hunting grounds in the whole section. Here, as elsewhere, the sportsman must turn a little aside from the main thoroughfare if he would find reward commensurate with his endeavors. The adjacent country is hilly, though not strictly mountainous; but there is an isolated peak called "Bald Mountain," which is everywhere the most prominent feature of the landscape.

From the west there are [other] entrances to the wilderness via Lowville and Carthage, stations on the Black River Railroad, by tolerable wagon roads which converge at Lake Francis, a distance of 18 or 20 miles; thence by road and stream 22 miles to Beach's Lake, and thence 9 miles to Raquette Lake. This route is not much traveled, and the sport will not pay for the hardships of the journey. Boonville is the better starting-point.

OTHER ROUTES INTO THE ADIRONDACKS

Moose River wasn't the only way into the heart of the Adirondacks. About the time (1799) John Brown was having his dam built across the Middle Branch, a few farmers had penetrated the northeastern corner of the mountains by following the valley of the Saranac River and were homesteading in North Elba, just south of Lake Placid. Nine years later they discovered iron ore, and a mining conglomerate built an iron smeltery on location. The discovery of iron sent a flurry of prospectors everywhere into the wilderness in search of other deposits.

North Elba's miners established a wagon road between Keesville and the Port Kent terminal on Lake Champlain by paralleling the Ausable River. About midcentury, the Delaware & Hudson Railroad built a spur line to Ausable Forks that connected to the New York & Canada along Lake Champlain. The wagon road from Ausable Forks to North Elba was the first access, other than foot trails, into this corner of the mountains. It also opened the Ausable's fabulous brook trout fishery to anglers, who could now take a coach from Ausable Forks to North Elba and fish Mirror Lake, Lake Placid, and the headwaters of the Saranac as well as the Ausable River.

The next incursion from the east was stimulated by the discovery of large iron ore deposits farther south of North Elba, near what became Henderson Lake. However, the way chosen into this spot was from the south. The Adirondack Railroad formed and built a line from Saratoga Springs north, following the course of the Hudson River. It got as far as the North River (the original name for the Hudson River) before running out of funds. The rest of the route was along a foot trail that eventually became a wagon, then a coach, road to Lower Iron Works at Tahawas. This road opened the brook trout fishery on the upper Hudson and Boreas rivers, and on numerous lakes, ponds, and tributary headwaters of the Cedar River.

The discovery of iron and other minerals early in the 1800s meant that the area had to be mapped. William Learned Marcy, in his third term as governor of New York, persuaded the legislature that the mountains should be surveyed. He's credited with the statement, "To the victor belong the spoils," and that's how he viewed the mineral wealth of the mountains. Professor Ebenezer Emmons, a Williams College geologist, mineralogist, and botanist, was given the task, and in the summer of 1832 he led a party into the High Peaks region. They cut a trail along the Opalescent River, the Hudson's eastern branch, and noted that there were no brook trout in the stream. Brook trout had never successfully ascended the cataract leading to it, and it was too high for glacial refugia to reach it with their lodes of brook trout. It was later stocked. Two days after leaving base camp at the McIntyre Iron Works, at 10 A.M. on August 5, 1837, Emmons reached the summit of New York's highest mountain (5,344 feet), naming it Mount Marcy after his patron.

"The cluster of mountains in the neighborhood of the Upper Hudson and AuSable rivers, I propose be called the *Adirondack Group,* a name by which a well-known tribe of Indians who once hunted here, may be commemorated." The tribe he referred to was the Hurons, who were often so destitute for food that they were relegated to eating tree bark and buds. *Adirondack,* in their language, meant "bark eaters." Emmons continued his work until 1842. His contribution to the topography and geology of the area left much to be desired.

One of the better journalists of the pre–Civil War period who visited the area was H. Hammond. He fished the Raquette River for brook trout, and in 1857 published a book about the Adirondacks, *Wild Northern Scenes.* He wrote of the river: "It flows on its tortuous and winding way for a hundred miles though unbroken forests, with all the old things standing in their primeval grandeur along its banks. The woodsman's axes has not marred the loveliness of its surroundings, and no human hand for all that distance has been laid upon its mane, or harnessed it for the great wheel, making it a slave, compelling it to be utilitarian, to grind corn and throw the shuttle and pin." He knew, however, that such wilderness wouldn't last much longer. His book contributed to the Reverend William H. H. Murray's motivation to visit these mountains a decade later.

The real job of mapping the Adirondacks was eventually given to Verplanck Colvin. On his own, Colvin had already started the task in the late 1860s. In 1870, the state gave him the contract for an official topographical survey. By this time, however, it wasn't the mining industry that needed to know what the mountains contained but a new business, the waterpower industry. Colvin worked incessantly in the mountains for nearly a decade and accomplished much, but he didn't quite finish the work (Colvin). Today, there are more lakes and ponds in these mountains than when the French first entered the interior in the 1700s, thanks to the water demands of canals and hydroelectric power. Sadly, each fall they're drawn down—to the detriment of brook trout and, now, salmon.

That the trout in the Adirondacks were not monsters has been pretty well established. That they were numerous might still bear support. Here's a tale from Wallace's guidebook about fishers and would-be fishers in the mid-1870s:

FISHY, BUT TRUE—Professor H., of Mass., with A. M. Sabin for a guide, started from Poplar Point, a noted camping ground near Spring Cove, on the St. Regis River; went to the head of the Level, passed around the rapids, took a boat and went to the head of the 4 Mile Level, supplied with the needful tackle to take the finny tribe with that exciting device—the fly. The Professor with his 224 lbs. of mortality, did not aspire to wet feet or a tramp; so the boat was anchored on the rifts, and out went his fly for a victim. The instant it touched the water it was taken by a trout; the Professor pulled—but no trout; again he made the effort—but to no purpose. Friend H. had "fish" on the brain, his tackling was all right, but no lazy pull takes a trout with a fly. In this dilemma he called his guide, who was near by, bagging trout at every pull—"I say, tell me how to catch them; they snap and are off like lightning." The guide, with a knowing wink, says, "twitch when they bite." The short lesson was soon learned, and an hour's time supplied them with 300 nice trout. They then landed, made a bough cabin, did justice to a bountiful repast of trout, and camped by a rousing fire for the night. In a few moments the Professor made the solitude sonorous, if not melodious. At early dawn, they added to their stock, and at sunset reached camp with 500 trout; pretty good for a 2 days' trip.

In 1873, Charles Hallock wrote this in his own fishing guidebook, *The Fishing Tourist*:

Last summer [1872], the *New York Times* published an article deprecating the "ruinous publicity" given by Rev. W. H. H. Murray to the sporting attractions of the Adirondacks, and lamenting that this exceptional region should have "fallen from that estate of fish and solitude for which it was originally celebrated." Railroads, stages, telegraphs and hotels, it says, have followed in the train of the throng who rushed for the wilderness. The desert has blossomed with parasols, and the waste places are filled with picnic parties, reveling in lemonade and sardines. The piano has banished the deer from the entire region, and seldom is any one of the countless multitude of sportsmen fortunate enough to meet with even the track of a deer.

It is not without a careful consideration of the question in all its aspects, that I have ventured to publish my Reference Book. But, there is not much danger of the musquito swamps and inaccessible fastnesses of the Adirondacks being invaded by "good society." The crowd comes only where the way is made easy, and because it is easy. It follows the natural watercourses and avoids the tedious "carries." It halts where the sporting-houses invite, and selects those which provide the most abundant creature comforts.

Hallock had hoped his book would be as successful as Murray's, and tried to avoid being criticized for its similarities to the reverend's book. As a result, he was far less critical of Murray than other writers.

Murray's book attracted its crowds, not because a legion of uninitiated sportsmen and ambitious Amazons stood waiting for the gates of some new Paradise to open, but because it presented the wilderness in new aspects and fascinating colors. It showed how its charms could be made enjoyable even for ladies. It was a simple narrative of personal experience and impressions, written *con amore*, with a vigor and freshness that touched a sympathetic chord in the hearts of its readers. It aroused a latent impulse and provided a new sensation for those who had become surfeited by the weary round of watering-place festivities. It has accomplished much good by encouraging a taste for field sports and that health-giving exercise which shall restore the bloom to faded cheeks and vigor to attenuated valetudinarians.

What though the door-posts of Adirondack hostelries be penciled o'er with names of those who fain would seek renown among the list of mighty Nimrods; what though the wilderness blooms with radiant parasols, and pianos thrum throughout the realm; there yet is ample room for the sportsman, and solitude sufficient for the most sentimental lover of nature. The very contour of the land makes roads impracticable. It is everywhere broken up into mountain ranges, groups, and isolated peaks, interspersed with innumerable basins and water-courses, nearly all connecting. These are the heads and feeders of numerous rivers that flow to every point of the compass, and after tumbling down the lofty water-shed in a series of rapids, fall into the lakes or ocean. These are the sources of the Hudson, the Oswegatchie, Black River, Raquette, St. Regis, AuSable, and Saranac. It is only where a valuable iron deposit makes it pay to surmount the natural obstacles, that some solitary tramway penetrates into the heart of the mountains. The few fertile districts and tillable spots are likely to remain unoccupied for lack of highways to a market, unless, perchance, the growth of succeeding centuries drives an overflowing population to the very crags of this American Switzerland.

APOLLOS "PAUL" SMITH

No book about brook trout fishing in the Adirondacks would be complete without mention of Apollos Smith. Though a man of great foresight and an early Adirondack visionary, even he could never have imagined that the rickety frame house he built on the shores of Lower St. Regis Lake would someday become Paul Smith's College, then a part of the New York State university system specializing in hotel management. He turned a $300 investment into a hotel enterprise that made him a millionaire when he died in 1912.

Born in Milton, Vermont, on the eastern shore of Lake Champlain, in 1825, Apollos "Paul" Smith worked as a young man on the canal boats that plied the Northern Canal, connecting Lake Champlain with the Hudson River. During the off-season, Smith would cross the lake and head for the uninhabited Adirondacks to hunt and trap. He stayed at John Merrill's House, the only structure on Loon Lake, on the northern edge of the Adirondacks. Merrill's House became a place for fishers and hunters, and Merrill often called on Smith, while hunting and trapping there, to guide city "fellers." Smith was so successful in guiding that his sports suggested he build his own hunting place.

In 1852 he bought 200 acres near Loon Lake for $1.50 per acre. On the North Branch Saranac River, in a sheltered ravine, he built "Hunter's Home." Even before Smith arrived, the river and the numerous ponds of the small tributaries that feed it had developed a reputation for "superior brook trout fishing." There was a large array of brook trout waters in the area, and the headwaters of the St. Regis and Salmon rivers were just over the mountain. The house was described as being "very primitive," but that's what most of his sports, mainly city doctors and lawyers, seemed to prefer. It added to the "wilderness" experience. It had a large living room and kitchen, with 10 thinly partitioned sleeping quarters under the gabled roof upstairs. It was strictly a man's retreat, exactly what his elite clientele wanted.

Hunter's Home was an immediate success, in part because of the excellent brook trout fishing but mostly because of the atmosphere Smith created. Board and lodging was $1.25 per day, and a guide, Smith at first, was $2 per day. The bar consisted of a barrel of rye whiskey and a tin dipper on a "stout string." Drinking was on the honor system, and a dip cost four coppers (pennies), because nickels were not in general use at that time.

After the fishing and hunting was used up around Hunter's Home, Smith decided to relocate. In September 1858, on the shores of uninhabited Lower St. Regis Lake, just 12 miles to the southwest of Hunter's Home, he built another lodge, one that would accommodate the families of his fishers and hunters. With $300 and a loan from Dr. Hezekiah B. Loomis, a wealthy New York physician and constant client, he bought 50 acres on the lake. The following summer he opened a hotel that eventually became the best-known summer resort hotel in the United States. It developed its reputation because Smith was constantly expanding both the acreage and the size of the hotel. He eventually owned nearly 40,000 acres. Because he was "land-poor" at the time, he just missed buying another 40,000 acres, at $1.50 per acre; they were scoffed up by William G. Rockefeller.

Smith sensed the coming times. His transition from the wilderness home to a resort hotel reflected how quickly the Adirondacks were changing. The end of that 10-year period, in 1860, was also the end of the true wilderness. While it ushered in a new era, it also marked a decline in the brook trout fishery. One of the best writers of the day and an avid brook trout fisher, W. C. (William Cowper) Prime, editor of the *New York Journal of Commerce* and president of the Associated Press, was a witness to the change. One of the best-written fishing books of the era was his *I Go A-Fishing*, published in 1873; it contained two chapters about fishing at Paul Smith's. The first, "The St. Regis Waters in Olden Times," was an account of fishing on Follansby Pond (Lower St. Regis Lake) and connecting Spitfire Pond (Lake) in 1860, when the hotel was just a year old and brook trout fishing was near virgin. The trip from Port Kent, 55 miles away, was made by horse-drawn wagon. He had no trouble taking 2-pound trout with wet flies.

The second chapter was "St. Regis Waters Now." It described his return 12 years later, in 1872, at the age of 47, to the mountains in hopes of improving his health. He was most astonished at the growth of the hotel, which by then could accommodate 150 guests. Ironically, the fishing wasn't that bad, according to the daily record he kept. Brook trout were still plentiful, but the largest was only 1¾ pounds; he also had to travel farther from the hotel and fish longer to catch as many fish. But, that, too, was changing rapidly.

Another description of what life was like in a resort hotel was written by S. R. Stoddard in his guidebook *The Adirondacks: Illustrated*, published in 1879:

> Paul Smith's is a surprise to everybody; an astonishing mixture of fish and fashion, pianos and puppies, Brussels carpeting and cowhide boots. Surrounded by a dense forest; out of the way of all travel save that which is its own; near the best hunting and fishing grounds, a first-class watering-place hotel, with all the modern appliances, and a table that is seldom equalled in the best city hotels, set right down in the midst of a "howling wilderness." Around the house the timid deer roam, within the rest. Without, the noble buck crashes through the tangled forest; within, his noble namesake straddles elegantly over the billiard table and talks horse. Out on the lake the theoretical veteran casts all manner of flies; in the parlors the contents of huge Saratoga trunks are scientifically played, and the nets are spread for a different kind of fish. Poodles, pointers, setters and dandies and others of the species are found. Feathers and fishing rods, point lace and pint bottles, embryo Nimrods who never knew a more destructive weapon than a yardstick—hung all around with revolvers and game-bags and cartridge-pouches and sporting guns are fearfully and wonderfully made, and which would take a first-class engineer to work; for you must know that here danger is to be faced, that even the ladies bare arms, and are said at such times to be very dangerous sportsmen indeed.

THE NEW ADIRONDACKS

It seems inconceivable that anyone in 1873 could have imagined the drastic changes that would occur within a decade. By the 1880s, the Adirondack wilderness was a thing of the past. The mountains, lakes, and rivers had been badly abused by loggers, miners, railroads, tanneries, and water-oriented industries. The latter at first demanded canal water and later hydroelectric water. Tourism and hotel building on an unprecedented scale also took their toll on the pristine aspect of the area. Everyone was taking a share of the spoils before they were altogether gone. Only fishermen, and to a lesser extent hunters, finally came to the rescue as the mountains' first conservationists. They would eventually be joined by hikers, birders, campers, and naturalists.

It was the lure of the great plenitude of trout and game that drew sportsmen from the cities to the North Woods or, now, the North Country. They were the first to be disappointed by the loss, and among them were the first persons and groups to speak out against the abuse of the woods and waters and their fish and game. It was the abuse of the mountains' native brook trout that became the symbol for those wanting to preserve the mountains. The depletion of most of the rivers, pools, ponds, and lakes occurred in their lifetime, making the cause that much more poignant.

Charles Hallock, one of the first to decry the abuses, gained support from Fred Mather, a leading fish culturist, and others, even Governor Theodore Roosevelt. Artists such as William Tait, Frederick Remington, Winslow Homer, Louis Rhead, and S. F. Denton lent strong support to the idea of establishing the Adirondacks as a wilderness preserve. In their scenes of the area, of course, the fish were almost always leaping brook trout.

In 1868, this group's pressure forced the legislature to establish the state's first conservation agency, the Fisheries Commission. The commission was given the task of studying the sources of noted fishing streams in the Adirondacks and the ill effects of the destruction of the forests. By the 1880s, the commission had become infatuated by fish culture, probably because Seth Green was one of the commissioners. Green resigned after he created a hatchery department, was named its director, and built several hatcheries in the state. To the detriment of brook trout, he also stocked the Adirondacks' rivers and lakes with rainbow trout and black bass. The commission underwent several changes in name and direction in the following decades, but was instrumental in 1894 in establishing the Adirondack Forest Preserve.

Since the turn of the century, the history of the brook trout and other fisheries in the Adirondacks has been one of a constant struggle for survival in an environment that continues to deteriorate under humanity's enduring abuses. Acid rain has accomplished what miners and lumber companies could not. In the last three decades, emanating from sources hundreds of miles away from the Adirondacks, acid rain has eliminated brook trout from more than half of the waters in which they existed in 1960.

15 MAINE'S RANGELEY LAKES

W ithin the borders of the United States, brook trout reached their greatest development in both size and numbers in the Rangeley Lakes region of northwestern Maine. The brook trout fishery in these headwaters of the Androscoggin River was probably on a par with that of the Nipigon region of western Ontario. It's difficult to say with authority which produced the most or the largest fish, because the environments were so vastly different. Suffice it to say that there were plenty of brook trout in both. And both produced superlative examples of brook trout that pushed the fish's maximum attainable size to the extremes.

Direct comparisons of the two systems are unrealistic, primarily because the Nipigon fish developed under riverine conditions and the Rangeley fish in a strictly lake-oriented habitat, although there were exceptions in both cases. While the Rangeley region never produced an authenticated brook trout of more than 14½ pounds, as did the Nipigon, it did produce a lot of fish nearly as big. In a 50-year period, from 1864 to 1914, the headwaters of the Androscoggin River produced 25 authenticated brook trout of over 10 pounds. This was also the period of concentrated sportfishing for brook trout on the Nipigon. No other area in Maine—or the United States—produced brook trout as large as did this unique environment, which evolved after the last glaciation in the Androscoggin River basin's numerous headwater lakes.

The brook trout fishing of the Rangeleys (actually the name of one of the most northerly of several lakes in these headwaters, but used also to refer to the entire group) was hardly known outside of Maine before the Civil War. There were a few fishing incursions into the upper Androscoggin region before the war, but those who made the trek through the virgin wilderness surrounding these lakes knew how to keep a secret. By war's end, though, Catskill trout fishing was in sad shape, the Adirondacks were becoming crowded, and serious anglers were looking elsewhere. When the extent of the Rangeleys' big brook trout became known, the region burst onto the American angling scene with a grand crescendo.

This was the land of the Oquossoc band of the Abenaki tribe. They lived most of the year just northwest of the divide that separates the Androscoggin's watershed from rivers in Québec. Long before Europeans came here, the Oquossoc knew of their waters' big brook trout. Each fall, until 1855, they set up a temporary camp where the Kennebago River meets Oquossoc (now Rangeley) Stream, the short outlet to Oquossoc (Rangeley) Lake. At that time, brook trout swarmed out of Mooselookmeguntic Lake and its arm, Cupsuptic Lake. Others would fall downstream out of Oquossoc Lake to spawn in the shallow rapids where the streams meet. On a huge rock ledge that overlooked the junction, the Oquossoc would spear, net, and trap trout, then split, smoke, and dry them for winter. When they had taken all they could haul, they ascended the Kennebago River, crossed the divide, and returned to Québec. For a long time, the village that sprang up just southeast of the rock was called Indian Rock, but eventually it was renamed Oquossoc. This and the lake names are the only traces left today of the area's original inhabitants.

The area saw few Europeans, other than during the disastrous trek by Brigadier General Benedict Arnold. During the winter of 1775, Arnold marched a disheveled army north in hopes of capturing the city of Québec, passing within 20 miles of Rangeley Lake. His men supplemented their rations with brook trout, but their journals didn't record fish of any size. During the ensuing years only a few hunters and trappers frequented the area, until James Rangeley, of Leeds, England, decided to investigate his inheritance in America.

Just how Rangeley acquired his piece of Maine is uncertain. There are three versions of the tale. One is that in 1796 he and two partners purchased more than 30,000 acres, at 20¢ an acre, of what was still a part of the state of Massachusetts. That sounds nice, but although Rangeley's family had wealth, he would have been only 24 at that time and not in possession of a large part of it. Nothing is ever mentioned of his two partners' role in Maine. Another version has him first settling in Virginia, then heading for Maine later, in 1825. Charles Goodspeed, in his classic book *Angling In America* (1939), interviewed Rangeley's descendants in Virginia, and they believed he inherited the Maine land. There may be a little truth in all three versions.

We don't know exactly when he first visited his 70,000-acre tract, an entire township that was eventually named after him, but we do know he liked what he saw, because he returned in 1825, at the age of 43, with his wife and children, ready to carve a fortune from the wilderness. To do so he needed a source of power, and his first task was to build a dam across Oquossoc Stream, where it exits the lake. Next to it he built saw- and gristmills, a large house, and all of the buildings a landed English squire needed to develop a

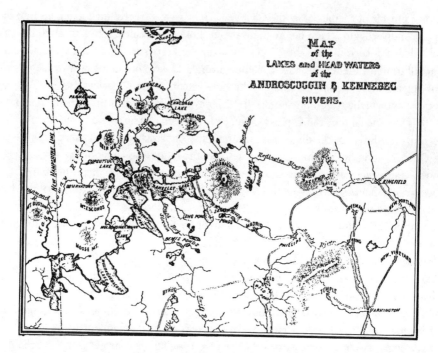

Figure 15.1   Now called "The Rangeleys," but during the exploration and subsequent discovery of their lode of huge brook trout they were referred to simply as the "Androscoggin Headwaters."

manor. We know he was a big man who loved to hunt moose, caribou, bear, and deer, but not much has been said about his fishing or the speckled gold that flowed at his doorstep.

Life in any wilderness is demanding, but his part of Maine had the added hardship of remoteness. While he made a modest living, he couldn't get his fortune out of the woods at a profit. Log rafting had not yet come of age. At age 69, in 1841, he abruptly abandoned the manor and enterprise and moved to "a 20-room house on State Street" in Portland, which his wife's brother had given her. They lived there for a few years, then moved to Henry County, Virginia, where he died in 1860. His descendants still live there.

While Rangeley may not have been particularly interested in brook trout, others were. Between 1830 and 1841, when Rangeley departed for Portland, Joseph Ellis Ware, a devoted fly fisherman also from England, settled in Farmington, 30 miles to the southwest. Ware came to Indian Rock to fish Oquossoc Stream and to talk with a fellow countryman. I don't know how Ware could have abandoned such pristine fishing, but in 1840 he also moved, to Nova Scotia. Maine was no longer English enough for him. He was described as being chauvinistic, and knew that Britain would never reclaim its colony.

Sometime shortly after Rangeley departed for Portland, the father of Henry O. Stanley (Henry O. eventually became Maine's first fish commissioner), of Dixfield, Maine, began exploring the area's lakes and surrounding streams. On one fishing sortie he discovered the great horde of brook trout in Oquossoc, by now known as Rangeley Lake. The younger Stanley began accompanying his father on these trips, and would eventually become the Rangeley connection with the outside world.

Even before Stanley, word was getting out of the area's fantastic fishing, but it wasn't documented in the journals of the day. Word-of-mouth must have reached an unidentified group of New York City sportsmen, however, because in the late 1840s they found their way to Indian Rock.

There's no record of their success, but the fishing must have been good, because they kept silent about it. They did have guides, river rafters out of work for the fall, who were astonished by the "dandy's" camping equipment. "They came with tents, silver knives, forks and spoons, fine cheeses, imported sausages, Madeiras and custom-made fishing tackle."

Obviously this was an affluent group, because such an expedition was then not only costly but also time consuming. But New York City at that time had a large cadre of "gentlemen" trout fishermen of means who were frustrated by the decline of trouting around Manhattan. They told others in New York about the fishing, and another group made the trip a few years later. An account of this latter trip appeared in the *Spirit of the Times,* a New York weekly "sporting sheet," on December 18, 1852. The group "walked from Bridgeton to Richardson Lake and captured a sackful or more of eight pounders," most likely in the fall of that year. These men probably weren't as affluent as their predecessors; it's a 45-mile hike from Bridgeton to Oquossoc.

A dazzling account of a great catch of large brook trout from the Rangeleys appeared in *Forest and Stream* magazine, the leading outdoors and conservation publication of the late 1800s. However, it appeared 20 years after the event, when the fishing was already on the wane. The magazine piece was a recollection of Joshua G. Rich's experiences on Rangeley. Rich was an interesting man of many trades, one being that of aspiring fish culturist; he rose to the rank of assistant to fish commissioner Henry O. Stanley. He also opened the first public fishing camp in the Rangeleys, at Middle Dam (Lower Richardson Lake, originally Welokennebacook), and named it Angler's Retreat. In the magazine piece he wrote: "I recollect seeing at a fisherman's camp one October morning in 1854, one hundred [brook] trout which had been speared the night before, weighing 600 pounds. An 8-pound trout was a common affair." In 1859, Rich wrote in a letter that "it was very common to take 100 pounds of red-spotted trout in one-half day's fishing."

Rich wrote a somewhat different version of the story that appeared in *The American Angler* in 1883, another outdoors magazine with an excellent reputation: "I remember one night in Trout Cove [Upper Richardson Lake], when an old hunter by the name of Leveratt and myself took in one night a hundred beauties, which weighed the next morning 600 pounds." He forgot to mention the spears.

The beginning of the end of the Rangeleys' great fishing occurred in 1860, when Henry O. Stanley, who had accompanied his father to the lakes 20 years earlier, organized an "expedition to penetrate the lakes from the upper end." He took with him George Shepard Page, of Stanley, New Jersey. This was Page's first exposure to the Rangeleys, but this was no real expedition—just a more convenient route from Stanley's home in Dixfield to Oquossoc.

By the 1860s, the Rangeleys had become widely known and were in the midst of a tourist boom, a spillover from the Adirondacks, where the boom was well underway. Most tourists came for clean air and water and to escape the city heat in Boston and Manhattan. Few if any were fishing tourists—at first. Hotels, cottages, and private "camps" dotted all of the numerous lakes. Meanwhile, the locals were still netting and spearing brook and blueback trout for the markets in Portland and Boston.

Page was president of Page, Kidder & Company, a Wall Street brokerage firm. He was an excellent angler and fly caster, and later considered himself a serious fish culturist, a devotee of New York's Seth Green, much to the detriment of the Rangeleys' strain of brook trout. On this trip, his first Rangeley brook trout was an unimpressive 2½-pounder taken on the apron of the Upper Dam. Later, he caught a 7-pound "giant." Some accounts say he returned every year thereafter, but the records don't show a return trip until 1863, along the same route he and Stanley had used.

Page was an egotist and publicist, a far cry from the reticent Gotham anglers who had first fished these waters. After fishing for a week, he carefully packed eight of the largest trout—fish between 5 and 8¾ pounds, a total of just under 52 pounds—and carried them to New York. As soon as he returned to Manhattan he showed the catch to William Cullen Bryant, editor of the *Evening Post* (later the *New York Post*), Henry J. Raymond, editor of the New York *Times,* and George Wilkes, editor of the *Spirit of the Times.* Even in 1863 the *Evening Post* liked big headlines. Bryant probably wrote the following piece:

> ENORMOUS TROUT—Mr. George S. Page, of the firm of George S. Page & Brother [sic], of this city, has shown us a basket of Trout, caught—he says it does not matter where, and he would rather not disclose the precise locality—but which are by far the largest of their kind that we have ever seen. In the basket before us, the heaviest fish weighs eight pounds and three-eighths; another weighs eight pounds and a quarter; and another, seven and a quarter pounds. Two others weighed six pounds and a quarter and six pounds.
>
> These fish are all the catch of two gentlemen, Mr. Page and Mr. H. O. Stanley of Maine, in the early part of the present month. In eight days they caught two hundred and seventy-three pounds, steelyard weight, and the fish caught averaged three and a half pounds each. Mr. Page desires us to say that all these fish were caught in fair play, with the fly. Trout fishermen must look out for their laurels.

Anyone who was part of the city's inner circle of "gentlemen anglers" knew where Page caught the trout. A furor arose as each newspaper printed an account of the huge brook trout. Many angler-readers found it impossible to believe that brook trout could grow so large. Most thought of the Adirondack brook trout as the species standard, and that region had never produced a brook trout of 5 pounds or better.

Even Dr. Thaddeus Norris, author of *American Angler's Book* (1864) and one of the more

Figure 15.2   Camp Kennebago a few years after it was taken over by the Oquossoc Angling Association.

knowledgeable writers of the time, couldn't quite believe they were brook trout. He hedged his way out of a full denunciation by saying: "If these fish were caught in the St. Croix River [Maine–New Brunswick border river] or its tributaries in Maine, they may have been Schoodic Trout, *Salmo Gloveri*. One who is not accustomed to mark specific differences, may easily have been deceived, though there are some instances of Brook Trout exceeding even the size of the Schoodic Trout."

Charles Hallock, then editor of New York's *Journal of Commerce* (founded by his father), wrote about fishing as well as commerce in the journal, and panned the stories. Later he founded *Forest and Stream,* and in 1895 become editor of *Field & Stream.* He was still only learning the outdoors trade, however, and still foolishly maintained that Page's fish weren't brook trout. Of course, nine years later he would take his familiarization tour around Lake Superior and ascend the Nipigon River, for his first look at brook trout of over 5 pounds.

Page knew his big fish would set off a sea of controversy. He may have even planned on it, because he sent his biggest trout to Cambridge, Massachusetts, where the period's most eminent ichthyologist, Louis Agassiz, held the chair of zoology at Harvard University. The Swiss professor speedily replied that these monstrous trout were genuine specimens of the speckled or brook trout family, and even knew that they were found in large numbers only in the lakes and streams of the headwaters of the Androscoggin River in northwestern Maine.

Figure 15.3 The original Oquossoc Club building today.

There were three doubting Thomases in New York who wanted to believe Page. Just to be sure, the next year (1864), R. G. Allerton (Reuben German Allerton; his friends called him Robert), treasurer of Goodyear's Indian Rubber Company, Lewis B. Reed, and L.T. Lazell fished Rangeley and confirmed Page's catches. They brought back several brook trout that weighed from 3 to 8 pounds.

Page himself was only getting started on this grand fishery. In 1867 he made another trip with Stanley and included a Mr. Fields, of Gorham, New Hampshire. In 10 days of fishing the trio caught an extraordinary number of big brook trout. Keeping nothing under 2 pounds, they still accumulated 50 fish that weighed 293 pounds—an average of nearly 5 pounds. The five largest weighed 8¼, 8½, 8¾, 9⅔ and 10 pounds.

Within the next year, so many new anglers came and so many new camps were built—thanks in part to the publicity created by Page and Allerton—that the gentlemen who fished out of C. T. Richardson's public fishing camp, opposite Indian Rock, were getting worried that they might be crowded out of their "find." In 1867, Page, who was a member of this group, called together the gentlemen anglers at Richardson's camp and those who had already built fishing cottages in the area. At the meeting were Lazell and Reed of Brooklyn, Allerton of Manhattan, Bowles of Springfield, Massachusetts, W. P. Frye, Maine's attorney general from Lewiston, W. S. Badger of Augusta, and Page's brother T. L. of New Orleans.

Figure 15.4 Interior of Camp Kennebago.

The next year, 1868, they formed the Oquossoc Angling Association; Page was named its president and continued in that office for 10 years.

Initially, their goal was to lease the grounds and buildings from Richardson and purchase his boats. The following year (1869) they changed their minds, and instead bought the entire fishing camp and a good bit of land surrounding the junction of the Kennebago River and Rangeley Stream, opposite Indian Rock. Richardson became their resident camp manager and immediately began building Camp Kennebago. The initial membership was 30, with a limit of 75. This was quickly filled by other affluent anglers from Maine, Massachusetts, New York, New Jersey, and Pennsylvania.

One of the milestones in the literature of trout fishing in general, and brook trout fishing in particular, was a unique little vanity book Allerton published that fall entitled *Brook Trout Fishing, An Account of a Trip of the Oquossoc Angling Association to Northern Maine in June 1869.* This 70-page book was the first devoted exclusively to brook trout. It also provided interesting insights into the national character of the time—and an often strange discourse on Allerton's moral ideas.

Mixed in with fishing accounts and a large dose of brook trout lore were a dissertation on Sunday school religion, touches of Indian history, and poems. Mostly it was an account of the trouting exploits of 11 club members, and as many guests, in camp that June. The book even included a lengthy discussion of trouting in the Adirondacks. Especially interesting is a reproduction of the menu Allerton had printed to commemorate their end-of-the-trip banquet, the "Grand Trout Supper" held at the Lackawanna

Hotel, Northern Maine, at which C. T. Richardson showed up as proprietor.

Have you ever wondered what Americans actually ate in 1869? Wonder no longer: The Oquossoc anglers started with *Soup:* tomato or oxtail; *Fish:* two brook trout weighing 15 pounds (it was noted that they were caught by Allerton), which were stuffed and baked in cream; *Meats:* boiled ham, corned beef, and fried pork; *Vegetables:* green peas and potatoes, either fried or boiled; *Pastry:* doughnuts, sponge cake, and apple pie; *Bread:* white bread, toast, and hard tack; *Napkins:* birch bark; *Toothpicks:* trout ribs; *Fluids:* coffee, tea, and Kennebago pura. The latter is a mystery or a misspelling. It might have been puree, a "thick liquid." Or it may have been pure Kennebago water.

The book was richly illustrated with numerous etchings and woodcuts, but the pièce de résistance was a three-panel colored engraving of a brook trout that Helen D. Findlay "rendered expressly for R. G. A. from a living Oquossoc Trout, furnished by Mr. Geo. Shepard Page."

Even though printed in limited numbers, this little book had a big influence on American anglers, revealing as it did the closely kept secret of the Rangeleys' big brook trout. Today it's much sought after by collectors of brook trout memorabilia.

Allerton's book also recorded the party's catch of fish on this trip. Counting only brook trout over 4 pounds, there were 30 fish that weighed in the aggregate 181¼ pounds, an average of better than 6 pounds. The biggest was a 9-pounder, caught by J. D. Badgley (of Badgley & Mead, N.Y.C.). The book noted that Allerton stayed on "for a considerable time" after the rest departed. He may have been looking for a private campsite of his own.

The following is an interesting account of life at Camp Kennebago in the formative years for members of the Oquossoc Angling Association. The account was written by Professor Edward Seymour, who may have stayed there more than once. It appeared in *Scribner's Monthly* (February 1877). If you've ever been in a communal fishing or deer-hunting camp, or even boot camp, it was a lot like this. You can sympathize with those members who had the means to build their own camps elsewhere around the lake. The club is still in operation today and its main structure still stands:

> There are some peculiar features in the arrangement of the camp buildings which will be of interest to those who are not familiar with such institutions. The main camp is a substantial board structure 100 feet long by 30 feet wide. At its extreme westerly end is a well-equipped kitchen, and adjoining it is a dining-room. Then comes the main apartment, which is occupied as a sleeping and sitting room. This room takes the full width of the main building (30 feet), is about 60 feet in length, and from the floor to the gable is 30 feet in the clear, giving it a most spacious appearance and securing thorough ventilation. There are no partitions in this apartment, but twenty-five or thirty beds are ranged along its sides, and at its extreme easterly end is a large open fire-place, around which the weary anglers gather after their day's sport, and entertain each other with the rehearsal of their experiences and exploits. As one huge log after another blazes up,—for the nights are seldom so warm that

a fire is oppressive,—story after story passes around. It rarely happens that some one of the circle has not captured a six or eight pound trout during the day, and the one who has been so fortunate is of course the hero of the hour. With what kind of fly the fish was captured, how long it took to land him, the narrow escape which the lucky angler had from losing his prize just as the guide was netting him, are points which must be rehearsed over and over again. Before eleven o'clock the weary anglers are all in their beds, and the camp sinks into a silence which is undisturbed save by some obstreperous snorer, at least until daylight the next morning, when some fisherman who has had poor luck the previous day starts out with a desperate determination to retrieve his fortunes by testing the virtue of early fishing.

It seems odd that Henry O. Stanley's name didn't appear on the club's roster as a member or even a guest during this time. After all, he had opened the Rangeleys for both Page and Allerton. There was one reference, in an article in *Forest and Stream*, April 3, 1879, that in 1869 Stanley took an extraordinarily large male brook trout. The fish was 30 inches long and had a circumference of 18 inches, but wasn't weighed when first caught. Page took the fish live to his home in Stanley, New Jersey, and put it into one of his trout-rearing ponds. Because the summer was so warm, however, the fish died after three

Figure 15.5   C.T. Richardson opened the area's first public fishing camp, Camp Kennebago, where the Kennebago River meets the outlet to Rangeley Lake and where the Oquossoc Indians had a seasonal camp. Brook trout fishing there was so good that a handful of his wealthy customers, within three years of its opening, bought the camp for themselves, formed the Oquossoc Angling Association, and hired Richardson back as their first superintendent.

weeks, then weighing 10 pounds. Professor Louis Agassiz calculated for weight loss and said that the live weight of the Stanley-Page trout was between 11½ and 12 pounds. It was mounted by one of the leading taxidermists of the era, a Mr. Dickinson of Chatham, New Jersey, "and has since occupied a prominent place in the office of Mr. Page at 10 Warren Street, New York."

In 1914, Dr. William Converse Kendall, of the U.S. Bureau of Fisheries, stated in his *The Fishes of New England . . . The Trout, or Charrs:*

> There is but one other authentic record of a Rangeley trout weighing over twelve pounds, although from what Stanley [then Maine fish commissioner] wrote concerning the size of Rangeley trout it is quite possible that the weights may have been exceeded by some taken in the past but unrecorded. At Kennebago there is, indeed, a tradition that a brook-trout weighing thirteen pounds and four ounces was once caught in these waters at or near Indian Rock pool. It is also recalled by old club members that at a time when the identity of these monster trout was questioned, William P. Frye [later a Maine senator] confounded all critics by sending a large specimen, preserved in a cake of ice, to New York, where it was exhibited in a refrigerator in the office window of the *Spirit of the Times.*

In 1870 the association was incorporated under the laws of the state of Maine and run like a corporation, with shares and stock. Its members began keeping daily records of all of the brook trout caught. Even though it was a private club, the public could use the facilities of Camp Kennebago for a decade or so longer. As with more than two dozen other camps around the lakes, for $2 one got room and board and access to the boats and guides. A better guide cost $2, $1 a day for his board, and 50 cents for the boat rental. At this same time, Maine's first trout-fishing laws were established. The season began May 25 and closed October 1. Club members reserved the best fishing periods for themselves. The camp was open to the public between June 20 and September 10—roughly when the first black flies appeared and when the last left.

In Bugle Cove, on Mooselookmeguntic Lake at the foot of Bald Mountain, Allerton constructed "a thoroughly built house, fully equipped with all the comforts of civilization." According to Seymour's article in *Scribner's:*

> It is located on a rocky bluff 20 feet or more above the level of the lake, and commands a magnificent view. Since Bugle Cove [4 miles by water from Camp Kennebago] is one of the best fishing grounds on the lake, its proprietor, who is one of the most enthusiastic and persevering of anglers, never fails to make up such a score during his visits in June as to excite the emulation of all other visitors during the rest of the season. Exactly what Mr. Allerton has accomplished during his eight successive annual visits to the lake is summarized in the table below. [Allerton's Logbook—1869–79]

1869	247 trout weighing	234.25 pounds
1870	124 " "	172.5 "
1871	218 " "	135.0 "
1872	130 " "	285.75 "
1873	149 " "	205.5 "
1874	175 " "	231.0 "
1875	157 " "	177.5 "
1876	136 " "	182.25 "

Figure 15.6 "Catching a 5-pounder." Note the similarity of the Rangeley boat to the Adirondack guideboat, page 190.

Oddly, there was little or no mention of either Allerton or Page after about 1876, although we do know that Page was president of the association until 1879. Maybe they left when the fishing declined.

By 1870, the Rangeleys had become widely known, and while the camps were crowded, the fishing was still excellent. The first effects of the boom were described by two urbanites who visited Rangeley Lake during the fall of 1872 (from *American Sportsman*, November 1872):

Well, here we are at last, after two days and nights of incessant travel, some 600 miles from Gotham and fairly in the heart of the wilderness. Now, thought we, for once in our lives we shall have enough elbow room and for once in our lives cast our flies to the extreme limit which skill allows. But, alas, on the morrow at early dawn we paddled to a favorite fishing spot which lies almost directly in front of the camp, thirteen other boats were moored in almost provoking proximity. There were fifteen of us in all and throughout the whole day, we whipped the waters with unflagging zeal, the gross return for the entire flotilla being exactly five trout, none of which weighed over five pounds. One thing was certain, we were not to suffer the pangs of solitude during our stay.

There is a glorious pool at the foot of the dam. In this pool big trout were swimming, for we actually saw them, and breaking water with a nonchalance and a tantalizing sense of security which was positively maddening. Around this pool, which was about 80 feet in diameter, were seven, I do not exaggerate, ardent anglers, armed with huge bamboo poles, some twenty feet in length and three inches at the butt. They were fishing with minnows, worms, spawn, in fact, every lure that was illegitimate and unscientific, and in lathe-constructed cars, which were tethered near the pool, we saw dozens of magnificent trout, weighing from four to seven pounds. Getting up early, we were able to fish from good locations and caught five trout weighing 27½ pounds, the largest being 8½ pounds.

In 1873, one seemingly innocuous and insignificant move forever altered the brook trout fishing in the Rangeleys but it had to wait for Page's maturation as a successful fish culturist. Ten years earlier, Page had opened the floodgates of fishing tourists with his publicity stunts. Still, the system was able to continue producing big trout even with the wanton commercial exploitation by locals and the absurd catches by "sportfishermen." Sensing a decline in the fishery, however, Page, still president and founding father of the Oquossoc Angling Association, convinced its members to build a hatchery on property leased on Bema (Bemis) Stream, on the southeastern corner of Lake Mooselookmeguntic.

Page, influenced by Seth Green's attempts in 1853 to raise brook trout in an artificial hatchery, eventually established, as a hobby, his own hatchery and rearing ponds at his home in Stanley, New Jersey. This town, since absorbed by the hamlet of Chatham, is on the edge of Great Swamp National Wildlife Refuge, 6 miles southeast of Morristown. What made it unique, and what probably attracted Page, was its location on the Passaic River, really just a creek at that point. Even today the Passaic River is reputed to contain populations of brook trout. If so, they're probably descendants of the numerous Rangeley fish Page released into this stream.

Having had mixed results transporting live trout over great distances, Page secured 30,000 brook trout eggs and artificially fertilized them. These he carefully sealed in jars, packed between layers of moss in elaborate boxes, and carried from Maine to New Jersey. After six weeks' incubation the eggs hatched, and the following spring Page released the fry into the stream below his New Jersey hatchery. This was the first successful long-distance (over 500 miles) transportation of trout eggs. Thus began a movement that saw hatchery brook trout stocked in many states and provinces that the species had not been able to colonize by natural means.

At this same time, nearly every publication was promoting brook trout fishing in the Rangeleys, and every creditable guidebook of the day referred to it. One of the most popular and respected of them was Charles Hallock's *Sportsman's Gazetteer and General Guide,* published in 1877. Here's his abbreviated description:

> The chain of lakes consists of Rangeley, or Oquossoc, 9 miles long, Cupsuptic, 7 miles long, Mooselookmeguntic, or Great Lake, 14 miles long, Molechunkamunk, or Upper Richardson, 12 miles, Welokennebacook, or Lower Richardson and Umbagog, 12 miles. The last lies partly in Coos County, N.H. All these lakes are connected by thoroughfares; the distance between them is from 1 to 6 miles. The surrounding country with the exception of the northern shore of Rangeley and south shore of Umbagog, is an unbroken wilderness.
>
> The lakes are famed for their rare fishing; trout taken from them are the largest found in the country. Indian Rock—is at the junction of the Kennebago and Rangeley streams. Camp Kennebago, C. T. Richardson, $2 per day.

Hallock then listed a score of fishing camps (including Camp Kennebago, which was still taking customers), lodges, and hotels, but used twice as much space describing the various routes and means of getting there as describing the lakes. By 1877, most transient anglers came part of the way by rail, followed by a stagecoach or buckboard ride to a point on one of the lakeshores, where they could continue on by steamboat, rowboat, and sometimes foot and portage to the camp of their dreams.

By the mid-1890s, the Portland & Rumford Falls line had a terminus on Bemis Point, the extreme eastern end of foot-shaped Mooselookmeguntic Lake. Eventually, tracks were laid to Oquossoc. Bemis Point was the site of Bemis Camps, operated by Captain Fred Baker. Baker took over the hatchery buildings that Page and members of the Oquossoc Angling Association had constructed in 1873. Baker also operated a steamboat service from his camps that took anglers and their baggage down the lake to the other camps that had sprung up around Indian Rock (Oquossoc) and Rangeley "City." Later, the railroad was closed and the railbed abandoned. It exists today in some areas around the lake as a 4x4 road. State Route 17 from Mexico, near Henry O. Stanley's hometown of Dixfield, was built on part of the old railroad bed.

It's interesting to note that, even today, most wild strains of brook trout inhabit streams close to the Appalachian Trail, from Katahdin in Maine to Brasstown Bald in Georgia. The AT eventually crosses the old railroad at Summit and then Route 17 at

Height of Land, just "up the hill," behind Bemis Point. If one travels to Oquossoc today, this is a great route to choose. The view of Rangeley and the other lakes is over a sheer cliff and is breathtaking. When I was last there, in June 1993, a pair of "alpine" moose were on the side of the road. The old railroad bed and the present-day Route 17 run parallel to each other, less than a mile apart, where the AT crosses Height of Land at 2,420 feet. The railroad follows the valley created by Bemis Stream, then runs around the edge of the lake at 1,467 feet to Oquossoc.

No discussion of fishing in the Rangeleys would be complete without a mention of Thomas S. Steele. A businessman from Hartford, Connecticut, Steele, more often remembered for his skill as a fish painter, contributed a series of interesting letters on Rangeley to *Forest and Stream* in 1877. His first visit to the lake was in 1873, made with 30 "companions of the rod," and he described the holiday-like atmosphere of their trip. "On our arrival 15 guides transported the party over the lake in stout keel-bottomed rowboats. The flotilla passed over the lake [a 9-mile row] to the outlet, an American flag floating from the bow of each boat, the oars of the boatmen beating time to our merry songs."

Steele, a dedicated trout and fly fisherman, made several subsequent trips to the Rangeleys and began painting the fish he caught. Brook trout vary greatly in color depending upon their age, sex, food, the time of year, and their environment. As both an artist and a fisherman, Steele was keenly aware of these changes. Here he described the beauty of the Rangeley brook trout:

> The proportions of the large fish vary greatly. A trout over two pounds can be almost any shape, and the writer has, among a large collection, an outline of a ten-pounder which is almost as broad as it is long. I have said that the color of most of these Rangeley trout always provokes our admiration, and an artist who portrays them in their most gorgeous colors must expect to stand any amount of criticism. In some of these fish the strong red or yellow color sweeps from above the lateral line, past the ventral fins, and entirely under-meat, leaving none of the white which usually marks the belly of the fish, while it is not unusual to find the bright vermillion spots on the dorsal fins. [I've yet to see this. I think he might have been carried away a bit.] The trout in the Rangeley stream are remarkable for their silvery appearance, and the flesh is frequently as white as that of shad, but there is no difference in the taste. The trout often assume a purple, and sometimes a steel-like appearance, but this is much more noticeable as they increase in size.

A pair of such "steel-like" brook trout was the subject of his most famous painting, *Salvelinus Fontinalis*, of which noted lithographer Bleischevitz did the engraving. I have a Bleischevitz print of this and the fish do have a slightly silvery appearance. They look like a pair of 3- or 4-pound fish that only recently entered Rangeley Stream from Mooselookmeguntic Lake; the full spawning livery of orange, red, and vermilion is still muted. Brook trout take a week to 10 days to make a complete color change from one environment to the next. These fish were probably in the stream for but a few days. Actually, they look exactly like blueback trout in their full spawning regalia, which reveals the close genetic relationship between the two charr species.

Blueback trout are a glacial relic, a color variation of Arctic charr. I caught several in Maine from a series of high-country ponds at the head of the Red River watershed (south of Allagash) that looked exactly like Steele's brook trout. Bluebacks are at the zenith of their spawning color phase when brook trout are just getting started. A good rendering of the blueback at the spawning stage can be found in Plate 4 of Kendall's *The Fishes of New England,* one of the publications of the memoirs of the Boston Society of Natural History. The original of Steele's *Salvelinus Fontinalis* (sic) at one time hung in the Boston Museum of Art. It's no longer there, and has probably been returned to its owner.

According to Austin Hogan, in a magazine article entitled "The Greatest American Brook Trouts," Kendall gained all of his information about the lakes and the big brook trout through countless interviews between 1912 and 1914 with people of the area, through their diaries, and through researching popular sporting publications of the previous era. Kendall summarized all catches of big brook trout in the last chapter on that species in his monograph:

> The largest trout reported, was one of 12½ pounds caught by a boy, worm fishing, not verified. Others of 17, 15 and 12 pounds were also reported. Professor Agassiz was sent a fish that weighed 11 pounds. (1860). Luman Sargent, an Upton guide, took a fish of 11½ pounds, the largest ever seen by Fish Commissioner H. O. Stanley, who spent many years in the area. He said, as a boy his father would bring home trout that, though gutted, looked like codfish and may have been even larger.
>
> There was an inclination to exaggerate sizes for publicity purposes by hotel keepers and guides. A prime example was the announcement of the capture of a trout of 12½ lbs. by J. Frederick Grote of New York on June 11th, 1886. It was kept in a car for a week before it died, meanwhile being weighed several times at the Mooselookmeguntic House. It was 26½ inches long, 17¾ inches in girth, 7¾ inches deep and 4 inches thick through the neck. Jerry Ellis, Mr. Grote's guide, called it an 8-pounder and obviously the weight of 12½ pounds was a fraudulent claim.
>
> On June 7th, 1887, Dr. J. S. Mixter of Boston, caught by deep-trolling a minnow bait, three trout that weighed 11¾ pounds, 9½ and 6 pounds. In answer to an inquiry by William C. Harris, publisher of *American Angler,* regarding the largest of these fish, C. T. Richardson, said he saw the trout weighed after one pint of spawn had run out of her and the weight was absolutely correct.

Kendall listed 15 brook trout weighing between 10 and 11 pounds, 30 between 9 and 10 pounds, and 60 weighing 8 pounds caught from the Rangeleys between 1869 and 1910. Most amazing was the catch of T. B. Stewart at the Upper Dam of two fish of over

8 pounds taken on one cast. Some time later, in 1888, this same T. B. Stewart was arrested for snagging trout with a grappling hook. He paid his fine, then loudly protested, casting suspicion on just how he'd taken the two big trout.

By 1880, changes in the brook trout population began to appear. The first telltale sign was a shortage of small brook trout. There were still plenty of fish of above 8 pounds, but even here the numbers began to slide. Kit Clark—an advertising man, and a very opinionated and boisterous fly fisher who became outdoors columnist for the New York *Sun* and a regular contributor to *The American Angler*—was the first to complain about shortages of all sizes of Rangeley brook trout in the late 1880s. He said that the fish "don't come to dinner at the ringing of the bell." He continued his revelations well into his 80s, around 1918.

The last big brook trout recorded in the annals of the Oquossoc Angling Association was the 9-pound, 7-ounce fish caught July 14, 1914, by Henly H. Roehofs. It was taken on a Parmachene Belle. Equally noteworthy in the logbook, listed on the same page and date, were catches of a 9-pound, 4-ounce landlocked salmon by Dr. H. H. Haskell on a Dusty Miller, and another landlocked salmon, 10 pounds, 2 ounces, caught by Martha Lambert on a Silver Gray. In the Rangeleys, salmon now outnumbered big brook trout.

The turn of the century saw a lot of anger, guilt, and introspection at the club. The Oquossoc Angling Association had placed a limit of one brook trout per day on its members when they fished the Kennebago River or Rangeley Stream. Of course, only a fly rod was permitted. To protect spawning trout, as early as the late 1870s it had petitioned the state to close all fishing on Rangeley Stream, which the state did. However, the club members felt no compunction toward conservatism when it came to lake fishing, and that comprised more than 95 percent of their angling.

Fishing in the Rangeleys was very different from in the Nipigon; here the fishing was in lakes, and much of it was done by trolling live bait from rowed boats. Dry-fly and streamer fishing had not yet been developed, nor had wet-fly fishing come of age as an effective method for catching brook trout in lakes. Fly fishing had a growing following among "gentlemen" anglers, but it was primarily a tactic of the spring, when fish were on the surface or in the shallows soon after ice-out, and again in the fall, when fish were in the streams looking for spawning sites.

In the early days there were no dams on the headwaters of the Androscoggin's watershed. The five lakes of the lower Kennebago River tributary—Oquossoc (Rangeley), Mooselookmeguntic (Cupsuptic was really an arm of this lake and not a separate lake), Molechunkemunk (Upper Richardson), Wellekennebacook (Lower Richardson), and Umbagog—were all connected by short rebirths of the river, except for the latter two, which were connected by 5 miles of what was called the Rapid River. After Rangeley built the first dam for his mill power, dams were constructed at the outlets of all of these lakes by logging companies seeking to create heads of water for their spring log drives. These dams are still in place. The dams elevated lake levels and created larger reservoirs, and for a time brook trout were able to spawn successfully in the short, tailwater rapids below each one. All of these outlet streams (except the lower reaches of the Kennebago River), even Rangeley Stream, were too deep for most wading, so fishing primarily was from boats anchored in the fast-moving waters.

Most fishermen in the Rangeleys used a trolling rod with a multiplying reel and at least 600 feet of strong linen line, a single gut leader, and a very small hook. As Allerton said in his book, fly fishing for the big fish was unsuccessful until late summer or early September, when they were taken with artificial flies and the most delicate of rods—as light as 6 ounces. Canoes weren't widely used for fishing in Maine until after the turn of the century. Instead, unique cedar boats, often double ended and similar to Adirondack guide boats, evolved on these lakes: light, well rounded, easy to row, and extremely seaworthy. They needed to be, because the lakes could look like the ocean in heavy northeast winds. A fleet of similar boats used today by Oquossoc Angling Association members can be seen at their docks opposite Indian Rock.

Allerton fished primarily with bait, although there's a fly named after him, while Page was a dedicated fly fisher. According to *Samuel Farmer's Guide to the Rangeleys 1880*, Page had a "portrait" on the wall of his cottage of a 12-pound, 2-ounce fish. Although no doubt this fish was caught on bait, there's at least one recorded fish of 7 pounds that Page took on a fly with his 7-ounce Murphy bamboo fly rod.

"Those who go to the lakes in spring and early summer determined to catch the biggest fish at all hazards must seek them with live minnows for bait, still-fishing, or by trolling in deep water," wrote Seymour in his *Scribner's* article. "In either case, the law rules out all gang hooks. The single-baited hook only is permitted, and any one infringing upon this wise restriction exposes himself to severe penalties. A larger hook, with a heavier leader than is used in ordinary brook trout fishing, is called for in these waters. In general, however, give preference in making your selection to the more subdued colors, and do not permit yourself to be stocked up with an immense variety. Five or six kinds well selected will be more than enough to give the fish ample range for choice."

This selection of fly patterns is in sharp contrast to Henry P. Wells's advice in an 1886 piece he wrote in *Fishing with the Fly*, edited by Charles F. Orvis and A. Nelson Cheney. But then Wells was the fly tyer who invented the Parmachene Belle. Then, as now, one cannot have a large enough selection of patterns and colors to suit the taste of the fish— or is it the fisher?

Even though Maine still offers brook trout fishermen thousands of miles of good angling on rivers, streams, and brooks, the largest fish are still taken from the hundreds of small lakes and ponds. As a result, stillwater fishing with flies saw its greatest development in these waters. Until the beginning of the 1880s, most wet-fly fishing was in moving water—rivers and streams. It wasn't very effective on these lakes because the fisherman or guide had to move the fly, usually by rowing the boat and dragging the fly through the water—trolling, in other words.

Wells, as it happened, was in the right place at the right time and had enough fishing acumen to recognize the significance of a new wet-fly technique that produced big brook trout. It may have evolved with the guides, or with the guides in concert with a sport or two. He wrote that, in 1886, on an early trip to the Rangeleys, "I was fishing under the tute-lage of that prince of guides, John S. Danforth—a man, though unexcelled as a hunter, trapper, and woodsman, and an angler, [who was] still not unknown in the literary world. I then knew I had much to learn about fly-fishing and the habits of trout, as I still have."

He asked Danforth, "Who catches the most big brook trout from these waters?" Danforth told him it was "a Mr. S., of Boston" (possibly Professor Edward Seymour), and went on to show him the system they had developed. Danforth had also guided Seymour, a regular on these lakes during the previous decade.

> A single large wet fly was used in contrast to two or three dropper flies which had been in vogue until now. Dry flies, streamers and nymphs were yet to evolve although the dry fly was in the formulative stages in the Catskills. It was cast and not trolled and if it straightened out without a loop or kink, it was allowed to rest where it fell until it had sunk a foot or so below the sur-face. Then slowly, it was moved about three feet, followed by another pause of five or six seconds, then the fly was slowly drawn to within a distance where it could be lifted, and in one quite, smooth lift it was taken off the water and without false-casting was ready for another cast—if nothing struck.
>
> "A marked change in the size of the fish taken attended the adoption of this method," said Wells. "I have never known or heard of a trout of over three and one-half pounds being taken in those waters upon a fly moving on the sur-face. It may happen, but it is surely rare."

Wells interviewed other guides, and they all agreed that this was the only technique that produced large brook trout on the open waters of these lakes. Regardless of the tech-nique used, though, big brook trout were beginning to disappear from the Rangeley Lakes at an alarming rate by the end of the century. In 1901, Maine passed the first brook trout limit: no more than 25 pounds per day. Many of the fishing clubs, "as a conserva-tion measure," changed their contests and quit awarding prizes for catching the most fish, switching instead to the largest fish. But the increasingly restrictive laws were all ineffective in halting the decline of the Rangeleys' monster brook trout. Of course, there was really nothing anyone could have done; the damage had already been done.

The culprit was the Atlantic salmon, which Page had introduced in 1875 and which gradually displaced the special variation of brook trout in the Androscoggin drainage system. Fish culturists at that time had little knowledge of a system's complex ecology, and either didn't care or didn't want to know how different species interacted. They did realize that the Rangeley Lakes had developed a unique balance between their two indigenous salmonids, both charrs. Brook trout were the predator charr, and blueback trout the prey charr. To attain the full size encoded into their genes, brook trout switched from feeding on insects to feeding on fish, when available. And in the Rangeleys were multitudes of small, fat, oily bluebacks.

Most anglers were unaware of the blueback trout's existence, or even recognized it as being a trout. Blueback trout seldom grew beyond 9 inches, and throughout most of the year they stayed in the depths of these deep, oligotrophic lakes, moving into the shallows of Kennebago River, Rangeley Stream, and several other small streams that feed the chain of lakes only to spawn.

Like clockwork, regardless of water temperature or the exact declination of the sun, they arrived by the millions in the shallows every October 10. It took two to three weeks before all had their turn at spawning. For years they were mercilessly netted, speared, and trapped by the thousands by area residents. Even so, their numbers showed no signs of declining. Nor did their steady consumption by brook trout affect their populations in the lakes. Bluebacks could easily compensate for these losses because they were extremely fecund, reproducing in large numbers. All they asked for was a steady supply of zooplankton on which to feed. And the lakes were rich in this near-macroscopic commodity.

Salmon liked bluebacks as much as did brook trout, and would sink to unbelievable depths, literally, to fill themselves. As a result, salmon grew and prospered to the detriment of brook trout, which were often outbid for this rich source of food. Someone even thought the salmon needed more food; perhaps it was Page. In 1891, smelt were introduced.

This was a double blow to the bluebacks and, eventually, to the brook trout, because smelt competed directly for zooplankton, the blueback trout's primary food. Thereafter, bluebacks began a steep decline; their complete demise took only a decade. Further complicating the matter were lake trout, introduced either accidentally or intentionally. Lake trout are another charr that had limited original distribution in Maine, but where they occurred there were no blueback trout. The problem was that they preferred the same habitat as bluebacks, and the larger lake trout won the battle. By 1905, blueback trout had disappeared from the Androscoggin basin.

At first it was believed that the Androscoggin watershed held the only population of blueback trout. However, they were rediscovered in the late 1950s in a few small drainages in the very northern part of the state, especially the Red River. They exist today in a series of small headwater ponds, but their populations are fragile and constantly threatened by incursions of lake trout from lower portions of the watersheds. They could again become an extinct strain of Arctic charr.

The Rangeleys' big brook trout didn't all disappear at once. From time to time during the first two decades of the 20th century, 6-, 7-, 8-, and even 9-pounders were caught. And these big fish were usually brought directly to Herbie Welch in the village of Oquossoc (actually Haines Landing on Mooselookmeguntic Lake) to be mounted.

Herbert L. "Herbie" Welch was born in Brownville, Maine, on September 6, 1879, and began guiding on the Rangeleys in 1902. He had come to the area as an apprentice to William D. Heinz, one of the foremost taxidermists of the time. Welch was already an accomplished fly tyer by the time he guided an English angler for two weeks on the Kennebago River. He had been trying to tie a fly to imitate smelt, which had become the main forage fish on the lakes. To do so he needed a long-shanked hook, difficult to obtain in the United States. The Englishman had several long-shanked salmon flies in his fly book, and Welch was able to tie the first of his smelt flies.

Welch moved to Oquossoc in 1902 or 1903, but was too late to get in on the easy catches of big Rangeley brook trout, most of which had disappeared by then—as had the everyday demand for guides. To augment his guiding income, he opened a tackle and fly shop and then a taxidermy studio. An innovative fly tyer, Welch invented the Black Ghost and a collection of well-known Maine salmon and brook trout flies (see chapter 20). However, Welch is best remembered today for his exceptionally lifelike brook trout mounts. He was a true artist. Fortunately, he taught the art to David Footer, of Lewiston, Maine, who recently mounted his 6,000th brook trout.

An extraordinary and invaluable collection of the last of these big trout mounted by Welch can be seen today surrounding the dining room walls of Stephen Philbrick's Bald Mountain Camps. The camps, less than a mile from Haines Landing on Mooselookmeguntic's shore, have been in existence since 1897, when they were Ed Wharf's fishing camps. Bald Mountain Camps typify the elegantly rustic style of that era's better fishing camps. Some of Welch's best mounts were eventually collected by Philbrick's grandfather Ray Turmenne, the camp's third owner, as well as by Philbrick, as summer homes around the lakes and their contents changed hands and were sold. It seems apropos that many of the mounts remain in the area where the fish were caught.

Welch became a well-known raconteur, champion fly caster, and guide. As a guide his reputation was national, giving him the chance to take part in the most-photographed event in the history of the Rangeleys. In 1939, ex-president Herbert Hoover, a recognized devotee of trout fishing, dropped in with Maine's Governor Lewis Barrows. Welch served as Hoover's guide, and as one newspaper report of the time said, "Trout they did catch."

But Hoover wasn't the most famous of presidents to stay at Bald Mountain Camps and fish the lake. In 1906, Theodore Roosevelt, also an avid trout fisherman, stayed at one of the lakeside cottages. There was no report of either Hoover or T. R. taking any big brook trout. Without blueback trout, the unique strain of big brookies continued to disappear. By 1915, the brook trout of the Rangeleys were the same size as most other brook trout in Maine, New England, New York, and Pennsylvania—something almost guaranteed by the massive stockings of hatchery brook trout derived from other waters in Maine. The Rangeley monsters entered history.

The Rangeleys still produce the occasional 4- and 5-pounders. These fish, like most of the state's stocked trout, are programmed for fast growth and are short lived, seldom even approaching the size of the original Rangeley trout. And while 6- to 8-pound brook trout have been taken in Maine over the last few decades, none have come from the Rangeleys.

"Hardly a man is now alive who remembers the Battle of '75. . . ."
—Ring Lardner

16 THE ASTONISHING NIPIGON

To paraphrase Lardner, hardly a man is now alive who remembers the fabulous brook trout fishing on the Nipigon River that so captured the imaginations of American and Canadian fishermen. Today, the fishery exists only in print and perhaps in a few scattered mounts in both countries. It need not have been that way. From this tragedy, there are real lessons to be learned, even today.

The Nipigon watershed possessed all of the ingredients necessary to produce the continent's best brook trout fishery, in both quantity and quality. Here, over a period of some 10,000 years, the species was able to achieve its greatest allowable genetic growth by fully utilizing an unlimited supply of both aquatic and piscivorous foods, all under ideal temperature and water-quality conditions. Life just didn't get better for the brook trout anywhere in its original range.

To say that the Nipigon watershed was unique would be a gross understatement. It was composed of a large river that varied in width from 50 to 200 yards, with a voluminous flow of water, 5,500 cubic feet per second. In its 32-mile southerly course from Lake Nipigon, it once descended 313 feet over 15 well-aerated rapids and seven waterfalls, losing its identity only temporarily when it flowed through four lakes. It has been described as having three ecologies: 10 miles of lakes, 10 miles of river, and 10 miles of rapids.

The watershed was divisible between the river and Lake Nipigon at its head. The lake was oval in shape—40 miles wide, 70 miles long, with a 580-mile shoreline—and filled with more than 1,000 islands ranging from oversized rocks to one 8 miles long. Flowing

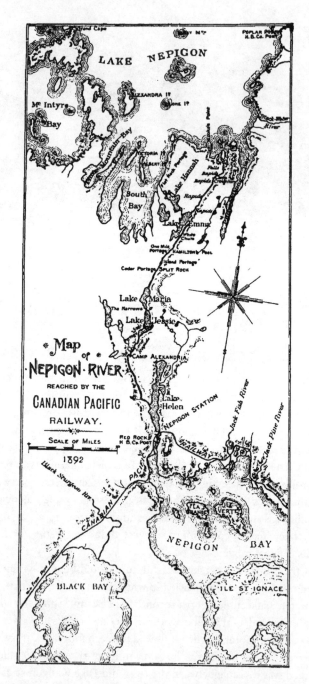

Figure 16.1 The Canadian Pacific Railway's 1892 map of the Nipigon River is quite useful and illustrates the rapid changes to the area in just nine years. Note that the railway was completed east of Nipigon on this map.

into the lake were a dozen small to medium streams and rivers. The Nipigon River itself had almost no tributaries other than Frazer Creek, and flowed into the northern side of Lake Superior, the largest of the Great Lakes; this acted as both a food source for the lower river's brook trout and a temperature haven when the river became too warm for riverine fish. In turn, the lower river offered the lake's brook trout excellent riverine spawning sites.

If you've noticed that I've been referring to the river in the past tense, there's a reason: The entire watershed is today a shadow of what it was 100 years ago. But that's getting ahead of the story.

Even before the first French explorers, trappers, and missionaries discovered the Nipigon River in the mid-1600s, the Ojibway, Chippewa, Hurons, and their precursors had used it for thousands of years as a route from the *gitchee gummee* ("big-sea water") to the interior plains of eastern Manitoba or north to James Bay. Portages and trails paralleling the river were already well worn in 1659 when Radisson and Des Groseillers used it to get to James Bay from Lake Superior.

In late spring each year, personnel from Nipigon House—the Hudson's Bay Company store, which had been on the shores of Lake Nipigon since 1792, succeeding its predecessor, the North West Company—hauled furs downriver on their travois, destined for London. On the return trip, they hauled provisions upstream from Red Rock, now the village of Nipigon, for the 400 Ojibway who lived around Lake Nipigon. Supplies came up the lake from Toronto by steamers to Red Rock Landing. Many considered Lake Nipigon, called by the natives Alemipigon ("deep clear-water lake"), the sixth Great Lake in the chain.

Although brook trout had long been familiar to settlers in Sault Ste-Marie (both the U.S. and the Canadian towns) on the St. Mary's River, which connects Lakes Superior and Huron, the first mention of brook trout in Lake Superior came from the eminent Swiss ichthyologist from Harvard University, Louis Agassiz, in his familiarization trip around the shores of Lake Superior in 1848, when he commented on the multitudes of these fish at the river's mouth near Red Rock.

Dr. Thaddeus Norris, author of the authoritative book of fish and fishing in the United States (*The American Angler's Guide*, 1864), wrote: "The rivers flowing into Lake Superior, as well as the outlet to that water, Sault Ste-Marie, contain brook trout of large size. A friend who was on a north-west tour, during the summer of 1860, brought me the profile of a [brook] trout, cut out on brown paper, with the following memoranda on it: 'Taken by J. E. Cady, of Sault Ste. Marie, July 30th, 1858. Weight six and a quarter pounds, length twenty-four inches, circumference thirteen inches.'"

Somewhere between 1840 and 1860, sportfishermen discovered the river's large and plentiful brook trout. This probably began with steamship passengers traveling from Toronto to Duluth, who temporarily got off the vessels to rest their sea legs at Red Rock Landing and found it easy to catch big brook trout in the lake and mouth of the river. Early sportsman's guidebooks, one dated in the early 1840s, lauded the size and number of brook trout that could be caught at the Nipigon's mouth. They also extolled the upriver fishing at Bashewana Rapids, Great White Shoot, and Split Rock. Even before the fishing tourists began trekking upstream in canoes with guides and all of their provisions for a week or two, many traditional campsites were well established along the river, and the numerous rapids, falls, and portages already had names.

WHEN SPORTFISHING BEGAN

Sportfishing on the Nipigon got serious in 1859, when the Hudson's Bay Company constructed its Red Rock House trading post at the river's mouth (Nipigon Harbor), at the present site of the village of Nipigon. It consisted of three log cabins, and for the first few years was not occupied year-round. The following year an independent fur trader named Clark set up a competing post at Nipigon. Now, fishermen could provision their trips here as well as at Sault Ste-Marie. Word of the fabulous brook trout fishery began to trickle back down the line, to Toronto, Cleveland, and even New York.

In 1865, Dr. Robert Barnwell Roosevelt, a renowned writer of the late 1800s and author of *Superior Fishing* (1884), sailed a barge around Lake Superior testing the fishing and happened upon another barge sailing in the opposite direction. They hailed each other:

> Our sail was hastily lowered, and the vessels being laid alongside of one another, we held an interesting conversation with our fellow-travellers. It appeared they had ascended the Neepigon, and gave glowing accounts of the number of fish, but not much of the character of the fishing; saying that the trout, which were large on the average, were collected in pools as we had found them in the Batchawaung, and were so numerous as to ruin the sport. They had had a long journey, and were out of whiskey, a deprivation that we hastened to supply; and were glad to see civilized beings, and to feel that they were once more on the confines of the land of the white man.

Four years later, in 1869, Professor Robert Bell headed a Canadian geological team that mapped the river, lake, tributaries, and nearby land. One of his crew, fishing at the mouth of the river in Nipigon Bay, caught a brook trout that weighed 19 pounds. With Bell's sophisticated equipment and his scientific techniques, surely this weight was accurate.

A. W. Flanagan was in charge of Red Rock House in 1872. He had just replaced Robert Crawford, who had set up operations as the river's fishing-expedition outfitter and opened his home to overnight guests. Prior to this, fishing tourists getting off the steamers (which by now had replaced sail-driven barges) had had to set their tents for the first night next to the Hudson's Bay Company store. Some found all the fishing they needed, without venturing all the way upriver to Lake Nipigon, in the mile of navigable rapids from the harbor north to Lake Helen, going upriver only as far as the first falls, where they fished from Camp Alexander.

One such angler was T. L. Morris, who was on the river in July of that year. In a letter,

Figure 16.2 The welcome sign today on the TransCanada Highway just west of the village of Nipigon touting it as the home of the world's record brook trout.

he wrote that in 48 hours of fishing he caught 108 speckled trout that weighed more than 1½ pounds each. "At least half were greater than 4 pounds. The cost of a canoe rental was 50 cents a day and guide $1.50 a day and included his board. The whole trip didn't cost more than $15."

Word of the 19-pound brook trout taken by Bell's geological team must have reached New York, but it was three years before Charles Hallock, dean of American outdoors writers, could get to the Nipigon. He was here in 1872, sharing the river with Morris, and was the first writer of repute to visit the river that was rapidly rising in fame. He wrote an account of the trip in his guidebook, *The Fishing Tourist* (1873):

> Arriving at Red Rock, we find a comfortable framehouse and store, which belonged to the Hudson's Bay company, in the palmy [prosperous] days of its reign, located on a grassy plateau, with a bright red-sandstone bluff in the foreground, and a range of wooded hills behind. Here we are received with an old-fashioned Scotch welcome by Robert Crawford, Esq., recently the agent, and his "gude wife," who spreads before us an entertainment that might propitiate the gods—I mean such heathen gods as depend upon their appetite and diet to shape the ends of their divinity. Here may be obtained everything needful for a protracted voyage, such as tents, canoes, guides, clothing, shoes,

blankets, and provisions, in great variety—everything but fishing-tackle; this, of course, the angler will provide for himself. Parties intending to visit the Neepigon should write Mr. Crawford sufficiently in advance of their arrival to secure canoes and Indians; as it may be necessary to send to the Sault [Ste-Marie] for them, where a number are always to be had. Or, a letter may be addressed to J. G. H. Carlton, Esq., Lock-master, Sault Ste. Marie, Michigan, who will arrange to have guides and canoes ready at any time to go aboard the steamboat with the excursion party.

Having enjoyed a night of refreshing slumber at Crawford's, we are ready in the morning for a start up stream. Our outfit is completed, the canoe laden with all essentials, and we only await the arrival of Pooray, our Indian guide, from his wigwam up the river. With commendable punctuality he presently puts in an appearance, bringing with him a specimen-trout from the regions above, which causes our eyes to dilate and our nerves to thrill with pleasurable anticipation. In size it resembles a good-sized shad; but its native characteristics are perfect, with every mark and line and color of the genuine Salmo fontinalis gleaming in royal splendor. It weighs 4¼ pounds, but we are quietly informed that "this is a common size here"!

Unlike most anglers, Hallock avoided the rapids that occur a quarter-mile above the landing, and had his guides load the gear—along with a guide's cocker spaniel, which helped them supplement a diet of fish with rabbits and ruffed grouse—onto ox-drawn carts. They started their trip at the head of the mile-long rapids, where the river exits Lake Helen. In Hallock's time, the success of day's catch was more often described by the total weight of fish caught and its average, and occasionally by the biggest fish "in the basket."

At the rapids and within sight of the steamboat landing one may tarry and fish to repletion of desire and basket, without going further. Passengers, while waiting for the departure of the steamer, have caught within an hour or so from off the dock, trout ranging from 1½ to 5 lbs. each. Of 150 fish which we have caught, the average, by actual test, was a little above 2½ lbs. The score runs thus, on exceptional occasions: 5 fish, 18¾ lbs.; 5 fish, 20 lbs.; 5 fish, 23 lbs.; 6 fish, 22½ lbs. And this is about as they run in the river. There are some small fish, but they are very scarce. Up in the Lake they have been caught weighing as heavy as 12 lbs. In short, one may hook and land on stout gear as many trout as he has flies on his line. I have known four to be landed at once weighing in the aggregate nearly 14 lbs.

Hallock didn't seem overly impressed with his catch, perhaps because he didn't find any really big brook trout. And he may have been premature in describing the Hudson's Bay Company post as past its prime—or he didn't appreciate the power of his word. Most authorities see the decade between 1870 and 1880 as the most prosperous period in the growth of Red Rock House as "an important outfitting station for gentlemen anglers visiting the Nipigon River." Red Rock House stood until 1903. In 1895, the HBC moved its operations into new quarters, the Nipigon Store, which was built near the new railroad station. It's still in use today.

Four years later, Hallock gave the Nipigon another shot in his voluminous 900-page book *The Sportsman's Gazetteer,* which appeared in 1877 and was more of a sportsman's guidebook than *The Fishing Tourist.*

> From Toronto there is a choice of routes either to Collingwood or Sarnia, whence good boats run to Sault Ste. Marie, and from there, to the north shore of Lake Superior, and the other to the south shore, touching at Marquette and other points, and on to Duluth. The North Shore steamers connect at Prince Arthur's Landing with other boats for Duluth, 140 miles distant. A favorite route for Americans is from Buffalo via Lake Erie to Detroit, on thence through Lake Huron to Sault Ste. Marie. Residents of States west and north of New York, will naturally make Detroit their objective starting point. A round trip ticket via the Collingwood route, costs $35 gold, which includes meals and stateroom. The fare from New York City via rail, to Niagara Falls, thence boat to Toronto, is $11.50; so that the cost of the entire trip from New York and return is about $65. The actual running time of the trip occupies ten days.
>
> Red Rock is a Hudson's Bay Company Post, where the sportsman will find excellent accommodations with Robert Crawford, the agent. From him must be procured the necessary fishing permits, without which no angler can fish in the Nepigon. He will furnish almost everything requested for camping out; cedar boats, and birch canoes, tents, blankets, woolen shins, Hudson's Bay overcoats, corduroys, cigars and tobacco, canned fruits, desiccated meats, condensed soups, milk and coffee, pickles, English ale, whisky for medicinal use, New Testaments, flour, pork and ham, cutlery, boots, shoe-packs—at ridiculously low prices. Good guides and Indian canoe-men can be had at a $1 per day each. The angler must take his own fishing tackle, including a stout rod, and red and brown hackles. From the middle of July through August and September is the best season for fishing.

This was the prime period for big brook trout on the Nipigon. Even though a world record was set in 1916, the quality and quantity of fish began to decline after 1880.

What probably stirred American anglers into fishing the Nipigon, before it was "all used up," more than either of Hallock's works, was a letter from Henry H. Vail of Cincinnati, written on June 2, 1884, to Charles F. Orvis of Manchester, Vermont. Vail told Orvis that his special order of extra-large trout flies had not arrived in time before his departure in July 1883 from Sault Ste-Marie to the Nipigon. Vail was a dedicated fly fisher and brook trout angler, and his letter was so full of information about the river that Orvis and A. Nelson Cheney included it in their *Fishing with the Fly* (1886), along with the best maps of how the Nipigon looked before its impoundment.

When Vail fished the Nipigon in 1883, the only way to get there from the east was by steamship. The Canadian Pacific Railway (CPR) had graded the future rail route from Port Arthur to Nipigon, but the tracks from the west ended in Port Arthur. Accommodations were as yet not plentiful at Nipigon. Vail and his partner tented alongside the Hudson's Bay Company post near Nipigon Harbor. The Euro-Canadian Nipigon community didn't begin to grow until 1885, when the CPR bridge (shipped across the lakes by barge and assembled on location) was completed over the river and Nipigon Station established. The following is an abridged version of Vail's letter:

> We commenced fishing July 11th, on the first rapids of the river, from our canoes, with two ordinary flies such as we have often used in Maine. This day I caught two pairs. After the second full catch I removed one fly. The trout were feeding in the rapids where the water was so active that it was almost impossible for a fly-rod to drag up two two-pound trout within reach of the landing net. Our total catch this afternoon in three hours for two rods was twenty pounds. The fish averaged a pound each. While we were camped at the Hudson Bay Post we had no difficulty in disposing of any amount of fish. Farther up the river we returned more than half of the uninjured fish to the water, except on such days as transient Indians camped near us. We took sixty-four pounds of trout one afternoon, and thirteen Indians consumed all of them before they slept.
>
> Our second camp was [Camp Alexander] at Alexandra Falls, fifteen miles up the river. Here there is a mile of rapid water and most excellent fishing. The trout were larger than were taken below, averaging nearly two pounds. We fished from our canoes.
>
> From Alexandra Falls we crossed a portage of two and a half miles, and afterward some lesser portages, to a point known as Camp Cincinnati. Here we had excellent fishing in about a mile of rapids, with falls above and below. There are two fine large pools above [Robinson and Hamilton pools], which we visited. In one of them I took three two-pound fish within ten minutes. One rod this day took fifty-six pounds of trout.
>
> At Camp Victoria, some miles farther up the river, we stayed several days, making excursions across to Lake Nipigon, about six miles away, and to the Virgin Falls, seven miles up the river, near where the river leaves the lake. At Camp Victoria the fishing grounds were on the rapids, in sight from our tent. I should think that the water fell twenty feet in about a hundred yards. A canoe could be anchored in almost any part of it, and the trout were found in every part. We took [in] one morning all the fish we could possibly use in the day; but the afternoon was perfect weather for fishing, and we could not lie quiet in the tent within sight of the leaping fish.
>
> Our day at the Virgin Falls, July 19th, was the successful termination of our northward journey. We paddled up the stream with both birch-bark canoes and

reached the falls at about 10 A.M. We carried our canoe around a sharp rapid at Miner's Camp [near Rabbit Rapids where Dr. Cook's 14½-pounder was taken 32 years later] and came in sight of the falls as we cleared the pine forest which covered our path. The falls, thirty feet high [22 feet], were right in front of us, half a mile away, and a great eddy, white with foam filled the space between us and the foot of the fall where the river turns at a right angle. We soon landed at the rocky point below the falls. The trout could be seen throwing themselves clear from the water in the eddy. I did not strike one until we had been there half an hour. I was greatly puzzled to place my fly far out on the deep water where the trout were to be seen feeding. It was too deep to anchor, too swift to hold the canoe with paddles, and too far to cast. I had with me a multiplying bass-reel. My fish was a five-pound brook trout. I reeled in slowly, and rarely did I have to repeat my cast without capturing a fish. At this place the largest flies were needed. There was no striking short or delay. The trout were there.

We then had in our pool among the rocks, dug out by some clever predecessor, the largest trout that the writer ever took. We weighed thirteen trout that aggregated 55½ lbs. We killed four speckled trout weighing: two of 5½ lbs, 5¼ lbs., and 5 lbs., and returned all the others in good condition to the water. These trout were from 22 to 24 inches long, and from 13 to 13½ inches in shoulder girth. They were all fine breeding trout, with the sexual differences strongly marked even, in the middle of July. We took trout with eggs fully developed in the middle of July.

Accounts of this kind of fishing eventually brought anglers to the Nipigon, first by the trainload and then by carloads. In 1887, the year after the Cheney and Orvis book was published, an article appeared in *Forest and Stream* (founded by Hallock; the article was probably written by him) that extolled the Nipigon as "the finest trout stream in the world."

"The Nepigon was one of the most famous trout rivers in the world," said Edward R. Hewitt in 1950, at the age of 84, "and it certainly lived up to its reputation of being the best river for large brook trout when I fished it many years ago."

Hewitt was born, you might say, with a silver hook in his mouth, into an extremely wealthy family. He was intelligent, well educated, and a global traveler, and used his wealth to fish throughout the world, whenever he wanted. He also spent years developing techniques for raising salmon and trout, and even bought a large part of the fabled Catskill brook trout river, the Neversink, and turned it into a living laboratory for his ideas on trout, fishing, fishing tackle, and flies.

He fished the Nipigon in 1887 and, because he "was sure many more large trout could be caught there," tried again during the last three weeks of summer in 1891. He chose this period because he believed larger fish were likely to be coming into the river, both from Lake Superior and Lake Nipigon, as the spawning season approached. A friend of Hewitt's was on Dr. Robert Bell's geological survey team and knew the angler who had caught the 19-pound brook trout. This firsthand knowledge may even have prompted him to search the Nipigon for big trout. Big fish were a passion of Hewitt's. Though born in 1866 and educated as a physicist, his inquisitive approach to sportfishing and his long life place him among America's modern scientific anglers.

He recounted his exploits after the 1891 trip:

> At the Hamilton Pool, one day, an Indian was fishing with a spoon and lead, casting the spoon out by whirling it around his head. The spoon was drawn across the current deep down and attracted the trout. He was securing his winter supply of fish he would smoke. He had taken a large number, cleaned them, and cut off the heads, and was preparing to smoke them when I happened to come along. I weighed the largest fish, which was dressed with its head off, on my scales. It weighed exactly eleven pounds. The fish was of the red, river variety, and the Indian told me that these red fish were not caught any larger than this one.
>
> At the Hudson Bay station at the head of Lake Nepigon, Mr. Anderson, the factor, told us that they took a large number of trout in nets near the spawning beds every autumn, which were used as their winter supply of fish, and were shipped by sleds to the other Hudson Bay stations within reach. They packed them in ice and kept them the year round. We went out to the icehouse, dug out four or five fish, and brought them into the store and weighed them on the scales. They were cleaned with the heads left on. They weighed from ten to twelve pounds apiece after being on the ice eleven months. He said the whole catch of many tons ran about this size. There were still about a thousand pounds of these fish in the ice-house.
>
> I spent a couple of days near the spawning beds in the lake in an endeavor to catch some of these larger trout, but it was too early in the season and we succeeded in getting only one, which weighed eight and three-quarter pounds.
>
> It was the middle of August when I reached the best fishing grounds, at Pine Portage. The big pool [Robinson] in front of my camp held some fine trout, many of them four pounds or more, but I saw none of the big ones. At the foot of the pool the river made a turn, with an island in the center. Large trout were preparing to spawn. At the foot of the island there was sure to be a gravel bar. I saw it was waist-deep, with small rocks. The current was swift, but not too fast to wade, if one waded with the current.
>
> I stationed one Indian below where I intended to cross so he could throw me a line if I got swept off my feet. I waded into the current to the foot of the island and started fishing. Big trout were on the gravel. Several rose to the fly and I hooked an enormous fish, far too strong to hold. It got into the current and down the rapids, and broke loose. I had another, which I kept out of the current and landed. This was a trout of about 6¾ pounds in spawning colors. I succeeded in landing two more, then made my way again back to where I started. This was my wonderful fishing experience with these big trout.
>
> At the head of the big Hamilton Pool there was an island, and the water

rushed down each side very swiftly, far too deep and dangerous to wade. The canoe crossed the current and I easily made my landing in the still water below the island. All the large trout in this great pool were collected on this gravel space and rose to the fly, several at each cast. Some that I hooked got into the main current and down into the big pool, and I was obliged to break the leader and let them go, but I managed to land five or six which weighed between six and seven pounds. During the Nepigon trip I got a large number of trout—more than I would have taken if Indians had not been camped along the stream catching their winter supply of fish. I caught all I could for them, and got a very excellent idea of the run and size of the fish in this river. All I took averaged 3¾ pounds. My notebook shows 63 trout of over 6 pounds, and 24 of over 7 pounds.

One afternoon we were camped at Virgin Falls where the river comes out of Lake Nepigon. Fishing along the bank did not raise a single large fish. The water was rather deep, about 8 to 15 feet, with large stones and boulders on the bottom. The best method we had found of getting the large trout had been to use a large fly, about No. 00 or No. 000 in size, with a small spinner above it [shades of Gapen's Cockatouche fly]. No trout appeared on the surface at any time. The falls were about a twenty-foot straight drop.

I had brought along a 17-ounce 15-foot salmon rod for just such an opportunity. The few casts failed to raise any fish. I put on a small lead above the fly, cast across the stern, and let the fly sink and swing around with the current. The line straightened out, and I was fast to a real fish. These trout always fight downstream, and could not be allowed to go over the falls. It was all I could do, with a big salmon rod and heavy salmon leader, to stop these fish. I never had as hard a fight with any trout in my life. It took some time to get one of these fish up to the boat.

That afternoon proved to be the greatest trout fishing in my life. Thirteen fish were taken in all, six over 6 pounds and one very much larger. I could not weigh them, as the scales had been lost, but measured them with my belt, which I afterward carefully measured. One was 26 inches long and 20 inches in girth. According to the well-known formula for the weight of fish, the length times the square of the girth divided by 800, it weighed 13 pounds. I have always found this formula accurate within a very small amount, and the fact that I saw a number of trout of this same size at the Hudson Bay station [icehouse] encouraged me to believe that I actually caught a 13-pound trout.

The last day in the season was spent at the swift water above Lake Superior, as I had an idea that there might be a big run of large fish up from the lake. This proved to be the case. There were six fish of over 6 pounds taken. I removed a scale from one which indicated the fish had six periods of poor feeding, which means six years in the stream, the additional six months or so of the season until it was caught. The fish was about six and a half years old.

Hewitt's well-developed fishing skills set him apart from other anglers who fished the Nipigon. He was a master angler—intuitive, inventive, inquisitive, and willing to vary his fishing techniques. He probably understood brook trout—their life cycle and requirements—better than anyone who had fished or written about the Nipigon. He was also driven to catch big fish, and was his own most challenging competitor. All of these characteristics allowed him to catch more fish than his predecessors from a fishery that, while still excellent by any standards, was beginning to decline.

Hewitt's guide on this trip was a young but experienced Indian named Andrew. It's too bad we don't know his last name. Wouldn't it be an intriguing coincidence if it was Lexie, the same as Dr. Cook's older guide? A year later, in 1891, William McKirdy became the overseer for the HBC's Nipigon House. His son Jack later became an outfitter and put together Dr. Cook's memorable trip.

The best description of fishing the river and its many rapids and falls appeared in an 1895 promotional brochure, "Fishing and Shooting on the Canadian Pacific Railway," since published annually by the Canadian Pacific (now National) Railway. The brochure was designed to encourage fishermen and hunters to use the railway and to fill the growing number of CPR resort hotels that stretched from the Atlantic to the Pacific. Several of them, such as the hotels at Banff Springs, Jasper Park, and Montebello, remain in operation today, rustic log cabins similar to the Old Faithful Inn at Yellowstone. In 1895, there was no CPR hotel at Nipigon. One was built eventually; Dan Gapen's father managed it in the 1930s and '40s. It remains today as a private hotel.

Though the 1895 CPR brochure could be construed as biased, it really does give a fair account of fishing at that time, which was still so good that little or no puff was needed to convince anglers to travel by rail to great fishing destinations:

> On a fishing day—for even Nepigon has its "off days," and occasionally gets the sulks—you will take veritable giants: great trout of beauty and weight, that even the rankest enthusiast ne'er dreams of 'till he has tried this stream. Two-pounders, three-pounders, four, five—yea! and, by the unlying scales, eight-pounders are there ready to spring upon the deadly fly and fight to the last gasp against your practised hand. The station for it is Nepigon, where will be found a comfortable and well-managed little hotel, Taylor House, with accommodations for a limited number.
>
> On some days the fishing is fairly good from the railway bridge down to the mouth, particularly in the rapids; but to fish this river properly you must camp, and fortunately there is no difficulty about obtaining guides (Indians) and canoes at Red Rock, Nepigon, Ont., a Hudson's Bay Company's post. All necessaries for ordinary camping parties can also be obtained there. The rates for two Indians and a canoe being from $2 to $4 per day. Intending visitors must bear in mind that a trip up the river means living under canvas, and govern themselves accordingly. Necessities can be obtained on the spot; luxuries must be brought from the towns. There are many beautiful sites for a camp

Figure 16.3   A modern Nipigon River brook trout taken on a Cockatouche fly.

all along the river, and to say that it is a veritable anglers' paradise is quite within the mark. Trout scaling from two to five pounds can be readily taken on any of the best pools, and whitefish are plentiful and afford fine sport, rising eagerly at "gnat flies." Their mouths are as tender as wet paper, and a light hand must have hold of the rod to land them; but a two or three-pound whitefish is not to be despised, as he will fight bravely on the hook, and is wondrous toothsome on the platter.

The Nepigon falls 313 feet in its course of thirty-one miles, and varies greatly in width, narrowing to about 150 yards one mile from its mouth, but broadening at other points into a noble stream. Four lakes mark its course the first being lake Helen, only a mile from Red Rock, the crossing at its outlet. The current at this outlet is very fast. Lake Helen extends due north, and is some eight miles long by one wide. The river proper leaves this lake on the west side, and for six miles above it is broad and deep, with a moderate current, till the bend at Camp Alexandria is reached. A quarter of a mile above are the Long Rapids, continuing for a couple of miles. These are avoided on the upward journey by paddling up a brook on the west side for three-quarters of a mile, and from thence portaging to the second lake, Lake Jessie, reached by a portage of a mile and a half. Lake Jessie is three miles long and dotted with numerous small islands, and is separated from Lake Maria by the tumbling narrows. The latter lake is two and a half miles long.

From this lake to Cedar Portage, or Split Rock, the distance is a couple of miles, the portage being 250 yards long. A mile and a quarter above is another portage over an island in the centre of the stream, called Island Portage, which is about fifty yards long; and three miles above it is One-Mile Portage. At a trifle over a mile above the head of this portage the stream rushes down in a foamy chute; and immediately above is Lake Emma, nearly four miles long. A narrow arm of the river extends beyond the White Chute, which the canoer will follow for about a mile, and then portage 230 yards to Lake Emma. The distance between this lake and Lake Nepigon is only six miles; but the river is broken by four rapids not to be essayed by canoe. In order to avoid this, canoes turn aside at the northwest angle of Lake Emma, and follow a small stream, flowing from Lake Hannah, for a quarter of a mile, and thence onward for four miles to the head of Lake Hannah, where Flat Rock Portage, one mile long, extends to the shore of Lake Nepigon.

By now (1895), the river had all the fame and notoriety it could stand. In fact it had too much, and was beginning to show signs of wear and tear. Within two years of the time the first railroad bridge had spanned the river, in 1885, the West Coast and Toronto were linked through Nipigon Station. (An automobile bridge was not constructed until 1937.) With the trains came fishermen of every kind. The first of the tourist-angler-writers to begin sounding the river's death knell was A. R. Macdonough, who fished the entire river during the summer of 1895. His chapter in *The Out of Door Library: Angling* (1897) painted a lucid picture of the river's use and abuse just before the turn of the century. His catch was only fair, but perhaps this was because he was too quick to philosophize. Certainly in print he was verbose, almost evangelistic. But such was the style of the times.

Macdonough began by lamenting that the Adirondacks were now filled with inns, and that tanners and lumbermen had stripped Pennsylvania and the Catskills; so now Canada had become "the goal for American sportsmen, as for cashiers." Macdonough needed a dozen pages just to launch his canoe. He'd just cleared the rapids above the growing village of Nipigon when he resumed musing:

> To these tempting waters, anglers of every grade and from all regions throng. At the Mission [a Jesuit settlement for the Ojibway], nestled in a nook of green, carved out among the rocks on the lower edge of Lake Helen, parties of Indians, catching a wind right aft, pile squaws, pappooses, and numberless dogs into rickety birches, to skim along under a dirty blanket sail, pursuing for food the snaky pickerel and coarse Mackinaw trout of the lake.
>
> The young novice, too eager to delay, drops his fly and lifts his two-pound fish even under the shadow of the railway bridge. The expert, trained for many years in many waters, and epicure of the best, his canoe trimly packed with a month's supplies in rubber bags and light boxes, manned by a steersman and a sturdy oarsman, presses steadily on his three days' course for the upper river. He will overtake a flotilla, bearing some millionaire and his household goods, feigning to rough it with actually a complete cooking-stove and a huge negro cook aboard. Or at the head of a portage he will come upon some noisy break-fasting party of ten or twelve from one of the inland cities, enlivening these calm solitudes with the clamor of the sociable West. Camps dot the shore

ahead of him, and camps astern—some charming with the gay colors and bright presence of women, some loud and dirty with pot-hunters on a picnic.

On the day he started, Macdonough had just ascended the rapids under the new Canadian National Railway bridge a little after noon as trains approached the Nipigon from the east and west, bringing their hordes of anglers. "The best months are July and August," he wrote. "At that season, there are often thirty anglers at once, scattered in camps along the stream. Each pair, if properly equipped, have at least two men [guides] to pilot them." That, according to Macdonough's calculations, was 90 people a day on the river—for 60 days. By now, the Nipigon was rapidly losing its wilderness character, and this was best evidenced at the portages. He called the numerous land routes along the Nipigon "the social exchanges of the river."

> If no one there meets the voyager, scraps of newspaper or marks on wrappers disclose what native of what town lately crossed the trail. More often [the portages are] occupied by flying camps at either end, and always convenient baiting-points after the toil of reaching them, the guides here meet their friends, and the angler makes acquaintances. New-comers produce the mails and the latest papers for those who care for them; descending parties bring notes of the sport promised or failed. Fly-books are compared, scores sometimes confided, cocktails, cigars, and addresses exchanged, and after a half-hour's joint lunch each goes on his way, wishing the other good-speed.

It took Macdonough only three days to cover the 30 miles of rapids, falls, and portages to Lake Nipigon. I doubt he had much time for serious fishing.

> Americans on either side the border concern themselves little about coming generations. Yet interest, if not duty, should prompt them to take some care that this superb river shall not lose its preeminence as the finest trouting water of the world. It is no longer possible, as it was reported to be twenty-five years ago, to take in one day a barrel of trout averaging four pounds, nor can the angler now quickly fill his basket within sight of Red Rock Landing. But that the fish are there, neither few nor small, is certain, from this record of one rod for two hours each day, wielded not to make a score, but merely to supply the wants of three men.

Year	Average Weight Each Day lbs.	Average Weight of Whole Catch lbs. ozs.	Number Taken Over Three pounders
1886	16	2 2	22
1887	11	2 0	14
1888	10	2 4	14

One hundred and fifty-five visitors camped on the river last year [1895] with the usual proportion of careful and accomplished anglers to ignorant or greedy fishermen.

A gauge of the number of fishermen coming to the Nipigon was reflected in William McKirdy's (HBC manager) report for 1890. It was the best revenue year in the history of Nipigon House; it sold $1,040 in merchandise. He estimated that visitors spent more than $9,000, which didn't include transportation or hotel accommodations. A year later, the 1901 report of the Fisheries Branch of the Ontario Department of Game and Fisheries noted that no reliable fishing was to be had from Nipigon Harbor upstream to Camp Alexander. However, above Alexander Falls brook trout fishing was still considered "good."

Another gauge that measured the rise and fall of the river's popularity was the sale of nonresident Ontario fishing licenses. They were required before 1900, but in that year McKirdy's store made just over $1,000 in license sales. Sales peaked in 1906, at just under $1,600. By the time Dr. Cook fished the river in 1915 (according to some authorities, and 1916 according to others; he may have fished both years), sales had declined to $957. In 1912, the cost of a license for Canadians outside of Ontario was $5 for two weeks and $10 for four weeks. For nonresidents it was $15, $20, and $25 for two, three, and four weeks.

By this time, the season on brook trout closed September 15 and didn't reopen until May 1. The limit was 50 per day or 15 pounds, whichever came first, with no brook trout of less than 5 inches.

With the fish population now in decline, the Fisheries Branch began some misguided attempts to rejuvenate the brook trout fishery, starting with a program of coarse-fish destruction, removing northern pike, pickerel (walleye), and suckers. "Some thousands of pike [a few to 10 pounds each] were destroyed." The Fisheries Branch also began removing brook trout from spawning grounds in Lake Nipigon to be used as brood stock in other waters, both in Canada and the United States. It believed these fish were unneeded in the river because it was a "vast spawning bed." At the same time (1902), it opened Lake Nipigon to commercial fishing. "Lake Nipigon," according to a Fisheries Branch annual report, "was overflowing with whitefish, lake and brook trout." In 1906, one man employed for six weeks by the Fisheries Branch netted and destroyed 7,632 northern pike, 2,282 suckers, 228 walleye, and 145 whitefish, for a total of 10,287 fish.

About this time, transient anglers were discovering that Lake Nipigon also held huge brook trout, and some of the pressure began shifting from the river to the lake. Over the next few years, a dozen fishing camps sprang up around its periphery. Today, only three remain.

Though brook trout fishing was faltering, the number of outfitters in Nipigon increased. William McKirdy left the HBC and set up a rival store, and in 1905 Revillion Freres set up his own Nipigon post. Upriver, brook trout were falling on hard times. Indians annually netted thousands of pounds of big river fish to feed their dogs. At Virgin Falls, they placed their nets across channels, which kept the fish from their spawning sites. On the lake, one Indian was reported to have taken 2,000 brook trout, from 2 to 7 pounds each, by netting them in the shallows on lakeside spawning sites. If that wasn't bad enough, an extreme drought in 1906 and 1907 lowered water levels in both the lake and river, and many spawning grounds went dry. Despite the netting of coarse fish, their numbers remained high.

But these problems were nothing compared to what was soon to come. In 1910, after a visit to the Nipigon, A. W. G. Wilson of the Geological Survey Branch of the Ontario Department of Mines made a statement, the ramifications of which few people at that time realized or understood. "The water-powers of the Nipigon River will be of more than local importance, when utilized, as they are probably one of the largest and best of the readily more accessible undeveloped water-powers of Canada." Wilson was well aware that the river moved 5,500 cubic feet of water, and that it dropped 313 feet over a course of 30 miles.

By the time Dr. Cook arrived on the river in 1916, the Nipigon had changed internally. Black bass had been introduced to the lake and worked their way into the river. Rainbow trout had been stocked regularly since 1894. More than 300,000 Atlantic salmon were planted in the river and were spawning at the base of Alexander Falls. The coarse-fish eradication program had just ended. Poachers and pot-fishermen had taken heavy tolls on brook trout, often using dip nets or dynamite in the pools. The Native peoples were now more dependent upon fish than before, and had netted huge quantities in the preceding decade.

It's amazing that, under the circumstances, a fish could grow as large as 14 ½ pounds in 1916. One ichthyologist recently speculated that it was probably a coaster, a fish from Lake Superior that had entered the river to spawn. This is unlikely for two reasons: First, coasters don't begin entering the river until late August and September. Dr. Cook caught his fish on July 22. And second, the fish was caught just below Virgin Falls, which is nearly 30 miles, 15 rapids, and six falls above Lake Superior. Brook trout can't jump, or at least not very high. The falls would have been insurmountable for a gutty 14 ½-pound brook trout.

After 1916, the river began to change physically.

With the increase of Euro-Canadian residents came the establishment of railways. Then commercial and illegal fishing began to take their toll. To this add irresponsible logging operations, which began in 1923 and didn't end until 1973. The loggers used the river to transport logs to the mills, and the effluent destroyed the water quality. The introduction of non-native fish species also caused a decline in brook trout populations (heightened in the past few decades by the addition of Pacific salmon to the Great Lakes). This was further compounded in 1921 by the fisheries department's overstocking of hatchery-reared brook trout fry, which competed with existing brook trout for the remaining spawning grounds. In 1940, aerial spraying with DDT began in the area in an effort to stop spruce budworm—but it also destroyed the river's aquatic life. In the mid-1940s, workers around the Cameron Falls dam complained of the black flies. Unlike mosquitoes, black flies can only mature in moving water. The province responded by dripping DDT directly into any creek within a half mile of the area twice a week during blackfly season. Frazer Creek was treated at three stations. This program was continued until the 1960s.

However, the worst was a move by Ontario Hydro, which heeded A. W. G. Wilson's advice and began to harness the river's hydroelectric potential—cheap power for area aluminum, chemical, and pulp plants. In 1918, dam construction began at Cameron Falls, just below where the Nipigon leaves Lake Jessie. The dam was completed in 1920, raising the level of the lake until it backed up 12 miles to the base of Pine Portage—flooding Cameron Pool, the basin of Lake Marie, and obliterating Bashewana Rapids. At The Narrows, the river became an even narrower passage with just a hint of current, between what was now called Lake Marie and Cedar Portage, Split Rock, Island Portage, and Camp Cincinnati. A fish ladder constructed alongside the dam in 1922 was closed because of "no perceptible use." But a log slide was provided next to it for the lumber companies. Despite the flooding of many brook trout spawning and fishing areas by this dam, some of the better areas of the river remained in their original state and offered fair to excellent fishing. By changing one's standards, it was still a fishery.

In 1926, the Hydro Commission built a second dam on the river, this time just above Virgin Falls, at the outlet of Lake Nipigon, "to control the outflow and regulate the levels," while the Cameron Falls dam was extended to satisfy the increasing energy demands of pulp and paper companies in Thunder Bay (Port Arthur/Fort William renamed). Instead of objecting, the Ontario Fisheries Branch responded by stocking more brook trout fry and fingerlings into the river. The little wooden dam above Virgin Falls and another smaller dam to the east, over a secondary channel, backed up Lake Nipigon by 16 inches, creating what was at that time the world's largest storage reservoir.

In 1930, a third but smaller dam was built on the lower Nipigon River at Alexander's Landing, just a mile below Cameron Falls. It flooded Alexander Falls and the long-used Camp Alexander.

The greatest blow to the Nipigon and its brook trout began in 1948, with the construction of the Pine Portage dam, which took 1,300 workers two years to complete. This dam, 10 miles downstream from Lake Nipigon, was just ½ mile above the spot where the waters of Lake Marie were elevated by the Cameron Falls dam. It backed water so far upstream that it flooded out the wooden Virgin Falls dam and even elevated Lake Nipigon another 4 inches. The Virgin Falls dam was partially dismantled to aid navigation.

Not only did this last dam form a complete barrier to any fish migrating upriver, but also it flooded out all of the river's remaining brook trout spawning areas. These included Robinson and Hamilton pools, Flat Rock Portage (on the river), Great White Chute, Camp Victoria and Victoria Rapids, Canal Rapids, Miners Camp, both MacDonald and Rabbit rapids, Pine Island, and even Virgin Falls. During the summer of 1994, the water was so clear over Virgin Falls that, drifting over it with the current, I could see the falls' old granite precipice drop away into the dark depths of the river. It was an awesome experience, even without the 22-foot-high falls.

The Pine Portage dam was the last phase in the ecological destruction of the greatest brook trout watershed on the continent. It eliminated Lake Hannah and created a vast, shallow reservoir now called Forgan Lake. It raised the level of Lake Nipigon so that it flooded the portage trail at the northwestern corner of Lake Hannah and created a new, small outlet over Flat Rock Portage; this is navigable, though tricky, by a small boat. This was the route followed by most trappers, explorers, and Hudson's Bay Company personnel packing supplies into the trading posts on Lake Nipigon. Today, all of these places and names, once everyday words in the vocabularies of brook trout fishermen, are buried in history and under water.

By 1960, according to Dan Gapen Sr., who grew up in Nipigon in the 1930s and '40s, 6-pound brook trout had become a thing of the past, and the average brook trout dropped to under 2 pounds. The river still produces the occasional trophy trout, but these are few and far between. About 1950, Lake Nipigon, which hadn't been fished as intensely as the river, rose to prominence, though it was then just a shadow of what it had been 20 to 30 years earlier. Despite the conversion of brook trout to dog food by Native peoples netting the spawning grounds, and the removal and transport of spawning fish to the provincial hatchery in Thunder Bay, there were still big fish in the lake. Frank Goodman, in an interview in 1979, stated that commercial fisherman Art Sutherland had a few years earlier taken a 21½-pound brook trout in a net.

Field & Stream magazine maintained a registry of the world's largest sportfish until 1956, when the International Game Fish Association inherited the task, and it also conducted an annual fishing contest. Studying this contest's results is a great way to discover where the big fish were being taken. Between 1943 and 1953, of the 50 largest fish in the Brook Trout Fly Casting Division, 7 came from Lake Nipigon and 6 from the Nipigon River. They ranged from 8 pounds, 14 ounces down to 7 pounds, with most of the larger fish coming from the lake. In the Brook Trout Open Division, 27, more than half, came from here—20 from the lake and 7 from the river. The division's two leaders were fish of 10 pounds, 2 ounces and 9 pounds, 4 ounces. River brook trout were ranked third and fourth—a 9-pounder and an 8-pound, 12-ounce fish. Eleven of the last 14 fish were also lake brook trout, which ranged from 7 pounds, 9 ounces down to 7 pounds, 4 ounces. The most effective fly was the Mickey Finn, and the most effective lure was Gapen's and Prescott's Cockatouche (with spinners).

By the 1970s, brook trout in both the river and the lake had declined to the point that a catch was almost incidental. Most anglers were after lake trout or the occasional walleye. In the reservoirs and in shallow areas of flooded land adjacent to the river, northern pike had become the epitome of fishing for most anglers. The run of rainbow and brown trout at the mouth of the river caught the attention of many anglers. Stocking Pacific salmon in Lake Superior tributaries pushed brook trout even farther down the list of desirable species. Still, a few dedicated anglers remembered the better days of the fishery and continued to fish for them. There was one important difference now, however: Most of them released the fish.

Since about 1980, the Ontario Ministry of Natural Resources or OMNR (the successor to the Department of Game and Fisheries) has been able to manage a fragile brook trout fishery from below the Alexander Falls dam downstream to the mouth of the Nipigon River. For management purposes, it's divided into two areas: one from the dam to the entrance to

Lake Helen, and the other from the beginning of the river, where it exits Lake Helen, to Nipigon Harbor. The brook trout population has fluctuated annually in these areas, but always showing a slight loss.

It wasn't until 1990, when OMNR regional fisheries biologist Rob Swainson tackled the problem, that a future for the fishery began to seem possible. Swainson had spent seven years in the 1980s studying speckled and lake trout in eastern Canada's Algonquin Park and was quite familiar with the species. His new task was to determine why brook trout were declining and to identify their spawning and nursery grounds in the lower river. Doing so led him to some startling observations. Swainson monitored Ontario Hydro's practice of storing water during winter for later use in generating, which reduced river flows below levels safe for the fish. This, he determined, was causing the decline in brook trout populations. Ontario Hydro denied it. Not until Swainson video-taped river spawning redds filled with brook trout eggs that were exposed to subfreezing winter air after the drawdown was he able to support his claim.

By now, Swainson had gained support from area anglers and fishing clubs. A novel idea—a return to native species of fish—was beginning to permeate the thinking of many dedicated trout fishermen, spurred in part in the United States by organizations such as Trout Unlimited and by new policies in the National Park Service. The idea caught on in Canada as well. Swainson helped establish the Nipigon District Cooperative Angler Programs and got the fishermen involved. In 1990, a provincial court got Ontario Hydro to agree to a one-year guarantee of sufficient minimum flow to the lower river to ensure that brook trout redds would remain covered with water. Though the term has expired, Ontario Hydro, on the strength of a handshake, has continued to keep the water coming.

"Yes, the specs are struggling in the Nipigon," wrote Gord Ellis of Thunder Bay, "but all is not doom and gloom. The Fall of '88 saw numerous large brookies again caught in the river, perhaps the best season in five years." Ellis and his two fishing buddies managed to catch and release four brook trout in the 4- to 6-pound range in three days of fishing in August of that year. Many other anglers enjoyed similar successes.

Catch-and-release fishing had really come to the Nipigon. A lot of the credit for this also must go to Molson's Big Fish Contest, 1984–89, which was jointly sponsored by the brewery and the Ontario Federation of Anglers and Hunters. The contest, which had a catch-and-keep as well as -release category, awarded prizes to the top 15 anglers and pub-licized their names. From 1984–89, Nipigon dominated the release category. Because of the great number of brook trout he had released, Ray DuPuis Sr. was named Angler of the Year in 1986. The largest of that year, however, was a 25-inch brook trout with a 16-inch girth, caught by Dan Klatt of Nipigon. It probably weighed more than 7 pounds.

Swainson, like many anglers, believed that these fish were coasters, which spend most of the year in Lake Superior and use the lower Nipigon only to spawn and as a nursery for their progeny. Their biggest threat today comes not from anglers but from Pacific salmon, which vie for the small amount of spawning area in the river.

Today, the Nipigon is nothing like it was in the past. Hydroelectric engineers have managed to harness 240 of a potential 250 feet of the river's 313 feet of vertical drop, turning most of the river into two large reservoirs. Semblances of the old river remain in only a few locations—at the site of the flooded Virgin Falls dam, in The Narrows that inundated Split Rock, just below the Pine Portage dam, and at the only remaining portage, Island Portage—all within a mile of the dam. Below this the old river is lost in the reservoir. The only remnant of the original fishery is for coasters in the lower river.

In June 1994 I fished with Ray DuPuis of Nipigon, an environmental chemist now retired, and Kaarlo Kjellman, also of Nipigon, who operates Osprey Charters. The first day we fished in Lake Superior, among the islands outside of the river's entrance. Ice had been off the lake for a week, and brook trout were still warming up along the shores. We caught several fish, all under 2 pounds. The bigger fish are here in August and September.

We spent another day fishing the lower river from the village to the foot of Alexander Landing dam. We caught a few brook trout and several whitefish. The following day we fished The Narrows and saw a big brook trout in the shallows, but it wasn't feeding. We passed several other boats drifting over what once was the famed Bashewana Rapids. One angler told us he had caught a 4-pounder two days earlier, and let it go. Later, we discovered that Ray's equally capable son had fished this same water with a friend the previous day and had caught and released nearly two dozen brook trout, the largest weighing 4½ pounds. Perhaps they all still had sore mouths when we were there. Another day we fished around the flooded remains of the Virgin Falls wooden dam, with no success. We then worked our way into the lake, fishing the shoreline around the numerous islands that glut the entrance to the river. Brook trout usually lie on the flooded edges around the islands, just inside of the deep water. DuPuis caught two of between 2½ and 3 pounds.

On the last day we fished Lake Nipigon again, around larger islands farther out in the lake. For about 45 minutes I thought I was battling a new record brook trout. We had been pulling small trout off the island using DuPuis's unique version of the Cockatouche fly. Kjellman had even managed to trap a few live sculpins (the English translation of the Ojibway *cockatouche*) in case the flies didn't work. By midmorning the wind on the lake began churning up whitecaps, and it was impossible to throw a fly into the near gale. I switched to a small spoon and began combing the ledges for brook trout. In a flash, a huge trout came out from the shadow beneath an overhanging bush and hit my lure, almost the moment it landed in the foot-deep water. It turned out to be a lake trout that weighed just under 30 pounds. There are big brook trout in the watershed, but they aren't numerous.

A week later I got a call from Kjellman. He had been fishing Forgan Lake when he was flagged down by two anglers in a boat who had been after northern pike in the shallows beyond what once was Lake Emma. They wanted to borrow a scale to weigh a big pike they had caught.

Kjellman looked into their huge cooler, and there, beneath several pike and their slime, were three brook trout—5, 6, and 7 pounds. The two pike fishermen didn't know what they had really accomplished. Oh yes! They took all the fish on a trolled Dardevle spoon.

17 THE LAURENTIDES: PARADISE LOST—BUT MAYBE NOT FOREVER

One of North America's least-known major brook trout areas was a 6,000-square-mile triangle of rugged terrain on the North Shore of the St. Lawrence River. As the continental ice sheet retreated from southeastern Canada 12,000 or more years ago, an eastward extension of the Great Lakes flooded the glacially depressed upper St. Lawrence Valley. Riding the crest of these flooding waters came a horde of brook trout, populating every niche except for the highest and most inaccessible waters. As the tremendous glacial weight disappeared, the land rose slowly and the waters flowed off the elevated lands. Remnant depressions in these Laurentian Mountains filled with water, brook trout, and other salmonids. Brook trout continued to colonize every watershed possible, and were stopped only where cataracts kept them from reaching a watershed's sources.

Through 8,000 to 12,000 years of isolated development, this unique area evolved a population containing many large brook trout, some of up to 10 pounds—or even more. Then, within the short span of 24 to 30 years, they disappeared, leaving in their wake brook trout of 2 to 3 pounds at most. Today, small sections, under strict management, have yielded a few big fish.

As one crosses this land today, it seems unimaginable that such a great brook trout fishery ever existed here. Only a comparatively small number of trout fishermen ever experienced it. Eighty years after its demise, none can recall this fishery except as tales from the elders. It's almost as if this brook trout angler's Shangri-la never existed.

The rugged Laurentian Mountains stretch from just north of Lake Superior east to southern Labrador, but the superlative fishing was restricted to a much smaller area—the large, irregularly shaped triangle in Québec, bounded on the north by the tidal Saguenay River and Lac St-Jean (St. John); on the west by the broad, south-flowing St-Maurice River; and on the southeast by the St-Lawrence. The area's core, where most of the larger brook trout once abounded, is an ovate plateau roughly 70 miles wide and 80 miles from north to south, somewhat smaller than the Adirondacks but possessing many characteristics in common. Its glacially beveled peaks rise on the average about 2,000 feet, punctuated by several of more than 3,000 feet.

The plateau receives an inordinate amount of rain compared with the surrounding area, and is drained by numerous watersheds that carved routes in the ancient granitic Canadian Shield. From its higher elevations, a center roughly 10 miles northeast of Lac Jacques-Cartier, nine large rivers start as small trickles or in lakes and flow in all directions. These include the Rivière Jacques-Cartier and its three branches: the Northwest, North (R. Launiere) and Northeast; the Montmorency and its tributary the Rivière des Neiges; the rivières Malbaie, Cyriac, and Chicoutimi, with its tributary the Pikauba; the rivières aux Ecorces, Métabetchouane, Batiscan, and Ste-Anne. Each of these is fed by countless brown waters draining the spruce and fir forests that cover the rocky land in a verdant velvet blanket.

Located just north of Québec City, these mountains, with their labyrinth of rivers and lakes and their horde of large brook trout, remained essentially closed to the outside world for 275 years after the French established their first permanent settlement at Tadoussac on the St. Lawrence River. The streams were large and swift, filled with rapids, chutes, and waterfalls that made them impossible to navigate more than a few miles above their mouths.

North of the mountains, Roberval and other communities sprang up on the shores about Lac St-Jean. They were connected with the outside world by a trip of 100 miles down the Saguenay, then another 120 up the St. Lawrence to Québec City. From December to March, ice cut off the people of Lac St-Jean from the outside world. What was needed was an overland route (today's Route 175) from Québec to Roberval. Construction of the St. John, or Post, Road, as it was called, began in 1875 in Stoneham and reached Roberval in 1878. It cut directly through the heart of the Laurentides. While it saved travelers more than 80 miles, it also opened the wilderness and brook trout to poachers.

An excellent account of the earliest brook trout fishing in the southern half of the triangle came from America's foremost naturalist, John Burroughs. The intrepid philosopher and brook trout addict was born in Roxbury, in New York's Catskills, and regularly fished the Neversink, Beaver Kill, Willowemoc, East Branch, and Esopus. Now he wanted to expand his fishing prowess into Canada.

"When the dog-star [Sirius] began to blaze [early July], we set out for Canada," wrote Burroughs in *The Halcyon* (Kingfisher) *in Canada,* published in 1879, two years after the trip. Burroughs and a companion traveled by train from New York to Montréal, then by steamer to Québec City. There they hired "Joe" and his buckboard for the trip along the uncompleted road.

Five miles into the forest upon the new road is the hamlet of La Chance, the last house till you reach the [St. John] lake, 120 miles distant. Our destination the first night was La Chance's [a farmhouse]; this would enable us to reach the Jacques Cartier River, 40 miles farther, where we were supposed to encamp.

We are now fairly well among the mountains, and the sun well down behind the trees when we entered upon the post-road. It proved to be a wide, well-built highway, grass-grown, but in good condition. After an hour's travel, we saw a clearing, and about six o'clock drew up in front of the long, low, log habitation of La Chance.

La Chance was one of the game wardens, or constables appointed by the government to see the game laws enforced. Joe had not felt entirely at his ease about the duck he was surreptitiously taking to town, and when, by its "quack, quack" it called upon La Chance for protection, he responded at once. Joe was obliged to liberate it then and there, and to hear the law read and expounded, and be threatened till he turned pale beside. It was evident that they follow the home government in the absurd practice of enforcing their laws in Canada. La Chance said he was under oath not to blink at or permit any violation of the law, and seemed to think that made a difference.

[The next day] we passed many beautiful lakes; among others the Two Sisters, one on each side of the road. At noon we paused at a lake, fed the horse and had lunch. I was not long in getting ready my fishing tackle, and upon a raft made of two logs pinned together floated out upon the lake and took all the trout we wanted. Early in the afternoon, we entered what is called *La Grand Brulure* or Great Burning. All the mountains and valleys, as far as the eye could see, had been swept by the fire. For three hours more we rode and came upon Morancy [Montmorency] River, a placid yellow stream 20 or 25 yards wide, abounding with trout. We walked a short distance along its banks. The mountains on either hand had been burned by the fire until in places their great granite bones were bare and white.

At another point we were within ear-shot for a mile or more of a brawling stream in the valley below us and caught a glimpse of foaming rapids cascades through the dense spruce, a trout stream that probably no man had ever fished. It would be quite impossible to do so in such a maze and tangle of woods.

We neither met, nor passed, nor saw any travelers till late in the afternoon, when we descried far ahead a man on horseback. When he saw us he drew rein and awaited our approach. He proved to be a young Canadian going to join the gang of workmen at the farther end of the road. About four o'clock we passed another small lake, and in a few moments more drew up at the bridge over the Jacques Cartier River, and our 40-mile ride was finished.

A hundred yards below the bridge, amid the spruces on the bank of the river, we bedded. The river at this point was a swift, black stream from 30 to

40 feet wide, with a strength and a bound like a moose. Three miles above our camp was Great Lake Jacques Cartier, the source of the river, a sheet of water nine miles long and from one to three wide; 50 rods below was Little Lake Jacques Cartier [Lac Sept-Îles], an irregular body two [one] miles across.

The spruce have colored the water, which is a dark amber color, but entirely sweet and pure. There needed no better proof of the latter fact than the trout with which it abounded, and their clear and vivid tints. In its lower portions, near the St. Lawrence, the Jacques Cartier River is a salmon stream but these fish have never been found as near its source as we were.

When I was a boy and used to go a-fishing, I could seldom restrain my eagerness after I arrived in sight of the brook or pond, and must needs run the rest of the way. Then the delay in rigging my tackle was a trial my patience was never quite equal to. After I had made a few casts, or had caught one fish, I could pause and adjust my line properly.

I found some remnant of the old enthusiasm still in me [he was then 40 years old] when I sprang from the buck-board that afternoon, and saw the strange river rushing by. I would have given something if my tackle had been rigged so that I could have tried the trout that had just broken the surface. I had anticipated this moment, and surreptitiously undone my rod-case and got my reel out of my bag, and was a few moments ahead of my companion in making the first cast. The trout rose readily. Almost too soon we had more than enough for dinner, though no "rod-smashers" had been seen or felt. Our experience the next morning, and during the day, and the next morning in the lake, in the rapids, in the pools, was the same; there was a surfeit of trout eight or ten inches long, though we rarely kept any under ten.

The third day, in the afternoon, we had our first and only sensation in the shape of a big trout. It came none too soon. It was a dull, rainy day; fog rested low upon the mountains, and the time hung heavily upon our hands. About three o'clock the rain slackened and we emerged from our den. I began preparing dinner while my companion took his rod and stepped to the edge of the big pool in front of camp. At the first cast, and when his fly was not 15 feet away, there was a lunge and a strike. Apparently the fisherman had hooked a bowlder. I was standing a few yards below engaged in washing out the coffee-pail, when I heard him call out:

"I have got him now!"

"Yes; I see you have," said I, noticing his bending pole and moveless line; "when I am through, I will help you get loose."

"Does that look like a stone or a log?" said my friend, pointing to his quivering line, slowly cutting the current up toward the centre of the pool. My skepticism vanished. I could hardly keep my place on the top of the rock.

"I can feel him breathe," said the fisherman, "just feel the pole."

I put my eager hand upon the butt and could easily imagine I felt the throb or pant of something alive down there in the black depths. Whatever it was moved about like a turtle. I rushed for the landing-net and I skipped about from bowlder to bowlder as the fish worked about the pool. I saw a shadowy, unsubstantial something emerge from the black depths, then vanish. I saw it again. This time the huge proportions of the fish were faintly outlined by the white facings [pipings] of his fins. The sketch lasted but a twinkling; it was only a flitting shadow upon a darker background, but it gave me the profoundest Ike Walton thrill I ever experienced. I had been a fisher from my earliest boyhood. I came from a race of fishers; trout-streams gurgled about the roots of the family tree, and there was a long accumulated and transmitted tendency and desire in me that that sight gratified.

The fish yielded to the relentless pole, till, in about 15 minutes from the time he was struck, he came to the surface and made a whirlpool where he disappeared again. Presently, he was up a second time, lashing the water into foam as the angler led him toward the rock upon which I was perched. As I reached toward him, down he went again, and, taking another circle of the pool, came up more exhausted. Between his paroxysms, I carefully ran the net over him and lifted him ashore. Much larger trout have been taken in these and other waters, but this fish would have swallowed any three we had ever before caught.

"What does he weigh?" was the natural inquiry of each; and we took turns "hefting" him.

"Four pounds," we said; but Joe said more. We improvised a scale: a long strip of board was balanced across a stick, and our groceries served as weights. A four-pound package of sugar kicked the beam quickly; a pound of coffee was added: still it went up; then a pound of tea, and still the fish had little the best of it. We called it six pounds. Such a beautiful creature. He graced the stump that afternoon and was the sweetest fish we had taken. The flesh was a rich deep salmon color. Two varieties of [brook] trout inhabit these waters, irrespective of size, the red-fleshed and white-fleshed, and the former were the best.

One afternoon, quite unexpectedly, I struck my big fish at the head of the lake. I was first advised of his approach by two or three trout jumping clear from the water to get out of his lordship's way. The water was not deep just there, and he swam so near the surface that his enormous back cut through. With a swirl he swept my fly under and turned.

My hook was too near home, and my rod too near a perpendicular to strike well. I struck, but not with enough decision, and before I could reel up, my empty hook came back. The trout had carried it in his jaws till the fraud was detected; and then spat it out. He came a second time, but failed to take the fly and so to get his weight and beauty in these pages. I will place my loss at the full extent and claim that nothing less than a ten-pounder was spirited away from my hand. I might not have saved him, netless as I was upon my cumbrous raft.

These trout are not lake trout, but the common brook trout (S. fontinalis). The largest ones are taken with live bait through the ice in winter. The Indians and the *habitans* bring them out of the woods from here on their toboggans, from two and a half to three feet long. About half a mile above camp we discovered a deep oval bay to one side of the main current of the river, that abounded in big fish. It was a favorite feeding ground, and late every afternoon they rose all about. A trout, when he comes to the surface, starts a ring about his own length; most rings in the pool were like barrel hoops. The haughty trout ignored all our best efforts; not one rise did we get. We were told of this pool on our return to Québec, and that other anglers had a similar experience. But occasionally some old fisherman, like a great advocate [lawyer] who loves a difficult case, would set his wits to work and bring into camp an enormous trout from the pool.

This core of the Laurentides, 2,500 square miles of Québec, was set aside in 1895 and later expanded as one of Canada's first parks—a "forest reservation, fish and game preserve, a public park and pleasure ground." It contains an estimated 1,500 lakes and ponds. As with the Adirondacks, its charter also had a "forever wild" clause, but this wasn't written into stone that was hard enough, nor into either provincial or federal constitutions: "No person shall, except under lease, license, or permit, locate, settle upon, use or occupy any portion of said park, nor shall any lease, license or permit be made, granted, or issued which will in any way impair the usefulness of the park." It began as Laurentides National Park, but in 1981 was renamed Le Parc des Laurentides, or Laurentide Park. In the introduction to the act that established the park, E. J. Flynn, commissioner of Crown lands in 1896, described one aspect of the potential recreation: "As regards river fishing, there is no finer brook-trout stream than Jacques Cartier, the fish running up to 5 lbs., taking the fly readily." He should have fished the lake. Brook trout there were twice as heavy (Blake).

But as early as July 1912, an order-in-council authorized a pulp and paper company to build and maintain a dam in the heart of the park, because "it needed a constant supply of water throughout the year to sustain its operations" (Longstreth). The company didn't have to buy timberland; it could lease timber rights from the province.

The motto of the government, claimed one conservationist of that era, was Commerce Before Sport. More recently, when logging interests couldn't resist the stands of virgin timber within the park, they lobbied the provincial government to change its designation to Reserve Faunique des Laurentides. This new designation judiciously used only *faunique* ("animals") and omitted *fauna* ("plants"), so the park became a reserve for the forest industry. True park areas were reduced to two portions that comprise less than one-tenth of the original park, and include Parc de Conservation des Grands-Jardins des Ours and Parc de Conservation de la Jacques-Cartier. A flight over the park reveals the true condition of the land. A driver on Route 175 from Québec City to Chicoutimi sees only the façade created by the rows of trees that line the road, not the lumber industry's devastating clear-cutting concealed behind.

Though some interior waters had been fished since the early 1800s, mainly by trappers and later by fishermen exploring for new brook trout waters, they remained in the mid-1800s virtually untouched. But by that time, as fishing south of the border began a slow deterioration, anglers with time, money, and a willingness to rough it begain making forays into the interior of the Laurentides. These jaunts lasted at least three or four weeks, requiring guides and all of the paraphernalia needed to camp and fish in the wilderness, as well as strong backs for the innumerable portages. The fishery for big brook trout was short lived, lasting only about a dozen years, from roughly 1890 to 1902, followed by a decline after the entry of pulp companies. By 1915, big brook trout in the Laurentides were history.

The first road to skirt the area was St-Urbain Road (Route 56, now 381), a rough dirt path on the eastern side that ran from Baie-St-Paul on the North Shore of the St. Lawrence to La Baie, midway up the Saguenay. Only the most dedicated angler took this tortuous trip by horse and wagon, but it provided the first access to the park from the east. From La Baie, anglers followed the Malbaie River west into the heart of the lake district. Along with the anglers came hordes of poachers, who defied provincial fish and game laws considered generous even then and devastated the fish on the eastern edge of the plateau. The fishery was saved from wholesale destruction only by the formation of the park.

Enforcing fish and game laws over so vast a land was considered impractical at that time by the government. But the practice of leasing these lands to private clubs almost completely stopped the abuse. Shortly after 1895, seven clubs came into existence and formed a cordon along the park's entire eastern edge. To maintain their leases, the clubs had to adhere strictly to the laws, patrol their lands, and prevent poaching. They did all of this so effectively that the fish and game came back, although they never attained their former stature. The 10-pound brook trout of Lac Jacques-Cartier were history before the park was formed.

Beginning in the early 1870s, inroads were made from the south, following the course of the Jacques-Cartier River. However, the most rapid expansion, before completion of the St-Jean Road into the Laurentides, occurred along its western edge near the end of the decade, when the Québec & Lake St. John Railway was completed, linking Québec City with Roberval on Lake St. John. Almost immediately, more than 30 "whistle stops" sprang up en route. Most were jumping-off places for hunting and fishing camps. Almost for pennies, the provincial government leased large tracts to hunting and fishing clubs. The more famous were the Triton, Talbot, Jacques-Cartier, and Iroquois hunting and fishing clubs. Many are still in existence, having held the land for more than 100 years.

The Canadian Pacific Railway, now Canadian National, was the main east-west trunk line. In those early years it actively promoted hunting and fishing along its routes. The railroad periodically issued pamphlets or guides extolling the great hunting and fishing of the lands adjoining its tracks. The following is an excerpt from the 1897 promotional booklet *Fishing and Shooting on the Canadian Pacific Railway*:

Eighteen rivers, large and small, empty into Lake St. John; but only one drains the high plateau to the south, the Metabetchouan River. It offers excellent [brook] trout fishing, some as large are four and five pounds. At its mouth, on Lake St. John, is Poole's Hotel, with room for a limited number. This house is the headquarters of the Fish and Game Club of Springfield, Mass., and may be reached by steamer from Roberval, or from Chambord Junction, on Lake St. John, a distance of five miles.

The outlet of Lake St. John is Grande Décharge and Petite Décharge, which finally unite and form Saguenay River. Perhaps the greatest pleasure connected with a trip to Lake St. John would be, when leaving, to hire canoes and guides and descend the Saguenay to the Chicoutimi, which drains the northeastern Laurentides into the Saguenay River.

Between the city of Québec and Lake St. John, the Québec & Lake St. John Railway traverses a country of wild beauty, the route leading amid the picturesque Laurentian Mountains, crossing several streams and touching upon fine lakes noted for the abundance and large size of their trout. Quite a number of these lakes are controlled by fishing clubs, but two of the largest, Lac Edouard [Edward] and Lake Kiskissink, have been leased by the railway company and are open to all visitors. Each contains plenty of big [brook] trout.

Upon the shore of Lac Edouard, and but a few yards from the railway, is a comfortable hotel, Laurentides House, where fishermen can obtain camp outfits, guides, canoes, skiffs, etc., at reasonable rates. Two small steamers ply upon Lac Edouard, and may be used as means of reaching camping grounds close to the shadowy haunts of trout. A summer vacation can be very pleasantly spent in visiting these waters, and killing brilliantly colored trout weighing as high as five pounds.

Lake Edward became one of the Laurentides' better-known brook trout waters, even though it's situated less than 10 miles west of the park's western border. It's a relatively large lake, and as the new railroad line passed along part of its eastern shore, its fame was guaranteed. A large lake whose western shore is also the western border of the park is Lake Batiscan. It had no direct railroad link; access was over a poorly cut logging road. While Lake Batiscan, not far from Edward, produced big fish, its river became equally notable for its large numbers of brook trout.

It's amazing that it took nearly 300 years of fishing in America before the first book was written dedicated solely to brook trout and how to catch them. In 1902, Louis Rhead edited *The Speckled BROOK TROUT*, a compilation of 11 chapters. Rhead also illustrated it. A noted artist and a prolific outdoor writer of that period, he illustrated other books on fishing in this era as well. It's surprising that such a voluminous writer contributed only the preface and a small chapter on cooking brook trout. However, his striking full-page line drawings and numerous sketches in the margins have assured him a place in posterity for assembling this classic work. The book is noteworthy here because it offers us the only firsthand descriptions of brook trout fishing in the Laurentides, in a chapter written by E. T. D. Chambers.

Let us carefully examine a newly caught specimen of the Lake Edward trout, fresh from the rapids of the River Jeannotte—the outlet of the big lake—where its monster fish descend in the latter part of August, in search of spawning beds. During the heat of midsummer we angle in vain upon the surface of the water. Minnows compose his daily menu, and with a cool summer-resort and plenty of good food, he has no inclination to trouble himself with what is disturbing the surface of the water. In the comparatively swift rapids of the picturesque discharge, *fontinalis,* finding no minnows upon which to feed, is successfully tempted by the fluttering fly to "spring from the deep and try aerial ways." Here the giant specimens of the Lake Edward charr, which attain a size rarely to be met in running water, rise freely to the artificial lures. Here, too, as in the Nepigon and the Montmorenci, at this season of the year, the American [misplaced chauvinism] brook trout is found in his most gorgeous apparel.

During the latter half of August and September, these large fish rise to ordinary trout flies in the Jeannotte, and have been taken there over 7 pounds. Fish from 2 to 5 pounds are quite common in all the upper pools of the river at this season. In spring and summer, not one of these large fish is to be found in the stream, though there are plenty of fingerlings. The big fellows are all in the big lake. They grow big because of the abundant food supply furnished by innumerable shoals of minnows.

The lack of much insect food at Lake Edward is perhaps responsible for the habits of its trout. At all events, the large ones are not to be seduced by insect lures until they withdraw to the shallower water of the spawning-beds in the stream. In spring time they often come near to the surface of the lake, when chasing shoals of minnows into shallow water. A live minnow is a good bait, and catches of four and five pound fish are of daily occurrence in spring. Worms and other baits are used with good result, and so are mice, frogs, and even pieces of pork. Trolling, either with the spoon, the phantom minnow, or a dead-fish bait, is also very successful. These monster charr will readily take a very large size pike-spoon, and will not even refuse to make a meal of the young of their own species.

In all probability there are larger fish in Lake Edward than any that have been taken out of it, and if reliance can be placed upon the stories of the big ones which have been hooked and lost there, the size of its speckled trout is not exceeded in any Canadian stream or lake. Much confusion has been caused by the application of the name "trout," as well to the namaycush as to Salvelinus fontinalis. Reports of large trout in these waters were found, upon investigation, to be gray or lake trout. However, speckled trout of 3 to 9 pounds in weight are reported taken in nets in Lake Wahwanichi, a beautiful mere about the size of Lake Edward, namely, 20 miles long by 1 to 3 wide.

Lake Batiscan, also noted for its large trout, is less than 20 miles southeast of Lake Edward, and only a few miles distant from the line of the railway. Dean Robbins, of Albany, N.Y.; Dr. Robert M. Lawrence, of Lexington, Mass., and a number of friends secured 12 brook trout in Lake Batiscan in 1895, whose aggregate weight was 72 pounds. The dean caught, by trolling, an 8.25 pound trout, and another of the party one 8.5 pounds. The latter was 26 inches long and 17 in girth. The Hon. W. B. Kirk, of Syracuse, N.Y., has to his credit a 9-pound trout taken from the lake. Alfred Harmsworth, proprietor of the London Daily Mail, saw 7- and 8-pound fish from this lake at the Garrison Club, in Québec, in 1894. He guessed their average weight at 10 pounds, as related at the time by the late A. N. Cheney, in the columns of Forest and Stream. Almost all the waters of the Triton Tract, in which Lake Batiscan is situated, are noted for the large size of brook trout which inhabit them. The late Colonel A. L. Light killed 14 trout in one hour on the tract in 1892, their total weight being 45 pounds. Mr. Cheney and Mr. W. F. Rathbone, of Albany, took 25 speckled trout in the Moise River, on the fly, in September, 1897, which weighed in all 101 pounds. Ten of Cheney's fish weighed 45 pounds and ten of Rathbone's 41 pounds.

Except in the fall of the year many of the heaviest trout caught in lakes are undoubtedly taken upon the troll. Even those that are killed upon a fly often seize it as it is trolled behind a boat. Lake Batiscan trout are exceptionally handsome fish. They are almost always in good condition. So, too, are those of the Montmorenci River, which are among the most gamy specimens known to Canadian anglers. They feed and fatten largely upon insect food.

In the Montmorenci, some 20 to 30 miles above its famous falls; in the Ouiatchouan, the stream which carries the surplus waters of Lake Bouchette into Lake St. John; in La Belle Riviere, and in other northern waters that might be mentioned, brook trout feed largely upon insect food, and 6 and 7 pound fish have not infrequently fallen victims to the fly-fisherman's skill.

Space forbids lengthy reference to the huge trout of the great lake Jacques Cartier, a splendid body of water now hidden in the almost impenetrable depths of the Canadian forest; but those familiar with the works of John Burroughs will recall the story, in Locusts and Wild Honey, of the 6-pounder taken by him at the very source of the Jacques Cartier River, when there was a passable road for a buckboard from Québec to the lake. Since the building of the railway to Lake St. John this pathway has become so deserted that it is in parts quite overgrown with shrubbery, while many of its bridges have entirely disappeared.

Were it but so today. The overgrown buckboard road was eventually reopened, and today is Route 175 (old Route 54), a major, paved highway not only passing along most of the western shore of Lac Jacques-Cartier but also bisecting the park.

A pack-horse may get through to the big lake, and here, in its discharge, and in Lac des Neiges, only a few miles distant from it, are to be found some of the best waters still open to anglers in which the big red trout [a relic Arctic charr] of Canada may be fished for, and may be caught, too, if good luck wait upon the angler's efforts. Autumn fishing is surer, here, than any other, and September is the best month. But the lakes mentioned, as well as all the upper course of the Jacques-Cartier River, are comprised in the Government preserve known as the Laurentides National Park, which occupies much of the interior of the country between the Saguenay and the Québec & Lake St. John Rail way. The Government guards this preserve itself and charges $1 per day [remember, this was 1902] for the right of fishing its waters, and $1 for the use of canoes and camping equipment. Guides cost $1.50 and $1.25 per day each. Owing to the rapid nature of the Jacques-Cartier River in the upper part of its course, and to its extremely wild, precipitous cliffs, it is dangerous and well nigh impossible to ascend it to its source, but good trout-fishing may be had in some of the waters that may be reached by canoes.

A drive of 30 miles from Québec [City] over good country roads [today's Route 175] brings the angler to a farm-house, where he may obtain lodging and guides, close to the boundary of the park, and a few hours' poling up stream brings him to good fishing grounds. The afternoon of the second day should find him at pools where 3- and 4-pound trout have been taken, and if he prefers a shorter trip he may enjoy good sport in the Sauteriski, one of the tributaries of the Jacques-Cartier, which has yielded 5-pound trout in September. Fair fishing may be had in the rapids of the Jacques-Cartier River in the latter part of May and the first part of June, and though the largest fish do not always rise to surface lures in spring, trout of a good size are plentiful, and many anglers prefer to fight brook trout in rapid water, even though they may not secure the biggest fish. Smaller fish may be had all through the summer at the Jacques-Cartier rapids.

By 1902, most of the area's best brook trout waters were controlled entirely by private clubs. These were not as exclusive as the fishing clubs we know today, especially those in the United States. With the wealth of waters then containing big brook trout, clubs didn't guard their fish as jealously, and itinerant anglers could almost always get a chance to fish a club's waters—for a fee, of course. At this time, fishing rights on the famed Jeannotte River belonged to the Orleans Fish and Game Club. Rights on Lake Batiscan, the river, Lake Moise, and numerous other lakes and streams belonged to the Triton Fish and Game Club, one of the first clubs to lease the area's fishing rights. The Stadacona and Laurentide clubs of Québec leased at that time waters containing very large fish, within easy reach of the Québec & Lake St. John Railway. The magnificent angling on the Ouiatchouan was leased to the Ouiatchouan Fish and Game Club.

Few clubs contained all Québecois or even all Canadian members. The Laurentian Club counted many New Yorkers in its membership; it controlled long stretches of good water holding big trout in the valley of the St-Maurice, outside the western edge of the park. One club on a large lake at Van Bruyssel, a stop on the railroad, must have had many anglers from Boston—for the lake was named Grand Lac Bostonnais. In Lake Edward, trout fishing was free to everyone—provided they stayed at the hotel there. The hotel proprietor, who succeeded the railway as lessee of the lake, had the only hotel and controlled all the camps. Visiting sportsmen had no other place to stay. However, the fees for hotel and guides were reputed to be quite reasonable.

Today, as one drives north along Route 155, which connects Montréal with Lake St. John, the road partially follows the valley of the St-Maurice River. Once north of La Tuque, signs begin appearing along the eastern side identifying tracts of land belonging to various private fishing clubs, several advertising trout fishing to anyone for a fee. These days there seem to be few takers.

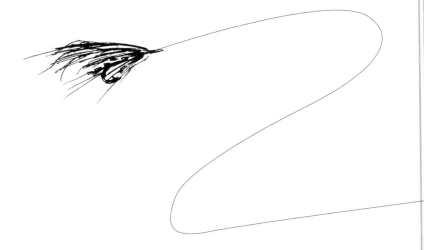

IV THE CURRENT STATE
OF BROOK TROUT

18 WILD BROOK TROUT FISHING TODAY

Despite the general deterioration of today's environment over a great part of the brook trout's original range, there's still excellent fishing, some of it on a par with that once possible in Maine, Nipigon, or the Laurentides. However, one has to travel north of the 49th parallel to find it. Several ecological niches in Canada allow brook trout populations within them to exhibit all of the potential characteristics of the species, those that few anglers in the United States ever see unless they leave their home waters.

The frontiers of brook trout fishing became literally bogged down—mired in mud, boulders, ice, and snow—from about 1915 until a few years after the end of World War II. The vast northern expanses of Canada, though explored by the turn of this century, went largely untapped because of the difficulty of travel beyond the limits of established communities. Few roads, even logging roads, extended north of the Great Lakes into the great, trackless spruce and fir forests or beyond the crest of the Laurentian Mountains. Even though Lower Canada, along the St. Lawrence River, had been well settled for three centuries, there were few roads along the north shore of this great river. Transportation to river-port communities was by ferry or steamer. River access north into the interior of Québec and southern Labrador was greatly limited by cataracts and rapids.

With the end of World War II, however, the means became available to conquer these natural physical barriers for northward movement: Large numbers of surplus aircraft were suddenly on hand and at fair prices. Even better were the great numbers of ex-military pilots, both Canadian and American, who took to bush flying like Canada geese.

But the ability to go north was still not enough to open new waters. What was needed was motivation. This, too, came on the heels of the war. The vast mineral resources newly discovered in the near and far north would pay the freight, and fishing and hunting flew in on their tailfeathers. There was also another factor: a newfound postwar affluence among America's middle class, an army of men and women who had traveled the world over.

Because of the nature of this northern terrain, often more water than land, most bush planes were equipped with floats. Most new brook trout waters were discovered by bush pilots with a penchant for fishing. They found waters that rivaled those their fathers and grandfathers had known. Many established their own fishing camps, and the more successful outfitters were usually also pilots.

The search for minerals—iron, nickel, aluminum—also led to the establishment of rail lines that headed directly north and returned with long skeins of ore-filled cars. Along with the rails came roads, rough and gravel covered only until recently. At their ends, mining towns sprang up, usually on large rivers or lakes. Busy floatplane bases did double duty, serving to funnel fishermen to camps on outlying lakes and rivers. The era of the northward expansion of brook trout fisheries that began in the late 1940s is still in progress. Though mining is still the prime motive for exploration, the search for hydroelectric power is an expanding secondary reason.

Not including the numerous rivers along northern Labrador and Ungava (Québec) that flow into Arctic waters, there are eight major rivers with excellent brook trout fisheries. In no particular order, they are the Broadback, Cocomenhani, Eastmain, and Rupert rivers in Québec; the Ashuanipi, Minipi, and Eagle rivers, and their tributaries, in Labrador; and Gods River in Manitoba.

GODS RIVER

Obsessions. Everyone has them, one or more, good or bad. They're part of being human. Some are constructive and make life easier. Others are the opposite and make it difficult. I've got one, and have never been quite able to categorize it. It's a dichotomy of pleasure and pain: to catch a big brook trout, at least 9 or 10 pounds, or perhaps even bigger than the 14½-pounder Daniel Webster caught on the Carmans River in 1827, or the one Dr. J. W. Cook caught on the Nipigon River in 1916.

I've been fascinated by this species since I was 11 years old and caught my first one on the Genegantslet River, a small stream north of Binghamton, New York. At first the attraction was their gaudy, glorious coloration, which is impossible fully to describe. It wasn't that alone, but at the time it was such things that fascinated me. Later, I think perhaps it was the unabashed ferocity with which a brook trout strikes that captivated me. But still there was something else, something undefinable. Brook trout didn't become an obsession, however, until the first time I fished Gods River, now more than 30 years ago.

Gods River Lodge was opened in 1955 by Tom Ruminski of Winnipeg. At that time,

Gods Lake was the northern limit for adventurous American anglers, and the river draining it quickly developed a reputation for its big brook trout. When I fished there in 1963, we went 34 miles downriver to Marshall Falls and overnighted in Ruminski's outpost cabin. I caught a 5-pound brook trout and was temporarily satisfied. But when he told me there were bigger trout farther downriver, I moaned. The seed was planted. Ever since I've been plagued with thought of what was "downriver."

In the ensuing years, I've fished many brook trout waters, and some have produced large fish. I caught what was close to a 7-pounder on the Minipi River in Labrador, but it only inflamed my obsession. The idea of going back and fishing the entire length of Gods River festered in my mind for years. The chance finally came in February 1993, when I got a call from Paul Zanewich. He still books fishermen for Gods River Lodge, as he has since he began with Ruminski in the late 1950s. Nine years ago, Ruminski died and the Cree band living at Gods River bought and today operates the lodge.

If you're going to search for a record, Gods River is a good place to start. I consider it one of the eight best brook trout rivers in North America. Like the others, it has a unique environment that produces the wealth of aquatic insect foods needed for fast fish growth. Also important, it's loaded with rapids. Rapids are the name of the game when it comes to finding brook trout. Trout demand cool, well-oxygenated water. I knew that the more rapids I fished, the better would be my chances of beating the river's 8½-pound record.

Zanewich found two other dedicated trout fishermen to accompany me. They also had an obsession—for canoeing. Dale Johnston works for the Canadian government as a community futures consultant; Bruce Brautigan is a federal skills development programmer. Brautigan is reputed to be the best wilderness cook on the river—any river. They'd gather the tents and camping gear, and the lodge would provide us with canoes and knowledgeable guides.

Figure 18.1   The runout at Big Bear Falls on Gods River, Manitoba.

"The big outboards never arrived," John Yellowback, the lodge's manager, told us minutes after the DC3 in which we had flown from Winnipeg landed on the lodge's airstrip. It was July 18, 1993. "The guides refuse to put on the smaller motors because the canoes cannot make it back up the rapids. They say currents now are too swift because the river is so low. They also say you might not be able to reach Shamattawa."

The lodge has two 21-foot, square-stern, Peterborough freighter canoes. They're fast, light to portage, and carry immense loads. It was these that we had planned to use. We had to modify our plans and instead use three broad-beamed, 17-foot aluminum boats.

Undaunted, that night we continued planning our assault on the river. Johnston had obtained a series of detailed topographical maps of the area, photocopied the river portions on a dozen 8x10 sheets, and put them together in a book. He waterproofed each page, and for good reason: It rained heavily that night. However, snug in the riverside cabin, we ironed out every detail of the trip. With dividers, I stepped off river distances on the map. We dry-ran the entire 128-mile course from Gods Lake to Shamattawa. After five days on the river, a floatplane would meet us at the old Cree village to bring us back.

The next morning, Sunday, as we departed under a cloud of black flies and drizzle, Yellowback told us the plane would follow the river looking for us in case we didn't make it all the way. It rained so hard I dared not open the waterproof maps to check our progress. Our Cree guides were John Okemow, Larry Kirkness, and Josiah and Stanley Wood. Josiah has been a lodge guide most of his life. Now in his 60s, he traveled the river as a young man to visit friends in Shamattawa. But for the past few decades, he has used airplanes. "They're faster and a lot less work," he said.

When I fished the Gods River in 1963, its lower section was still virgin water to sportsmen. Since then, the occasional floatplane has begun dropping onto the river at wide spots, but no one has ever fished all of the rapids and falls on one trip. Gods is a powerful river, not to be toyed with. From the lake, it cuts its way north through 228 miles of Precambrian bedrock to enter Hudson Bay at York Factory. At its beginning, it's narrow, circuitous, and studded with islands. Its waters are clear and swift.

Now, the river sparkled as we freely drank from it. Tall black spruce trees formed canyon walls along its banks. As we progressed downriver, poplar trees encroached among the spruce.

Despite strong headwinds and a pelting rain, we made good time. We passed Okemow Rapids at Mile 14 and Alan Rapids at Mile 19. We didn't fish them because they're flayed regularly by guests from the lodge. We stopped at the lodge's outcamp at Mile 31 to pick up extra gas and sleeping bags. It's used as an overnight shelter for trips that return to the lodge the next day. We stopped at Marshall Falls, really just a set of rapids, at Mile 34. I made three casts with a Mickey Finn streamer and netted a 2-pound brook trout. On the next cast, Bruce Brautigan caught its clone. We had trout for our first shore lunch.

At Oskatukaw Rapids, at Mile 38, the river is blocked by three islands. Josiah chose the tightest passage, through a narrow granite canyon that we dubbed "Hole in the Wall"; it's less than a dozen feet wide for about 100 yards. When we popped out the other side, I suggested we stop for a few casts. Josiah said we had a portage ahead and needed the remaining daylight to set up tents. Peter Burtons and Shorty Rapids, at Miles 47 and 48, looked like places where we should do some serious fishing. "Tomorrow," the reticent guide said. "This is all good water. Seldom fished."

Sturgeon Falls is a combination of 6 feet of falls and 6 feet of rapids. The portage around is a quarter mile long. It took us more than an hour to pack our gear and motors over the trail, then haul over one of the boats. Luckily, there was a third boat stored at the other end of the portage that we could use. It was nearly dark when we restarted, and the rain had become intense. Now, mosquitoes joined the trail of black flies following us. The thought of setting up tents in the rain was disheartening.

"Maybe trapper's old cabin still okay," Josiah said.

A mile below Sturgeon Falls, where tiny Timewee River enters, a deserted trapper's log cabin stood on the high bank. It looked warm and inviting. Inside, it was clean. We didn't pitch tents, but shared the cabin with a trio of mice that resented our presence.

Monday, our second day, dawned clear and cool as we headed upriver to fish Sturgeon Falls. We had no trouble finding trout; they were in almost every run in the rapids. Later, I walked the portage to the top and found even better brook trout fishing in the slickwater at the head of the rapids. Still, the biggest fish we found were just 4 pounds—good, but not enough to placate my obsession.

We were halfway to Shamattawa and figured we could make it in one long run if we had to. We had passed up sampling Peter Burtons and Shorty Rapids, so we opted to head back upriver again on the third day, Tuesday. After a light portage, we fished Peter Burtons in the morning and Shorty in the afternoon. The latter was by far the better.

Early on Wednesday we headed downstream, fully loaded. At Mile 56, a difficult portage around Muskeg Falls slowed us. We pulled the boats over a trail that was hardly visible, almost grown over from disuse. With the low water, the numerous portages were consuming valuable fishing time. Just 4 miles ahead lay Big Bear Falls and what we believed would be our biggest obstacle. We had been told it was a 30-foot drop. Rather than search Muskeg Rapids for trout, we decided to make a quick run to Big Bear Falls first to see what might be in store.

As I stood on a granite outcropping high above the falls and looked downstream, I suddenly realized we would never make it to Shamattawa. We had just run out of water and time. Big Bear, at Mile 62, is comprised of chutes, rapids, and steps that drop 15 feet, instead of 30—but over a 50-yard stretch. It wasn't so much the falls that stopped us but what lay beyond. Below these rapids, Gods River changes character. No longer a waterway 100 feet wide and 12 feet deep, it spreads over the land, and the same volume of water thins to inches. Dry boulders fill the riverbed as far as one can see. And beyond the river's bend, before Shamattawa, lie 10 more sets of rapids and one falls.

Disappointed, we worked back upriver. After thrashing the head of the falls, with little success, we fished the bottom of Muskeg Rapids, but with little enthusiasm. Then we portaged all of our gear back over the trail to Sturgeon Falls. On Thursday, the last day, we returned to Shorty Rapids. The Mickey Finn is always a deadly brook trout pattern, and had proved itself almost everywhere we fished. It seemed most effective at Shorty Rapids.

My companions alternated between fly gear and spinning tackle, hoping to dredge up a few of the river's famous walleyes. Barbless hooks are the law, so Dale and Bruce replaced treble hooks with singles, or cut off two hooks and crimped the remaining barb. Instead of walleye or trout, however, they came up with northern pike, one a 15-pounder. I hooked and released seven trout of between 3 and nearly 5 pounds, but the monster I was after eluded me. Still, anyplace that can produce seven brook trout of such size, without requiring me to move more than a few feet between casts, had to be a great trout river.

My eighth fish, however, seemed to have potential, and fought like a really big one. I later attributed this to the swift current in which it was hooked. I battled it from a granite boulder in the midst of the rapids. Even Josiah, who didn't get excited easily, came along with the other guides to watch the contest. In anticipation, he brought along the big northern pike landing net from the boat.

The fish used the swift-flowing water to its advantage and kept my rod constantly arched and vibrating. Finally, I worked the trout into a small eddy. It weighed a shade over 5 pounds. Ironically, this was the exact weight of the brook trout I had caught 33 years earlier to start this fever. While I was disappointed, in another way I wasn't. Maybe I really didn't want to end my magnificent obsession.

This was the lodge's first downriver outfitting attempt, but another year, perhaps with higher water and earlier in the summer, we can make it to Shamattawa. There are 10 more rapids I haven't fished. I'm sure the trout are larger farther down.

THE ASHUANIPI RIVER

Wednesday, August 4, 1993, was just another day in paradise, the fourth one in a row of cool nights, temperate days, and the kind of brook trout fishing one usually experiences only in dreams. By noon, however, Jim Muise, our 52-year-old guide, who spent most of those years in the bush, and my 29-year-old son Steve were beginning to worry. We hadn't caught a fish for our shore lunch, and the fishing lodge was 20 miles away.

We had already caught and released a dozen brook trout that ranged from 3 to 5 pounds. Though their spawning time was still a few months away, the females were already glutted with eggs. We didn't want to kill any of them. And the males were large, flaming red, and just too beautiful to wind up in a frying pan. We were looking for one or two 1-pounders to eat, but they were rare. Just when it looked as if we'd have to break open a can of Spam and some beans and potatoes, and fill the remaining stomach crevasses with Josephine's (the camp cook) homemade bread, I had another strike.

"It's a little one," Jim yelled from the boulder where he watched Steve and me work the western edge of a set of rapids called Middle Run, where the waters in Dyke Lake escape to once again become the Ashuanipi River, in western Labrador. Here, the rapids are 5 to 8 feet deep, 400 to 500 feet wide, and wadable on the edges even though the river drops 3 feet in a 1,000-foot run. About 3 miles farther downstream it re-forms as Birch Lake.

"We'll have to settle for one 2-pounder," I said, "instead of two 1-pounders." Muise was scurrying off the rock for the frying pan.

Ashuanipi River is probably the world's best brook trout water, but "best" is a subjective word. I've fished other waters and caught bigger brook trout. I've fished other waters and caught more brook trout. But I've never fished a river with more brookies between 3 and 5 pounds than the Ashuanipi. In four days of fly fishing, we three landed and released about 60 trout, using only barbless streamer flies. Of these, 45 ranged between 2½ and 5 pounds; 12 weighed between 4 and 5 pounds. Steve caught the biggest, a 5¼-pounder, but we lost a few—of course—that were nearly 6 pounds. We knew they were that large because we lost them at the net. The biggest caught here in the past three years had been a 7¼-pounder.

Just to retain our appreciation of the quality of fishing we were experiencing, after two days we took a day off and trolled for lake trout. A few miles from camp, the river is backed up by a dam 40 miles to the south. The water has only a whisper of current. We boated and released eight lakers of between 5 and 9 pounds. Bored with the ease of success, we quit. That wasn't quite fair to the lakers; they had accounted themselves well. But we were spoiled and preferred to meet fish in their own element, wading waist-deep in fast, cold water where the pace of life is so much quicker. Closer to the truth, we had to get some rest. After an early dinner, we planned to fish where the river slows to a lakelike pace and wait for the lemmings.

For unknown reasons, these shrew-sized rodents migrate en masse in late summer and fall, especially when there's a full moon. When they reach water they find the narrowest crossing, so that their swim will be short. The brook trout are waiting for them. Lemmings are a regular part of their fall diet.

The moon was full on Monday night. This time, however, the lemmings never showed, nor did the big trout. Nothing took the big mice we were casting. At dusk, Steve caught a 3-pounder. After that we saw neither lemming nor trout break the water's moonlit surface, and we quit near 11 o'clock.

This part of Labrador looks as if the last glacier retreated just a few years ago, not 12,000. The landscape is composed of expansive fields of gigantic boulders strewn randomly about or piled in rows by torrential rivers of ice melt. Sand eskers covered with black spruce and water-filled potholes dot the landscape. The tops of surrounding peaks, 1,000 to 2,000 feet above the lakes, have all been glacially honed.

Through this ancient granitic land flows the Ashuanipi River. It's big water where it passes Northern Lights Fishing Lodge. It's even large at its beginnings, where it escapes 40-mile-long Ashuanipi Lake next to the Labrador-Québec border, more than 75 miles southwest of the lodge, to flow 120 miles north toward Schefferville. Along its course it connects Menihek Lakes, then turns east for 20 miles to connect Marble and Ashtray lakes, then turns south in a tight loop known as Dyke Lake and connects Birch Lake with the Lobstick Lake arm of the Smallwood Reservoir. Before the dams that created this 2,200-square-mile impoundment were closed in 1971, the Ashuanipi flowed into Lobstick, along with several other rivers, and emerged as the Hamilton River, now renamed the Churchill, which flows into the Labrador Sea.

"I told you there were big brookies here," Yves Ste-Marie said the first afternoon we returned to the lodge after a day's fishing. I had met him at a cocktail party in Manhattan more than a year earlier.

"I know you did," I answered, "but you didn't tell me how many."

Ste-Marie and his uncle own a construction firm in nearby Labrador City, where they contract work for the world's largest open-pit iron mine. Five years ago he got a permit to build a fishing lodge on Crown lands. He knew that Dyke Lake's center rapids had excellent brook trout fishing, but the closest that provincial biologists would allow anyone to put a permanent camp was 20 miles away.

"Their reasoning was sound," Ste-Marie said. "It would have been nice to put a lodge at the rapids, but if guests could fish it every night the big brook trout there would disappear in a season or two." Now it's a 20-mile, hour-and-a-half run from the lodge and gets fished once a week, twice at the most. Dyke Lake is unique. It has three widely separated outlets that join to re-form Ashuanipi River. Though smaller than the center rapids, they also produce big brook trout. In the 20-mile run from the lodge, there are also a dozen other sites along the river's edge. Where points of land constrict the now lakelike water, the flow quickens past the jutting land, and brook trout take up residence.

If that isn't enough prime brook trout water, Ste-Marie also has two fly-out camps on nearby lakes that get fished even less. With his guides rigidly enforcing provincial restrictions—barbless hooks only, and only one trophy trout to be kept—the future of the fishery seems certain. Non-fly-fishing anglers use spoons and spinners with their treble hooks replaced by a single, its barb crimped.

Ste-Marie established the picturesque peeled-log lodge on an esker that separates Shaw Lake from the river by just 100 yards. Guests are brought in by floatplane from Wabush, adjacent to Labrador City, 106 miles away. Four summers ago, guide Jim Muise and three men built the main lodge, two guest cabins, a guide cabin, and utility cabins in 28 days. During the previous winter, they had hauled in a portable sawmill over frozen lakes and with chain saws cleared the area of ruler-straight spruce. This produced all of the peeled logs they needed for the walls. Plywood was hauled in only to build the floors, inner walls, and roofs.

One can catch any trout on a 6-weight rod and matching line, but it becomes a chore when the fish are over 4 pounds and there's no adjacent back eddy into which to persuade them. I fished with 4-, 6-, and 8-weight rods, and found it difficult to bring in a trout with the 4-weight in fast water. Most of the time I used the 8-weight with a fast-sink tip, a high-density connecting leader, and a 2X tippet. The fish were not leader shy. The 2X tippet had to be replaced regularly, because fish constantly played it against submerged boulders in the river.

Like matching the fly to the hatch, we matched the size of the hook to the fish. I used some particularly fully dressed Mickey Finn streamers tied on size 4 and 6 black salmon hooks with upturned eyes. They had been tied by Ronald Jones, a guide from Chicoutimi with whom I had fished for sea-run brook trout two years earlier on the Ste-Marguerite River. They were deadly. So were comparable-sized Muddler Minnows with white marabou feathers. I was also

Figure 18.2 The last few minutes of the season on the Broadback River, Québec.

surprised at how well a mouse worked, even during the middle of the day.

Unlike others areas in northern Canada that were opened by floatplanes in the late 1940s and early 1950s, western Labrador and eastern Québec were opened to anglers by a new railroad. In 1953, the Labrador Railroad was completed, running 365 miles north from the city of Sept-Iles ("Seven Islands"), on the North Shore of the St. Lawrence River, into the interior, to the mining town of Knob Lake (Schefferville). The railroad was built to haul out iron ore to the shipping port, but it also hauled in an armada of brook trout anglers.

At about Mile 190, the railroad meets Ashuanipi Lake, and for 165 miles parallels the lake and river. Through a series of lakes and name changes, the river reaches Hamilton Inlet at Goose Bay and, eventually, the Labrador Sea. For the first time, because of the railroad, anglers had waterborne access to all of central Labrador. It was like the discovery of gold in California. Within the next decade, nearly a dozen fishing camps opened, and most continue to offer today's anglers brook trout fishing the way it was meant to be.

BROADBACK RIVER

Since Dr. John W. Cook's world-record brook trout, no area in Canada or the United States has been able to mount a serious challenge to the title. One area, however, did came close, and the potential still exists there.

René Demers was a bush-wise French Canadian who had been bouncing around the edge of the wilderness north of Chibougamau, in south-central Québec, for years. He was either cutting pulp, evaluating timber stands for lumber interests, or helping mining company prospectors who were unraveling the store of minerals that lay hidden across New Québec and Ungava farther to the north. A product of the burgeoning use of bush planes that opened the country after World War II, Demers accumulated a good deal of time in the second seat on many floatplanes.

In his travels, Demers often heard pilots talk about exceptionally large brook trout, but they were always farther "to the north." One report of big speckles, in the waters just east of huge Mistassini Lake and north of Chibougamau, really interested him. These reports were from pilots who in the mid-1950s flew for Fecteau Air out of the large floatplane base at nearby Albanel. Early in September 1957, while flying to James Bay, Demers was able to talk one pilot into putting down for a few minutes on the eastern end of Assinica Lake, 60 miles northwest of Chibougamau. What he discovered was almost better than gold—thousands of huge brook trout, stacked like cordwood at the end of the lake, waiting to move into the headwaters of the Broadback River to spawn.

Demers returned in late spring at ice-out and began building his rustic fishing camp, a series of small cabins and a larger cooking/dining room, at the narrow base of a broad neck of land surrounded on three sides by water. He knew it was the right place because at the peninsula's distal end was the site of a seasonal Cree camp. For centuries they had come there to trap, net brook trout, and dry them for their winter food supply. The following year, 1959, Broadback River Fishing Camps was open for customers.

The first year was a bit slow in the outfitting business, but the brook trout fishing was fantastic. It didn't take long for word to spread about the Broadback's big brook trout, especially when they filled the first three places in the 1960 *Field & Stream* annual fishing contest. In 1962, a young mason from Lewiston, Maine, who was apprenticed to Herbie Welch, the country's best brook-trout taxidermist of that time, made his first visit to Demers's camps. He already had an attachment to brook trout and fell in love with the river and its fish, which were even more gaudy than those in Maine, if that was possible. For nearly a decade, Dave Footer spent several weeks each summer guiding for René Demers and fishing when he had the chance.

The Broadback is really two rivers; both produce excellent catches of big brook trout. The North Branch rises in a series of interconnected lakes 25 miles east of Lake Mistassini, but doesn't take on real riverine characteristics until it escapes Lac Troilus and flows west. The South Branch forms as it escapes Lac Assinica (Cree for "lake of rocks"), 75 miles west of Lac Mistassini. Both branches meander extensively, though ever westward, occasionally forming long, thin bodies of water more like lakes than rivers. They join 30 air miles west of Assinica, but it's more like 100 miles along their courses.

There's fishing on both rivers, but numerous rapids, chutes, and fast water make the better sites difficult to reach in anything but a helicopter. A few sorties by Demers down the South Branch and beyond the union of the branches produced lots of fish, but none that could match the size of those that came from the lakes, especially in late August and early September, when the fish move into the rivers to spawn.

There are only two fishing camps on the Broadback's entire watershed. Square-Tail Lodge was built by Bob White at about the same time Demers built his camps. Its main camp is on the outlet of Lac Troilus; an outpost camp is on Lac Frotet. Square-Tail accommodates only eight anglers, and Broadback River Camps house 12. The season in this part of Québec begins June 3 and ends September 5. The limit is 15 brook trout or 2½ kg (5½ pounds) plus one fish, whichever comes first.

In terms of both numbers and size of brook trout, the South Branch, now renamed the Assinica River, seems to have the edge over the North Branch. Lake Assinica is a lot like Minipi and Minonipi lakes in Labrador, also known to produce exceptionally large brook trout. Assinica is much larger than Troilus or Frotet, and has a uniform shallowness, about 8 feet, that makes the lake especially fertile and productive. It has populations of northern pike as well as walleye, and a huge population of stickleback minnows. Big brook trout seem to prefer fish to insects as they get older and larger.

The largest brook trout the Assinica-Broadback has produced is an 11½-pounder taken August 28, 1962, by Edward H. Hall of Fitchburgh, Massachusetts. "He was a nice, old fellow," his guide, Footer, recalled. "He was getting along in years and I believe that was his last trip because I never saw him again in camp. It was kind of fitting that he caught the large fish." Footer also did the mount for Hall. The second largest brook trout the river produced was a 10-pound, 14-ounce fish that René Demers caught in 1963. Footer mounted that fish, too, and it hangs in the main camp.

Just to give you some idea of the size of the fish that have come from the Assinica River since the camps were established, here's a list of the largest brook trout caught there each year. It's incomplete because René suffered a stroke in 1982 that left him paralyzed. His son Richard, who spent all of his summers working and guiding in camp, and probably knows the lake and river better than anyone, took over the operation of the camps from his father in 1982 and has managed them ever since.

1959	Leo A. J. Gaudry	7 pounds, 14 ounces		
1960	Effe M. Thierry	10 "	4	"
1961	I. M. Black	9 "	10	"
1962	Edward H. Hall	11 "	8	"
1963	Donald C. O'Brien	10 "	8¼	"
1964	Walter G. Kuzer	8 "	8	"
1965	Nichiolas A. Somma	8 "	8	"
1966	Marcel Basque	9 "	4	"
1967	D. M. Roch	9 "	9	"
1968	Dalton M. Schaad	9 "		
1969	W. E. Minnig Jr.	8 "	14	"
1970	Ronald C. Brooks	8 "	1	"
1971	Newell Auger	9 "	15½	"
1972	Arnold B. Avery	10 "	2	"

1973	Donald Eisen	9 pounds, 15 ounces
1974	Foster Carter	10 " 4 "
1979	Steve Klopacz	9 " 7 "
1982*	Jim McGarry	10 " 8 "
1988**	Roger Caron	9 " 2 "
1989	Richard Demers	9 " 4 "
1993	Brian Kendale	9 " 8 "

* IGFA world fly-rod record.

** Only fly fishing has been allowed in the river since 1989.

These names and dates were taken from a large trophy cup kept in the lodge. The records are incomplete because René didn't always take the cup into Chibougamau at the end of a season to be engraved. After his father's death, Richard was going to fill in the missing dates but couldn't find his father's book, though he knew René had religiously kept a record of each year's biggest brook trout.

It's interesting to note that, discounting the first year's fish, a range of only 3 pounds separates the lightest from the heaviest fish: from 8 pounds, 8 ounces to 11 pounds, 8 ounces. While the four heaviest were taken in the first four years, brook trout of the last few years approximate the weight of those throughout the 35-year period. The average weight of the biggest brook trout (excluding 1959, when both Demers and his anglers were still learning where and when the biggest brook trout appeared) is 9.68 pounds.

When Richard took over the operation in 1982, he noted that big brook trout (8-pounders) were still being caught, but not in the same numbers as in the first decade. It wasn't, however, until 1989 that he instituted measures to save the fish once they were in the river and more vulnerable to anglers. Dr. Dwight Webster and William Flick, biologists with Cornell University, spent a summer (1976) in camp studying the lake's unusually large fish. They discovered that the brook trout of Assinica were a unique population of unusually long-lived, slow-growing fish. The ages of the biggest were eventually determined by counting annual rings in the otoliths (inner ears). The largest were eight to nine years old, with a rare 10-year-old. Most brook trout in New York, part of the same strain, are old by the time they reach four or five years. The stock is so unique that New York and a dozen other states and provinces eventually took eggs from Assinica Strain fish, which become the backbone of their brook trout hatchery stocks.

Most Assinica brook trout of 8 pounds or heavier are probably in their last or next-to-last year of life. And while they're still capable spawners, removing them from the overall brook trout population is unlikely to have any marked effect. It's the 4- to 8-pound fish that are the most prolific spawners and produce the most progeny, and it's these fish that must be released to ensure the future of the population.

Richard Demers responded by restricting all fishing in the river to fly tackle and closed barbs. More important, guests are allowed to take home only one trophy fish after a week's fishing. In a move to placate his customers, he built a large, covered holding pen at the dock. All boats are equipped with a large, water-filled plastic box. When a big fish is caught that is to be kept, it's immediately rushed to the dock, weighed, marked, and placed in the holding pen. If, during the remainder of the trip, the angler catches a larger (and thus older) fish, it can be swapped for the earlier one, which is then released. Thus the more productive trout are returned to the fishery. When I fished here in early September 1994, most anglers didn't bother keeping a trophy brook trout unless it was larger than one they already had hanging on the wall at home. There's no doubt that the fishery is only a shadow of what René Demers discovered in 1958, but while the quantity is no longer there, the quality is. Each year, one to four fish of over 9 pounds are landed.

It was with great anticipation, in 1994, that my wife and I decided to see if there were still big brook trout in the Broadback. I had heard very little of the river and its fish in the past few decades and believed they were history. One reason, we later discovered, is that there's seldom an empty cabin, and word-of-mouth is all the publicity Demers needs.

We could have driven almost all of the way into camp. One end of a series of river-connected lakes leads to Lake Assinica. Our destination was next to a 50-mile washboard gravel road from Chibougamau that Québec Hydro built when constructing its dam on the Eastmain River. From there it's a three-hour boat ride, if it isn't windy and wet, to the Broadback. It was wet when we took off in a two-seater floatplane from a lake just outside Chibougamau. As we readied to land on Assinica, the clouds parted and the lake shone like a deep azure gem in a black spruce forest.

Affable 50-year-old Richard Demers was on the dock to greet us. So was Dave Footer, whom I had known since 1987. I believe he's the best brook trout taxidermist in the world. He has mounted over 6,000 brook trout, and almost all of the trophies that have come from the Broadback. This was early September, the last week of the brook trout season, and the fish would be in their most resplendent nuptial livery. Both Footer and I wanted wall-hangers. Our first stop after landing was the in-water holding cage. There were six fish in the pen, two of them of over 7 pounds.

During the first week of September, brook trout started to leave the lake, readying to spawn in the river. (In the summer, only small brook trout inhabit the river, but bigger fish are taken on the lake.) The river has no shoals and is impossible to wade. Along its course are nine pools, which are fished from shore. We either fished pools on both sides or from a boat anchored in the 100-yard-wide stream between the lake and the first impassable rapids. Brook trout had moved into the river only a few days before we arrived, and were holding in the glazed-over fast water just above the rapids. Big fish, many over 6 pounds, rose repeatedly in the current, broke the river's surface with a splash, then disappeared. They looked like porpoises but fed like salmon. They were bent on spawning, not feeding, and only occasionally took a fly. However, six trophies from a dozen guests were already in the holding cage.

I hooked and released a 6-pounder on the first day but went fishless thereafter. My wife, Shirl, hooked and lost several fish. On the next to last day, our number came up in the rotation among guests to fish the coveted pool just ahead of the rapids. Shirl cast a

Figure 18.3   Dave Footer preparing a brook trout for skinning and eventually mounting. He has mounted over 6,000 in his career as the nation's leading fish taxidermist.

large Mickey Finn into the fast-moving water. As she retrieved it toward the small casting platform, a huge trout took it. The fish dashed into fast water but Shirl eventually pulled it back into the pool, where both the guide and I were ready with landing nets. The fish was just 2 feet away and every bit of 9 pounds. The morning had been cool, and frost covered everything at sunrise. Shirl wore a pair of light, fingerless woolen gloves. In the excitement of landing the fish, she tried to unburden herself of them. One became entangled around the fly line as the fish drove away, it jammed in the rod's first guide, and the behemoth snapped the tippet's frail leader.

"I didn't want to mount it anyway," she said. "But it would have been a nice anniversary gift. After all, how many women get a 9-pound brook trout for their 40th?"

MINIPI RIVER

The Minipi River's watershed is not especially large when compared with many other northern Canadian streams; its full length is under 80 miles. It rises in a series of shallow lakes on a glacially scoured plateau that averages about 1,200 feet above sea level. The plateau is relatively flat except where the river, after it leaves Minipi Lake, cut into it a deep valley and canyon, aided 10,000 years ago by a torrential glacial melt. The better brook trout fishing is in the interconnected lakes that form its headwaters, including Little Hairy, pond-like Minonipi Lake, Johnny Lake, The Nursery, Petch's Pond, and Anne Marie Lake—all small waters that feed 22-mile-long Minipi Lake, the largest of the lot.

While most big brook trout are taken from the lakes by fly casting, there are two riverine sections that produce large fish. Especially productive is the river portion between Anne Marie and Minonipi lakes, which is navigable, and 6 miles of the Minipi River between Anne Marie and Minipi lakes, which isn't navigable because it's marked with a half-dozen wild rapids. The key to the high fish productivity of these lakes is that they're relatively shallow, between 6 and 10 feet, and only lightly colored by leachings from surrounding bogs; thus they're very fertile for aquatic insect production. Surrounding watersheds usually drain deeper, clear, oligotrophic lakes, which are nearly sterile in fish production.

The entire watershed curls on itself before the Minipi River falls through numerous cataracts and enters the Churchill River, 50 miles upriver from the city of Goose Bay. Lake Minipi is 30 miles above the 52nd parallel, the border between Labrador and Québec, in the south-central part of the province. Most watersheds in this area drain south into Québec and the St. Lawrence River. The Minipi's watershed must be unique, because it has produced five of the six current IGFA line-class fly-rod records, and three of the six freshwater line-class records. This means that eight brook trout caught here on rod and reel were larger than any produced elsewhere since such record keeping began 100 years ago. The average brook trout released here by anglers weighs 5¼ pounds.

It's a unique experience to be in an environment dedicated solely to the propagation of one species of fish. There are small landlocked Arctic charr and a fair population of northern pike in the watershed. But there are no brown trout to be glorified in the Minipi's watershed, no rainbow trout by which to be awed, no Atlantic salmon before which to genuflect. There are only sagacious, unsophisticated, brawling brook trout—tons of brook trout, small brook trout, big brook trout, even some of over 10 pounds. The Minipi River's nonpareil watershed is the brook trout devotee's mecca, the very center of the world of *fontinalis*.

Recently, I stood waist-deep in the cold, clear, acid-tan river, armed with an 8-weight fly rod and trying to understand how all of the water, trees, rocks, air, and land in lower Labrador had conspired to make brook trout this river's only progeny. I had been educated in the ways of trout on reclaimed brook trout rivers and streams, where the multiple-species concept—trout-fishing's troika, brown, rainbow, and brook trout—was always in vogue.

The following notes from my fishing diary may help explain the Minipi experience. On August 18, 1992, I began my quest to catch a brook trout, a really big brook trout, a brook trout heavier than any I had ever before caught. I would have six unencumbered days in which to do it. I would have settled for a 10-pounder, an 8-pounder—even a 7-pounder.

> *Day 1, Monday:* I started small this morning by losing a 5-pounder almost at the net. I fished the tail of a chute that slowed into Woody's Pond, a temporary widening of the Minipi River. Thereafter, I sorted through a dozen trout

under 12 inches and silently hailed each one; even world-record trout must begin as small fish. I also silently thanked Lee Wulff, a longtime friend now gone, for discovering the Minipi in the early 1950s. He was on one of his many sorties into the Labrador bush, looking for off-base recreation for U.S. Air Force personnel stationed at Goose Bay.

I cautiously waded among boulders and through fast water to the last eddy and worked a Muddler Minnow into the rip. On the second cast a maw opened a hole in the water and sucked in the fly. Ten minutes later, Herb Morris, my guide, slipped the net under a 3-pounder. After that, we trekked down the portage to Halfway Pond, 4 miles, or about halfway between Anne Marie and Minipi lakes. I was fishing out of Jack Cooper's Matinek Lodge on Anne Marie, one of three fishing camps he operates on the Minipi system. When Cooper, a trained biologist, took over operation of the lodge in 1979, he realized that the superb brook trout fishing he had bought into wouldn't last if the fish weren't conserved. He immediately imposed a one-fish-per-trip limit, either to take home to eat or to have mounted, during the length of one's stay.

Day 2, Wednesday: Departed Anne Marie camp at 5 A.M. with guide Ron Hopkins for the lake's inlet 4 miles away. Cooper's policy is to rotate guides daily, and three of the four guides are Inuit from Goose Bay. It was a clear, windless day with air and water at 66 degrees. Fishing with me, where the river enters the lake, was Don Vannice of Orlando, who immediately hooked, weighed, and released a 4-pound female. There are so many trout here that records are kept only of fish over 3 pounds. Guides record them in a book and carry accurate Cotillion hand scales. Trout of over 3 pounds are called "book" fish. The average weight of book fish is 5¼ pounds. The largest ever caught weighed 10 pounds.

At its northern end the lake narrows into a winding, twisting arm a mile long and 300 yards wide before re-forming as the river. At the rapids, Don took another 4-pounder. I caught my second book fish, a 4¾-pound female decked in brilliant spawning colors. Also in camp were Dan Vogel and Dan Rife, both of Lakeland, Florida. That day they went downriver, as we did the first day, and released trout of 4, 6, and 6½ pounds. That afternoon the world changed. Rain squalls caught us on the lake and dropped the thermometer to 63 degrees. After supper, we searched the lake's surface near camp for fly hatches. Bill Lundrigen, my roomie and a Newfoundlander, took a 5½-pounder. At night it rained unmercifully with horrendous lightning and thunder. Sleeping was great!

Day 3, Thursday: A sullen, heavily overcast sky greeted us. The rain stopped only long enough to lull us onto the water. Muscles not used regularly ached as I readied my gear. Randy Best was our guide. We walked the half-mile portage at the lower end of the lake and fished the head of a small set of rapids. As I waded deeper into the river I bemoaned the fact that my quest for a big trout wasn't going well. The trip was half over and I wasn't near my goal. I was brought back to reality by the strike of a very small trout that took a No. 10 Muddler, half its size. As I pulled it into shallow water, a large trout rushed the fish, its back breaking clear of the water, mouth agape. It missed its prey. I cast to where the cannibal disappeared. The strike was immediate, the fish strong. I battled it in the fast-flowing water for nearly 10 minutes before bringing it to net. It bolted in response, tearing at the reel's drag, catching the power of the rapids and running 200 feet downriver to the next pool. I stumbled after it, somehow managing not to fall, and netted a 4¼-pound male. I was going backward in size. It rained throughout the day and fog compounded the dreariness.

Day 4, Friday: I had two trout for breakfast, small fish hooked too badly yesterday to be released. My fishing partner was John Johnston of Moncton, New Brunswick. We fished Anne Marie's outlet, where Johnston released a 4-pounder. It was our turn in the rotation among the guests to again fish downriver. We hiked the two portages and fished three sets of rapids to Halfway Pond, then worked back. I was without a strike until we were about to make the last portage back to camp. At the base of Harvey's Pool, in three casts I caught two 5-pound trout, and 10 minutes later a third that weighed 5¼ pounds. That night the weather cleared, the air cooled, and the aurora borealis obliterated the stars.

Day 5, Saturday: Each day since I got here I've witnessed the slow but inevitable approach of winter. Daily, the air temperature has fallen. This morning it was 50 degrees. The water chilled to 59 degrees and the first migrating Canada geese were on the lake. The number of fish taken by the seven anglers in camp also fell. We knew this would happen. It occurs every year at this time as brook trout enter their spawning period. But as the number of fish caught declines, their average size usually increases—the rewards of a summer of ferocious feeding. And it's size, not quantity, I'm after. Today we fished Lover Boy Run, a narrowing of the lake on its northern end before it opens into Burnt Lake and the long arm leading to the inlet. Just before lunch, Joel Sowers of Orlando, fishing next to a large boulder in the middle of the run, boated a 5½-pounder. After lunch, I took a 5¾-pounder from the same spot. At last I was moving in the right direction, but at the rate I was going the lake would freeze before I got an 8-pounder.

Day 6, Sunday: This is our last day; we fly out tomorrow. Over the years I've spent a lot of time in waders, but never six continuous days in these neoprene "pantyhose" and wearing a 4-pound fishing vest, a 2-pound camera, a landing net, and a wading stick. Who said fishing isn't work? Knights had their pages; so should trout fishermen.

The air temperature at the dock was 42 degrees and didn't rise above 47 all day. Fall has arrived in southern Labrador. It would be nice to say that I've achieved my goal, or even got close to it. But I went fishless today and so did most of the other anglers—except for Walter Tilley of Orlando. An experienced fly fisherman, he went almost fishless in the last five days while we caught trout, but today would be his day. At Lover Boy Run, he waded off the sandbar, tossing a No. 14 Adams dry fly, and netted brookies of 4½ and 3¾ pounds. That would have been enough to make anyone's day. But in the afternoon he was on the other side of the lake, at the outlet, tossing a Muddler Marabou, and connected with a 7-pound, gaudily colored, hook-jawed male.

"I thought of keeping him," Tilley said. "He looked too beautiful to kill. I let him go."

In all, we landed and released 44 book fish that averaged 4.9 pounds this week. That's great fishing in anyone's book. My 7-pounder will have to wait until next year. Luckily, I didn't set a time limit.

Jack Cooper has in his hands the future of the last great brook trout fishery in North America. For the past 15 or so years, he and his wife, Lorraine, have managed it adroitly, but they and the brook trout here are also benefactors of a few people who came before them. That big brook trout lived in the interior of Labrador was known for more than 200 years. Early explorers probed the highlands through Hamilton Inlet (Lake Melville) and entered the Hamilton (now Churchill) River, where Goose Bay was eventually established. Their first barrier was 70-foot Muskrat Falls, and after that the first major tributary was the Minipi River. They brought back reports of big brook trout, fish exceeding 10 pounds.

Getting to Labrador was a problem even after World War II. While the expansion of bush floatplane service took place elsewhere in Canada, it was slow here because Labrador was still considered a territory, and private aircraft were restricted. Even in 1938, when Lee Wulff first visited the area, the only way to get here was by ship. Only two settlements were along the coast: the Grenfell Mission on the Northwest River and the Moravian Mission (Adlatok River) at Hopedale. Restrictions on the use of private planes may have delayed the exploration of Labrador's interior, but this was a boon to the preservation of the fishery.

Wulff had special access to the region in the early days because he worked as a consultant for the Newfoundland government, which politically controlled Labrador, and his task was to discover the extent of its salmon and sportfishing to attract tourists. In 1947, he brought the first private plane into the territory. In 1949, Newfoundland (including Labrador) became Canada's 10th province. Fear of a Soviet invasion of North America prompted Canada and the United States to establish a series of SAC (Strategic Air Command) bases. One was built at the head of Hamilton Inlet and became the Goose Bay Air Base. By 1957 there were 13,000 U.S. Air Force personnel stationed there. Wulff got the job of locating places for them to fish on their days off.

This gave him a base from which to operate his float-equipped Super Cub and explore all of Labrador. In doing so he discovered three major watersheds with enormous brook trout—the Minipi, Eagle, and Adlatok rivers. In his hundreds of hours over the province he had come to recognize a series of land and water features that told from the air that a lake had worthwhile brook trout fishing. (All had some number of brook trout.) The first feature he looked for was light brown, even tan, water—but not dark brown. He felt dark brown water was too acidic, and, while it produced some fish, it usually didn't have enough food to produce a lot of big fish. Clear lakes also had some fish. But clear lakes are usually deep lakes, which have very little food and fish production because the shallow shorelines are so narrow. Wulff was looking for shallow, light brown lakes. If there were numerous boulders poking through the surface around their edges and on shoals in their middles, this meant they were shallow. Lakes 6 to 12 feet deep are best, because sunlight penetrates to the bottoms and food production is usually greatest. Even better is when these lakes contain patches of aquatic grasses; this means insects and more food.

Wulff discovered one such lake in the late 1950s and named it White Lake, after General Thomas D. White, the air force chief of staff. Wulff took General White in to fish and they found a tremendous horde of big brook trout. Wulff immediately realized that he had found "the greatest brook trout fishing in North America," and petitioned federal and provincial governments to set aside these watersheds, to give them and their fish special protection. His efforts failed.

"A trout is too valuable to be caught only once," he pleaded, "and that goes double for the giant brookies of Minipi."

Ray Cooper was one of Wulff's guides when Wulff owned the Sandhill River salmon camp on the southeastern Labrador coast. Wulff got a permit in 1967 to establish a fishing camp on White Lake and Cooper managed it. During the first year it operated from tents. That year, Wulff returned with Dick Wolff of the Garcia Corporation to make a movie with his old guide. In one week they caught and released several hundred trout. The only brook trout smaller than 4 pounds was a 2½-pounder. Cooper was already aware of the short life-span of a fixed camp if the fish weren't conserved. Wulff had preached this message to him often throughout their association. As a result, Cooper immediately established a kill limit of one trophy fish per week. He also changed the lake's name to Anne Marie, after one of his daughters.

In 1979, Ray Cooper sold his camps to Jack and Lorraine Cooper, no relation. There was no question that the new Coopers were even more concerned about ensuring the future of their investment. Jack Cooper's father was an American, Master Sergeant Eugene R. Cooper, who had been stationed at Goose Bay for 11 years and married a Canadian woman. Jack was born in Goose Bay and educated at Memorial University, Newfoundland. He received a degree in biology, and has used his knowledge to manage the fishery even more restrictively than the province requires.

The Minipi watershed's brook trout are unique, though not so different that they can be labeled a strain. The first study of these fish was done by Cornell University researchers in 1973. They discovered that the watershed contained two populations of brook trout with different characteristics. One was basically a riverine fish that spent most of its life in the streams, matured by Age II or III, and seldom lived beyond IV. A second group was slow to mature—as late as Age IV or V—spent most of its life in the lake, except when spawning, lived to 8 or 9 years of age, and grew to 6 to 8 pounds, a few even more.

To take pressure off Anne-Marie's fish, Cooper opened up surrounding lakes in the 250 square miles of Labrador under his aegis. He established a fixed camp on Minipi Lake and fly-out tent camps on others. All fishing is done with closed barbs. Cooper's guides are as adamant about conserving brook trout as he is, and handle the fish with TLC. They're kept in the net and in the water as they're unhooked, and weighed in the net. If they look spent, they're resuscitated before being released. During the area's short fishing season, a maximum of 100 anglers usually occupies the camps. Only a small percentage use their option of carrying out one fish.

With such a philosophy, the future of this fishery seems assured.

EAGLE RIVER

The Eagle River's watershed is similar in physical characteristics to Minipi's, and its production of big brook trout is also on par. From its beginnings in Eagle Lake, Eagle River trends northeast and runs in a fairly straight course between the Mealy Mountains on the north and the Laurentians on the south for about 125 miles, before it flows into Sandwich Bay and the Labrador Sea south of Hamilton Inlet. A series of small streams drains the height of land 40 miles east of the Minipi's watershed into Eagle Lake. Through most of its first half the Eagle is fed by other streams and rivers that drain a land mass covered in numerous shallow lakes. There are so many lakes that only a few, the very largest, have been named.

Four fishing camps are on the Eagle's headwaters—Eagle Lake, Labrador Wilderness, and Igloo Lake lodges, and Osprey Lake Camp—whose primary fish is brook trout. Two camps or lodges are located on the lower portion of the river and offer anglers salmon and charr as well as sea-run brook trout fishing. However, these brook trout don't approach the proportions of the ones taken from the river's headwater lakes. In 1993, on Osprey Lake, brook trout of 9 and 10 pounds were taken.

While the physical characteristics of the lakes are very similar to those of the Minipi system, shallow and rock strewn, the acid-stained waters are considerably darker. The surrounding land is flatter, and numerous intertwining lakes and coniferous swamps seem to produce a greater amount of leachates. This reduces the sun's ability to penetrate the shallow bottoms, and aquatic vegetation and insect production is considerably reduced. As a consequence, the main food source for brook trout here is other fish, mainly smaller brook trout, and the occasional lemming feast. While the size of big brook trout from this watershed is comparable to that of trout from the Minipi, the number of such fish is somewhat less.

Because of the land's relatively flat nature, waterways connecting the lakes are not very riverlike, and they produce only a few real rapids to attract or concentrate brook trout. As a result, the most popular fishing technique among guides and camp operators is trolling streamer flies. Of course, any brook trout caught in this manner are ineligible for IGFA recognition in the fly-fishing division. As a result, fewer fish reach the record books or garner the publicity they otherwise would.

In July 1994, I fished Osprey Lake out of Roland Reed's camp. The camp is quite rustic, almost primitive, and accommodates only eight anglers a week. It was opened in the mid-1980s by Reed, a Maine fishing-camp operator who moved his outfitting activities to Labrador. He now operates two caribou-charr camps along the coast as well as Osprey Lake camp. The camp opens at the end of June or first of July, depending on ice-out, and usually closes in late July, when Reed shifts activities to his other camps and caribou hunting, which in Labrador begins in August.

During his first decade of operation, brook trout fishing here was so good that Reed advertised that if you didn't catch a brook trout of over 6 pounds during your stay, you didn't pay. In the past few years this feat has become more difficult, even though Reed had limited the kill to one trophy trout per angler per week. He has withdrawn the guarantee, too, but trout of over 6 pounds are still taken every week.

During the week I was there, beginning July 11, there were only five other rods in camp; it was Reed's last week of operation for that year. I wanted to fish it in late July or early August, but Reed and his guides would have moved north by then. The biggest fish was trolled (and released) by George Payson, of Skowhegan, Maine, who had fished the lake several times in the past. Jim Holland, Payson's fishing companion, also from Skowhegan, released a 6½-pounder. No one that week would have gotten free fishing, because each angler caught at least one fish of over 6 pounds.

I caught one that weighed 6 pounds, 2 ounces, and kept it because it was such an unusual-looking fish, with double halos on its sides. Bored with trolling, Neil Bowie, a Scotsman who practices medicine in San Antonio, Texas, and I convinced our Newfoundlander guide, Gordon Snow, to take us down Osprey River to the next lake in line. Osprey Lake isn't large, just 4 miles long and 4 miles at it widest, and the river, which begins here, is only 10 to 12 feet wide. It was too shallow and rock studded at that time of year to navigate, so we made a half-mile portage to Trap Lake, into which it flows.

Several years ago, Reed had his guides take one of the camp's 22-foot fiberglass Gander River guide boats downstream when the water was high and it was left there for anglers to fish Trap Lake. Snow carried a small outboard on the portage, and we fished several rock clusters atop a shoal in Trap Lake, where Snow and his anglers had been successful on past trips. Catching 2- and 3-pound trout by trolling was no problem, but that was not why we had trekked the portage. Snow then took us around a point and into the bay where Osprey River emptied.

Over the years, the river had gouged a deep hole at the inlet—a natural spot for big brook trout from the lake to lie in wait for food flushed to them by the river's brisk flow. As we approached I saw a large trout roll on the surface as it took a fly. I switched to a small Marabou Muddler and fished it as a dry.

On the first cast, the brook trout returned to the top and inhaled the big fly. To its surprise, the fly fought back. It took nearly 15 minutes to boat the fat female, full-bodied all the way back to the tail fin and in good color—unusual color. Many of the red spots encircled with blue halos on her flanks were joined together in pairs. I had never seen or heard of such a pattern on a brook trout. It was certainly one for the wall.

Trap Lake was an unusual experience. We were the only anglers on a body of water 4 miles long and 2 miles wide. It felt so rare to keep scanning the lake's shores without seeing some form of habitation or even an artifact of the past. There was nothing on the lake but wind, waves, sunshine, and the occasional herring gull—and brook trout in its waters. Snow told us that no one from the party in camp the week before had been down the trail. We were the only ones who fished the lake that week. It gave one a feeling of total desolation. I'm sure that's what its brook trout preferred.

UNGAVA

Ungava is not a river but a region of northern Québec, often referred to as Nouveau Québec or New Québec, a north-jutting peninsula created by Hudson Bay on the west and Ungava Bay on the east. It's brook trout fishing's newest and last frontier. Many of its rivers, especially at their mouths, have only been fished by Inuits. In most, their headwaters are still virgin. Because of the harsh environment, the northern tip of this vast area is unpopulated by brook trout. On the western side, a half-dozen small streams provide fair to moderate brook trout fishing. On the eastern side, from the George to the Leaf, nearly a dozen major rivers and a host of smaller streams flow into semicircular Ungava Bay. All contain brook trout, and most contain Arctic charr and Atlantic salmon.

Fishing in the smaller watersheds can be as good and often better than in the big, brawling rivers that drain most of New Québec. Fifteen camps, several on the same river and often operated by the same outfitters, make fishing possible for recreational anglers in summer, overlapping the caribou-hunting season, which begins August 1. All operators provide some fishing for big brook trout, and four—on the George, Tunalic, Finger, and Dancelou rivers—provide excellent fishing.

The newest camps are on the Dancelou River, operated out of a lodge on Diana Lake— a widening of the river near its source—by ex-bandleader and -banker Joe Stefanski, of Jaffrey, New Hampshire. He's in a partnership with Isaac Angnatuk, who has been able to trace his ancestry back more than 1,200 years to occupiers of the Dancelou River watershed. The partners began constructing the small lodge building in 1994. During the summer of 1995, they completed the last of eight 10x20-foot three-man satellite tents. The tents are on permanent platforms with 4-foot sides; each is heated by a propane stove. When it rains, one finds it difficult to leave the coziness of a sleeping bag. A generator provides electricity for the tents and fish freezers. The sun hardly sets during the fishing season.

I fished here in late August 1995 with Ed Sutton, a well-known fish illustrator and one-time sales manager for Shakespeare fishing equipment. Sutton met Stefanski when they both lived in New Hampshire and were active fly fishers. Sutton was acting as a guide and explorer for Stefanski, because many of the waters are still unfished and the depth of the fishery has yet to be fathomed. The lodge is located in the midsection of the 24-mile-long lake at The Narrows. Here the lake is 200 yards wide; other parts of the attenuated body are no more than a mile wide. The Dancelou is not a long river with a vast watershed—it's only 40 or so miles long, including the lake—but it's marked by numerous rapids with only short passages between the white water. And brook trout live in all of them. The biggest so far was a 6½-pounder, but the lake and river have only been lightly fished.

Most fish range between 1 and 3 pounds, but one would be hard pressed to find more colorful brook trout than those in this river in fall. It's probably the clarity of the water and its relatively low acidity—even though the river and its tributaries drain a vast area of muskeg on the tundra—that contribute to the fish's brightness.

On the first day, Sutton and I ran one of the lodge's 20-foot freighter canoes south, almost to the end of the lake. With topo map in hand, we tried to find a falls that Isaac and other Inuits claimed was the lake's main feeder. It was difficult to locate where streams entered the lake because of the numerous small bays and indentations in its shore. The bay we finally entered was guarded by a field of boulders, and we didn't think we could reach the far end. It wasn't until we were near its southern tip that we detected a current. Eventually we found an inlet, guarded by a small set of rapids that were just navigable, and made our way up a slow-moving stream only 30 feet wide. When we rounded the bend, a shallow, wide cascade of tumbling water greeted us. It narrowed down to a huge, elevated boulder that seemed stuck in a narrow pass. It was split in the middle, and from it the river poured forth in 10-foot falls.

We caught fish after fish, on almost every cast, until it suddenly shut down. None was larger than 2½ pounds, but all were in glorious full color. "Just think," Sutton said, as he hooked his green-headed Muddler Minnow to the rod's keeper ring, "we're probably the first people to ever fish this with rod and reel. And, probably the first in many years to even fish the pool."

During the next four days we ran the canoe downriver, and where it widened enough and the water was sufficiently boulder-free to land a floatplane, Stefansky flew us downstream for more virgin fishing. The biggest book trout we caught was a 3½-pounder. We also caught several landlocked charr, in full fall regalia, and were there to witness the beginning of the charr migration. These charr summered in Ungava Bay and were returning to winter in the lake. Our largest were two 12-pounders. Last year, Stefanski took some as large as 18 pounds from the lake, at the spot where the river escapes.

We had hoped to fish the short, tidal section of the river, but the water level was so low that Stefanski dared not take the chance of ruining the floats. He brought in a bulldozer last winter to clear a dry-land strip behind the lodge, and plans to build a strip on an island in the middle of the river's mouth, Angnatuk Island. "When that's in," he said, "I plan to offer three- to four-day downriver trips ending on the island and then flying back to the lodge. While the river has its share of rapids, most are navigable and on those that aren't, we can easily line-down the canoes.

"Most of the rapids have never been fished."

ARGENTINA

Nowhere outside of its original range, even in the United States or Canada, has the brook trout been stocked as successfully as in Argentina. The numerous big and small lakes along the eastern side of the Andes Mountains, and the streams and rivers that drain them, are perfect habitats for brook trout and other salmonids, but salmonids were never able to cross the equator on their own. Many watersheds in the southern part of this country, in areas of equivalent latitude to salmonid-producing areas in the Northern Hemisphere, are clear, cold, and filled with the foods capable of supporting large populations of trout and salmon. Most were devoid of predator fish species except *perca*. It was an unpopulated brook trout Eden just waiting to happen.

The story of brook trout and other salmonids in Argentina's Patagonia, a land very similar to western North and South Dakota, began with a 23-year-old Argentinean surveyor and explorer, Francisco Moreno. In 1875, he was sent by his government to Patagonia to survey the Chilean frontier and establish the border between the two nations, a border that was also the Continental Divide. During his work, he visited most of the large lakes and their rivers that flow out of the Andean cordillera. Some lakes even straddled the border, and some rivers flowed into the Atlantic while others flowed into the Pacific.

Moreno returned to Buenos Aires with great tales of the huge, clear lakes with almost no fish in them. He suggested to the government that they had great potential to produce fish, for both recreational anglers and commercial. This got people thinking, but the concept of introducing trout and salmon to Argentina stalled. In 1893, members of

Figure 18.4   Emilio Clari with an 8-pound brook trout taken from the Corcovado River in southern Argentina.

the British diplomatic community living just outside of the capital city—and missing their fishing on the Test and Itchen—introduced trout to a small stream outside of Buenos Aires, but the attempt failed.

Argentine officials were fascinated, however, and the government invited Frenchman Ferdinand Lahille to study its waters with the idea of stocking them with fish. At about the same time, 1892, the Argentine minister of agriculture hired Italian biologist Felipe Silvestre also to study the headwaters of the Rio Santa Cruz to see if it could hold fish. Both investigators examined only a limited number of waters, and both reported that they were uncertain stocking would succeed. In the meantime, the same minister became ambassador to the United States. While in Washington, he hired the foremost American fisheries biologist of the time, John W. Titcomb.

Titcomb landed in Argentina in 1903, took the train to what was then the frontier town of Neuquén, and spent 19 days on horseback and wagon exploring waters along the eastern base of the Andes, sampling and testing them. He concluded that they were perfect for a great variety of freshwater fishes and began building a temporary hatchery. The Argentine government gave him the task of introducing salmonids to the country. With the aid of other American biologists, who together lived in this frontier wilderness for the next decade, they began bringing salmonid eggs from the United States.

The first shipment included 1 million whitefish, 102,700 brook trout, 53,000 lake trout, and 50,000 Sebago salmon. They were all hatched, and all but the whitefish (which disappeared) immediately established themselves. During the next six years, eight major shipments of eggs, mostly brook and rainbow trout and landlocked salmon, arrived, were hatched, and were planted. More than 36 Argentine waters were stocked, from ponds to huge lakes and streams and rivers, some with all three species, some with only one. Brown trout were introduced but were not successful until stockings in the 1930s. Today, brown trout are the most numerous of all of the salmonids.

Browns and rainbows currently get most of the attention in the lakes in northern Patagonia. A dozen or so lakes farther south, higher in elevation and closer to Antarctica's cold, were all but forgotten. Several held only brook trout, and little was heard of this species until the first American sportfishermen trekked the gravel roads farther and farther south from the established trout center of Bariloche, and then even farther south, to the ranching town of Esquel, where the Sundance Kid had left his mark.

The first angler to discover brook trout fishing on the edge of Patagonia was Canadian writer Roderick Haig-Brown. He spent several months fishing Patagonia during the winter (our winter) of 1951-52. The world learned about brook trout in Argentina in 1954 when his book *Fisherman's Winter* was published. It wasn't until 10 years later that the outside world had a chance to see just how big the brook trout were, when angler and TV host Mort Neff ran a segment on his *Michigan Outdoors* show of the fish Argentineans called *truchas de arroyos,* Spanish for "brook trout." Today, most Argentine anglers refer to brook trout as *fontinalis* rather than the Spanish term.

The best description of what it was like for a brook trout devotee to fish Patagonia when its waters were still almost virgin was a chapter in the book *Squaretail,* by Charles Kroll, published in 1972. Since then, there have been numerous books and travel guides written on trout and salmon fishing in Argentina. Fortunately, most still deal with browns, rainbows, and salmon.

It wasn't until 1991, when the International Game Fish Association (IGFA) published the winners of its annual fishing contest, that the world of brook trout fishing was knocked on its heels. First place was captured by 15-year-old Ken Bohling Jr. with a 12-pound, 2-ounce brook trout he caught on March 9, 1991, on an unknown little lake, Lago Engaño, in south-central Argentina. Bohling, who was fishing with his father, wasn't able to weigh the fish until three days after catching it, when they returned to Esquel, about a 120-mile drive north of where they were fishing. The fish surely lost at least a pound between catching and weighing. His brook trout failed to make the IGFA record book because the elder Bohling left it to his son to submit it to the association. When Ken Jr. finally did, the 90-day submission period had expired.

Originally from Utica, New York, and a devoted brook trout angler who regularly fished the Adirondacks, Ken Bohling Sr. is a computer specialist who carried his love of fishing wherever he was stationed, accompanied by his wife and son. He worked for the federal government in Cuba and in Uruguay, and had taken two previous trips to Chubut Province to fish, frequently as extended vacations because of the great distances they had to drive and the poor roads over which they had to travel. Fortunately, they had a 4x4.

Lago Engano, 1½ miles long, is one of six small lakelets just north of Lago Vintter, 60 miles south of Esquel. Its northern shore lies against the base of a mountain that contains patches of snow at its top even in March (the end of summer in the Southern Hemisphere), while its southern shore is on the edge of the arid pampas and in the heart of gaucho land. It's surrounded by pure wilderness, the frontier, and is reached only by a gravel road from Esquel that's twice the distance a crow would fly.

The Bohlings were prepared to camp out, but discovered a gaucho who had a few out-cabins on nearby Corcovado River. They had brought with them an inflatable raft and had the good fortune of fishing for three or four days when the winds on Patagonia had stopped—exceptionally rare on the pampas at that time of year. Usually, they move at a steady 30 knots across the open, treeless plains. The elder Bohling was at the oars and both were trolling Flatfish when the fish struck his son's lure. They also took several other brook trout of up to 6 pounds. Their fish set a new Argentine record for *fontinalis,* and overnight the lake became famous. The next summer, an Argentinean caught a 10-pounder from its waters.

The majority of Argentine anglers are avid fly fishers and dedicated conservationists, and they immediately demanded and got a series of new restrictions to preserve the fishery. During the first week of March 1995 I fished Engaño and the Corcovado River with 41-year-old Emilio Clari, who now owns the out-cabins on the Corcovado. Clari, an architect, built the Sol del Sur Hotel in Esquel. I believe the only reason he did so was to provide a steady income so he could fish whenever he wanted. And it seems his passion is yet to be satisfied. I've never seen anyone who fly fishes as long and as hard as Clari. He is possessed, consumed by fly fishing.

"If you want immediate pleasure, for a little while, take drugs," said Clari.

"If you want to be happy for a few days, kill a pig," he added.

"If you want to be happy for a week, get married. But if you want constant pleasure and to be happy your entire life, learn to fly fish for trout!"

Also with us was Roque Vertone, of Wachung, New Jersey, an Argentinean, who 30 years ago had emigrated to the United States as a cabinetmaker. He, too, is a devoted fisherman, but his first love is the dorado, a brutish freshwater fish that inhabits the rivers of northern Argentina. He operates New Horizons, a U.S. guide service that takes anglers to Argentina, but this trip was a busman's holiday. The third angler was 58-year-old Paulino Aris, who works for a utility company in Rio Pico, about 30 miles south of Lago Vintter, and who is Clari's partner in the cabins. He, too, is an accomplished fly caster.

Unlike the Bohlings, we were hampered by high winds on Engaño and couldn't launch the rubber raft I had dragged from New York. However, from shore we were still able to catch a dozen fish, although none was over 2 pounds. Aris's fantastic ability to make long casts from shore made him high hook. But the place where the big fish resided, and where Bohling had caught his monster, was on the windward side. We did, however, fish the Corcovado River, where it emerges from 24-mile-long Lago Vintter. The western part of this cobalt blue lake is in Chile. The water flowing from it is so clear that the first time I gazed upon the river, which is about 75 feet wide and 10 to 12 feet deep, I couldn't see any water.

This made the fishing extremely difficult, and brook trout would bite only between daybreak and sunrise and again after sunset for an hour. They were there but came sparingly, only one or two a day. The biggest was an 8½-pounder taken by Emilio just after sunset. Brook trout in the Corcovado are the most unusual I've ever seen. In shape they are almost perfectly round, full-bodied all the way to the caudal peduncle because of the great wealth of freshwater shrimp upon which they feed. Even though we were there at the beginning of their spawning season, few brook trout, even those farther downriver, exhibited the traditional gaudy nuptial livery of their ancestors in North America, or even in Lago Engaño. They were bright and silvery, lacking real color, and the blue-surrounded carmine halos were very faint. Even the telltale vermiculations on the back were faint or nearly missing. They looked like coasters or sea-run trout.

If there's ever to be a brook trout to beat the 14½-pound current record, it will come from Lago Vintter or in the first few hundred yards of the Corcovado River, where it leaves the lake. But it will be a hard-earned and well-deserved trophy. The lake is long, deep, and wide, and seldom is its surface calm. Pampas winds that originate in Tierra del Fuego blow unmercifully for days on end. Brook trout have been well protected by regulations ever since Bohling's fish brought fame to the species and the area. Most waters are restricted to fly fishing with barbless hooks. Rivers with big brook trout are usually no-kill waters, and boats, canoes, rafts, and even float tubes are prohibited. In lakes with a creel limit, it's two fish per day. Even trophy limits are passé here. On many lakes where boats are allowed, trolling with outboards is prohibited. While these restrictions might seem severe, especially for someone who has flown almost halfway around the world to catch a big fish, they almost guarantee the future of the fishery. And that's what counts!

Figure 18.5   Argentinian guide Paulino Aris.

19   ACID RAIN AND THE BROOK TROUT'S FUTURE

Today, two major problems affect the future of brook trout: encroachment by stocked rainbow trout and, more insidious, the acidification of their environment by airborne pollution. The first is a management problem, and while the solutions are complicated, drawn out, and influenced by local preferences, encroachment can be reduced or even eliminated.

The problem of acid rain is another matter altogether. The deposition of airborne acids—acid rain—is not only causing the decline of many brook trout populations but is also threatening the ambient supporting environment and, thus, the existence of some genetically unique strains of brook trout. In most of the brook trout's range, waters are already naturally slightly acidic; that is, on the pH scale of 0–14, they rate less than 7, which is neutral. In the typical brook trout waters at higher elevations of the Appalachian Mountains, most of the trees are conifers, intrinsically rich in tannic acid. The terrain is pocked with ponds and lakelets stained coffee brown by decaying wood and by the conifers' matted root systems, which leach tannic acid into the watershed through trickles and seeps. North of the Appalachians, the terrain flattens somewhat, and conifers are the dominant trees all the way north to the tree line. Over time, brook trout have adapted to life with tannic acid, and they can occupy an environmental niche that has lower pH levels than other salmonids, and most other fish, can tolerate.

Coniferous forests aren't the only natural source of acids in the brook trout's world. A certain amount of airborne acid deposition is natural: erupting volcanoes, lightning, forest fires. Because of these, rainwater is often slightly acidic (has a pH lower than 7). But in the last 40 years, brook trout waters have slowly grown more acidic. Within the last two decades, entire populations in some lakes in the Adirondacks, New England, Ontario, and Québec have been eliminated.

Acid rain—the term was coined by Robert Angus Smith—is not new. It's a byproduct of the industrial revolution created when fossil fuels (coal, oil, and natural gas) high in sulfur and nitrogen are incompletely burned. These gases escape into the atmosphere, where they combine with water droplets to form sulfuric and nitric acids. These are carried with the wind for hundreds, even thousands, of miles, and washed from the air and clouds by precipitation—rain, snow, and fog—or even fall dry when they become too heavy for air currents to support. The industrial revolution began in Great Britain in the early 19th century. Smith, a chemist appointed the country's first alkali (or lack of it) inspector, connected the Sceptered Isles' coal-blackened skies and "killer fogs" with smoke pouring from the chimneys of its multitude of new industrial plants.

The problem of acid rain lay unnoticed until 1960, when Svente Oden, a Swedish soil chemist, realized his country's soil was becoming acidic. He believed the source was Great Britain and the vehicle was southwesterly winds carrying pollutants across the North Sea. Three years later, two American researchers in New Hampshire discovered acid rain falling over their study plots in the Hubbard Brook Experimental Forest.

A more appropriate name for this phenomenon is acid deposition, not acid rain, because it doesn't all fall with the rain. But however it fell, enough of it landed on the 1,469 lakes and ponds in the Adirondacks for Cornell University researchers to conclude that the water in more than half of the high-elevation lakes had become too acidic to support aquatic life. At times, they discovered, cloud droplets over these Adirondack watersheds had a pH as low as 2.6. The pH (potential of Hydrogen) scale ranges from 0, at the acidic extreme, to 14, at the alkaline. Neutral water is in the middle at 7. Vinegar has a pH of 2.25, lemons about 2.3, apples about 3, seawater about 8.2. Soil can vary between 4 and 9.

Acid deposition blankets an entire environment, affecting all plants and animals and collecting in a watershed's most minute dendritic tributaries. The worst problems come with the thaw. When the snows melt their lodes of accumulated acidic elements rush suddenly into streams and lakes, and their environments can quickly turn lethal. This first affects smaller fish, those that have just hatched, then yearlings. Eventually adults succumb. This phenomenon is called "acid shock."

Acid deposition is especially detrimental to the conifers, mountain laurels, and rhododendrons that dominate high-altitude forests in the Appalachians. These plants are all acid loving, but too much acid is as bad as not enough. With the subsequent loss of forest cover, land and water temperatures rise, further compounding problems for brook trout, the principal salmonid at these elevations.

While the deposition of acidic compounds is widespread across the Northeast, there are pockets where it hasn't affected fish or plants (McGlade). These are areas where limestone deposits in a watershed are exposed by stream erosion and counteract the acidity.

Such areas occur in Pennsylvania, along the Mohawk Valley, and in parts of the Catskill Mountains in New York. However, they aren't sufficiently widespread to have a significant impact on acid deposition. There's no limestone in the Adirondacks, and heritage strains of brook trout there are threatened with extinction. Liming of ponds was tried, but this is practical only on a small scale where the threat to brook trout is imminent.

At first only the forest watersheds of New York, New England, and eastern Canada appeared threatened, but within the past few years the problem has become apparent throughout the Appalachians, and brook trout populations as far south as northern Georgia are now affected. Acid deposition also occurred in the Appalachians south of New York, but went unrecognized because the deeper soil typical of this region acted as a buffer, absorbing the acid fallout without letting it run into the watershed. More than three decades of deposition finally saturated it, however, and in the last few years the effects on brook trout and the surrounding forest have become as acute as they were two decades ago in the Adirondacks. They're most evident in the defoliation of conifers in the national parks.

Attempts to correct the problem began in Europe. Sweden, at the United Nations Conference on the Human Environment in 1972, raised the issues of responsibility and of how the release of pollutants then carried across borders could be stopped. The result was international legislation to reduce airborne pollutants by 30 percent. The United States began a massive 10-year study, the National Acid Precipitation Program (NAPP). If that sounds a lot like pap, that's what much of it is. NAPP completed a 6,000-page report on acid deposition in this country but sat on it until after the passage of an amendment to the 1990 Clean Air Act. Program members were fearful that legislators might pass even more stringent regulations controlling emissions than those proposed in the bill. In effect, this deprived legislators of the information needed to make decisions on the bill before it was passed.

Seventy percent of sulfur dioxide comes from utilities burning high-sulfur coals and oils, which are less expensive than higher-grade fuels. Forty percent of nitrous oxide comes from car, bus, truck, and train emissions, about 25 percent from utilities generating electricity, and the remainder from industrial and residential users of fossil fuels. The amended 1990 Clean Air Act, which calls for annual reductions of nitrous oxide of 2 million tons and sulfur dioxide of 10 million tons, didn't satisfy anyone. Utilities claimed it was too much and environmentalists claimed it wasn't nearly enough.

Although these restrictions have slowly reduced emissions by measurable amounts, acid deposition continues unabated—in fact, it is on the increase. This puzzled everyone until just recently. British researchers discovered that another byproduct of burning fossil fuels is alkaline particles, such as ashes from industrial smokestacks; these help neutralize the acid emissions. Other alkalkine particles come from cement dust and soil erosion. Alkaline particle production at the sources of emissions also dropped, 70 percent between 1960 and 1990, based on analysis of precipitation data. Because the alkaline particles are heavier than the almost weightless acids, they fall out first, and their con-

Figure 19.1   Areas sensitive to acid rain.

centration is in direct proportion to the distance from the emitting source. This is why acid deposition has increased even as emissions have been reduced.

Investigators and legislators are now faced with the even more complicated problem of finding ways to reduce sulfur dioxide without reducing the buffering alkaline particles. And caution is necessary, because elevated pH readings on the alkaline side of the scale can be as detrimental to brook trout as increased acidity. Ironically, greater reductions of sulfur emissions might do more harm than good: They would re-create the dilemma of acid rain. The goal of researchers is to find ways to reduce both acid and alkaline emissions. The answer is simple but costly. Using low-sulfur fuels—or eliminating fossil fuels altogether—would end the dilemma.

HOW ACID RAIN KILLS

Brook trout have a higher tolerance for acidic water than other salmonids. In gradually acidified waters where they once cohabited with rainbows, brook trout have been able to survive while rainbows eventually disappeared. Individual brook trout can tolerate a pH as low as 4.25 for a while, but the long-term effects of such an environment will eventually eradicate the population.

Exactly how low pH kills brook trout is not entirely understood, although much has been learned recently. The acidic environment disrupts body functions, including salt balance and transportation of oxygen in the bloodstream. The most apparent explanation of death by low pH is the coagulation of excessive mucus over the gills, causing suffocation. Gills are the organs most sensitive to an acidified environment. Superficial damage occurs to them before it does to other parts of a fish's body. As the pH decreases or duration of exposure is extended, the opercula (gill covers) and then corneas respond, followed by the fish's nostrils, skin, and esophagus. The effects of the acidic environment on sodium ions in the blood disrupt the fish's isotonic balance and lead to kidney failure. Not a very nice way to die.

Low pH affects a population in ways different than it does an individual. Prolonged exposure to pH levels of 5 or lower has been shown to reduce initial growth in fry and to increase death rates. It also reduces the number of viable eggs in a female as well as their hatchability. Spawning is further impaired by acid stress. Sometimes, death can come rather quickly in an environment where the acid level is already high and stressing the population. This can occur during the first spring melt or runoff—the acid shock referred to earlier. This happens most frequently in higher-elevation watersheds or in the northern part of the brook trout's range. Many watersheds in Labrador, Québec, and northern Ontario, for example, rely on snowmelt for most of their water. Snow laden with acid, which accumulates over the winter, is suddenly released into streams and lakes with the first thaw, elevating acids to lethal levels.

The need for a solution to acid deposition grows daily. The problem affects not just brook trout but our entire environment, and everything and everyone living in it. Answers must be forthcoming—and soon.

My rod and my line, my float and my lead,
My hook and my plummet, my whetstone and knife,
My basket, my baits, both living and dead.
My net, and my meat, for that is my chief,
Then I must have thread, and hairs green and small,
With mine "Angling Purse"–and so you have all.
I. Walton

20 THE COMPLEAT BROOK TROUT ANGLER

Izaak Walton, contrary to what what most fly fishermen would have you believe, was a bait fisherman. He used worms, minnows, even paste baits made of bread dough. Above all, "Ol' Izaak" believed in catching fish. Although Walton is responsible for imbuing the gentry of his day with the ethics of sportsmanship—by codifying the appropriate behavior and manners for a fisher afield or astream—and was the first sportfisherman of note, proselytizing for fly fishing was left to his protégé and "adopted son," Charles Cotton. Also contrary to popular belief, neither Cotton nor the English invented flies and fly fishing. That took place on a Mesopotamian river in the second century.

Bait fishing was an accepted and honorable means of catching trout, and the practice came to America with the first colonists. It was not just *la mode populaire* in this country for more than 150 years, it was the only *mode* until after the Revolutionary War, when some of the occupying forces left behind their fly rods. Bait fishing has endured to the present day in the populace despite the aftereffects of *A River Runs Through It*.

SPINFISHING FOR BROOK TROUT

While goodly numbers of brook trout are caught with trolling and bait-casting equipment, the majority are taken by spin casting. Introduced to the United States and Canada by returning World War II servicemen, who had discovered it in Europe, spinning took off in the early 1950s because of the ease of mastering it and its simplicity of tackle, especially after the invention of monofilament lines. Anyone with the slightest degree of coordination can become sufficiently proficient to catch fish after a few simple lessons and a few minutes of practice.

Any serious-minded spin fisherman will need at least two outfits for brook trout fishing. The first is an ultralight rod, 4 to 6 feet long. While fiberglass is still used extensively in many low-cost rods, graphite has become so inexpensive that it's worth the few extra bucks just for its lightness and superior action.

Matching the size of a spinning reel to the weight of the rod is important, but more crucial is the quality of the reel's drag system. By its very nature, an ultralight system means light lines—usually 2-, 4-, or 6-pound-test monofilament. If one hopes to land a big brookie on a gossamer line, the drag must start easily with the fish's first lunge and remain uniform throughout the fight.

Terminal tackle beyond the simple bait hook usually consists of small spoons and spinners, most likely size 0 or 1, and small plugs. Weighting light lines with lead when using live baits—worms, minnows, grubs, grasshoppers, crickets, and so on—can be a problem. Crimped too tightly, a lead split shot can reduce the line's strength. Instead of 2-pound-test line, you might be fishing with 1-pound-test or less.

The second spinning rod is often little more than a slightly larger version of the first. In fact, it's a good idea if it's the same brand of rod and reel, because familiarity with equipment is a plus when fighting an unusually large fish. The second rod should be between 7 and 8 feet long and have a tip with a medium to stiff action. Of course, the reel should be proportionately larger. You should have several spare spools, each with different-test lines ranging from 4- to 6-, 8-, or even 10-pound tests.

If you're heading to Canada for trophy brook trout of 5 pounds or heavier, it behooves you to take a still-larger rod, especially if you'll be fishing in big, fast-flowing rivers. Again, it's a good idea to continue with the same brand of rod and reel. The rod should be between 8 and 9, or even 9½, feet, and have handles or grips in front of as well as behind the reel seat. You won't need this heavier rod so much for overpowering brook trout as for the lake trout that often inhabit these same Canadian rivers, where they can grow to 20 or more pounds. Such rivers are also favorite haunts of northern pike, and they, too, can surpass 20 pounds.

TROLLING FOR BROOK TROUT

Dragging a lure or bait behind a slowly rowed boat or a paddled canoe is an old fishing technique. During the heyday of brook trout fishing in Maine's Rangeley Lakes, the most popular and efficient method was for an angler to be rowed around the lakes, trolling a large chub or minnow in the boat's wake. The big brook trout in these lakes fed on an almost limitless supply of small blueback trout. These charrs remained too deep to be caught for bait, except when they swam into the creeks and rivers to spawn, so anglers used large live baits netted or trapped in streams.

Trolling wet flies and streamers from a slow-moving canoe or powerboat is still one of the most popular techniques for catching trout on Maine ponds and lakes. Trolling large streamers is also the dominant technique on Labrador's famous Osprey Lake. Osprey is shallow, and the brook trout are spread out; trolling allows anglers to cover a lot of water and show the streamer to as many fish as possible. Each year, one or more brook trout of as much as 9 pounds is taken from Osprey, or from rapids on the small river that connects Osprey with other lakes, by this method. However, a big fish taken by trolling won't make it into the IGFA record books.

Trolling on the hundreds of small lakes and ponds in the Adirondacks is also a popular and productive technique. Here a spinning rod is used, with a lightweight 2- to 3-inch flasher spoon connected to a snap swivel at the end of the main line. An 18-inch length of slightly weaker monofilament runs between another snap swivel, at the distal end of the flasher, and a small hook with bait-holding barbs; a garden worm is skewered thereon. This deadly combination sends more brook trout into the frying pan than any other technique. The key to this method is a very slow troll. The flasher has great action, and as long as it vibrates the rod tip you can be sure it hasn't collected weeds.

FLY FISHING

It was opening day several years ago on the Carmans River, the spring-fed trout stream on the southern side of Long Island that drains into Great South Bay and, eventually, the Atlantic Ocean. A half-dozen anglers fished a wide, pool-like expansion of the slow-moving, spring-cooled river—the same one where Daniel Webster supposedly caught his 14½-pound brook trout in 1827. Two anglers were in the water, wearing waders, but only one of the six used flies. The others used worms, Power Baits, pickled salmon eggs, or corn.

By midmorning, the fly fisherman slowly worked his way out of the pool; he had taken his limit of 10 brook trout. I saw only two other trout taken by the other five anglers.

"What kind of bait was he using?" one bank angler asked.

"It was a Gold-Ribbed Hare's Ear Nymph," I answered.

"Is that a kind of grub?"

"No. it's an imitation of an insect larva," I said.

"I'll bet the real thing would catch more trout," he responded.

"How much better do you want to get than a limit?"

He didn't answer.

The moral of the incident is that flies that match the size and kind of foods fish feed upon can often outfish bait. Terrestrial foods such as worms are part of the brook trout's diet so infrequently that recognizable imitations of nymphs, and so on, are more likely to be taken.

Any angler serious about fly fishing for brook trout in their varied habitats will need a minimum of three rods. Balancing the outfits is extremely important. Mismatching even a single component can make casting difficult and inefficient. If you're a beginner, let a knowledgeable person or professional help you balance a fly-fishing outfit.

The size of the fish you hope to catch governs the equipment you'll choose. While big fish will strike small flies, they more often strike big flies. And the size of fly you can cast reflects the size of your line, rod, and reel.

Your primary outfit should be determined by the average conditions where you'll do most of your fishing. Typically, a first outfit is a 6-weight system, which can handle most brook trout in the United States, from small stream or river to pond or lake. The most popular system consists of a graphite rod between 7½ and 9 feet long, a single-action reel with a spare spool, and two 6-weight lines—one a weight-forward floating line for dry flies, the other a floating line with a 6-foot sinking tip for nymphs, wet flies, and streamers. Full-sink lines can be difficult to handle; a sink-tip line is easier to cast and fish. Sink-tips are available with tips of different densities to sink at different rates, ranging from slow sinking (often marked 1 or I) to extremely fast sinking (6 or VI).

You may need more than one sink-tip line to fish streams of differing depths. In shallow water, 2 to 4 feet, I prefer a slow- or moderate-sink tip, in 3-foot lengths if I can find them. These so-called "minitips" keep the nymph on the bottom as it crosses the stream; as the line swings, the current rapidly lifts the nymph toward the surface. This is when most fish strike, because they can't resist what appears to be a helpless emerging insect.

The next step is usually to a heavier rod, in part because you hope to encounter bigger fish, which are easier to land on a heavier rod, and in part because in strong rivers a light rod can't work the heavy lines needed to get down deep, especially with full-sink lines. A third reason is wind. If you fish in consistently windy environments you'll need a heavier line. Most brook trout anglers choose an 8-weight system for their heavier rod, because it's heavy enough to do the job but is more manageable than a 9-weight. With this rod, you can easily work an 8-weight line with a 6- or 9-foot medium-density sinking tip. High-density tips are for special situations and experienced fly casters.

The third rod should be a lighter one, either a 5-weight or—especially if most of your fishing is for small brook trout on small streams with minimal room for back casting—a 4-weight. As in both previous systems, a reel with two spools is used. Since lighter rods are used mostly in shallower water, the sinking tips are often of the slowest sink rate.

Some anglers who fish for brook trout primarily on big waters start with a 7-weight instead of 6-weight. Regardless of where you start, though, with three outfits you should be able to fish all of the environments where brook trout are found.

FLIES

Too often, I've heard anglers claim that one species of trout is more sophisticated than another in its feeding habits or the kinds of flies it will take. I think the basis for this rests not with the fish but with the angler, and stems from a lack of understanding of the fish's

Figure 20.1   Don Gapen, Sr., with a pair of brook trout taken on his Muddler Minnow from the Fawn River in Ontario. (Courtesy Dan Gapen.)

habits. When it comes to choosing a trout fly, there are two distinct and separate schools of thought that go back as far as the early Macedonians: One favors exact imitations of a fish's food, while the other relies on the fish's curiosity about sparkle and color.

> I have heard of a Macedonian way of catching fish, and it is thus: They fasten red wool around a hook and fit onto the wool two feathers which grow under a cock's wattles, and which in color are like wax. Their rod is six feet long and the line the same length. Then they throw their snare, and the fish, attracted and maddened by the color, comes up, thinking that the pretty sight is a mouthful; when, however, it opens its jaws, it is caught by the hook and enjoys a bitter repast, a captive."
>
> Ælian (second century)

The first flies were wet flies, and as fly fishing began to rise in popularity in the mid-1700s in Great Britain, and the late 1700s in Canada and the United States, most patterns

Figure 20.2 The Cockatouche (a sculpin) and the Muddler Minnow fly invented by Don Gapen. (Courtesy Dan Gapen, Sr.)

closely resembled the real foods that anglers found brook trout eating. These flies were quite simple. The list of original brook trout patterns includes the White Hackle or White Miller, March Brown, Pale Yellow Dun, Orange Dun, Coachman, Hare's Ear Dun, Black Gnat, Red Ant, Stone Fly, Green and Gray drakes, Black Palmer, Ginger Hackle, and Cinnamon Fly.

Many of these patterns are still in use, attesting to their original effectiveness. Some have become the basis for entire families of flies. Most had a lot in common: They were lightly dressed and easy to tie. Over time fly patterns changed, becoming more embellished. However, such change was less a reflection of the brook trout's tastes in food than of the angler's perceptions of what the fish preferred.

Fly fishermen seek their own Holy Grail: the Perfect Fly, one that will catch fish on every cast and under every condition. To this end, thousands upon thousands of fly patterns evolved over the last century, yet the quest remains unsatisfied. One man did come close, at least for a while. He was Henry P. Wells. When Wells fished in Maine, from about 1880 to 1890, his selection of popular brook trout flies included the No Name, Montreal, Silver Doctor, Grizzly King, Yellow Professor, and Brown Hackle, as well as many from the earlier list.

Wells's favorite fly, and that of many of his contemporaries, was the Parmachene Belle. The above list of flies was one he developed during "ten protracted [fishing] trips" to the Rangeley Lakes, including the Magalloway River as well as Parmachenee Lake, which it feeds and drains. The list was based on interviews with area anglers about which fly patterns they used to catch their brook trout. Wells admitted that trout from different waters preferred different flies, but felt that an angler really needed at most only a half-dozen different patterns.

Figure 20.3 The legendary cockatouche tied by Ray DuPuis of Nipigon, Ontario. The head is made of the interdigital hair of a wolverine and does not collapse when in the water.

He also believed that "trout looked upon artificial flies not as insects but as some other form of live bait." This was in the days before nymphs and streamers. Thus inspired, Wells set out in the summer of 1880 to tie his idea of the perfect fly, the Parmachene Belle. He based its design on his theory of how brook trout perceived the artificial fly, but also on the idea that to be most successful its colors should closely resemble those of some favorite trout food.

"Why, I cannot now recollect," he wrote in an article on fishing the Rangeleys, "but the belly fin of the [brook] trout itself was selected as the type. Place all the other known flies on the one hand, and that single fly on the other. Then force me to elect between them and to abide by my choice and I should take the Parmachenee Belle every time for fishing these waters. In sunshine and in rain, at high noon and in the gloaming, I have tried it under all circumstances and conditions for years, and in every season it has gained in my esteem.

"As I tie it," continued Wells, "the tail is two strands of white and two of scarlet; the body of yellow mohair, with silver tinsel; the hackle double; first white, with scarlet hackle wound over this—capping the former, so to speak; then wind white, striped with scarlet. By scarlet, the color of the red ibis is to be understood."

A MODERN SELECTION OF BROOK TROUT FLIES

Do fish—especially those caught and released—become so familiar with a fly pattern that its effectiveness suffers? Or is it that anglers gradually lose confidence in a pattern, causing it to fade away and be found only in the pages of old books? I think the latter. After all, several patterns have been around for many years and still catch fish.

The search for that perfect fly continually lures many anglers away to new concepts. Some of the newer flies are well proven, though, and have joined the established list of flies that should be in every brook trout angler's tackle box, if not in the fly box in his wading vest.

One such avid brook trout angler, both a tyer of traditional brook trout patterns and an innovator of new characteristics and materials, is Howard Eskin, of Stony Brook, New York. The following is Eskin's list of his favorite flies. He also tied the flies in the photographs accompanying this chapter.

BLACK GHOST

"The Black Ghost is one of the relatively few Maine streamer flies which have enjoyed national acceptance by anglers throughout the United States," wrote Joseph D. Bates Jr., in 1950. "In Maine waters, nearly every fisherman will acknowledge it to be one of the most productive, especially for landlocked salmon and squaretail trout. Its popularity has caused its origination to be misunderstood and, in some cases, to be misrepresented." The fly was invented, according to Bates, by Herbert L. Welch, of Mooselookmeguntic, Maine, in 1927.

ESKIN'S FAVORITE BROOK TROUT PATTERNS

	PATTERN	IMITATES	TIED IN THE STYLE OF
I. DRY FLIES			
	Gray Fox	*Stenonema fuscum*	Preston Jennings/Art Flick
	Quill Gordon	*Epeorus pluralis*	Theodore Gordon/Art Flick
	Light Hendrickson	*Ephemerella subvaria* female	Rod Steenrod/Elsie Darbee
	Red Quill	*Ephemerella subvaria* male	Rube Cross/Elsie Darbee
	Am. March Brown	*Stenonema vicarium*	Walt Dette/Art Flick
	Light Cahill	*Stenonema canadensis*	Rube Cross/Elsie Darbee
	Royal Wulff	*Search pattern*	Lee Wulff
II. WET FLIES			
	Muddler Minnow	Sculpin	Don Gapen
	Owens River Stone	Stone fly nymph	Bob Soderberg/Howard Eskin
	Damsel Fly Nymph	Immature damselfly	Pat Barnes
III. STREAMERS			
	Gray Ghost	Smelt	Carrie Stevens
	Supervisor	Brook trout	Joseph Stickley
IV. BUCKTAILS			
	Mickey Finn	Attractor pattern	John Alden Knight
	Brookie Parr	Brook trout parr	Howard Eskin
	Magog Smelt	Smelt	Frier Gulline

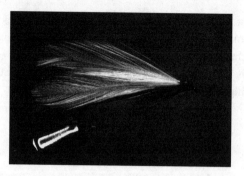

Figure 20.4   Black Ghost.

It was first tied under his direction at the Boston Sportsmen's Show in the spring of that year by Nellie Newton, a fly dresser of the Percy Tackle Company, of Portland, Maine, which had an exhibit there.

Evidently Nellie Newton took a great interest in promoting the fly, as this letter to the author [Bates] from Mr. A. W. Ballou, one of Maine's expert and old-time anglers from Litchfield, Maine, will testify. Ballou says: "On my trips to Maine it was my custom to stop at the Percy Tackle Shop in Portland, and to spend several hours having dressed new types of streamer flies which I had developed during the winter. On one of these stops in 1927 Mr. Percy asked Nellie Newton, one of his fly dressers, to work with me. Nellie tied a fly with a black body and several white feathers and said it was called the Black Ghost. I didn't think much of it.

"I went on from Percy's to Thompson's Camps at the mouth of the Songo River [on Sebago Lake]. I had been there ten or twelve days when one morning I pushed the boat out into the river and anchored it there. I hooked into a beautiful trout and had him up to the boat several times, but finally lost him. Just then a Mr. Merritt from Connecticut came along in his boat with his guide. He had seen me with the fish on and shouted that it looked like a Pierce Pond trout. Just then he cast his fly about three feet from my boat and hooked a large fish. When he landed it he pulled up to my boat to use my scales. It was a nice five and one-half pound trout and the fly was still in his mouth.

"When I stared at the fly, Mr. Merritt said, 'Do you want a copy of this fly, Mr. Ballou?' I said I didn't, but asked him where he got it. He said he stopped the day before at a place in Portland where they tied flies and bought half a dozen, but that he didn't think the fly had a name. I said it had a name all right and that it was a Black Ghost; the same fly that Nellie had tied for me. After telling her that I didn't think much of it, and then seeing Mr. Merritt catch a five and one-half pound trout right under my boat with it, I swore I never would use one of those darned Black Ghosts as long as I lived, and I never have.

"As you know, it turned out to be one of the best streamers that ever was developed. I think Mr. Merritt gave it a big start by giving samples away."

The evidence is that Nellie Newton also gave away many Black Ghosts that year. Guides and sportsmen duplicated them, which contributed to the erroneous impression that the fly was invented by several people at about the same time. In checking up on the matter, I wrote to Gardner Percy. He replied: "With regard to the Black Ghost streamer fly, Herbie Welch was the originator of the pattern. Nellie Newton tied the fly for Herb at the Boston Sportsmen's Show back in 1927 when we had a display booth there."

MICKEY FINN

On a trip to Gods River, I was looking for big brook trout. I'm a firm believer that, while big brook trout will take small flies, they'll take big flies with more gusto. Two years before that trip I had fished with Ronald Jones, a guide and first-rate fly tyer from Chicoutimi, Québec, for sea-run brook trout on the Ste-Marguerite River. I was impressed by the size and quality of streamers he used. He'd tied them himself. I asked him to tie me a batch of especially fully dressed Mickey Finns. He later sent them to me, tied on No. 4 and 6 black salmon hooks with upturned eyes. They proved deadly, but I had even bigger flies in mind.

"Can't tie them any bigger than the bucktails I sent you. Get me some bigger bucktails," he said, "and I'll tie you bigger streamers."

That fall I booked a trip to Saskatchewan, where the biggest bucks in North America are taken. I shot two and collected a few tails from companion hunters' bucks as well. All of the deer were 300-pounders or better. Jones couldn't believe the size of the tails. In return I got the biggest Mickey Finns you ever saw, tied on No. 1, 1/0, 3/0, and 4/0 black salmon hooks, again with upturned eyes. They were so fully dressed that even the fastest currents on the Ashuanipi River in Labrador couldn't compress them. The big trout thought they were candy. He also tied up some Muddlers that looked more like mice than sculpins. They weren't bad either. Now, I'm looking for big bucks as well as big brook trout.

Regardless of size, I believe the Mickey Finn is one of the best brook trout flies in any angler's fly book when it comes to river fishing. The progenitor of the Mickey Finn is lost somewhere in the annals of fishing. It may have been an offbeat design by one of William Mills's group of commercial fly tyers. It's one of the earliest of streamer flies, and gave rise to the generic name *bucktail*, used erroneously today by many anglers as a synonym for a streamer.

It was used for years without any real name, other than the "Red and Yellow" bucktail. It wasn't until John Alden Knight fell in love with the fly and popularized it in his writings in the 1930s and '40s as the Mickey Finn that it assumed its new name. One of the best accounts of the fly's rise to fame and how it was named came from its promoter, Knight, in a letter he sent to Joseph D. Bates Jr., who in the late 1940s was compiling his classic book on streamers and streamer fishing. Knight wrote:

In the spring of 1932, when I was living in Rye, New York, I was invited to fish the waters of a trout club a short distance out of Geenwich. My host, Junior Vanderhoff, gave me a small bucktail which he found most effective for catching stocked square-tailed trout from this little stream [the Mianus River]. It delivered the goods that day; in fact, it was the only fly that did so.

I learned from Mr. Vanderhoff that this fly was one of a series of six small bucktails in various color combinations which were at one time put out by William Mills and Son. Then, the fly was known only as the Red and Yellow bucktail. I used the fly for a couple of years quite successfully.

In 1936 I had occasion to go to Toronto, Canada, on business, and there I met the late Frank Cooper, of the firm of Larway, Temple and Cooper, and his friend, Gregory Clark. Mr. Cooper and a friend of his took me as a guest to the Mad River Club, where we fished for native squaretail (by "native" I mean the unstocked variety). The club members had been taking these fish, not without a little difficulty, by [the] greased-line method with small salmon flies. I showed them the one pattern of (what later was to be called the Mickey Finn) that I had with me but they were not impressed. Finally I prevailed on one of them to give the fly a trial.

On the first cast I cautioned the angler to let the fly sink three four feet below the surface before starting the retrieve. He did so, rather lackadaisically, and then started the fly across the pool in short, well-spaced jerks. On the second cast, fished in this way, he hooked a two-pounder. I used the fly on the Mad River that afternoon and with it managed to hook and release about 75 trout; a feat which was unheard of on the part of a guest in those waters.

On the way home we christened the fly the *Assassin*. Later that year it was rechristened by Gregory Clark, noted feature writer and war correspondent who was with the *Toronto Star*. He called it the *Mickey Finn*.

In the fall of 1937 I made an arrangement with *Hunting and Fishing* magazine and with The Weber Tackle Company to write a story about the *Mickey Finn* for *Hunting and Fishing*. The Weber Company took a full column advertisement in that issue and featured the fly and yours truly in it. The magazine appeared on the newsstands when the Sportsmen's Show was on in New York. In the space of two days not a single copy of *Hunting and Fishing Magazine* could be found on the New York news stands. I suppose that the name and the flashy colors struck the public fancy. In any event the fly tiers at the show were busy for the entire week tying *Mickey Finns*. Each night bushel baskets of red and yellow bucktail clippings and silver tinsel were swept up by the cleaning crew at Grand Central Palace, and by Friday of that week not a single bit of red or yellow bucktail could be purchased from any of the New York supply houses. It was estimated that between a quarter and a half million of these flies were dressed and distributed during the course of that show. How accurate that estimate is I have no way of knowing but I do know that almost everybody encountered in the aisles had a *Mickey Finn* stuck in his hatband.

During the next few months the entire facilities of the Weber company were stretched to the breaking point in their frantic efforts to keep up with *Mickey Finn* orders. One outfit in Westchester actually saved itself from bankruptcy proceedings by specializing intensively in the manufacture of *Mickey Finns*. As matters now stand, it is a difficult thing to find any angler on any stream anywhere who has not at least one *Mickey Finn* in his kit. The "Mary Pickford" trophy for the prize brook trout taken annually in Ontario was won for the next two consecutive seasons with *Mickey Finn* flies. I still use the fly and find it to be a consistent fish-getter."

Bates added:

Mr. Gregory Clark, mentioned by Mr. Knight in the letter above, adds this: "A day or two after I named the fly the *Assassin* I recollected a story that recently had been published in *Esquire Magazine* about how Rudolph Valentino had been killed by Mickey Finns administered to him by the resentful waiters of New York and Hollywood and I rechristened the fly the *Mickey Finn*. All we did up here was to make it respectable and legitimate and give the nameless waif an honest name."

At that time, the Mickey Finn was a popular mixed drink, but the waiters who served Valentino his drinks are alleged to have increased their kick with a narcotic. These did him in at the age of 31. From this came the term "to slip someone a mickey."

THE ULTIMATE FLY

No examination of brook trout would be complete without a discussion of the Muddler Minnow—a fly pattern, not a fish species. While hordes of wet-fly patterns were designed, from the late 18th century on, strictly to catch brook trout, there's never been a fly so effective for its intended species as the Muddler. It can be fished as a dry fly, a wet fly, and even as a streamer. It's effective cast or trolled. Only the technique of fishing a Muddler as a nymph has evaded anglers.

A large Muddler treated with flotant can be fished as a mouse or a lemming trying to cross the water. But when worked under the surface, especially with a bit of added marabou, the fly is at its most effective, closely resembling the small bottom-feeding fish it was designed to imitate.

The Muddler Minnow was invented by Don Gapen Sr., while he still managed a Canadian National Railway hotel on the eastern bank of the Nipigon River in Ontario. According to his son Dan, his father tied the fly on August 27, 1937, while on the banks of the pool formed below Virgin Falls on the Nipigon. The event was witnessed by three Ojibway—Dan Bushard, Benny Wawi, and John Sheboyer—two of whom are still alive.

For the previous two years, Gapen had been fishing the river, looking for a fish big enough to topple Dr. John W. Cook's 14½-pound record, a fish that was taken just a long cast, some 20 years earlier, from where they were fishing. As a reminder, Gapen had hanging in the hotel half of that famous fish, mounted on birch bark. He was also lured on by stories from Indians of still bigger trout to be had on the Nipigon—trout bigger than Dr. Cook's fish that they had taken in gill nets set for suckers.

Always a fly-fishing purist, according to his son, Gapen refused "to belittle himself" by using the favorite live bait of the region. Gapen knew that big trout fed heavily on a sculpin the natives called *cockatouche,* and Dr. Cook had used one to catch his world-record brook trout. A descendent of English and Scottish fly-tying families, Gapen "persistently clung to many family traditions" and became an accomplished fly tyer in his own right.

Two of the Ojibway, Dan Bushard and John Sheboyer, worked for Gapen as guides and often accompanied him on fishing trips, such as the one on August 27. Throughout the trip they had harangued him that, if he wanted to catch a big speckle, really big, he'd have to use a live *cockatouche.* He finally relented, "just this once." The guides immediately set about turning over stones, according to the son's account, looking for *cockatouche.*

In the next 20 minutes, Gapen caught three brook trout between 5 to 8 pounds on the minnows. "These were the first and only trout he ever caught on live bait," said Dan. "My father told me [Dan was only four at the time of the invention] that if big brook trout preferred an ugly, bullhead-looking minnow over brightly colored fly patterns, that's what they'd get. He tied a fly of equal ugliness."

With a crude vise tied to a forward canoe thwart, Don Gapen began creating his masterpiece. It took him two hours to complete his imitation of the *cockatouche,* but when he was finished, though he couldn't have realized it at the time, he had created the fly that would catch more trophy trout of all species than any other. The two guides nodded their approval as Gapen made the finishing touches under the light of their campfire. Tests of the fly had to wait until the next day.

It was almost like a soap opera unfolding. The anglers paddled their canoes into the pool and Gapen cast the new fly. It wouldn't sink! How could it imitate a fish if it wouldn't sink? he was said to have cried out. The hollow, buoyant deer hair kept it high and dry. All kinds of thoughts must have flashed through Gapen's mind, but the word *saliva* kept coming back. He mouthed the fly, crushing some of the deer hairs and thoroughly wetting them. Then another cast and the fly hit the water. It slowly began to sink.

The first fish was a 2-pounder, proving that the fly worked. The second was a 4-pounder. When the third fish hit, Gapen knew he had a winner. A few minutes later, Dan Bushard lifted an 8-pound, 1-ounce brook trout from the water with his landing net. At the time, it was the largest brook trout Gapen had ever caught. He kept it. It was later mounted by Benny Wawi over an "ax-hewn cedar frame."

"In the next two days at Virgin Falls," said son Dan, "my dad told me the guides landed more than 50 brook trout, on more Muddlers he tied. The biggest was estimated to be near 9 pounds. All were released except those small fish that went into the frying pan." Don Gapen's largest brook trout caught on a Muddler was a 10-pound, 4-ounce fish taken from the Nipigon in 1939. He died in 1986 without having broken Dr. Cook's record. However, he did capture the world's largest collection of anglers devoted to one fly.

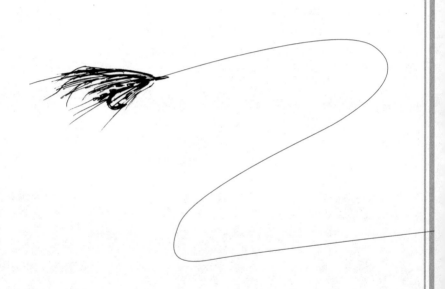

APPENDICES

A   Original Distribution of Brook Trout in the United States

While there are still brook trout in almost all of the watersheds they inhabited when the Pilgrims first discovered them in Town Brook, their numbers have fallen sharply, especially in the waters of southern New England, New York, and states farther south. Where altered environments have drastically reduced or eliminated populations, brook trout have often been able to retreat upstream, to less desirable ecosystems in small tributaries where some semblance of their original habitat still exists. The fish have completely disappeared only where mining effluents have polluted entire watersheds, as in parts of West Virginia and Pennsylvania, or in areas such as New York where entire watersheds have become a vast reservoir system to provide municipal drinking water.

Brook trout also have expanded their range, not with the aid of retreating glaciers and interconnecting refugia but by overt human action. In the United States, brook trout were moved west, beyond the restrictions of the Mississippi River, and now inhabit 13 new states. In some states, stocking them in already productive

trout waters was a mistake that led to the destruction or reduction of other species, especially the cutthroat trout. This genuine trout acts more like a brook trout and has carved out a niche for itself in Rocky Mountain environments similar to those that brook trout like. In some states and provinces, control of the readily adaptable brook trout is now being managed by stocking sterile, triploid brook trout that can't overpopulate a system.

Brook trout were also carried west in Canada, and today are found in varying numbers in three provinces. They've been transplanted abroad, too, and are found in Central and South America, Europe, and Asia. The following is the result of a survey to determine the status and location of brook trout in their original ranges and in new locales.

CONNECTICUT

Brook trout are indigenous to the Nutmeg State and were food for Indians and early colonists. They are still well dispersed throughout the state, especially in the numerous small, north-south flowing streams that start at higher elevations in northern-tier counties. Except for some impoundments in the south, the better brook trout waters are in the central and northern half, especially the tributary headwaters of many small streams that are characteristic of Connecticut.

Streams that empty into the Long Island Sound at one time had small populations of sea-run trout, but industrialization and the need for power caused even the smallest of these to be dammed and harnessed. As a result, few if any streams that flow into salt water now harbor sea-run brook trout. Connecticut was also heavily farmed and its forests cut long before the great lumbering wave began to sweep westward across more northerly states in the mid-1800s. The result was an elevation of stream temperatures in all but headwater sections; most streams and rivers became too warm for brook trout. Because brown trout took readily to these environments, today they dominate the state's stocking program.

The return to native species gaining popularity elsewhere in the United States is having a slow start in Connecticut. One reason is that most trout fishermen don't differentiate among species. To many, a trout is a trout, whether brown, rainbow, or brook. While there are stocking holdovers among browns and rainbows, few brook trout hold over because of the marginal environment. As a result, most Connecticut brook trout fisheries are put-and-take, with 50th- and 60th-generation hatchery fish.

Connecticut, however, is not without its wild brook trout waters. Most are in the headwaters of streams with self-propagating populations. These include the Tankerhoosen River in the Belding Wild Trout Management Area, Salmon and Taylor brooks, and Haley and Latimers brooks near the coast. The state's Fisheries Division is currently conducting an assessment study of its catch-and-release fishery for wild brook and brown trout in the Belding area. It's also considering restricting fishing to artificial lures and flies in several small streams. And it's nearing completion of a six-year statewide

stream survey, and hopes to develop a new trout management plan that may include dedicated brook trout waters.

Connecticut's managed trout waters usually have a mixture of the three trout species with a combination of wild and stocked fishes, as do those of most other states on the southern periphery of the brook trout's range. The most productive trout streams are the Farmington, Salmon, Housatonic, Mianus, Hammonasset, Willamantic, Saugatuck, and Moosup rivers, and Salmon Brook. Ponds and lakes include Candlewood and East Twin lakes, Saugatuck Reservoir, West Hill Pond, Crystal and Highland lakes, Beach and Mashapaug ponds, and Wononskopomuc and Quonnipaug lakes. The state's largest brook trout was caught in 1983 from Muddy Pond (New Haven) and weighed 4 pounds, 15 ounces.

GEORGIA

One of the best-kept secrets in the expansive world of brook trout is the fishing available in Georgia. Most devotees of this speckled fish cast their eyes northward when they ponder a trip, and only a few are even aware that brook trout inhabit a state so far south. But Georgia has an "up" as well as a "south," and the "ups" are elevations above sea level that top even those in New York and New England. The Appalachian Mountains begin in New Brunswick and Maine, paralleling the East Coast and ending in Alabama and Georgia. At one time, Appalachian peaks in the North may have been higher than those in the South, but the last four glaciers did a real job of cutting them down and leveling them off.

From a toehold in the Allegheny Mountains in southwestern New York to their end in northern Georgia, however, the Appalachian Mountains have always been glacier-free. Of the 11 highest peaks in the Appalachians, 7 are located south of the Mason-Dixon Line. The highest is in North Carolina, Mount Mitchell at 6,684 feet, but Georgia's Brasstown Bald, at 4,784 feet, ranks fourth. These seven closely located peaks form the backbone of the high country known as the Allegheny Front.

As the last great glacier began retreating in the North, waters at lower elevations in the South began to warm, and brook trout, which at this time were probably spread throughout Georgia, began heading upstream into watersheds that originated at the tops of the Alleghenies. In the strictest biological terms, those fish that survived the glacial phenomenon are referred to as *relic* populations, because such populations became isolated from the main body of fish. In this case, elevated summer temperatures prevented downstream migration and interwatershed communication. In effect, each watershed was heat-isolated from the next one up the line.

Today, a broken range of brook trout distribution occurs from Georgia to Maryland and some areas of Pennsylvania and New York. While the quality of the fishery may vary greatly between the geographical extremes, it would be difficult to convince Georgia's 100,000 trout fishermen from across the state's northern-tier counties that catching brook trout isn't a lot of fun. There are more than 60 trout streams with over 4,000 miles of water in the Peach State, though today they aren't all brook trout waters.

The headwaters of the Chattahoochee River in northern Georgia are the farthest south that these fish remained dispersed after the demise of the last continental ice sheet. Because Georgia has always had an indigenous brook trout population, which in some areas is still self-sustaining, there's little need to stock these waters. In the late 1800s, fish culturists were stocking brook trout everywhere in the country that offered a chance of survival. Georgia also got its share of domesticated brook trout, especially from federal hatcheries. However, it's unlikely that many of these fish survived. If they did, their hatchery ancestry was still so new that their contributions to the gene pool of indigenous brook trout were little different from those of native fish.

Nor did stocking usually take place at the heads of watersheds, because getting to them was difficult in those days. In many instances, upstream wild populations were protected from hatchery fish by the terrain's steep gradi-

ent and by such natural barriers as waterfalls. However, researchers with the Department of Natural Resources, Fisheries Section, and several universities are currently conducting DNA tests to determine how closely related are the genes of their wild trout to populations farther north or to DNA samples of preserved or mounted Georgia brook trout from the past.

Today, brook trout as well as browns and rainbows are stocked in lower portions of watersheds, where fish of catchable size are desired. These fish constitute a comparatively small portion of the state's brook trout population and are easily caught.

Georgia classifies its trout-fishing (all species combined) opportunities as: Stocked Streams (best for beginners); Wilderness Streams (located in rugged terrain, not readily accessible by road and not generally easy to fish; these are mostly brook trout waters); Streams with Special Regulations that provide variety and achieve specific management objectives; Small-Impoundment Trout Fishing (small reservoirs in mountain streams that may be fished from bank, canoe, or float tube); and Large-Reservoir Trout Fishing (reservoirs with year-round trout habitat).

The following is a list of Georgia's stocked waters where brook trout can be taken: Stamp, Amicola, Rock, Johns, Panther, Dicks, Nimblewill, Holly, Wildcat, and Mill creeks; the Tacola, Tallulah, and Middle Fork Broad rivers; Coopers and Chattahoochee rivers and West Armchee and Smith creeks. Waters classified as Wilderness Streams include the headwaters of the Chattahoochee River, and Conasauga and Jacks rivers. Small lakes with trout include lakes Conasauga and Winfield Scott, and Dockery and Nancytown lakes.

Georgia's record brook trout is a 5-pound, 10-ounce fish taken by Russell Braden from Waters Creek on March 29, 1986. Waters Creek is located in the Chestatee Wildlife Management Area, not far from the beginning of the Appalachian Trail in Lumpkin County. It's jointly managed by the Game and Fish Division, U.S. Forest Service and the Georgia Council of Trout Unlimited. Waters Creek and its tributaries are open Wednesdays and week-ends. Fishing is only with single, barbless-hook lures. The minimum size for brook trout is 18 inches; the daily limit is one fish per angler and three for the season.

ILLINOIS

There's little doubt that at one time the natural range of brook trout included in its southern limit a series of short, small streams that flow north into Lake Michigan, off the slight rise of land surrounding the southern periphery of the lake. As metropolitan Chicago began engulfing two-thirds of Illinois's 60-mile lakefront, not only did the land disappear but so did the trout and even some streams. The original lake-oriented population of brook trout in Illinois disappeared almost with the first settlers to Fort Dearborn, later called Chicago. As late as the early 1930s, there were still a few brook trout in the very northern part of the state, next to the Wisconsin border, including the Apple, Pecatonica, and Kishwaukee rivers. But by 1935 they, too, had disappeared.

Even though the land on the other side of the slight, circuitous elevation that parallels the lakeshore is the birthplace of such waters as the Des Plaines, Chicago, Skokie, the Calumets, Illinois, Piscasaw, Rock, and Fox rivers, they all flow south or west to the Mississippi. Quite a few years ago, these were stocked at their headwaters with brook trout, and for a few years natural production took place. It didn't last, however, and the practice was ended. Most weren't good brook trout habitat: in summers they're warm at their sources, and they become even warmer as they meander over the flat lake plain characteristic of states on the southern side of the Great Lakes.

There are brook trout taken today in the state, but only in its share of Lake Michigan waters. Illinois never really had a brook trout stocking program, except for the period between 1976 and 1980, when it stocked 39,000 brook trout in its remaining tributaries to Lake Michigan. Nothing was ever heard of them and the program was stopped.

Any Illinois brook trout caught nowadays come from Lake Michigan, and these are usually coasters, stocked in neighboring Wisconsin and Michigan streams, that work their way into the lake and treat it much as sea-run brook trout do the ocean. The state's brook trout record is a 4-pound, 1-ounce fish caught in Lake Michigan by August F. Bulleri on November 29, 1970. He released it!

INDIANA

The situation in this state is the same as in Illinois. With even fewer streams flowing into Lake Michigan, stocking them with brook trout was never considered. Like Illinois anglers, those who catch trout on Lake Michigan are catching fish stocked by other states.

IOWA

Brook trout were naturally dispersed in most of Iowa at the end of the last glacial period; however, as the level of remnant glacial lakes receded, the brook trout habitat gradually diminished. After farming began to dominate the terrain, the environment changed again. Streams warmed rapidly, silt from runoff covered spawning beds, and brook trout died off. Today, the fishery encompasses only a few small watersheds of the Upper Iowa River in the northeastern corner of the state.

Iowa eventually began to restock small streams in north-central and western parts of the state, in the slightly hilly (1,670 feet) terrain that borders Minnesota. At best, this is primarily a put-and-take fishery. There's some holdover in a few streams, especially South Pine and North Cedar creeks, where natural production augments stocking efforts by about 20 percent. Brook trout are the top predator fish in South Pine Creek. With catch-and-release practiced here and on Spring Branch Creek, Hawkeye anglers have a high regard for the fish. The state record is a 3-pound, 3-ounce brook trout taken by Melvin Yerkes from Lake Despair in July 1993.

Better brook trout waters in Iowa include Waterloo, French, North, South, and Middle

Bear creeks; the Trout River; Coldwater, Bloody Run, Magill, Pine, and South Pine creeks; Silver, Grimes Hollow, North Cedar, Ram Hollow, Spring Branch, Upper Bankston, Monastery, North Canoe, and Ten-Mile creeks.

MAINE

Nowhere in the United States have brook trout achieved as much of their maximum potential, in both size and numbers, as in the state of Maine. The environment offers two distinct choices: a relatively flat terrain along the coast and inland, covering about a third of the state, and a fairly mountainous and hilly extension of the Appalachian Mountains in the west. Both produce a habitat suitable to the wide demands of brook trout.

Of the state's many ponds and lakes, 1,010 have been designated brook trout waters. However, not all of these contain descendants of the original stock that colonized Maine in postglacial times. Some 457 are stocked annually with more than 800,000 fingerlings, either wild fish, Assinica Strain, or a hybrid of these two. While these waters may have ideal habitat for adult brook trout, they're often muddy-bottomed bog ponds with no pebble-bottomed spring holes or small-graveled feeder streams to provide the aerated spawning beds needed for natural reproduction. Maine has thousands of rivers, streams, and brooks, but stocks fewer than 100 because the remainder have an abundance of spawning habitat.

Maine has a long-established policy of stocking that many states should have adopted years ago. It gives preference to wild (original-strain) brook trout populations where they exist, and efforts are made to preserve them through regulatory protection. The goal is to prevent a possible loss of genetic integrity from hatchery-reared brook trout derived from nonindigenous stocks and to ensure that these aren't introduced into waters where wild populations are reproducing successfully.

Despite these efforts, the status of the brook trout population has changed drastically since the turn of the century. The causes are the same in Maine as elsewhere. Most prominent is the change in habitat caused by lumbering and poor forestry practices. Lumber-road erosion into streams has destroyed many spawning sites and increased mean water temperatures because of increased runoff and loss of streamside cover. Add to this the growing dominance of agriculture, with its inherent pollution, especially on the coastal plain, and you have vanishing brook trout populations.

Add overfishing, compounded by the introduction of such non-native species as brown and rainbow trout, and brook trout have lost another round. Even worse has been the introduction of native species—lake trout, landlocked salmon, and smelt—into what was once exclusively brook trout habitat. The biggest single threat today is the unauthorized introduction of warm-water fishes, especially small- and largemouth bass. If this continues, brook trout will be relegated entirely to higher elevations and upper watersheds, as has been the case in many states in the fish's southern range.

Some losses have been tempered or slowed by more restrictive legislation. The bag limit now is usually five brook trout per day—less in many waters. In 1915 it was 25. The number of waters with two-trout limits has increased sharply since 1957 and is now over 200; and the number requiring special minimum lengths of 10 and 12 inches has increased dramatically. Another boost has been the restriction of some waters to fly fishing only. Since 1965 the number of such waters has increased by 40 percent, and the number of lakes where only artificial lures may be used has increased to 50. Plans are underway to further increase this number. But is all of this enough to turn the tide? Heartening to many people is the active role individuals, private clubs, and Trout Unlimited have taken in Maine to improve the fishery and to change the attitude of many Mainers toward conserving the resource.

In a state with so much brook trout water it's almost impossible to list the better or even best waters. Maine has 10 streams where catch-and-release is required. These offer bigger fish than those found elsewhere. In 1994, five ponds were added to this category: Mountain

View, Mirror, Notch, Bluff, Salmon, and Roach ponds. Maine has also named 180 waters to its Remote Trout Ponds program. These have been zoned to exclude permanent development and access roads within a half mile.

The most productive brook trout waters are found in the northern half of Oxford County and in Franklin, Somerset, Piscataquis, Aroostook, and Penobscot counties. The largest official brook trout in Maine—8½ pounds—was taken from Chase Pond in 1979 by James Foster. However, much-larger brook trout have been recorded as coming from the Rangeley Lakes in the last century. One weighed 11½ pounds; its photograph was published in 1890 in *With Fly-Rod and Camera* by Edward Samuels. Maine does have a sea-run brook trout fishery, but one hardly hears of it because of the preponderance of brook trout in its multitude of freshwater streams.

MARYLAND

It's amazing today that a state the size of Maryland, crunched in the massive urban-sprawl corridor between Washington, Baltimore, and Philadelphia, can offer its anglers any degree of trout fishing, let alone a fairly high quality of brook trout fishing. But it does. Though a small state, Maryland has 162 trout streams, with 816 miles of productive water in its 11 river basins. Of these streams, 89 are dedicated to brook trout, where they're the major or the only salmonid predator. Even more noteworthy is that these 89 brook trout streams have self-sustaining populations. Thirty other streams hold various combinations of brook, brown, and rainbow trout.

Don't look for big water to find brook trout in Maryland. In fact, brook trout waters, regardless where you find them, are seldom large. Brook trout streams in the Old Line State are small, from 10 to 15 feet wide and from 1 to 3 miles long. The better brook trout fishing is confined to five watersheds—the North Branch Potomac, Savage, Monocacy, Gunpowder, and Patapsco rivers--three located in west areas of the state, another north of Frederick, and the

fifth north of Baltimore.

The state has never run an extensive brook trout stocking program, because nearly 100 percent of its populations are self-sustaining. The only annual stocking is the 500 fish planted in Hunting Creek, but these aren't intended to create as a put-and-take fishery. Brook trout streams in the area north of Baltimore include the watersheds of Beaver, Morgan, and Piney runs; Jones, Little, and Gunpowder and Little Gunpowder falls; Beetree and Dead runs, Gwynns Falls, Herring Run, Deer Creek, and the main and south branches of the Patapsco River.

There are six watersheds containing brook trout in the group of small drainages north of Frederick that parallel the eastern side of the Appalachian Trail, in an area protected by several state parks and forests and the City of Frederick Municipal Forest: Hunting, Little Hunting, Fishing, Owens, Friends, and Middle creeks.

The best brook trout fishing is concentrated in a collection of watersheds in the far-western part of the state, almost exclusively in Garrett County. This is the state's highest terrain, with several peaks above 3,000 feet, including Backbone Mountain, the state's loftiest at 3,360 feet. It's also marked by numerous state forests and parks. The area contains 11 notable watersheds: the Savage and Youghiogheny rivers, Bear Creek, the North Branch Potomac and Little Youghiogheny rivers, Salt Block and Mill runs, Muddy Creek, Buffalo Run, the Casselman River, and Herrington Creek.

Lower sections of the Savage River offer anglers the state's best brook trout fishing. Because it's managed as a trophy trout stream, it gets added attention. It also includes good populations of brown and rainbow trout. Minimum size for brook trout is 12 inches, for browns 18 inches, but there's no minimum for rainbows. The daily limit is two trout per day in combined species. It's flies-only above Allegany Bridge to the Savage River dam, and lures-only (flies included) below Allegany Bridge to its mouth. The trophy trout management area extends from the Savage River dam downstream to the river's confluence with the North Branch Potomac River. Within this area are two large wooden suspension bridges designed to carry foot traffic across the stream. The lower bridge, known as Allegany Bridge, divides the upstream flies-only area (1½ miles long) from the downstream lures-only area (3 miles long).

The following is a description of the stream from Maryland's regulations:

> The Savage River is a moderate gradient, rough and tumble stream located downstream of the Savage River Reservoir in east-central Garrett County. Rocky runs and rapids are commonplace and the stream-bed is virtually lined with large boulders and cobble. Pocket-water and moderate-sized pools abound throughout the stream with occasional large pools available to test your casting skills. Cold, clear water is released at a relatively constant rate from the Savage River Dam. Spring and summer flows average 150 and 50 cubic feet per second, respectively, and only the largest storms will turn it off color. Savage River rarely exceeds 65 degrees F and it never freezes. The entire flies-only section flows through public lands while most of lures-only section flows through private land, some of which is posted against fishing. Savage River Road parallels the entire trophy trout area and has numerous pull-offs and gravel parking areas. Trout are abundant throughout the stream and are maintained solely by natural reproduction of brook and brown trout. Most brook trout caught average 9 to 11 inches long while browns average a few inches longer.

The state's largest brook trout is a 4-pound, 12-ounce fish taken May 30, 1985, by Rick Joyce from Western Run, near Cockeysville in Baltimore County.

MASSACHUSETTS

While brook trout were always well distributed throughout the Bay State and continue to be so, Massachusetts was never known for producing big fish even when the state was first colonized—or at least no one made note of it. Even Dr. Jerome V. C. Smith, the state's first recording ichthyologist, in his book *Natural History of the Fishes of Massachusetts* claimed that the average Massachusetts brook trout was only between 8 and 12 inches long. He called the sea-run brook trout, which is still present in the state, the salmon-trout, and erroneously identified it by the brown trout's scientific name, *Salmo trutta*. The European brown trout was more than 30 years away from being introduced to North America.

Alterations to Massachusetts's waters caused by changing land uses forced its fisheries managers to begin stocking the state's streams with hatchery-raised brook trout more than 125 years ago. Though the original stock of brook trout was derived from the state's wild fish, constant generations of breeding the same group removed most of the preferred characteristics of wild brook trout. Over the ensuing years, the state stocked brook trout in all of its major watersheds. However, there's a real possibility that, in the minute feeder streams to some of these headwaters, pure strains of wild brook trout may still exist. Brook trout can be a tough fish when life gets down to the nitty-gritty.

And while the state can still offer its anglers good brook trout fishing, most of it is put-and-take, with marginal winter holdover and reproduction. There are five waters—the Deerfield, Quasnet, and Millens rivers, the East Branch Westfield River, and Higgins Pond—where catch-and-release (artificial lures only) is the rule.

Cape Cod has always been famous for its small brook-trout ponds and didn't escape mention by Smith. Where they had access to the ocean the fish moved downstream for periods and became salters. There are even salters and trout on the state's two large offshore islands, Nantucket and Martha's Vineyard. The best known of these streams, which still produces some fair-sized salters, is the Mashpee River, on the Nantucket Sound side of the Cape. About 30 years ago, feeling the latent effects of chemicals used in the cranberry industry and of its land alterations, populations in these streams began to decline, which spurred an intensive investigation of salters. Since then, brook trout stocking and a halt to the use of DDT and rotenone has brought back some of this fishery. Today, there are sea-run fish in the Jones,

Childs, Coonamessett, Parker, Santuit, and Quashnet rivers, and Scorton Creek as well as the Mashpee River.

The Massachusetts state record is a 6-pound, 4-ounce fish taken from Otis Reservoir by Thomas Laptow in 1968.

MICHIGAN

When American settlers reached Michigan in the early 1800s, they were surprised to discover that the ubiquitous brook trout was found nowhere in Lower Michigan except in the Muskegon River's watershed. It was everywhere on the Upper Peninsula. Charles Hallock, later of *Forest and Stream,* traveled to the state in the late 1860s and recorded that the only fish in the Au Sable River, other than grayling, were suckers. Brook trout were absent from all streams on the Lower Peninsula, according to him, except "those running into [Little] Traverse Bay and all around the shore of Presque Isle on Lake Huron; but, they are found in but a few on the [Lower] peninsula, if any, that empty into Lake Huron south of Thunder Bay, or in Lake Michigan south of Grand Haven Bay."

But by 1870, the first brook trout had appeared in several streams in northern parts of the state. Some think they migrated naturally from the Upper Peninsula. There's also the possibility that early settlers, or even Native Americans, planted them in these small streams.

It wasn't until March 6, 1885, that the first brook trout were stocked in streams on the Lower Peninsula. At that time, R. S. Babbitt planted 20,000 in the Au Sable River in Grayling Township. All of the streams of the Lower Peninsula had contained great numbers of grayling, but they had disappeared long ago on the Au Sable and were fast disappearing from other streams. In April of that same year, O. D. Marks stocked 10,000 brook trout in waters in Menominee County on the Upper Peninsula.

With these efforts began one of the most intensive and successful stockings of the brook trout anywhere in its present range. The first results from these small stockings were so spectacular that within a few years every watershed that would support brook trout was stocked. The late 1800s were the heyday of brook-trout fishing in Michigan. By 1905, the decline had set in. The initial causes were heavy lumbering and increased agricultural use of the land, followed by urbanization. Brown and rainbow trout adapted better to the region's changed ecology, and stocking practices favored these species. In many once-famous brook trout streams, such as the Pere Marquette and Muskegon, brook trout are now missing or in low numbers.

Today, Michigan still maintains one of the nation's best brook trout fisheries, primarily through hatchery stockings. While few brook trout are trophy fish, their numbers are healthy. They still inhabit most of the state's cold-water streams, especially those that radiate from the hilly plateau in the north-central part of the Lower Peninsula. These include the Black, Au Sable, and Pigeon rivers and Hunt Creek. On the Upper Peninsula, the Fox River has self-sustaining populations supported by stocking efforts.

The waters surrounding both peninsulas also offer excellent fishing for coasters, brook trout that migrate from the streams to feed in the big lakes and return to spawn in the fall. The state's two largest brook trout, tied for the record, came from northern Lake Michigan. The 6-pound, 12-ounce brook trout caught by Leon Dube on February 25, 1991, was 26 inches long. The other, caught by Jeff Johnson on July 17, 1988, was a 24½-incher.

MINNESOTA

Minnesota's terrain is not ideal for brook trout. Relatively flat, it was once an ancient ocean bottom and, more recently, a glacial floodplain. Three-quarters of it is rolling prairies interspersed with oak groves. It's widely pocked by lakes and ponds, kettle holes created by the last ice sheet, except for the southeastern corner, which was never glaciated. The rest is heavily wooded and hilly, and gives rises to numerous tributaries that feed the Red River to the west and the Mississippi River to the east.

Minnesota is the western edge of natural

brook trout distribution. Today the boundary is the Mississippi River. There's some good brook trout fishing at the river's origins, however, in clusters of small lakes, ponds, and small streams and creeks in Itasca and Beltrami counties in the north-central part of the state. The Mississippi flows south in a large S-curve across the state to Minneapolis and St. Paul; the tributaries that form the river's western watershed, even in early times, contained very few brook trout. The exact western limit of the brook trout's range in presettlement days was the height of land that separates the Minnesota River, Bois de Sioux, and Red River of the northern watershed from the upper Mississippi River's watershed.

While brook trout fishing is today scattered throughout most of Minnesota, the better areas are concentrated in the northeastern part of the state, in St. Louis, Lake, and Cook counties along the North Shore of Lake Superior; in a series of small watershed streams southeast of Route 23 that flow into the St. Croix River; and in the southeastern part of the state in the watersheds of the Zumbo and Root rivers.

At one time, all of the streams in the state that flowed into Lake Superior had a lake-run or coaster brook trout fishery. Coasters are still taken inshore along Lake Superior by anglers trolling for lake and rainbow trout and Pacific salmon. Remnant populations probably still exist in streams such as the Brule, Cascade, Temperance, Manitou, Baptism, and Split Rock rivers, because coaster brook trout are taken near their mouths. These fish typically don't move more than a dozen miles from their nursery streams. Minnesota is taking part in a coaster brook trout program with other Great Lakes states and provinces. Because of the limited spawning habitat in its Lake Superior streams, it's unlikely that a restoration program here will be very effective, according to Department of Natural Resources biologist Mark Ebbers.

Minnesota has an active brook trout stocking program. Large numbers are planted annually, even though many of the state's waters have self-sustaining populations. Many others don't, however, especially lakes and ponds, where habi-

tat is often marginal for this species. Brook trout in such waters are managed as put-grow-and-take fish. To maintain vitality in domesticated trout, hatchery personnel here use a variety of brook trout stocks that include fish from Maine waters, Nipigon and other Ontario waters, and a combination of these populations. It must work, because the state record is a 6-pound, 4.48-ounce brookie taken from High Lake (St. Louis County) on August 10, 1991.

Even though the state's biologists rate the overall brook trout fishery as only "fair," Minnesota's recreational anglers prefer brook trout to other trout and even to walleye, the state fish. The state gives no special management to brook trout; they're treated as a group with rainbows and browns. However, a few streams are managed strictly for brook trout. Minnesota has a limited brook trout trophy program and has two lakes—Thrush and Turnip in Cook County—with a one-fish-per-day creel limit and an 18-inch minimum size.

The state is currently analyzing isolated pockets of brook trout that might have escaped interbreeding with domesticated brook trout, and it hopes to develop a program that will place emphasis on Minnesota's native brook trout populations.

NEW HAMPSHIRE

One hears little about New Hampshire brook trout fishing outside of the state. However, the state does a great job of managing 180 ponds and lakes and nearly 240 brooks, streams, and rivers for trout. And in more than 90 percent of these waters, brook trout are the only species; in others they cohabit with brown and rainbow trout. Brook trout are found in almost all of the state's cold-water streams. These waters offers anglers fair to good fishing; a few have excellent brook trout fishing.

Probably one reason that one doesn't hear a lot of about the state's brook trout, especially big brook trout, is related to its nickname, the Granite State. Most brook trout fishing is in the expansive White Mountains in the northern half of the state, part of the White Mountain

National Forest. Because of the area's igneous granite strata, the waters have few dissolved minerals and nutriments, and leachings from the predominantly forested land make them highly acidic. While brook trout survive better than any other salmonids in such environments, the low pH doesn't produce the abundant insect life that composes the major portion of brook trout diets elsewhere in their range.

According to Scott Decker, a regional fisheries biologist, the historically low productivity of the state's waters, combined with fishing pressure, has created a primarily put-and-take fishery. Brook trout account for half of all the salmonids stocked annually in the state. Only three major watersheds and one pond are managed for wild brook trout and not stocked. However, this doesn't mean that there are no New Hampshire waters containing the original-strain wild brook trout that colonized these waters with the retreat of the glaciers. But some of these are so remote that reaching them requires real dedication and a lot of effort.

In New Hampshire, one has to add "grow-" to "put-and-take," because there's no problem with holdover fish; they do grow, even though the state's brook trout seldom live longer than four years. About 60 of the more remote ponds are stocked with fingerlings. Because of their location and light fishing pressure, they produce brook trout of up to 4 pounds. The state is now in the process of surveying its trout streams to determine where wild strains dominate the populations; these are less likely to be stocked. Wild strains will be protected by more restrictive regulations to give them a chance to create self-sustaining populations.

The overall brook trout fishery in New Hampshire has, for the most part, been managed as a put-and-take fishery due to the limited amount of natural reproduction. Reclaiming ponds with rotenone or similar fish toxicants, then stocking them with hatchery-reared fish, was the dominant management technique for a 40-year period beginning in 1938, which opened with the reclamation of Back Lake in Pittsburg. Pond reclamation continued until 1978, when only two were treated. Rotenone costs and small budgets eliminated

the program. There are now 103 reclaimed ponds, all being managed for trout. The reclaimed-pond designation was eliminated in 1983 when all ponds were classified as trout ponds. In 1989, the New Hampshire Fish and Game Department, at the public's request, reclaimed Little Diamond Pond, Stewartstown, to remove an overabundance of yellow perch.

The most productive ponds include Munn Pond (Errol), Lower Trio Pond (Odell), Nathan Pond (Dixville), Big and Little Greenough ponds (Wentworth), and Jones Pond (Middletown).

Trout-stream management became more refined with the completion of the Hoover biological surveys, 1936–40. Specific recommendations for species, sizes, and numbers of trout to be stocked, based on habitat factors, were made for all of the major streams in the Connecticut, Androscoggin, Saco, Merrimack, and coastal watersheds. Management of trout streams has not changed drastically since the early 1960s. Sections of some streams have had special regulations placed on them in order to develop "quality" fisheries. These special regulations include fly fishing only, trophy trout (12-inch minimum length, two-fish creel limit), and catch-and-release. Recently, barbless-hook restrictions were proposed for several streams and ponds.

The state's top rivers include portions of the upper Connecticut River, and the Androscoggin, Dead Diamond, Dry, and Ammonoosuc rivers, some of which are "rivers" in name only and really more like streams.

In 1983, the department began a statewide inventory of all trout streams in order to develop a more quantitative method of trout distribution. The program, entitled "Fishing For The Future," classifies streams using several criteria, including wild trout abundance, recreational use potential, and stream width. Any streams classified as having an excellent wild trout abundance won't be stocked. So far, only five southern counties have been surveyed. The program has been reactivated after a five-year hiatus.

Several attempts were made over the years to produce a trophy brook trout fishery using fast-growing and/or long-lived hybrid strains. Splake trout (male brook trout x female lake trout), tiger trout (male brook trout x female brown trout), and Assinica brook trout (a long-lived Canadian strain) have been tried in several lakes and ponds. Apparently these hybrids didn't meet anticipated growth or size standards, and support for their continued management gradually dwindled.

Despite these concerted efforts in managing brook trout populations, they're still not what New Hampshire's fisheries managers or fishermen are hoping for. However, the state has an active program with a positive philosophy toward bettering the quality of its brook trout fishing. Decker, in evaluating the overall status of brook trout in New Hampshire, candidly summarized it as "good in stocked and poor in wild waters."

The current state record is a 9-pounder caught May 8, 1911, by A. Val Woodruff from Pleasant Lake (New London). With a heritage of fish this large, it's no wonder that New Hampshire's biologists are making such an effort to restore the fishery.

NEW JERSEY

The Garden State has taken the concept of a put-and-take brook trout fishery to its maximum. It never claimed to offer anglers the kind of quality fishing taken for granted by fishermen in better-located states or provinces, but it has achieved a fair semblance of what many people have come to believe is brook trout fishing.

Except for the first few millennia after the retreat of the glacier that covered portions of the extreme northern portion of the state, New Jersey has always been on the periphery of the brook trout's range. Most of the state is part of a coastal outwash plain. Only in the short western and northern piedmont that leads to the eastern base of the Kittatinny Mountains, folded hogback ridges typical of the Atlantic-slope side of the Appalachians, is there habitat suitable for brook trout.

Brook trout were not extensively distributed even in precolonial times, although there were brook trout in almost every county. Today, populations of natives exist only in the headwaters of small streams in the northwestern counties of Sussex, Warren, Morris, and Passaic. This closely mirrors the locations of streams today classified as "Wild Trout." These streams retain the needed requirements for brook trout reproduction: clear, cool waters whose temperatures don't rise above 68 degrees Fahrenheit, shaded banks and pools, and clean gravel beds for spawning. These waters aren't stocked by the state, but because extensive stocking of all New Jersey waters began in the 1880s, the primordial strain has surely been hybridized with hatchery fish, and truly wild or original-strain brook trout probably no longer exist.

Despite this, in several waters not listed as Wild Trout Streams natural reproduction and self-sustaining populations do exist. Few if any of the state's wild trout grow larger than 6 or 7 inches. This has caused its fisheries managers a bit of consternation. Most of the brook trout stocked by the state are 7 to 14 inches. Where wild and stocked fish appear in the same stream, the state has been accused of stocking small fish, but these are really the stream's progeny. Although some wild brook trout may grow larger than 7 inches, most fish over 10 inches are hatchery trout. Many New Jersey waters are stocked well above their capacity, because the fish are removed before that becomes a problem. And the stocked fish are larger than those most other states would plant, because these fish are put there to satisfy angler demands. Even if the fish aren't harvested, they usually die for a variety of reasons. By midsummer, most stocked fish are gone.

There's no such thing as the best waters to fish in New Jersey, because the best waters are where the hatchery trucks stop. And the best season is as soon as these waters are opened. Stocking takes place in two months, April and May. There are some holdover fish, but most hatchery fish have been caught by fall. The state also stocks a goodly number of "sugar trout," fish larger than 14 inches—up to 18 inches.

"The size attained by brook trout in rivers, large lakes and marine waters may be remarkable," hedged Harry Goodwin, in a piece he wrote in the April 1967 issue of *New Jersey Outdoors*. For example, the state-record brook—from Lake Hopatcong—was a 6-pound, 8-ounce fish taken in 1956 by George J. Hornung. However, Robert Soldwedel, chief of New Jersey's Freshwater Fisheries Division, believes this was one of his sugar trout, probably a hatchery breeder, because "brook trout would not be expected to survive a summer in this lake." More recently, another sugar trout was caught. This one was also a breeder that had done her job well and in 1963 was released into the Rockaway River in Morris County. The Rockaway has some pretty deep holes, and this huge fish was able to avoid being caught until June 1965, when Andrew DuJack drifted a live minnow into a pool and caught her, now 7 pounds, 3 ounces, setting a new state record.

The most productive brook trout waters in New Jersey include Flat Brook, the South Branch Raritan River, the Musconetcong and Pequest River drainages, and Van Campens Brook and other Delaware River tributaries in Sussex and Warren counties. Brook trout have been found in tributaries to the Delaware River as far south as Mantua Creek, south of Philadelphia, but the better brook trout streams flowing into the Delaware River begin with the Musconetcong and continue north.

The following streams, or portions thereof, are designated Wild Trout Streams: Bear Creek (Southtown), Bear Swamp Brook (Mahwah), Black Brook (Clinton Wildlife Management Area), Burnett Brook (Ralston), Cold Brook (Oldwick), Dark Moon Brook (Johnsonburg), Flanders Brook (Flanders), Hances Brook (Penwell), Hickory Run (Califon), India Brook (source to Mountainside Avenue, Mendham), Indian Grove Brook (Bernardsville), Ledgewood Brook (Ledgewood), Little York Brook (Little York), Lomerson Brook (Pottersville), Merrill Creek (Stewartsville, upstream of reservoir), Mill Brook (Montague), North Branch Rockaway Creek (Mountainville), Parker Brook (Montague), the Passaic River (source to Route 202, Bernardsville), Pequannock River (Newark watershed, Oak Ridge Road bridge downstream to railroad bridge upstream of Charlottesburg

Reservoir), Rhineharts Brook (Hacklebarney State Park), Rocky Run (Clinton Township), Stephensburg Creek (Stephensburg), Stony Brook (Stokes State Forest), Stony Brook (Washington Township, Morris County), Tetertown Brook (Tetertown), Trout Brook (Hacklebarney State Park), Turkey Brook (Mount Olive), Van Campens Brook (Delaware Water Gap National Recreation Area), West Brook (source downstream to Windbeam Club property), and Willoughby Brook (Clinton Township). Major trout-stocked lakes include Canistear and Clinton reservoirs, Lake Hopatcong, Monksville Reservoir, and Wawayanda Lake.

In these Wild Trout Streams, brook trout must be 7 inches or longer to be kept—12 inches in some waters—and only artificial lures may be used. The creel limit is two per day from the second Saturday in April to September 15.

At one time, New Jersey had fair populations of sea-run brook trout or salters. There may have been more in precolonial times, but the fishery was never as well developed as those on Long Island, on Cape Cod, or in coastal streams north to Labrador. There were salters in Hop Brook (the feeder stream to the Navesink River) and in the Shark, Metedeconk, and Cedar rivers as late as 1936, and in tidal portions of Manasquan River as late as 1968. The Cedar River, in modern times, seems to have been the southern limit of sea-run brook trout along the Atlantic Coast.

NEW YORK

Like most northeastern states, New York once had brook trout in every river, stream, brook, creek, lake, and pond with an outlet, and even on its islands surrounded by salt water. The state was in a pivotal position in the fish's recolonization of northern waters as the glaciers began receding 20,000 years ago. Various temporary glacial lakes flooded the terrain at elevations reaching the tops of most of today's highest watersheds. This flooding allowed brook trout access above barriers that today would restrict upstream and interwatershed migration.

Thus New York became unique among all of the states and provinces in the range of brook trout, because its waters were exposed at slightly different times to differing populations, including four of the five or possibly six recognized strains of this species. But no angler or even well-trained biologist can separate these by appearance alone. Strain recognition, a relatively recent tool, enables fisheries managers to identify and favor stocking those brook trout with characteristics unique to a watershed that have the best opportunity to survive and develop self-sustaining populations.

As in most states, brook trout in New York have lost more than half of their waters to lumbering, agriculture, urban expansion, and damming. Since the turn of the century, their range has been further reduced by the introduction of exotic species—rainbow and brown trout, perch, and smallmouth bass; this continues. Within the last 40 years, more than 500 high-elevation lakes and ponds in the Adirondacks have lost their brook trout populations because of acid rain.

Because of its long history of hatchery brook trout production, New York is probably the best example of a fishery whose product bears little resemblance to the original fish. After the introduction of brown and rainbow trout, it was also guilty of managing trout as a single fishery, irrespective of the unique needs of each species. The losers were brook trout. In 1979, New York's Department of Environmental Conservation (DEC) took a hard look at its trout fisheries and reevaluated its approach to brook trout management (see chapter 7). The result was a multifaceted plan intended to return parts of the fishery to their previous state, to manage others as wild trout waters, and to manage the remainder for put-and-take trout fishing.

Today, between a third and a half of the state's trout population is a self-sustaining mix of all three species. However, in about 30 streams, mostly headwater rivulets, brook trout are the only predator salmonid. There are three primary areas for brook trout fishing in the state, centered on three mountain groups: the Alleghenies in the western part of the state, the Adirondacks in the north, and the Catskills in the southeast. This doesn't mean that there are no brook trout waters elsewhere; to the contrary. Good fisheries exist along the eastern side of the Hudson, on Long Island, and on the lake plains in the west-central part of New York.

The DEC rates the brook trout fishing in New York as fair to good. At one time, the majority of brook trout caught were stocked or domesticated fish. However, almost all brook trout stocked today are hybrids composed of Témiscamie and Crown Point Strain domesticated trout.

New York has more than 600 waters, from small rivulets to big rivers, that contain brook trout populations. The following is a collection of 50 of the better streams: Ausable River, East and West Branches (Essex), Batten Kill River (Washington), Beaver Kill River (Delaware, Sullivan, Ulster), Black River (Oneida, Herkimer, Lewis), Boquet River (Essex), Carmans River (Suffolk), Cattaraugus Creek (Cattaraugus, Erie), Cedar River (Hamilton), Chateaugay River (Franklin), North Branch Chazy River (Clinton), Cohocton River (Steuben), Connetquot River (Suffolk), East Branch Croton River (Putnam, Westchester), Delaware River, East and West Branches (Delaware, Sullivan), Esopus Creek (Ulster), Fish Creek and its East Branch (Oneida, Oswego, Lewis), Genesee River (Allegany above Wellsville), Hudson River (Essex, Warren), Independence River (Lewis), Indian River (Hamilton), Ischua Creek (Cattaraugus), Kayaderosseras Creek (Saratoga), Kinderhook Creek (Rensselaer, Columbia), Lansing Kill (Oneida), Limestone Creek (Onondaga), Little Salmon River (Franklin), Mettawee River (Washington), Mill Creek (Warren), Mohawk River (Oneida), Moose River (Lewis, Herkimer, Oneida), Neversink River (Sullivan, Orange), Nissequogue River (Suffolk), Oatka Creek (Monroe), Oriskany Creek (Oneida, Madison), West Branch Oswegatchie River (Lewis), Otter Creek (Lewis), Roeliff Jansen Kill (Columbia), St. Regis River (St. Lawrence, Franklin), Salmon River (Clinton, Franklin), Salmon River, East and North branches (Oswego, Lewis), North Branch Saranac River (Clinton, Franklin), Schenevus Creek (Otsego), Schoharie Creek

(Greene), Schroon River (Warren), Trout Brook (Warren, Essex), Trout River (Franklin), West Canada Creek (Herkimer, Oneida), Willowemoc Creek (Sullivan), and Wiscoy Creek (Wyoming, Allegany).

While brook trout populations are large and widespread in New York, in modern times the state has never produced really big fish. Even in early colonial times, few brook trout exceeded 6 pounds, with the exception of sea-run fish. Most brook trout inhabited rivers, streams, and brooks with environments that don't produce the kinds of food needed to grow big trout. Big brook trout come from lakes or from large rivers with lakelike sections. Most of New York's big lakes are oligotrophic—deep, cold, and with little food. The smaller lakes and ponds, mostly in the Adirondacks and some in the Catskills, are usually at higher elevations and, due to the surrounding conifer forests, highly acidic, which minimizes both insect and forage-fish production.

Until a few years ago, the state record was an 8½-pound fish taken by William Keener in 1908 from Punchbowl Pond, located on the edge of the Catskills in Sullivan County. Though the "Druids of eld" (after Wadsworth's Acadia) have long been timbered off in the Catskills, their offspring are now full adults. The walls of many of the ravines formed in these hills by centuries of spring freshets are now so steep and close together that sunlight never penetrates the dense hemlock–white pine canopy, except perhaps during the height of day, and then only for a few moments.

Abe Wood Creek plunges more than 900 feet to meet Willowemoc Creek at Roscoe, just a tad above Junction Pool, where the Beaver Kill also enters. But this is not about Abe Wood, Willowemoc, or Beaver Kill creeks, but about a large trout and a small, obscure, sapphire blue pond that sits in a sea of soft, spring green, velvet mountains.

The Punchbowl came into existence about 1880. Just above the gorge, across a rivulet that even today has no name, Sullivan County built a bridge that stood atop several tall flagstone pylons. Upstream of the bridge is a natural basin, gouged from the surrounding land by the

last glacier. Here, in the bowl, the stream widened. There may even have been a pond here created by beavers, which today still cut back trees from along the water's edges. William Underwood, who at one time owned the land, saw that the bridge's pillars could form the base of a dam and built one. He used flagstone because of its immediate abundance, and cleared hemlocks and pines from the depression's edges to increase the size of his impoundment.

There was only one kind of trout in the no-name stream. Eons ago, ancestors of these natives worked their way upstream, out of the Willowemoc and up the lower reaches of Abe Wood, only to be stopped by the falls. Underwood, however, helped them overcome this hurdle and set them free in his new pond. As the impoundment increased in size, trout, dace, and golden shiners found themselves in a hyper-rich environment. And, as is natural in such situations, their populations exploded in numbers and size.

Bill Keener—a cousin of Frank Keener, who built and operated Antrim Lodge, a hostelry long famous as a gathering place for anglers, just a mile or so away down the precipitous gorge in Roscoe—was a friend of Underwood. Together, they fished many streams and ponds in the area. Late one afternoon in 1908 (we don't know the month or day), as the story goes, Keener landed an 8½-pound brook trout while fishing in the Punchbowl, as the impoundment has become known. We have no more details than that. For years this alleged feat remained obscure, recorded not in one of the Catskills' many weekly newspapers but in the minds of the Keeners. For a while, nothing more was heard of this, the largest trout taken in recent years from New York's waters.

The state had never taken the time to record its largest fish, so Cecil Heacox, a fisheries biologist who in the 1950s rose to the rank of secretary of the Conservation Department, the predecessor of the DEC, took it upon himself to form such a list. His department had little such information to fall back upon, so Heacox turned to *Field & Stream* magazine, which had been keeping such records since before the turn of the century. He took the biggest fish he found recorded that had been caught in New York State and created the state's record book. For brook trout, he listed a 4-pounder. This was the champ for a few years until Clayton Seagers, editor of *The Conservationist*, published by the DEC, met Bill Keener in Keener's Pool, the bar in the basement of Antrim Lodge. As the story goes, Keener told him of his catch from the Punchbowl. The next time the state's fish records were published, Bill Keener's trout was at the top.

"There's no record of the big trout being caught," said Ed Van Put, a DEC fisheries aide. Van Put is into the history of trout fishing in the Catskills and researched all of the Catskill-area libraries' newspapers for 1908. He found no mention of the catch. "Even then, trout fishermen here and in the City were keen on record fish. I couldn't find mention in any City column or local weekly. Still, that doesn't mean the fish wasn't caught, it's just unlikely."

Nevertheless, it's an interesting tale.

Keener's fish was deleted when the state began reviewing its records because it lacked corroborating evidence. Today, the biggest brook trout on the official list is only a 4-pound, 13-ounce fish taken by Rick Mace on May 16, 1992, from Deer Pond. It was probably a released hatchery brood fish.

NORTH CAROLINA

More than likely, brook trout were spread throughout the entire state of North Carolina in early postglacial times. Today, they're restricted to a small corner in the far-western part of the state, at elevations above 5,000 feet. This area encompasses the high peaks of the Great Smoky Mountains and part of the southern end of the Appalachian Mountains, which extend as far north as Canada's Maritime provinces. Most watersheds still holding brook trout are in Great Smoky Mountains National Park and Pisgah, Nantahala, and Cherokee National Forests, some of which straddle the border between North Carolina and Tennessee.

Wild brook trout were much more widely distributed in Southern Appalachian watersheds, to as low as 1,500 feet, prior to the late 1800s, when lumbering operations denuded the forests on all but the highest peaks and drastically changed the fish's habitat. The forest canopy over the streams was lost, water temperatures rose, and siltation obliterated spawning sites. By the 1930s, few brook trout were found in streams below 3,000 feet. This situation was further aggravated by the introduction of brown and rainbow trout, and by intrastrain hybridization of wild brook trout with hatchery stocks that had lost most of their wild characteristics. Much of the stock for North Carolina's early stocking efforts came from New York hatcheries. From 1935 to 1975, more than 800,000 hatchery brook trout were stocked in Great Smoky Mountains National Park.

In 1976, the National Park Service, under a mandate to protect native species, stopped stocking the remaining brook trout streams under its aegis. Of approximately 1,000 miles of suitable waters in the park in 1976, brook trout were able to inhabit only 123. However, even this small mileage wasn't necessarily safe for brook trout. Only 40 or so miles were protected by barriers, some natural and others man-made in prepark days, to keep brown and rainbow trout from encroaching upon wild brook trout populations. At these high altitudes, even in waters below the barriers, there's little more than insect food available, and brook trout can't compete effectively for this with other trout. As a result, they were unable to grow beyond 5 or 6 inches.

About 4,000 miles of brooks and streams with waters suitable for trout exist today in North Carolina. About half are on state lands, but only 1,100 miles are managed as Wild Trout (all species) Waters. Of this, only 200 miles are believed to hold the state's original strain of brook trout. If this is correct, then these fish have been resident in the area since preglacial times, because none of the last four major ice sheets ever flowed farther south over the Appalachian Mountains than southern New York and northeastern Pennsylvania. These aren't relic stocks of brook trout that moved north to colonize postglacial lands, but an integral part of the population that existed on the northern edge of their distribution (Pennsylvania), which supplied the progeny for the northward expansion of the species.

North Carolina has stopped stocking hatchery fish in streams that might contain wild populations not hybridized with earlier hatchery stock. Of the dozen or so such streams, the best-established populations occur on the Hiwassee, Tuckasegee, Little Tennessee, New, and Nolichucky rivers. Stocking still occurs on other waters, most of which also contain brown and rainbow trout. James Borawa, a biologist with the state who's involved with the coldwater fishery, rated the remaining quality of brook trout fishing in the state as fair. "However," he added, "we believe we're still continuing to lose brook trout populations to habitat degradation and competition from brown and rainbow trout."

Despite the dour outlook, North Carolina does maintain just over 200 streams that are designated Hatchery-Supported Trout Waters and regulates the trout take on 33 streams designated Wild Trout Waters. It also has nine Special Regulated Trout Waters where one can fish only with lures and single hooks; all fish must be released. It also has four watersheds with similar regulations, except they're fly fishing only.

All brook trout populations are managed to be self-sustaining, even though only catchable-sized brook trout are stocked. Essentially, these become a part of the put-and-take fishery, and no waters are set aside strictly for brook trout other than those wild populations. Because none of the watersheds stemming from the mountains of western North Carolina are very productive, brook trout of over 10 inches are rare. The statewide minimum is 7 inches. The state record is a 7-pound, 7-ounce fish taken from Raven Fork River on May 15, 1980.

OHIO

Today, there's no brook trout fishery in Ohio. At one time, after the retreat of the last glacier, which exposed Lake Erie about 12,000 years ago, brook trout probably inhabited the dozens of small streams in the northern part of the

state that flow into Lake Erie. But there was postglacial warming of the area, and northern Ohio lacked cooler elevations to which these fish could retreat to find suitable habitat. By the time French explorers passed along the shore of Lake Erie, there were probably only token remnants of these populations. The last fish held out in a few small streams in Ashtabula and Geauga counties. Clearing the land for agriculture and lumber and removing the leafy canopy over the streams caused water temperatures to rise above levels brook trout could tolerate, and they disappeared.

Biologists with Ohio's Division of Wildlife recently conducted an inventory of all these north-flowing waters to see if remnant populations of brook trout might still exist, especially in isolated headwater sections. According to Vincent LaConte, a fisheries manager, only one small tributary to the Chagrin River, in the northeastern part of the state, had a small population of brook trout. The Chagrin rises near the town of Chardon and works its way through the eastern outskirts of metropolitan Cleveland before it enters Lake Erie at Timberlake.

LaConte believes that brook trout here are part of the original wild stock that populated the river from Lake Erie, but because the Chagrin, like many of these other streams, was stocked at one time, the pedigree of these fish is in doubt. However, because stocking hasn't occurred for a number of years and these fish are a self-sustaining population, it seems unlikely that the population has been diluted by hatchery (domesticated) brook trout.

The study did find other waters in this area suitable for brook trout stocking. Plans are now under way to stock this area, and Chagrin fingerlings will be used to reintroduce brook trout to other headwater tributaries of the Chagrin. The goal is not to create a fishable population, however, but to establish a source for expansion of the original strain where suitable waters are found.

Ohio has no regulations designed strictly for brook trout; they fall under general trout restrictions: a daily creel limit of five trout, 12 inches or longer. The best opportunity for catching brook trout, though slight at best, is on

Lake Erie, where coasters from other state and provincial waters have adapted to lake living.

The state's largest brook trout is a 2-pound, 11-ounce fish caught from the Chagrin River by S. Graboshek on June 30, 1955.

PENNSYLVANIA

It's no wonder that Pennsylvania, like New York, designated brook trout its official state fish. The Keystone State is divided into 67 counties, and every county has at least one trout stream—even tiny Philadelphia County, which is almost entirely consumed by the city. Pennsylvania claims to have more miles of trout waters than any other state in the Northeast and some of the finest trout fishing in the country. Half of its counties offer fishing for wild trout. More than 100 streams, with over 400 miles of water, have been identified by biologists as having exceptional populations of wild trout and are rated as Class A waters. An additional 90 streams are part of the Wilderness Trout Streams program.

Pennsylvania can lay claim to so many brook trout superlatives because of its northerly location and unique geology. Much of the central Appalachian Mountain range consists of long, steep, parallel ridges ("hogbacks") with deep, river-filled valleys between them. These were created when the earth's crust was compressed and the land buckled and folded. The best of these hogbacks are found in Pennsylvania, and trend southwest to northeast. Eons of time and rain have created a plethora of small and large streams along the lines of natural erosion patterns. As erosion created this great number of freestone streams, it also exposed valley floors rich in limestone, a real plus for stream fertility and aquatic insect production.

The tops of these mountains were spared the glacial peneplaining that blunted the northern Appalachians. The four most recent glaciers covered only the northeastern corner of the state, filling the valleys with glacial till and smothering their streams. Brook trout were distributed everywhere over what's now Pennsylvania in preglacial times; they now represent some of the oldest examples of this species. When the southern periphery of the glaciers in New York began to melt, water at its base emptied into the headwaters of the Susquehanna River. This became a temporary highway for the northward recolonization of the land and its waters, and brook trout from Virginia and Maryland were among the first fish to move northward. This gave brook trout in Pennsylvania a head start in moving up the state's numerous river systems, whose headwaters had probably been locked in snow and ice for millennia.

Though distribution may have changed little since the first colonists cleared Penn's Woods, brook trout numbers have been reduced sharply. Even as late as the turn of the century it was possible to catch 3- and 4-pound brook trout. The state record is a 6-pound, 5.75-ounce fish taken in 1984 by Anthony Taliani from Little Sugar Creek, Venango County. It was identified as a hatchery breeder. Logging and agriculture, as was the case elsewhere in the fish's range, took a devastating toll on natural populations. The changed environment is now more suitable for other trout species, and where water temperatures really increased, warm-water species have claimed streams no longer inhabited by brook trout.

Like other states, Pennsylvania took the quick-fix route and stocked more and more hatchery-raised brook trout. In the last 75 years, some habitat has improved with reforestation and control of agricultural runoff and chemical use. Today, 60 percent of the state's brook trout populations are self-sustaining. But where they aren't, the Pennsylvania Fish Commission annually stocks about 5 million trout, not all brook trout, in about 5,000 miles of cold-water streams and nearly 100 trout lakes. Unlike states where stocking is only a springtime activity, in Pennsylvania the commission stocks during all seasons. It also discriminates as to where it releases hatchery fish and has evolved a unique philosophy.

Many of Pennsylvania's limestone streams and a number of its freestone streams contain healthy populations of wild trout. Some of these streams are classified as Class A Wild Trout Waters. To avoid interference with natural strains of wild trout, the Fish Commission does not stock hatchery-reared trout in Class A waters, a policy adopted several years ago under the commission's Operation FUTURE program. It's applied to waters where natural populations are sufficient to provide a quality trout-fishing experience. Fishery management techniques allow these streams to sustain themselves through natural reproduction. In addition, protection of the habitat is a major objective.

Some Class A streams are included in a Wilderness Trout Streams program. Not all Wilderness Trout Streams are rated Class A, although all have populations of wild trout and are managed as natural-yield waters. Like Wild Trout Waters, Wilderness Trout Streams aren't stocked. The most important criteria in designating Wilderness Trout Streams are that they produce sufficient populations of wild trout to provide a recreational fishery and that they be remote. Access is walk-in only.

A great deal of Pennsylvania's success with stocking trout is the unique water quality of its streams. Its better trout streams run over limestone beds that enhance both plant and aquatic insect growth. Pennsylvania's limestone streams, such as Big Spring Run, LeTort Spring Run, the Falling Spring Branch, Yellow Breeches Creek, and Penns Creek, enjoy a reputation for quality trout fishing. Anglers from other states as well as abroad have also discovered chalk waters that, in their richness of aquatic insect and plant life, remind them of classic English streams. According to one spokesman, "Their pristine, clear waters produce trout that are reportedly bigger, wilier, and often more brightly colored than the trout living in non-freestone streams."

"In simple terms, limestone streams are defined as streams that flow over a bedrock of limestone or begin as a large spring from an underground stream," said Martin Marcinko, a state fisheries biologist whose specialty is brook trout. "They are generally meadow streams emanating from calcium-rich rock on the valley floor, and are considered among the most fertile of trout streams. In central and southeastern Pennsylvania, limestone streams meander

slowly through quiet valleys and past the rolling hills of fertile farmland.

"It is generally accepted that most freestone streams in Pennsylvania begin from springs in the sandstone bedrock that forms the ridges and mountains. Freestone streams make up the majority of our streams and cover a much bigger area of the state than do the limestone streams. Freestone streams vary more in chemical and biological makeup than limestone streams. Compared to limestones, freestone streams may have fewer insects, but a greater variety."

For management purposes, the Fish Commission divided the state's trout waters into 12 regions based on drainage or watershed. The list of streams classified as Trout, Wilderness Trout, and Wild Trout looks almost like a telephone book. A copy can be obtained by calling the commission at (717) 657-4518. The majority of these waters are located in the north-central portion of the state and are comprised of the watersheds of the West Branch Susquehanna River or the Western Susque-hanna River Basin.

It's sad not to see Loyalsock Creek, a 40-mile stream that in its lower reaches is 50 yards wide, listed among the state's top streams. During the first quarter of this century, it was to many Pennsylvania trout fishermen what the Beaver Kill and Willowemoc are today to New York anglers. The Loyalsock, along with its dozen major tributaries, was the state's classic trout stream. Also no longer a top trout stream is the Tobyhanna. And not even listed is the state's first trout stream, the Schuylkill River, where the nation's first fishing club was established.

Pennsylvania has set aside 19 streams where fly fishing only is permitted, with a minimum size of 9 inches. In these, the restrictions may include all or parts of the streams. They are Conewago Creek, Mud and Trout runs, Young Womans Creek and its Right Branch, Green Spring, and Big Mill, Dunbar, East Branch Antietam, and Little Lehigh creeks; Slate and Grays runs, Bushkill and Cross Fork creeks, Lyman Run, Clear Shade Creek, Francis Branch tributary to Slate Run, Slate Run, and Butternut and Muddy creeks.

The commission designated 10 Pennsylvania

streams catch-and-release only. These are open throughout the year, and while fly fishing is the most popular technique, others are allowed as long as artificial lures with barbless hooks are used. Here, too, restrictions may apply to the entire stream or only to parts, so check the regulations. Included are Hickory Run; Fishing, Yellow Breeches, and Spruce creeks; Roaring Brook; Penns, Bushkill, Toms, and Kettle creeks; and West Branch Calder Creek.

The commission has also set aside parts of six streams as trophy waters. Fishing on these is open throughout the year and only artificial lures may be used. There's a daily creel limit of two fish 14 inches or longer. These are Lick Run, Fishing Creek, Lackawanna River, Cedar Run, and East Branch Tunungwant and Monocacy creeks.

RHODE ISLAND

While brook trout were indigenous to the many streams, lakes, and ponds of this smallest of all states, fishing for this species was never especially noteworthy for either quality or quantity, nor is it today. The state's waters are at best marginal brook trout habitat, and any pressure on the fishery is immediately felt. For this reason, an active stocking program has always been needed to support the fishery. Its management, other than maintaining a put-and-take fishery, has never been aggressive or productive. Even the state objectively rates its brook trout fishery as poor.

Like most coastal states, Rhode Island had a small sea-run fishery in colonial times, but agriculture denuded many watersheds and the industrial revolution, with its demand for mill power, placed dams on almost every stream with a head of water; today, no discernible salter fishery exists. Still, there's ample opportunity for brook trout fishing during the early part of the season, when the number of stocked fish is relatively high. On only one stream are brook trout managed for quality fishing. This is Falls River, a small headwater of the Pawcatuck River in the Arcadia Management Area.

Rhode Island stocks more than 60 streams and ponds throughout the state. These are concentrated in western and northern sections. The largest brook trout taken in Rhode Island was a 3-pound, 12-ounce fish landed in October 1984 from Wyoming Pond by Raymond Boucher Jr. The pond isn't on the state's stocking list but is connected by a quarter-mile-long outlet stream to the Pawcatuck River, which is stocked, near Hope Valley.

SOUTH CAROLINA

While it's still possible to catch a trout in South Carolina waters, this state is today on the extreme southern edge of brook trout distribution. There's no doubt that during the height of the last glacial period, when the brook trout's range was displaced far to the south, these fish inhabited all of the mountainous area in the western part of the state and probably a good bit of the Appalachian Plateau south and east of the mountains. By the time the first European settlers moved inland, however, brook trout were probably already relegated to higher elevations of the Chattooga and Blue Ridge mountains and to such waters as the Chattooga, Little Keowee, South Saluda, and South Pacolet rivers. In this case, it wasn't humanity but a change in mean average temperatures that reduced the fish's natural range. As the continent continued to warm, only those populations at higher, cooler elevations survived.

Even though brook trout in South Carolina are on very fragile footing today, this species receives no added protection and for management purposes is grouped with all trout. Despite this, existing populations are self-sustaining. The state is in the process of determining if these fish are unadulterated examples of the southern brook trout strain or if they've been hybridized with domesticated brook trout, which were widely stocked in waters of neighboring states—Georgia and North Carolina—during the late 1800s and early 1900s. As a result of these studies, biologists hope to effect a change in the fish's status to protect this heritage stock, and special regulations for this species are likely. There's little interest in brook trout fishing in the state, probably because few anglers know that a small population exists. South Carolina's fisheries managers would like to keep it that way, for a while at least.

TENNESSEE

At one time, all of the streams draining the western side of the Appalachian Mountains in Tennessee had brook trout. They occurred in all waters, from the beginnings of the smallest tributaries down the mountain slopes and into the valleys and the northeast-to-southwest-flowing Tennessee River, and eventually the Ohio River, just before it joins the Mississippi. During the mid-1800s, intensive lumbering and farming eliminated most fish at lower elevations, and populations have declined since the early 1900s. Habitat degradation is still a major factor in the fish's distribution, but the introduction of exotic species (rainbow trout) and acidification of many waters by acid deposition are new threats.

Today, brook trout in Tennessee are confined to 170 miles on 135 streams in eight eastern counties—only 20 to 30 percent of their pre-1900 distribution. The 135 streams are part of four watersheds that rise at the tops of the Appalachian Mountains. When one divides the number of miles by the number of streams, one realizes that the fish are restricted to small brooks and rivulets in the very beginnings of the upper drainages. These typical high-elevation streams are slightly acidic, low in fertility, and composed of soft water. The main river is the Tennesseee, which is formed by the confluence of the Holston and French Broad rivers at Knoxville and flows from northeast to southwest along the western base of the Appalachians. Draining into it from higher elevations to the east, from south to north, are the Hiwassee River, the Little Tennessee River and its tributary the Tellico, the Little River, and several tributaries of the French Broad, the most significant being the Little Pigeon River and, farther north along the base of the mountains, the Nolichucky.

Tennessee has always had an indigenous stock of brook trout, which belong to the southern or nondisplaced strain, one of six or seven recognizable strains within the species. After extensive lumbering of the Appalachians' western slopes, fish of northern-strain stocks were used to repopulate lower-elevation waters. In these low-gradient streams, brown and rainbow trout were stocked and immediately dominated this warmer habitat. As a result, most wild brook trout populations at these lower elevations were eliminated, and even northern-strain stocks fared poorly against the more aggressive rainbows. At the headwaters, most of this strain remained relatively free of crossbreeding, and even today has been able to maintain self-sustaining populations.

The state does a limited amount of brook trout stocking, but only with wild-strain fish and mostly in waters that have been renovated and in which brook trout are the only predator species. Stream renovation for brook trout in upper watersheds is the state's most active cold-water fisheries program. Fishing for brook trout, where allowed, is usually rated fair to good. There are no closed seasons and the catch is limited to three fish. Because these waters don't offer optimal growth potential, brook trout are usually small. The minimum size is 6 inches. The state record is a 3-pound, 14-ounce fish taken from the Hiwassee River on August 15, 1973.

VERMONT

If you're looking to catch big brook trout, try elsewhere. But if you're looking for lots of brook trout, a generous limit, and innumerable idyllic stream-fishing settings that combine clear, cold, tumbling brooks interspersed with short rapids and placid pools under heavy conifer and hardwood covers, come to Vermont. The average fish is 5 to 6 inches, with 10-inchers taken from ponds or lakes. They're plentiful, and most result from natural production.

Vermont's waters, like those of New Hampshire and New York's Adirondacks, don't produce big brook trout because the watersheds are primarily comprised of small, cold, clear, infertile, high-gradient mountain streams high in acid. The ingredients for producing the kinds and quantities of food brook trout need to grow large are just not here. Vermont has thousands of miles of trout water in hundreds of streams, ranging from mere trickles and rivulets to brooks, creeks, streams, and, in some cases, even rivers. The state's waters are divided into two main drainage systems. The smaller system is restricted to western and northwestern sections and flows into Lake Champlain and, eventually, the St. Lawrence River. Most of these streams, after initial short, fast runs from higher elevations, are low-gradient waters that warm too much for brook trout; competition with warm-water species is keen.

Most of Vermont's waters drain east or southeast into the Connecticut River, which begins in New Hampshire just south of the Québec border and flows due south into the Long Island Sound, along the way forming the border between Vermont and New Hampshire. The better brook trout fishing is in the upper limits of these watersheds, where they can outcompete browns and rainbows. Truly wild brook trout are restricted to the headwaters of a few remote streams in the Green Mountains and in the Northeast Kingdom region.

Nearly all of these waters contain brook trout populations sustained by natural reproduction. Numerous high-elevation ponds and lakes also contain self-sustaining populations. There are also many shallow ponds and lakes that have ideal conditions for growing brook trout but lack suitable spawning sites. Vermont stocks these waters annually with hatchery fish. It also plants hatchery brook trout in the lower elevations of many streams, where brown and rainbow trout were stocked more than 100 years ago. More than half of the state's trout-hatchery efforts today go into producing brook trout.

Because Vermont's lacustrine (lake) environments are more fertile than its stream, brook trout there grow a bit larger, averaging 7 to 8 inches. In stream environments, no more than 10 percent of fish grow beyond 6 inches. Despite this, brook trout are the most popular trout with the state's anglers. A recent survey revealed that nearly 80 percent favored brook trout over other species. An anomaly in this infertile habitat was the state record for the species, a 5-pound, 12-ounce fish taken in 1977 from Paran Creek by Dennis Hardwood. Richard Kirn, a biologist with the state's

Wildlife Laboratory, believes that while the overall status of the state's fish is good to excellent, this brook trout might not have been a true product of Vermont's streams but rather a large brood fish released from a hatchery after it became unproductive. The largest legitimate trout produced in recent times weighed a little over 3 pounds and was taken in 1948 by Percy Angwin from a tributary of the Mad River; it should be considered the state-record fish.

A list of Vermont's better brook trout rivers and streams in the Northeast Kingdom includes the Barton, Black, Clyde, Connecticut, Lamoille, Missisquoi, Moose, Nulhegan, Passumpsic, Stevens, and Willoughby rivers. In the northwest are the Brown, Dog, Gihon, Huntington, Mad, Rock, Trout, Tyler, Waterbury, Winooski, and Kingsbury rivers.

VIRGINIA

Virginia has the most sophisticated trout-management program in the East and probably the entire country. Few anglers outside of the state are aware of the excellent trout-fishing opportunities available here. The state annually spends more than a million dollars on trout-production efforts at three hatcheries and three rearing facilities, producing 800,000 catchable-sized (9–11 inches) trout for its streams. This number doesn't include the many subcatchables and fingerlings used in other programs. Virginia boasts 2,800 miles of trout streams, plus many ponds, lakes, and small reservoirs. Of all of this stream mileage, only about a quarter is stocked with hatchery fish; the remaining 2,200 miles are classified as Wild Trout Streams with self-sustaining populations.

In glacial and postglacial times, brook trout probably occupied almost all of the state's rivers and streams. But because of changed climatic conditions and later intrusions of civilization, today they're found only in western counties and in higher elevations of the Blue Ridge and Allegheny mountains. These mountains provide the elevation needed for cooler summer temperatures, and their valley rivers have also cut through to their limestone bases, making them highly productive habitat for brook trout and their natural foods.

Virginia's cerebral trout-management program is the result of a project, initiated in 1975 by its Department of Game and Inland Fisheries, to survey all of the regions in the state where trout occur. Armed with these data, the biologists were able to provide habitat protection, ensure that proper regulations were implemented, and create the best stocking program possible. One result of the survey was the discovery of a wild brook trout population more substantial than first estimated. The resulting program is composed of three schemes: the Catchable Stocking Program, the Wild Trout Program, and the Put-N-Grow-N-Take Program. All three are integrated into the total plan, which has a lot of happy, dedicated anglers.

The first program is the best known and most popular, because waters so designated are periodically stocked with keeper-sized fish, a few of which easily fill a frying pan. There are 35 waters so designated in 16 counties; from them anglers are guaranteed a fairly large domesticated trout. The Put-N-Grow Program is relatively small and so are its fish, but it's growing in both size and popularity because of the high-quality trout fishing it provides. Stocked fish are of sublegal size. Some streams have two designations, often Wild Trout Streams in their upper reaches and Stocked Waters at lower elevations. A few have a third—Special Regulations Water—thus utilizing the full potential of all of a stream's habitats.

The Wild Trout Program includes reproducing populations of brown and rainbow as well as brook trout. Here, the major effort is directed toward habitat protection. It's a big task, because the state has 2,200 miles of streams to manage. A secondary task is to design regulations that will protect the spawning stocks. It's this program that concerns brook trout anglers. Virginia's waters have been stocked with domesticated brook trout for so many years that the integrity of the wild strain has probably been compromised. However, those brook trout populations at the highest altitudes that have survived are probably little changed genetically from the original stock. The environment at these levels was the protective element. The only threats are acid rain and rainbow trout moving upstream into prime brook trout habitat. As in many states along the Southern Appalachians, natural barriers are the only means of containing rainbows.

Special regulations govern fishing on most of the Wild Trout Streams and include single hooks, artificial lures, and a minimum length of 9 inches. The exceptions are the Rapidan River and its tributaries, Stewarts Creek, the North Fork Moormans River, and East Fork Chestnut Creek, where all fish must be released. Wild Trout Streams with brook trout–only populations are Buffalo Creek (Amherst County), the Conway River/Devils Ditch (Greene County), the Dan River (Patrick County), East Fork Chestnut Creek (Grayson and Carroll counties), the North Fork Moorman River (Albemarle County), Little Stony Creek (Shenandoah County), Ramseys Draft (Augusta County), and several streams in Shenandoah National Park. The best-known Special Regulations Stream is the Rapidan River in Madison County. Other trout are here, but the brook trout is the dominant species. Brook trout share the St. Marys River (Augusta County), but here acidification has temporarily worked to the advantage of brook trout, which survive better in more acidic waters than do rainbows; the brook trout is again the dominant species. Brook trout also share Little Stony Creek in Shenandoah County with rainbow trout. Some of these waters annually produce brook trout of up to 14 inches.

Most lakes and ponds in Virginia are too warm in the summer to sustain brook trout populations. However, one that's almost exclusively a put-and-grow brook trout fishery is Laurel Bed Lake (Russell County). Similar brook trout waters include Mills Creek and Coles Run reservoirs and Skidmore Lake (Switzer Dam).

Virginia's biggest brook trout came from a stream, a 5-pound, 10-ounce fish taken in 1987 by Gref Orndorff while fishing in Big Stony Creek.

WEST VIRGINIA

The present distribution of brook trout in West Virginia is interesting and reflects population sources that reveal its past. At one time, brook trout occurred in every stream in the Mountain State. Their distribution, while still quite extensive, is now restricted to about 500 streams in seven eastern counties. These are in higher elevations along the Allegheny Front—the slightly less folded western parts of the Allegheny Mountains, part of the Appalachian Mountains that stretch from northern Georgia to the Gaspé Peninsula in Québec. Most of these trout streams are located in the Monongahela National Forest.

The Appalachians were formed by the buckling of the earth's crust, and the resulting Allegheny ridges run northeast to southwest. So do most rivers and streams, except those that were large enough at the time to erode through the land as the folds slowly rose, some to exceptionally high elevations. The highest in West Virginia is Spruce Knob, at 4,862 feet. Larger streams formed in the valleys between these ridges and were fed water from the slopes on each side. Tributaries rose near the summits of these long ridges, and today these are primarily the realm of brook trout. While most tributary streams are fairly large where they meet bigger streams on the valley floor, the portions near their tops—where brook trout are the main predators—are usually short, averaging but 1½ miles in length and often only 10 to 12 feet in width. None are stocked by the state's Division of Natural Resources, though they may have received fish at one time. Most brook trout here are wild, probably even endemic fish that have been here since time immemorial.

Well, maybe not quite that long.

Today, West Virginia's brook trout are derived from two primordial populations, which may not have differed enough from each other even 20,000 years ago to be called separate strains. One originated from a population on the eastern side of the Appalachians; the initial distribution route was both the James and Potomac rivers. Brook trout from the western side of the Appalachians, from the Ohio/Allegheny River, traveled primarily through New and Elk rivers, which flowed into the Ohio as the Kanawaha River, and the Tygart and Cheat rivers and their many tributaries. The Monongahela, at its union with the Allegheny, becomes the Ohio River. When the last glacier covered half of Pennsylvania, except for a small ice-free portion that extended into western New York, the state's brook trout were physically and geographically separated into two similar populations.

Today, brook trout in West Virginia are found in Pendleton, Randolph, Grant, Tucker, Pocohontas, Webster, and Greenbrier counties. They occur in the headwaters of the following major drainage systems: Potomac River (and the Capon River), the South Branch Potomac, and the Gauley, Elk, and Shenandoah River systems, which also include six downriver streams draining into the Potomac River before Berkely Springs: the Ohio River system in the Panhandle, and the Monongahela, Tygart, Little Kanawha, New, James, Cheat, Coal, Guyandotte, Greenbrier, and Big Sandy river systems.

West Virginia began its own brook trout hatchery in the mid-1930s, and today annually stocks about 100,000 adults and from 150,000 to 200,000 fingerlings in non–wild trout waters. These don't include waters where self-sustaining populations exist. The only streams where solely brook trout are stocked are those with low acidity levels.

The heaviest brook trout taken in West Virginia was a 6½-pounder landed in 1981 by Tom Barnisky from Stoney Creek. It was 22 inches long. The longest brook trout caught in the state, however, was 23½ inches long but weighed only 4.78 pounds. It was also caught in 1981. The angler was Jack E. Foltz; the fish was taken from the Lost River.

WISCONSIN

"I have lately been shown a letter," wrote Thaddeus Norris in 1864 in *The American Angler's Book*, "which stated that a party of three anglers went last summer from Chicago by rail and boat, to the town of Green Bay, and there packed their luggage on mules and travelled a distance of 40 miles to a stream not over 20 feet wide, within 12 miles of Lake Superior. They fished two pools where there was neither tree nor bush to interfere with their fly-cast, and during their stay of ten days, each of them killed from 50 to a 100 pounds of Trout per day; the fish weighing from 2 to 4 pounds each."

I have often wondered, when I read of such past catches, just what they did with all of those fish. Who knows. If they had limited themselves only to what they could use, there might still be 4-pound brook trout in the Peshtigo River. If the letter writer's distances were accurate, the anglers probably fished the Peshtigo. If they were a little off, it could have been the Menominee River, which today separates Wisconsin from Michigan's Upper Peninsula. However, the stream seems too narrow to have been the latter. Even today, Wisconsin considers the Peshtigo one of its better trout streams. Today, however, brook trout must share it with brown and rainbow trout. It's classified by the state as a Category 5 water, which means one may fish it only with artificial lures, the daily creel limit is two fish—less than on the state's other streams—and brook trout must be at least 10 inches to be kept.

Wisconsin is one of these fortunate states that has the bulk of its terrain in low-rolling hills, along with thousands of potholes, and as many small streams to drain them, left behind by the retreating glaciers. The streams gather size and depth as more join before they arrive at either Lake Michigan to the east, Superior to the north, or even the Mississippi River to the west. While brook trout streams are scattered everywhere across the state, most are concentrated in the hilly northern half and in east-central portions. The fish's primary range has been reduced since 1900, but state fisheries managers consider it stable. In central Wisconsin (north of Madison) and in the southeastern quarter of the state, the habitat has so changed that brook trout waters have become rarities.

While warm-water fisheries are popular in Wisconsin—the state fish is the muskellunge—brook trout still provide an intensive fishery; anglers annually harvest more than a million fish. Management has been key to the fish's survival. The big problem facing both fish and management personnel is continued habitat deterioration and destruction. About 80 percent of the brook trout population is self-sustaining. This has been enhanced by restrictions placed upon size and creel limits. Add to this an expanding program of pond reclamation and the brook trout's future doesn't appear quite as bleak.

To support populations in streams and ponds without natural reproduction, Michigan developed its current brood stock in 1973 with brook trout from the Nashua (New Hampshire) National Fish Hatchery; about 500 waters are currently stocked. Wisconsin believes it still has waters with endemic stocks and has embarked upon a program to determine their genetic heritage. It hopes to use this stock, in a hybrid cross with Témiscamie stock, to repopulate its reclaimed ponds as well as streams, and to bolster its domestic populations. The wild trout concept is catching on here as in other states.

Wisconsin has a very viable coaster fishery for those brook trout that prefer to spend most of their lives in lakes Superior and Michigan. While anglers on inland waters annually creel more than a million brook trout, those who fish the bigger waters boat from 5,000 to 11,000 coasters. Brook trout in these two lakes grow larger than those from inland waters. The state record almost made 10 pounds—a 9-pound, 15-ounce fish taken from near the center of the state, in Prairie River, Lincoln County, on September 2, 1944. The river must still be a good place to catch big brook trout, because it's classified as a Category 4 water, with portions of Category 5, where the minimum legal length for brook trout is 14 inches.

The state's better brook trout waters have greater restrictions to ensure the continuation of the fishery. The Peshtigo is one of the state's top waters, along with the Oconto River, both of which flow into Green Bay (Lake Michigan). Most Category 5 streams flow into one or the other Great Lake. Draining into Lake Michigan proper are Stony Creek, the Ahnapee River, Scarboro Creek, and the Manitowoc and Pigeon rivers. Draining into Lake Superior is the Bois Brule ("Burnt Wood"), a Category 5 river for its entire length. To this add Nemadji Creek; the Amnicon, Poplar, Flag, Cranberry, Bark, Sand, and Sioux rivers; Fish Creek; and the White and Bad rivers.

These are but a sampling; there are hundreds more.

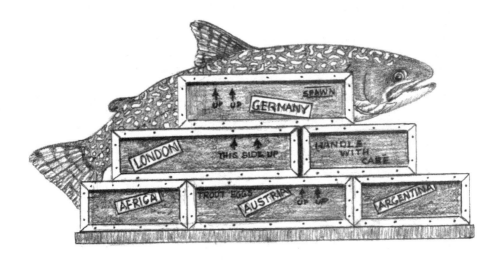

B EXPANSION OF THE BROOK TROUT'S RANGE
WITHIN THE UNITED STATES

With the fish being so beautiful and so easily raised in hatcheries, it's only natural that brook trout were chosen both for repopulating reclaimed streams and for introduction into new habitats. In the era of the great fish culturists, from about 1850 to 1900, brook trout were planted in almost all of the waters of the West. In many of these they couldn't survive, either because the waters were too warm or because they lacked physical features needed for natural reproduction. In others, brook trout were unable to compete with endemic populations that had been there for thousands of years, filling every bioniche available. In still others, culturists and fish managers knew little or nothing about the effects of exotic fish on native populations, or didn't care to find out.

Two species, the cutthroat and bull trout, the latter a charr closely related to the brook trout, suffered where brook trout were introduced. Today, efforts are underway by the National Park Service and state and provincial governments to halt all brook trout stocking in waters where they compete with indigenous species. In some areas, where these native species are in danger of extinction, fisheries managers are attempting to remove brook trout. The latter task, however, is likely to prove costly and ineffective. In truth, the damage has already been done and can't be undone.

ARIZONA

Brook trout provide only a minor fishery in Arizona. They weren't introduced during the initial wave of brook trout stocking that swept across the West during the late 19th century; Arizona then had minimal aquatic habitat, not only for brook trout but also for all species of fish. The demand for hydroelectric power in the second quarter of the 20th century, however, spurred dam building on the Colorado River, which crosses into the northwestern corner of the state then serves as the border with Nevada and California. Damming the Colorado at Page, south of the Utah border, backed the river into Glen Canyon to form expansive Lake Powell, most of which lies in Utah.

The tailrace of Glen Canyon Dam, with its lower water temperatures, created an excellent trout fishery, and brook, brown, and rainbow trout were stocked. Prime trout waters also occur in the main river, the Paria River, and several small tributaries downriver to Lee's Ferry, at the entrance to Marble Canyon. The state's largest brook trout, a 5-pound, 4-ounce fish, was taken at Lee's Ferry by Moe Beck on March 6, 1982.

Most of the brook trout fishery is in the center of the state, on the elevated plateau between Phoenix and Flagstaff, which is studded with many small ponds, lakes, and reservoirs. The area acts as a headwater for many streams that flow northwest into the Little Colorado River. It was from Big Lake, in this area, that Skip Tabor caught the state's largest brook trout taken outside of the Colorado River, on May 17, 1986. It weighed 4 pounds, 10¼ ounces.

Because no more than 10 percent of Arizona's brook trout population is self-sustaining, the state maintains a stocking program, which offers a primarily put-and-take fishery. Two of its better waters are Rucker Canyon and Boneyard creeks. The state also stocks Big and Luna lakes, Nelson Reservoir, Bear Canyon Lake, Concho and Willow Springs lakes, and Black Canyon, Crescent, and Woods Canyon lakes.

CALIFORNIA

As early as 1872, the Golden State began stocking brook trout, when 6,000 trout were brought in by the California Fish Commission and planted in the American River, Alameda Creek, and San Andreas Reservoir. During the next seven years, thousands of eggs were shipped from New Hampshire and Wisconsin to be raised at the Berkeley hatchery. By 1890, large numbers of brook trout were being raised in California and distributed throughout the state. They became established from the San Bernardino Mountains north to the Oregon border. Fish planted in coastal streams failed to reproduce, but a few annually stocked populations exist today. Only comparatively

small numbers are raised nowadays in the state's hatcheries.

Anglers immediately embraced the "Easterners" and were enthusiastic about their beautiful colors, and table and angling qualities. The fish responded by adopting California as if they had always been here, including mountain lakes that had been devoid of trout. More than 600 mountain lakes and more than 1,500 miles of streams now have self-sustaining populations. The state's top brook trout streams or rivers—the Clarks Fork Stanislaus River; the Tuolumne River within Tuolumne Meadows in Yosemite National Park; the Rubicon River within Desolate Wilderness; the West Walker River above Pickle Meadows; and the West Fork Carson River in Faith Valley—don't produce what most fishermen would consider good angling. In these waters, brook trout are often considered a nuisance.

The low rate of growth among California brook trout is caused by the inability of infertile waters to produce sufficient trout foods. As a result, brook trout are numerous but small; fish over 8 inches are rare. In some state lakes with self-sustaining populations, brook trout do grow a bit longer, and 8- to 12-inch fish are more common. California does grow large brook trout. These are found in shallower lakes, where populations are maintained entirely by the stocking of fingerlings due to a lack of suitable spawning habitat. An example is Kirman Lake, which is managed for trophy-sized fish with a 16-inch minimum length, and flies-only and barbless-hook regulations. The state's biggest brookie was a 9-pound, 12-ounce fish taken in 1932 from Silver Lake in Mono County. However, bigger fish have been netted during Bunny Lake fish studies.

Better brook trout lakes can be found in the Sierra Buttes–Lakes Basin Recreational Area (Tahoe and Plumas national forests), and the Dinkey Lakes and Marble Mountain Wilderness Area. Alpine County also has some productive brook trout lakes. However, the brook trout's future in some of these wilderness mountain lakes may be in jeopardy, as a movement is afoot within the U.S. Forest Service to prohibit trout stocking of any kind within designated wilderness areas. If the state also adopts this management philosophy, at least 300 of California's most productive lakes will revert to a fishless state, because these lack suitable spawning areas for brook trout or for any other species.

California's most fertile lakes are Kirman Lake, Mono County east of Sonora Pass, fish of 1–3 pounds, 2 miles by the roadside; McCoy Flat Reservoir, Lassen County, near Susanville, good for big fish during wet years, 1–2 pounds, roadside access; Red Lake, Mono County, 1–2 pounds, roadside access; Castle Lake, near Mount Shasta, Siskiyou County, 9- to 12-inch trout, roadside access; Medicine Lake, Siskiyou County, 10- to 14-inch brook trout, roadside access; Toad Lake, near Mount Shasta, Siskiyou County, 10- to 15-inch brook trout, difficult to catch, reached by ⅔ mile of trail; Dinkey Lakes, near Shaver Lakes, Fresno County, a backcountry hike of 2 to 4 miles, 9- to 13-inch trout numerous; Triangle Lake, Caribou Wilderness, Lassen County, 2-mile hike, 10- to 14-inch brook trout.

Many California anglers today are more gourmet- than sportfishing-oriented. Given a choice, they prefer to catch brook trout to eat and other trout for the fun of it.

COLORADO

As in California, Colorado brook trout today are relegated to the high country, mostly in headwaters--ponds, lakes, and streams—of the river systems that begin above 5,000 feet. While brook trout aren't native, they were stocked almost everywhere there was water, moving or not. The first introduction was made in 1872 (the same year as in California) by James M. Broadwell, who early that year had 10,000 eggs shipped to him from Boscobel, Wisconsin. After hatching, fry were released into the South Platte drainage 10 miles downriver from Denver. Subsequent stocking covered almost all of the waters of the state. Today, these waters are without brook trout; either they were unsuitable ecologically or the competition from warm- or other cold-water species was just too great—or these native fishes too

entrenched. At higher elevations, however, brook trout held their own with rainbow trout and in many places outcompeted native cutthroats. This often places these colorful easterners in a bad light with fisheries managers. For the last decade, some anglers, acting on their own, have tried to eliminate brook trout in watersheds where possible, especially in headwater streams, and replace them with wild, native species.

Brook trout here don't need stocking to support their populations. Where they exist they've become self-sustaining. Aerial stocking in high mountain lakes does still take place, and in some streams fingerlings are stocked. Many of Colorado's headwaters are managed as "wild" waters, meaning that self-sustaining populations are left alone. In many of these small streams brook trout are thus managed by default, because they're the dominant species, or the only species, and the state doesn't actively manage these waters for other species.

Despite the drawbacks of brook trout introduction, this species, according to the Colorado Division of Wildlife, does occupy an important niche in aquatic management in the state. However, there's increasing pressure in Colorado, on the state as well as the federal level, to promulgate a policy of replacing the nonindigenous brook trout with native trout species such as greenback and Colorado River cutthroats. Even if this policy is adopted, it will be a long time before it can become effective. More than likely, brook trout will never be eliminated from some of the areas where they're now well entrenched.

As a result, brook trout will continue to be important fish for many Colorado anglers. For many, they rank with cutthroats and rainbows for aggressiveness and fighting ability, and top them when it comes to the frying pan. Colorado's better brook trout streams include the Upper Colorado, Fryingpan, Blue, Gunnison, Roaring Fork, Rio Grande, and North and South Platte rivers. Top reservoirs include North, South, and East Delany Butte lakes, Lake John Spinney Mountain Reservoir, and Rams Horn Lake. Most of these rivers and impoundments are part of the state's Gold Medal Waters, considered the best waters in the state, and contain browns and rainbows as well as brook trout. I've fished the Gunnison, Roaring Fork, and Fryingpan, and they're not just good but excellent brook trout waters. I guess you could also say that they're pretty good for noncharrs, but I'll admit to being prejudiced.

Colorado's biggest brook trout was a 7-pound, 10-ounce fish taken from Upper Cataract Lake in 1947.

DELAWARE

In glacial and for a while in postglacial times, brook trout may have occupied some of the low-gradient streams in Delaware. Today, however, the state suffers from a decidedly flat topography and has no large groundwater springs to maintain streams with water sufficiently cool throughout the summer to support a viable brook trout habitat. Because of this, brook trout don't occur here naturally. There's a short spring season in the state, but the fish are stocked as a put-and-take fishery with no holdover or reproduction.

IDAHO

It's easy today to look back and condemn the zeal with which fish culturism swept across the United States in the late 1800s. In Idaho, as in many western states, stocking brook trout into waters that already contained healthy populations of other trout was a mistake. Blame the beauty of these speckled charr or the ease of raising them in hatcheries. By the beginning of the 20th century, almost all of the watersheds in Idaho were stocked to varying degrees with brook trout.

In most systems they became self-sustaining, and now can be found in all but one or two major river drainages. The brook trout's ability to adapt to a wide range of environments, its omnivorous penchant for eating anything that moves, and the fecundity of its brood fish allowed it to displace or become a major cohabitant with cutthroat and bull trout; in some systems it even holds its own against rainbow and brown trout.

Today, brook trout are looked down upon by some state and federal fisheries managers in Idaho. If given free rein they would begin an eradication program that would in the end probably be unsuccessful in all but the most contained watersheds. It seems ridiculous to blame the fish. Despite this attitude, which has filtered down to many resident anglers, brook trout are doing well, and in some places—such as Henrys Lake—are sought after for their own attributes. Nearly half of the anglers in Idaho are nonresidents, transients, or new residents who only lately have taken Horace Greeley's advice and abandoned the East to head for the mountains. Many of these anglers still maintain a love affair with the brook trout and support its position in Idaho.

While the Snake and other great Idaho trout streams attract many anglers, Henrys Lake is still a must on the fishing tourist's itinerary. Today the lake's trout fishing, for either cutthroat or brook trout, isn't what it was during the 1970s, when the state-record 7-pound, 1-ounce brook trout was landed. Nor is it the equal of the 1980s, when large numbers of Assinica and Témiscamie Strains of brook trout were stocked and a lot of brook trout of over 4 pounds were taken. Still, it's exciting to watch 4- and 5-pound brook trout milling about the lake's shallows in September, waiting at the concrete entrance to Hatchery Creek for enough water to run over the spillway into the dilapidated hatchery.

Because brook trout have done such a good job of maintaining their populations in Idaho, much to the chagrin of some of its fisheries managers, there's currently no stocking underway in the state except in Henrys Lake. Brook trout never were the dominant predator species in the lake, and their proportion of the annual creel census ranged from a low of just under 10 percent in 1980 to a high of nearly 33 percent in 1978, when the state-record fish was taken by D. Stratton.

Even before the record was set, Henrys Lake had a reputation for producing big fish from the domestic stocking that took place years ago. "Henrys Lake, in Fremont County, is still producing big brook trout," said James

Simpson, fish culturist, State of Idaho Department of Fish and Game, in 1950. "Their average size in streams throughout the state will run from 12 to 15 inches with a weight of .75 to 1 pound, but we find some exceptionally good trout fishing in Henrys Lake in September and October. Several fish are taken each year which weigh as much as 9 or 10 pounds. The majority average 2 or 3 pounds." He may have been a bit overzealous, because no fish this large were ever documented. However, two brook trout larger than the current state record were taken from Henrys Lake in the 1950s and documented in *Field & Stream*'s annual fishing contest. The bigger fish weighed 7 pounds, 4½ ounces and was taken on a nymph by H. McCaughy. A 7-pound, 4-ounce brook trout was taken by T. Foode on a Mickey Finn.

Word of Idaho's new state record in 1978 rejuvenated attention to Henrys Lake and created a lot of national interest in trout circles. The number of fishing tourists rose dramatically, and they brought in as much as a half-million new dollars annually to the Sunup State. Hoping to continue capitalizing on the reputation, its fisheries managers began stocking more domesticated brook trout from the Ford Hatchery (Washington County). Looking for bigger brook trout, they eventually turned to Québec and in 1980 were able to stock 6,000 Assinica Strain fish. These were the fish that were to catapult the Broadback River's brook trout to prominence. For several years they dominated in *Field & Stream*'s fishing contest. In subsequent years, Témiscamie brook trout fry, from a watershed adjacent to the Broadback, were also stocked.

Big brook trout, but no record-breakers, continued to be taken from Henrys Lake. In 1982, a 6.8-pound, six-year-old fish was landed, the largest to date. The brook trout fishery in the lake is still viable, and some of the fish have worked their way out the outlet into the Henrys Fork (North Fork of the Snake River) to provide some good fishing down the length of the Henrys Fork to Box Canyon, below Island Park Reservoir. During the 1980s a series of droughts, compounded by problems with agricultural runoff pollution, hurt the sportfishery. Though Idaho continued for a few years to introduce Québec-strain brookies, the lake's overall fishery never regained the status it enjoyed in the late 1970s.

Today, self-sustaining populations of brook trout can be found in headwater tributaries of the Clearwater, Spokane, Kootenai, Salmon, and Boise rivers. These streams offer excellent fishing, and include the Snake River and the South Fork of the Snake River, the Henrys Fork (North Fork of the Snake), and the Big Wood and Big Lost rivers; Silver Creek; and the St. Joe, North Fork Clearwater, Lochsa, and Selway rivers. Lakes and impoundments include Brownlee and Cascade reservoirs, Lake Pend Oreille, and Henrys, Mirror, and Priest lakes; Strike, Ririe, and Anderson Ranch reservoirs; and Spirit Lake.

MONTANA

As in other western states, brook trout were heavily stocked in Montana during the late 1800s and early 1900s. Most of those stocked in the waters of the High Plains disappeared because the area didn't offer suitable habitat. Nor were watersheds in the western part of the state all suited for brook trout. Many already had better-adapted species, and brook trout disappeared or moved upstream, where they competed with strains of native cutthroat trout. In some watersheds they hybridized with the bull trout, a closely related charr species, and have endangered its existence.

Brook trout are found today in 52 rivers and streams in Montana, most in the mountainous western part of the state, especially south of Helena. In nearly all of these streams, to the consternation of fisheries managers, brook trout have developed self-sustaining populations. Only a dozen small lakes and reservoirs, where they're quickly caught, especially by children, are regularly stocked with brook trout.

Most western fisheries people view brook trout as a nuisance and a threat to native species. Many streams are so overpopulated with brook trout that few fish grow larger than 6 inches. Consequently, bag limits are generous—20 fish per day and open every day in some waters—to encourage harvest and reduce fish numbers. Because of this management stratagem, few brook trout ever attain the sizes that would interest sportfishermen. However, some anglers do prefer brook trout and like fishing for them. Maybe it's the gourmet in them.

With all of this going against them, it's surprising that a few brook trout do grow to trophy size in Montana. The state record is a 9-pound, 1-ounce fish taken in 1940 by John R. Cook, from Lower Medicine Lake.

NEVADA

Like many western states, Nevada was first stocked in the late 1800s. This was done by private clubs, and, while the stock originated in the East, it's not known from which hatchery. At one time the state had a small brook trout stocking program, but plantings were sporadic because of the species' recognized competition with native trout. All Nevada brook trout populations are self-sustaining and today offer anglers a fair fishery. Nevada currently has no stocking program and is unlikely to inaugurate one; brook trout outcompete cutthroat trout where they occur in the same environment.

Opportunities for fair catches are possible in Blue, Marlette, and Spooner lakes, and Knott Creek and Hobart reservoirs. Nevada has a catch-and-release and trophy brook trout program on Spooner Lake. The biggest caught from Nevada waters was a 5-pound, 10-ounce fish taken by Richard Baker while fishing Bull Run Reservoir in 1980.

NEW MEXICO

Brook trout have adapted so readily to parts of New Mexico that one would believe they were always present. The first fish were introduced to the headwaters of the Rio San Jose near Laguna during the mid-1850s, but no serious attempt to introduce the species was made until after 1900. In the following 50-year period, it was introduced to the headwaters of

streams in the Sangre de Cristo Mountains in the north-central part of the state, Gila National Forest in the southwest, and Lincoln National Forest in the south-central region. After 1960, stocking efforts were concentrated onto headwaters, lakes, and ponds in north-central New Mexico. Because all current populations of brook trout are self-sustaining, there's been little or no stocking since 1990.

Some of the best brook trout waters in New Mexico include Whitewater and Beaver creeks in Gila National Forest, Hopewell and Cabresto lakes in north-central New Mexico, near the Colorado border, and Bonita Lake just north of Ruidoso. Other good waters include Sacramento River, Diablo and Canones creeks, the Rio Costilla, Lake Fork Creek, and Long Lake. The state record is a 4-pound, 6¼-ounce fish taken June 3, 1979, by Donald Bensten from Long Lake. The only restriction on fishing for brook trout is a six-per-day creel limit.

SOUTH DAKOTA

On their own, brook trout were never able to make it "across the wide Missouri," nor across the flatlands of the High Plains plateau to the west of the river. With a little human help, however, they had no trouble establishing themselves in the Black Hills, in the extreme southwestern part of South Dakota, where they took up residence around the presidents on Mount Rushmore. The Black Hills afford the state its only elevated relief, especially where Harney Peak rises to over 7,200 feet. The land and all of its waters are under the aegis of the Black Hills National Forest.

Two main watersheds contain brook trout, though these are small in comparison with other waters draining the Black Hills. The largest, in the center of these hills, is the Rapid River, with its main tributary, Castle Creek. These drain east into the Cheyenne and then Missouri rivers. Beginning near the source of the Rapid River but on the north side of Crooks Tower (7,140 feet), is Spearfish Creek, which flows north into Belle Fourche River. Small streams include Beaver Creek (North), which flows though the U.S. Fish Hatchery just before it meets Redwater River, and Beaver Creek (South), which winds through Wind Cave National Park and eventually into Cheyenne River. Other small streams that flow east out of the national forest include French, Grace Coolidge, and Battle creeks.

Not all brook trout fishing in South Dakota is restricted to streams. The fish are also found in Iron Creek Lake, Roubix and Sheridan lakes, and Pactola and Deerfield reservoirs. Deerfield Reservoir, a damming of the upper reaches of Castle Creek, a tributary to Rapid Creek, produced the state's largest brook trout. It was caught by Bill Anderson on May 19, 1990, and weighed a whopping 7 pounds, 10 ounces.

Today, the brook trout fishery is well managed, even though the fish are grouped with other trout, splake, and salmon in regulations. Mostly confined to streams in the Black Hills, the fishery is self-sustaining; there's no brook trout stocking program. There's no closed season, either, and anglers are allowed eight brook trout of 8 inches or longer, only one of which may be over 12 inches. Brook trout of under 8 inches may be taken inside the Black Hills Fire Protection District—basically the Black Hills National Forest, along with some peripheral land. Parts of Spearfish and Rapid creeks are restricted to catch-and-release fishing. These sections contain brown trout, which may be kept, but brook, rainbow, and cutthroat trout must be released.

UTAH

The future of brook trout in Utah is tenuous. As in many western states, fish culturists in the late 1800s and early 1900s indiscriminately stocked brook trout wherever they found clear water. In many streams, fish survival was short lived because of competition from native populations that had the edge in the habitat. Unfortunately, one fish didn't—the cutthroat trout, which has habits and niches very similar to those of charr, especially brook trout, but lacks the brook trout's aggressiveness and reproductive abilities.

Utah's Bureau of Fisheries Management currently has a program to remove the eastern import from stream and lake environments where cutthroat trout are competing with it. However, Utah has thousands of small ponds and lakes at high elevations where the brook trout is now the sole predator species. Some waters probably contained cutthroat populations; others may have not. In these niches, the future of brook trout is relatively safe.

Unfortunately, these are usually the least-productive environments, and the fish are often small and, to their own detriment, too numerous. These streams are inaccessible except by foot, but they do offer the trouter willing to backpack a real wilderness experience. And few fish provide better eating than high-altitude brook trout. In these waters, from 25 to 50 percent of the populations are self-sustaining. Those that aren't are often stocked from the air.

A few lakes, especially those on a flat, alpine plateau (11,602 feet) known as Boulder Mountain, are managed for trophy brook trout. The program hasn't expanded, because so many areas that trophy brook trout inhabit are inaccessible and thus difficult to manage. More than two dozen small lakes and ponds pock the top and upper slopes of this mountain, and most are stocked, or were once stocked, with brook trout. Some of the better ponds are Blind, Horseshoe, and Grass lakes. Streams include Donkey, Fish, Pleasant, Oak, Frisky, West Deer, and West Fork Boulder creeks. The Utah state-record brook trout, 7½ pounds, was caught by Milton Taft in 1971 from "atop Boulder Mountain"—he didn't reveal which lake or reservoir. The Boulder Mountain complex is located in the south-central part of the state (north of Boulder), on Route 12.

WASHINGTON

With the amount of brook trout stocking that took place in Washington over an 80-year period, it's a wonder they don't live in every body of water in the state. It was the U.S. Bureau of Fisheries and not the state that started the brook trout rolling in. In 1894, fingerlings were placed in Lakes Twin, Mountain, Kelly, Hooker,

Cranberry, Johns, and Washington. Much of the early brook trout stock was shipped from the Paradise Brook Trout Company in Henryville, Pennsylvania. By 1913, brook trout from stocked waters were being using as brood stock at the Little Spokane Hatchery. Within two years, more than a million fry were raised and released. Using added facilities, by 1977 nearly 28 million eggs had been run through the state's hatcheries.

By the early 1960s, the effects of brook trout on native cutthroat and bull trout populations were coming to light, and almost all hatchery production of brook trout was stopped. Today, brook trout are stocked, but to a very limited extent. Regulations are designed to increase the harvest of brook trout where they compete with native species, and the brook trout's future looks bleak as the demand to favor wild or indigenous populations gains momentum. A program to eradicate brook trout in some waters is likely.

While most brook trout populations in Washington are self-sustaining, the fish aren't dispersed in all watersheds. The biggest concentration occurs in the northeastern part of the state, in Colville National Forest (N.F.) in the north; in Okanogan N.F. and Wenatchee N.F. in the central part of the state, as well as a few streams in Mount Baker–Snoqualmie N.F.; and in the south in waters in Gifford Pinchot N.F. A few streams in Olympic N.F., on the eastern side of the Coast Range Mountains, also contain self-sustaining populations of brook trout.

Despite the attitude of many state fisheries managers toward brook trout, a lot of Washington trout anglers still view the fish with favor. This is amazing when you consider that most brook trout waters are in the upper reaches of the watersheds, where conditions don't favor growth and which often are crowded with small fish. I guess a quintet wrapped in bacon and smothered in onions makes a mighty tasty breakfast, especially at 7,000 feet. Or maybe it's the scenery that surrounds brook trout fishing among the high peaks.

However, in lower watersheds that contain no other salmonids, or where brook trout are the dominant predator and thus grow larger,

they're given more protection: two-fish limits, minimum sizes, and even fly fishing only with barbless hooks. No waters are solely dedicated to brook trout, but they've made a few streams their own by their aggressive nature.

Some of the state's better brook trout waters include the Methow, Entiat, Wenatchee, Yakima, Naches, Klickitat, White Salmon, Dungeness, Elwha, and Solduc rivers. Streams with brook trout only are located in Ferry, Stevens, and Spokane counties and include Red, Deer, Rock, Trout, Beaver, and Pine creeks. Washington's biggest brook trout is a respectable 9-pounder, taken by George Weeks on May 7, 1988, from Wobbly Lake in Lewis County, just south of Mount Rainier National Park.

WYOMING

While the Equality State offers many angling opportunities and a great variety of species, it's not known for its brook trout fishing. Not only are they not indigenous, but they're also relegated to the highest elevations by their demand for near-pristine environments, which often puts them out of reach of the great majority of anglers—even the most dedicated trout fishers. The typical brook trout habitat in Wyoming is alpine beaver ponds and the trickles and creeks that drain them.

The initial stocking of brook trout occurred about 1880, with a shipment of eggs from Wisconsin. Most early stocking was done by private individuals, with fry packed in on horses and, finally, on anglers' backs. Just how many watersheds were stocked isn't certain; few or no records were maintained. Since the 1930s, some stocking has taken place by drops from airplanes. Wyoming has never had a very extensive brook trout stocking program, and even today the work is carried on mainly by volunteers.

Despite this, there are established populations in 45 creeks, streams, and rivers, in 28 high-altitude ponds and lakes, and in three reservoirs. The majority of these occur northwest of Casper. Almost every stream in Yellowstone National Park has been stocked with brook trout. In waters at higher elevations, especially above falls and natural barriers, no species of trout existed in modern times.

Some of the reluctance of Wyoming's fisheries managers to encourage the expansion of brook trout is based on the devastating effects that the introduction of this species has had upon cutthroat trout. The two fish are quite similar in characteristics, especially when it comes to the ecological niches they prefer, but brook trout are more aggressive, have greater fecundity, and mature slightly earlier than cutthroats. These factors have allowed brook trout to overwhelm and outcompete cutthroats, and in some streams eliminate them.

Nowhere in the state do brook trout grow especially large, because they're consigned to a watershed's least fertile waters. If they try to drop to lower elevations, they're stopped by rainbow trout, which can outcompete them for food and habitat. In areas where they're the dominant predators, they're often their own worst enemy, producing so many young that they consume the limited food supply typical of alpine environments, consequently retarding growth.

Where brook trout are stocked in Wyoming, they're planted in limited numbers; primarily maintenance stocking is done in ponds, lakes, and reservoirs where natural reproduction doesn't occur or can't keep up with the rate at which the fish are harvested. Elsewhere in the state, brook trout have no trouble with natural reproduction and maintaining self-sustaining populations. Where they're stocked, they're seldom released at lengths large enough to be legally taken; the state relies on further growth before the fish are harvested. "Virtually no catchable-sized brook trout are stocked in Wyoming," according to state biologist Robert W. Wiley.

The current brood stock is derived from a facility maintained on Soda Lake, 6 miles north of Pinedale and open to fishing. One of the better brook trout streams is at the head of Pole Creek, which begins in the Wind River Range near the Continental Divide and Wall Lake, and passes through a series of small ponds before entering Half-Moon Lake, just northeast of Pinedale.

Despite all of these disadvantages, brook trout are highly regarded by many anglers in Wyoming, and the state rates the fishery as good. And while the Wyoming Game and Fish Department has no trophy brook trout program to encourage the development of larger fish, the state record is a whopping 9-pound, 11-ounce fish that was 24½ inches long. It was caught in 1976 by Max Long on Green River Lake, in Bridger-Teton National Forest. Ironically, this lake isn't supposed to contain a recognizable brook trout population, but the Green River above the lake and as far upstream as the Wind River Range, where it begins, is prime brook trout water.

C. Canadian Brook Trout Distribution in Original and Expanded Ranges

LABRADOR

While brook trout are well distributed throughout this region, there's a limit as to how far north they can complete a full cycle of life. This limit seems to be just a few minutes south of the 58th parallel. Here, along the Labrador Sea, four moderate-sized streams flow east and, at different points, enter a large marine estuary, Hebron Fjord. This constitutes the most northerly brook trout population along the East Coast.

Several researchers have suggested that the delimiting factor is probably the maximum mean water temperature during the month of July. The most northerly limit along the Atlantic Coast for salmon production is just 100 miles farther south, at the Fraser River. Here, the mean isotherm never rises above 60 degrees. Brook trout can tolerate water somewhat colder than salmon, and their isothermic limit is reached just above Hebron Fjord. Waters from here north never rise above 48 degrees on average. In both cases, if the eggs don't hatch by the time the rivers open for the two-month summer, fry are unlikely to survive the onset of winter because they lack the time to store enough lipids for cold-weather survival.

At one time Labrador included all of Ungava; it was known as the Ungava District of the Northeast Territories and encompassed all of the Labrador/Ungava Peninsula. In 1809 the east coast was made a part of Newfoundland and has been administered by it ever since. Today, Labrador's western border with Québec follows the Continental Divide from Cape Chidley in the north southward to just below the 52nd parallel, thence in a straight line eastward to the Atlantic. This also uniquely separates east- and west-flowing watersheds, making fisheries management easier.

A single major watershed, located in southern Labrador, drains most of the region's rivers and streams. The Churchill, originally called the Hamilton River, starts in Ashuanapi Lake in the western part of Labrador, almost on the Québec border near Labrador City. The Ashuanipi River first flows north, gathering water from many large streams. It expands over the relatively infertile land at natural constrictions into several lakes. Near Schefferville in Québec it suddenly reverses direction, turns southeast, and moves through more lake-like waters (now accumulated by a huge system of hydroelectric reservoirs) before eventually tumbling over 245-foot-high Churchill (Grant) Falls to enter brackish Lake Melville (Hamilton Inlet) at the town of Goose Bay.

Throughout its watershed, this system produces some of the best brook trout fishing on the continent. The Ashuanipi River part of the watershed still yields many 4- to 6-pound brook trout. The comparatively small Minipi River system, which enters the main portion of the lower Churchill River from the south, just 60 miles west of Goose Bay, has consistently produced some of the region's largest brook trout, some over 10 pounds. Today, Minipi's big fish dominate line-class records maintained by the International Game Fish Association, which inherited the freshwater record-keeping task from *Field & Stream* magazine in 1979. If you want big brook trout, there aren't many places better than the Minipi watershed.

Challenging the Churchill River's big brook trout are those in the comparatively small watershed of the Eagle River. Just 135 miles long, from its beginning in Igloo Lake to its end in Sandwich Bay at the town of Cartwright on the Atlantic Coast, this river system flows west to east and parallels the Churchill River. It contains several lakes, whose tributaries flow into the Eagle from both north and south, which have produced some 10-pound-plus brook trout.

The remainder of Labrador's brook trout rivers north of the Churchill all flow east from the Continental Divide to the sea. They diminish in length as one heads north toward the tip of the peninsula. All have good brook trout fishing, mostly for sea-run brook trout of up to 6 pounds, but none compares to the region's southern waters.

Labrador's current brook trout record is a 10-pound fish taken by Sal Borelli, using a fly rod, on June 29, 1987, from Lake Minonipi, part of the Minipi River watershed. However, a 10-pound, 8-ounce brook trout was taken in August 1994 from Osprey Lake, part of the Eagle River watershed, and is awaiting IGFA confirmation.

MANITOBA

It was the discovery, in the late 1940s and early 1950s, of big brook trout in the Gods River that stimulated a renewed interest among anglers in both the United States and Canada in searching for this coveted species. This effort was aided by a surplus of aircraft after World War II and a corps of experienced pilots who turned to the bush to earn a living. This allowed entrepreneurs such as Tom Ruminski to switch from running a Hudson's Bay Company post on Gods Lake to setting up the first sportfishing camp in Manitoba's northern wilderness, at the head of the Gods River.

There are plenty of waters in Manitoba other than the Gods River that produce big brook trout, and all have many characteristics in common. They rise in numerous interconnected lakes located on an expansive, fairly flat, semicircular plateau in northern and central portions of the province. From this pie-shaped terrain they drain toward a center in Hudson Bay. En route, they cut gorges though Precambrian granite where they escape the plateau, and are marked by numerous chutes, rapids, and waterfalls. Then they meander across the old coastal plain until they meet tidewater in Hudson Bay, the big inland sea.

If not for the lakes at their origins where floatplanes can land, it would be nearly impossible for most anglers to fish these rivers. This is genuine wilderness. There are no roads, communities, or facilities of any kind along the rivers until they meet the coast. Even here there are only two, the ports of York Factory and Churchill. These are served by aircraft, which allows those who may have canoed downriver a chance to fly out. Because of these headwater lakes, a dozen sportfishing camps now utilize the upper headwaters of these rivers. But unless an expedition is organized, the farthest downriver it can go is an overnight stay at an out-camp and a return trip the next day. A few rivers do have lakelike widenings along their courses, which allow small floatplanes to drop in and deposit fishermen and camping gear then pick them up later with their fish.

Brook trout are found at every set of rapids and falls in these large rivers. And there are also numerous smaller feeder streams that originate along the descending edge of the high plateau and later join larger rivers. The big rivers include Gods, Hays, Fox, Nelson, Churchill, North and South Knife, and Seal, with a host of small streams in between. The flat, run-out sections of these rivers, along the coastal plain, have lesser numbers of brook trout. Another part of the brook trout population, closer to the river's distal ends, is anadromous. As air and water temperatures warm in early summer, these fish drop down to tidal sections or enter Hudson Bay. In late August they begin trekking upstream to spawn. Smaller spawners usually stay in the river until late spring, but bigger fish return to the estuarine environment after spawning.

Within these watersheds you'll find a wide range of brook trout sizes. Most grow to 4, 5, and 6 pounds, and there are occasional 7- and 8-pounders. There are larger brook trout in the province, but rivers don't seem to produce them. Manitoba generally keeps track of its superlative brookies by length and weight. On September 30, 1992, Ted F. Wasylyshen landed a brook trout in Garson Pond that measured 27 inches; its weight wasn't recorded. The heaviest brook trout recorded is a 10.01-pounder caught by Syl Shwaykosky from East Blue Lake in 1988. Its length wasn't recorded, so there's no way to compare it with Wasylyshen's fish. The 27-incher was probably close to 10 pounds.

Not all of Manitoba's watersheds contained natural populations of brook trout. Streams and lakes in the southern part of the province possess good waters, but for some reason weren't colonized naturally by brook trout. In 1942, the province obtained eggs from hatcheries in Dorion, Ontario, and Spokane, Washington, and used these to establish fisheries in the Birch and Steeprock rivers in Porcupine Mountain Forest Reserve, streams in Duck Mountain Forest Reserve, and in Stony Creek near Neepawa.

Manitoba has a Master Anglers program to recognize fishers who catch the province's big fish. It has been maintained for years and serves as a guide to where its biggest fish were caught. To be recognized, brook trout must be at least 20 inches long. The greatest number have come from Gods River. The five largest were from lakes or ponds: Garson Pond and Camp Lake, and three from Gull Lake. Other waters include French Creek; the South Knife, Kashkattama, Churchill, and Limestone rivers; and Tugby and Two Mile lakes.

Overly generous book trout limits in the 1950s and '60s severely depleted brook trout populations even in isolated watersheds. Since then, more enlightened management by camp operators as well as by provincial fisheries personnel has slowed population losses. More than 85 percent of the province's brook trout are self-sustaining, and the majority of these are from riverine environments. In waters such as the Nelson River, catch-and-release is the only fishing method allowed. One trophy brook trout may be taken out on a fly-in trip. On others, creeling fish is restricted to the last day of fishing. In watersheds where access is easy and heritage brook trout have been identified, brook trout may not be killed.

NEW BRUNSWICK

In terms of climate, topography, and fish, this Canadian Maritime province is in many ways an eastward extension of Maine. The Appalachian Mountains here are approaching their northern terminus, and other than being nearly bisected by the south-flowing St. John River, they gradually lens under the Gulf of St. Lawrence and Atlantic Ocean. The majority of New Brunswick rivers tend to flow eastward, in parallel watersheds from the height of land, except a few that trend to the north to Baie de Chaleur. All of these streams were once prime brook trout waters and share their habitat with another predator salmonid, the Atlantic salmon. In many lakes and ponds at the headlands, brook trout also cohabit with landlocked salmon.

It seems ironic that in such a land of plenty the province should be forced to maintain a pair of active hatcheries to sustain brook trout populations. One reason is that many lakes and ponds, while ideal habitat for growing trout, have few or no spawning and nursery areas. To fully utilize the habitat, New Brunswick annually stocks 30 percent of its lacustrine waters with nearly 17,000 pounds of hatchery-reared brook trout. This amounts to about 125 lakes in addition to seven streams. Stream stocking is in waters close to urban areas, where fishing pressure is too intense to allow holdover fish to reproduce.

Despite these efforts, the brook trout fishery is in a downward slide, one that could be easily corrected. The Federal Fishery Act, allowing the Fish and Wildlife Branch of New Brunswick's Department of Natural Resources adequately to manage Atlantic salmon by quotas, season, size, limits, and tackle, doesn't allow such management for brook trout. Anglers are allowed to harvest brook trout so small that they've spawned but once or at most twice. When hatchery fish are released, they suffer a higher hooking loss than the salmon's 40 to 60 percent mortality, because bait and worms (deep-hooking) are allowed.

This poor management scheme is reflected in a steady loss of fish and a blow to the province's economy. In 1985, the province recorded a harvest of 4.3 million brook trout; in 1990 it dropped to 2.2 million; and the 1995 harvest was projected to be less than 1.5 million fish. A drop in license sales paralleled the brook trout decline. In 1985 there were 109,000 active brook trout anglers; this fell to 61,342 in 1990. Could it be that the mismanagement is intentional, a philosophy of the federal government to enhance its salmon fishing? Salmon fishermen are often heard complaining that brook trout caught on salmon streams have been feeding on salmon eggs. The irony is that brook trout successfully cohabited with salmon for the last 10,000 years, but are now a thorn in the sides of affluent salmon anglers.

The province is very specific about which stocks of fish are planted and where. It has long had a policy of stocking sea-run heritage fish only in waters where they appear naturally. For lakes and ponds where brook trout spawn naturally, stocks of fish with the same behavior are used to produce fingerlings. And in lakes and ponds where managers want to maximize the size and growth of the fish they stock, the source is usually a hybrid of Assinica Lake (Québec) fish crossed with indigenous local stocks.

About 40 lakes drain west and east in the mountainous region in the north-central part of the province. Here, the headwaters of the Tobique River watershed and tributaries of the Miramichi watershed are set aside as dedicated brook trout waters, with strains of fish undiluted by stocking. Brook trout are given added protection on private lands by limited entry; some permit only catch-and-release fishing. On others there's a two-fish limit, with bait fishing prohibited and an 8-inch minimum size enforced. A trophy brook trout program is scheduled for 1996, and catch-and-release will be instituted on sections of the Cains and Little Southwest Miramichi rivers.

New Brunswick had an extensive sea-run brook trout fishery until recent years. Today it exists in varying degrees only on the Restigouche, Caraquet, Tracadie, Pokemouche, Bartibogue, Tabusintac, Kennebecasis, and Burnt Church rivers. The Miramichi River has a vast watershed that drains a large portion of the center of the province. It's divided into two large branches that are tidal for a considerable distance inland, and this impressive, unique watershed has several fair-sized tributaries that house sea-run brook trout. These are Beattle Brook and Cains, Little Southwest Miramichi, Northwest Miramichi, Dungarvon, and Main Southwest Branch Miramichi rivers.

Some of the province's better brook trout streams include the headwaters of the Tabusintac, Beattle, Northwest Miramichi, Kennebecasis, Millstream (north of Bathurst), Big Brook, Mamozekel, Little Tobique, Odellach, and Southwest Miramichi rivers. The better brook trout lakes include Island, Moose, Sisters, Peaked Mountain, States, Mains, and McDougal lakes. The province has no record-keeping program, but according to biologist W. E. Hooper, a brook trout of over 9 pounds was caught in 1960 on the Restigouche River and a similar-weight fish was caught in the mid-1960s on Tabusintac River.

NEWFOUNDLAND

All of the great islands in the Gulf of St. Lawrence and the Canadian Maritimes—Anticosti, Prince Edward Island, Cape Breton—were colonized by brook trout almost as the last glacier retreated. But while the continental ice sheet began retreating 20,000 years ago from Manhattan Island, it was 4,000 years before these northern islands were completely free.

Brook trout could not have made a better environmental choice than the island of Newfoundland, teeming as it is with hundreds of small rivers, streams, and brooks that flow seaward in every direction around its entire periphery. "The species occurs in all suitable waters," said Pat Ryan, a federal biologist with the Department of Fisheries and Oceans, "including roadside drainage ditches!"

All of today's Newfoundland brook trout are descended from the original colonists, and there has never been a need to augment any streams with stocked fish. They're all wild brook trout. Unlike Labrador to the west, really large examples of brook trout seem to be missing here, even though the biomass is quite large. There's some compensation for this in the island's well-developed sea-run fishery.

Almost every stream has free access to the surrounding ocean and has developed seagoing populations. These food-filled marine environments produce large "salters." According to two researchers, "There are reports of sea trout of seven pounds in Alexander Bay, [and] eight and nine pounds from Deer Harbour." Record sea trout were landed in 1908 when fish of 10¾, 12, and 15 pounds were taken from the Fox River and Romains Brook. The largest, from Romains Brook, was 31½ inches long and 8½ inches (a girth of 17 inches) deep.

More recently documented big brook trout don't match the sizes of earlier fish. A sports shop in St. Johns has been keeping track of big brook trout entered in a contest it has sponsored since 1947. Until 1991 the largest weighed but 4¾ pounds. Then, a 5¾-pounder was caught in Indian Bay, on the northeastern coast, by an angler using a worm and bobber.

Because almost every watershed has brook trout, it's difficult to list which might be the best. However, the most productive are the Humber, Exploits, Gander, and Terra Nova rivers. There has been some stocking of rainbow and brown trout, but brook trout are still the dominant predator in these waters. In inland waters they do have some competition from ouananiche (landlocked salmon); in some of the province's better salmon rivers brook trout populations are lower, but in others they seem to outdo young salmon in the competition for food.

NOVA SCOTIA

One would imagine that a province blessed with more than 6,500 lakes, both large and small, and hundreds of miles of streams, rivers, and brooks, most with seaward estuaries, would abound in brook trout. It does, but of late the overall brook trout fishery seems headed downward. Brook trout have long been the favorite of most Nova Scotian anglers, even though Atlantic salmon more often grab the spotlight. Brook trout have been and still are the backbone of the recreational fishery. However, the province's biologists rate the fishing as only fair.

Brook trout are widely spread over the province and occur in every watershed and a wide range of habitats, from large lakes in the interior to small ponds, large and small streams, and the province's numerous estuaries. The majority of these brook trout waters are located in the western half of the province and along the Atlantic-facing southern side.

Nova Scotia has a plethora of lacustrine environments; between 300 and 400 of these lakes support brook trout, but about 200 need annual stockings to sustain the fishery. To stem the downward trend in the fishery, a decade ago the province took over the management of its freshwater fisheries from the federal government and inaugurated its own hatchery efforts. During the past seven years, brook trout have accounted for more than 90 percent of production from its two hatcheries. Since 1988, brook trout distribution has increased by 88 percent, reflecting an increase in the stocking of fall fingerlings. Since 1992, the hatchery stock has varied and includes wild, hybrid, and domesticated stocks. Future hatchery plans are to place a greater emphasis on wild and hybrid stocks to enhance existing wild populations.

The Department of Natural Resources believes that hatchery production alone won't return the brook trout fishery to its earlier status. It believes harvesting restrictions must be used in conjunction with increased stocking efforts, and in 1994 reduced the brook trout creel limit to five fish per day. Minimum size restrictions are also planned for the near future. Opening day varies from April 1 to April 15, but all waters close on September 30. Anglers in the province are aware of the decline in the fishery but are resisting stricter regulations to reduce the harvest.

While records of big brook trout haven't been kept in Nova Scotia, the average inland fish ranges between ½ and 3 pounds. Sea-run brook trout are considerably heavier and range up to 5 and 6 pounds. The number of the province's productive waters is still so great that a list of the best is impossible to create. However, most will agree that there are few better brook trout rivers than the Shubenacadie and Margaree or lakes that can surpass Lake Ainslie and Grand Lake.

ONTARIO

At one time Ontario had the best brook trout fishery in the species' entire range. It was concentrated along the North Shore of Lake Superior in a series of rivers that flow into the lake, including such classic waters as the Batchawana, Montreal, Agawa, Magpie, White, Steel, Aguasabon, and Nipigon rivers. All regularly produced trout of 7, 8, and even 9 pounds, and the Nipigon to 19 pounds. By the turn of the century, these fisheries had been depleted of their big fish by the combined onslaught of logging, recreational and commercial fishing, and the demand for cheap hydroelectric power. Today these waters offer brook trout fishing that's fair at best. Despite these problems, Lake Superior still offers a fair fishery for coasters—brook trout that use the

lower reaches of these rivers, where still possible, for spawning, but spend most of their lives in the big lake.

Ontario is a vast province, stretching east to west for more than 900 miles and north to south almost as far. There are almost innumerable miles of rivers and streams and almost innumerable numbers of lakes and ponds. Many still produce some degree of brook trout fishing, but quality angling is now reduced to a half-dozen waters in the northern interior of the province, most of which flow into James or Hudson bays. Not all of the province's waters contained brook trout. The southwestern edge of Ontario, west of the Nipigon and Sturgeon rivers to the Lake of the Woods area, was never naturally colonized by brook trout. If they ever were here, their population disappeared long before the first French explorers pushed through looking for the source of the Mississippi River.

In the first part of this century, Ontario and its numerous universities were at the forefront of brook trout research and management. However, as the fishery waned, so did interest in effectively managing this species. The reasons are understandable but inexcusable. Lobbies representing lumber, pulp, mining, and hydroelectric interests were powerful and influential. What was done to the Nipigon is a classic example of total government disinterest in protecting an irreplaceable resource.

Even though the province today maintains a well-developed hatchery system, almost all brook trout populations are still self-sustaining, except in urban areas. Ontario's hatcheries were a major source of brook trout stock for developing fisheries in western Canadian provinces and several states. Most hatchery stock originated as Lake Nipigon eggs, and this contributed to the depletion of that watershed's brood stock.

Serious brook trout fishing today requires a drive as far north into the province as possible, then a floatplane trip into one of a dozen lodges that offer brook trout fishing as an adjunct to walleye and northern pike fishing. Most are located at the heads of the watersheds, usually lakes where floatplanes can land for downriver excursions. These include the Severn, Fawn, Winisk, Attawapiskat, and Albany rivers and their numerous tributaries. The Albany is a big river and contains brook trout, but the numerous tributaries in its vast watershed offer most of the better brook trout fishing.

There's also a sea-run brook trout fishery at the lower ends of these rivers, where they enter Hudson and James bays. Access is usually along the coast, from the communities of Fort Severn, Peawanuck (Winisk River), Attawapiskat, and Fort Albany. Only the latter has an Ojibway reservation where guides and boats can be obtained. In the interior, the province lists its best brook trout waters as the Nipigon, Credit, Boyne, and Sutton rivers, and a number of small, spring-fed lakes in Algonquin Provincial Park. To this list I'd add the Ogoki, a tributary to the Albany River just north of Lake Nipigon. It was an excellent brook trout river, but a hydroelectric dam changed that. Even so, it's still a fair fishery.

Nor would I overlook the coastal fishery in Lake Superior. Brook trout of up to 9 pounds are still being taken on their fall run as they stage around St. Ignace and a series of smaller islands that define Nipigon Bay. Guide services in towns along that section of the lake specialize in coaster catching. The fishery is rated as only fair in more southerly parts of the province, and it's understandable why most Ontario anglers and visitors rate it behind fisheries for lake trout, walleye, and smallmouth bass.

PRINCE EDWARD ISLAND

If there's a Valhalla for brook trout fishermen it must look like Prince Edward Island. About the size of Long Island (New York), this bastion of brook trout fishing is just 10 to 20 miles offshore, cradled in the seaward arms of mainland New Brunswick, Nova Scotia, and Cape Breton Island. More than 200 streams run seaward in all directions along the periphery of this island province, which is about 120 miles long and averages 20 miles in width. Because of its relatively small size, there are no major rivers or watersheds on P.E.I. The Hillsborough River, the longest at 25 miles, is really a tidal estuary that's fresh in only its first 5 or 6 miles. The rest of the island is drained by numerous rivulets

and small and large streams, all called rivers. Several gather at their mouths to empty into a dozen or so well-protected estuaries, which create prime habitat for sea-run brook trout.

While there's excellent brook trout fishing along thousands of miles of streams, this is really the domain of the salter. It's rated tops by the horde of local anglers, and almost everyone on the island seems to be a trout fisher. The island's largest fish weighed 7 pounds, 14 ounces, taken at the mouth of the West River, and is believed to have been a salter. The island is unique in that it's groundwater rich and its streams are full-flowing throughout the year. In addition, they're rich in nutriments and thus very productive trout waters. Because of this, all streams have self-sustaining populations, and brook trout are the major predator species except where Atlantic salmon occur; even here, dominance is shared.

Because of the gradient of the island's terrain, few lakes and ponds developed. About a half dozen are large enough to provide good fishing, and these are concentrated on the eastern third of the island. Two, one near Avondale and the other north of Tarantum, have fishable populations. With good brook trout water so common, it's difficult to select the better streams; most are pretty good. However, five receive special consideration in their management: the West, Dunk, Morell, Mill, and Trout rivers. To these should be added the Tyne, Flat, Sturgeon, Valleyfield, and Naufrage rivers. The season is April 15 to September 30, and the creel limit is 10 brook trout per day.

QUÉBEC

There are more good brook trout waters within the borders of Québec than in any other province or state. At one time the province tried to count them all but quit after a million. And many of them offer the last opportunity for pristine brook trout fishing, just as it was in "the good old days." There are two reasons for this: Québec is huge, nearly 800 miles wide and 1,000 miles from north to south, and Québec is north. But not all of Québec is inhabited by brook trout. A small, northerly tip of the

Labrador Peninsula on the eastern side of Ungava Bay and the most northerly 100 miles of the Ungava Peninsula on the western side of Ungava Bay have no brook trout. There's water and good habitat, but the mean summer temperature, 48 degrees, is so cold that eggs don't hatch until late in the summer, and the fry haven't time to grow and fatten enough to survive the long winter. However, a recent examination of the range of brook trout by Québec biologists showed that this northern tip of the Ungava Peninsula is inhabited by brook trout. Whether these are seasonal visitors or attempts to establish new populations farther north will take several years of observations to determine. One or two exceptionally cold summers could force them to retreat south along the coast. This is an area in transition for range expansion. Further, all tidal sections of these rivers support anadromous brook trout populations; these fish, however, may winter in streams farther south along the coast. Aside from this area, there's more than enough habitat for brook trout in La Belle Province.

Brook trout fishing in Québec is both very old and very new. The first permanent French settlement was at Tadoussac, the site of an Indian trading place at the mouth of the Saguenay River, where it joins the Gulf of St. Lawrence. Sea-run brook trout have been on European menus there since 1599. The realm of the species and the quality of fishing it offers in Québec can be divided into five regions, based on the rate of the advance of civilization and the exploitation of the fishery.

The region south of the St. Lawrence River, including the Gaspé Peninsula, today offers only fair brook trout fishing at best because of heavy local angling pressure and heavy agricultural and lumbering activity. Because rivers of the Gaspé offer great salmon fishing, these streams are managed first for salmon; brook trout receive little attention unless there are no salmon in the rivers. Another area of southern Québec, bound on the east by the St. Lawrence River and the south and west by Ontario, was never prime brook trout habitat. After the initial stock of native fish was removed, it never recovered. Today, the area offers good fishing for bass,

walleye, northern pike, and muskellunge.

The exception to this region's conditions is found in the third area, located roughly between the North Shore of the St. Lawrence River, Québec City, Tadoussac, and Lake St. John. Most of this is on the Laurentian Highland, a plateau that spawns several rivers and was set aside more than 100 years ago as Laurentides Provincial Reserve, later Park. The original park covenants were neither respected nor enforced. Instead, the timber industry saw the reserve's virgin forests as a private pulp reserve. When land everywhere else was finally lumbered, this verdant gem in the heart of Québec's wilderness was sacrificed to clear-cutting practices. Its horde of large brook trout went unrecognized until after the turn of the century, because routes into its interior were on unnavigable rivers. But to those willing to paddle, portage, and walk, it offered brook trout fishing on a par with the Nipigon's. By the late 1940s, however, its fabulous brook trout fishing had become only pages in history. Today, brook trout fishing here is rated as fair. However, efforts are being made to regenerate this fishery using strains of hybrid stock, which grow faster than domesticated fish and survive better if caught and released.

Both the northern and southern shores of the Gulf of St. Lawrence and its many rivers still hold a goodly stock of sea-run brook trout, as does the big island of Anticosti. At one time, spawning brook trout entered all of the rivers that flow south into the St. Lawrence, from Blanc Sablon west to Montréal and the rapids at Lachine. Several rivers still provide a good to excellent fishery, including those from the mouth of the Saguenay east to Blanc Sablon. In 1992, I fished for salmon on the Ste-Marguerite River as I waited with guide Ron Jones of Chicoutimi for the sea-run brook trout to arrive. The Ste-Marguerite is the prettiest river in the world. It had rained for four days, and while the river had risen slightly the water was still crystal clear—a testament to the virgin watershed it drains. The river flows into the Saguenay, which is tidal at that point and still under the influence of the Gulf of St. Lawrence. The mouth of the Ste-Marguerite is blocked by a large sandbar where it joins salt water, and brook trout often have a difficult time clearing this bar in late August. It takes the combination of a fall freshet and a lunar high tide before the fish can gambol in. It took them three days to cover the 20 miles upstream to the beat I was fishing. For two days the pool I worked produced only ½- to 2-pound brook trout, gaudily colored in their darkening spawning garb. On the third morning, on my first cast, I almost had the rod torn from my hand. At first I thought it was a salmon, but it turned out to be a 3-pound sea-run brook trout that looked more like a salmon than a "speckle."

The fourth of Québec's brook trout fisheries, discovered after World War II, centers on several streams that drain the large plateau, in south-central Québec, around huge Lake Mistassini. A few flow southward but the better brook trout rivers flow westward, almost on parallel routes, to James Bay. Several rivers are in this realm, but the best are the Eastmain, Rupert, and Broadback. The Broadback, the southern branch that recently was renamed the Assinica River, after the lake from which it flows, produced more *Field & Stream* records in the 1950s than any other water. It still produces near-record brook trout. But while quality is still there, quantity isn't. The biggest brook trout caught on hook and line in Québec was landed near the outlet of Assinica Lake on August 28, 1962. It weighed 11½ pounds.

Equally good was the Rupert River, but permanent fishing lodges were never established on it and a big-trout fishery never developed. Still, the main river and its tributaries, such as the Martin and Cocomenhani, are capable of producing big fish. The problem for anglers is access. At one time, members of the Cree tribe maintained sportfishing camps on these rivers, but they were short lived. The Eastmain and its main tributary, the Opinaca River, were rising in prominence as producers of big brook trout, but grandiose hydroelectric dams flooded their headwaters into oblivion.

Lake Mistassini, which is drained by the Rupert River, has two unique brook trout fisheries. The lake itself has produced some 8- to 10-pound brook trout, but it's so large and deep

that fishing is difficult. Instead, anglers prefer to work a collection of tributaries at its northern end, where the fish spawn. These include the Papaskwasati ("Papa") and Little Papaskwasati (Nielson) rivers, and the River Cheno (alias DuFour), a tributary to the larger Takwa (Toqueco) River. The latter has two tributaries above its confluence with the Cheno that produce big brook trout. These all had fly-in satellite camps on them at one time. Like the Cocomenhani, they were serviced by Cree outfitters who operated out of Vieux Poste, a small village on the eastern shore of Lake Mistassini.

As well known for producing brook trout, but not quite as large as the Assinica/Broadback, is the Témiscamie River, the largest river feeding Mistassini. It rises to the northeast of the lake and parallels other watersheds that enter the lake's northern end. Before it does, however, it flows into long, attenuated Lake Albanel, which looks more like a huge arm of Mistassini than another lake. The outlet to Lake Albanel is a bit more than a mile long and enters Mistassini near its northern end. But before it does, it cascades down two waterfalls, which keep any brook trout from Mistassini and its feeder rivers from ascending the outlet. The isolation of this population of brook trout has created a unique variation of the strain. They grow large and have a singular migratory ability (they often spawn considerable distances up the length of the Témiscamie River). The population has been used as the source for brook trout stock in many states and provinces, and is in wide use today for creating wild hybrids or for crossing with domesticated trout.

The fifth brook trout region is a vast area that encompasses most of the area called New Québec. Even today it offers anglers willing to travel, and at times to "rough it," excellent brook trout fishing. Sixty streams, some small and others great rivers, flow west from Rupert Bay, a part of James Bay in the south, north along the coast of Hudson Bay to the Inuit settlement of Povungnituk. All have populations of brook trout, parts of which show preferences for salt water at certain times.

One of the best-developed populations of sea-run brook trout is in the triangular-shaped estuary of Richmond Gulf (Guillaume Delisle). Into this triangle, which is about 25 miles across its base, flow three fair-sized rivers and a half-dozen small streams. This water is trapped inside the triangle and squeezes out of a corner through a narrow granite passage formed between two cliffs, no more than ½ mile long. Through The Gullet, as this opening is called, tidewater enters the gulf; on the ebb, brackish water flows seaward. Inside the triangle the water is mostly fresh, though still affected by tides. Brook trout from the lower ends of the streams spend summers in the gulf feeding on herring and capelin. One August, more than a dozen years ago, I spent a week here catching and releasing untold numbers of silvery, salmonlike brook trout that weighed between 1 and 2 pounds. The largest was a 3-pounder. All of this while waiting for the first Arctic charr to begin their spawning run, entering the gulf then migrating up its rivers.

About 75 miles west of Richmond Gulf, in Hudson Bay, are the Belcher Islands. The Inuit village of Sanikiluaq is on the largest, an island strip about 60 miles long. At one time an outfitter operated a sportfishing camp on one of the islands and found the small streams filled with Arctic charr and sea-run brook trout.

From Povungnituk north brook trout are only coastal transients, to Ivujivik, the most northerly tip of the Ungava Peninsula. Because average summer water temperatures in the estuarine portions of more than a dozen more rivers never get above 48 degrees, brook trout haven't been able to colonize these watersheds. This restrictive condition is in effect for the 200 miles from Povungnituk to Ivujivik, then along the northern shore of the peninsula and south down the western shore of Ungava Bay to the mouth of the Leaf River. From here south, along U-shaped Ungava Bay and up its eastern coast to the estuary of the George River, brook trout are again found in all watersheds. These waters are shared with only two other salmonids—Arctic charr and, on the eastern side, Atlantic salmon.

Three rivers that brook trout share with Arctic charr and Atlantic salmon, on the eastern side of Ungava Bay, have produced some big sea-run trout. The Tunulic River, whose estuarine mouth is just south of that of the George River, has produced sea-run brook trout of up to 9 pounds. Several rivers flowing north into Ungava Bay have their origins as far as 250 miles away. In these watersheds, brook trout cohabit with lake trout and landlocked salmon. The southern ends of these waters were the first to be opened to sportfishing when surplus airplanes became available to outfitters after World War II. However, large numbers of their tributaries have still only been fished by a passing floatplane looking for new brook trout waters. Much of this fishery is untouched.

EXPANDED DISTRIBUTION OF BROOK TROUT IN CANDIAN WATERS

ALBERTA

Brook trout are not native to this province; they were introduced to the Banff area in 1910 in the form of stock from Lake Nipigon. In 1928, brook trout were also introduced into Maligne Lake, southeast of Jasper. Subsequently, they've been introduced into the western half of the province in the Peace, Athabasca, North Saskatchewan, Clearwater, Red Deer, Bow, and Oldman river drainages. They were also stocked in Wood Buffalo National Park, where they provided an excellent fishery for several years.

Brook trout sometimes naturally hybridize with brown trout in Alberta, and hybrids between bull and brook trout have also taken place. In 1962, forced hybrids between brook trout and Québec red trout (originally known as *Salvelinus marstoni*), actually a relic Arctic charr, were stocked in Lake Louise and Bow Lake in Jasper National Park. However, none of these hybrids survived.

Brook trout in Alberta compete directly with the bull trout (*Salvelinus confluentus*), another charr that at one time was regarded as a Dolly Varden Charr, but has since been given its own identification; some Canadian biologists still regard it as a Dolly Varden (*Salvelinus malma*), however. It's believed that through competition, brook trout have reduced populations of this fish, which is native to the province. Biologists here are now managing waters where both species appear in favor of bull trout. In such waters, according to provincial authorities, brook trout won't be protected with specific management strategies at the expense of indigenous species.

Despite this stratagem, brook trout are a popular species with Alberta anglers, and in over 90 percent of their range they sustain their populations by natural reproduction. However, to maintain this fishery in several small lakes where this doesn't take place, the province annually stocks about 400,000 brook trout.

The average life span of brook trout in Alberta is three years. In several streams they've been known to reach 6 years, and in one mountain lake a 13-year-old fish was found.

The province's biggest brook trout was a 5.9-kg (13-pound) fish that measured 75.5 cm (29.8 inches) FL (fork length); it was caught by D. Jenkins in 1967 from Pine Lake in Wood Buffalo National Park.

BRITISH COLUMBIA

In 1908, 35,000 brook trout eggs arrived at the Fraser River Hatchery from Québec. This was the first expansion of this species in Canada outside of its natural range. Populations were established in the southeastern part of the province and on Vancouver Island. The next eggs came from Lake Nipigon fish in 1913. An active brook trout hatchery is still maintained by B.C.'s Department of Recreation and Conservation.

At first, brook trout stockings were readily accepted by fisheries managers and anglers alike. But overzealous and inappropriate stocking of some waters caused a decline in native species because of the brook trout's greater reproductive abilities and competitive nature. In the past few decades, with the growing emphasis in many states and provinces on stocking and restocking their waters with only wild and indigenous species, brook trout haven't been looked upon as kindly as in the past.

B.C.'s Ministry of Environment, Lands and Parks recently issued a new policy guideline that allows hatchery brook trout to be planted only in closed systems where they already exist. This, according to the policy statement, is to ensure the continued health and productivity of native fish populations. The major concerns with brook trout are the ecological impact of their competition with native trout species, in particular the cutthroat trout, and the genetic implications they might have for bull trout, with which they can reproduce (although the resulting hybrids are usually sterile). Also working toward this goal, provincial biologists are developing a triploid strain of brook trout that would guarantee their sterility and pose no reproductive threat to native species.

Despite these concerns, brook trout do fill a niche in some of the waters of British Columbia, especially in lakes where the rainbow trout fishery is marginal or where native populations are affected by winterkill. Self-sustaining populations of brook trout here are slight and are annually supported by about 800,000 hatchery fish. The brood stock for these fish comes from Aylmer Lake, north of Chase, where brook trout are the dominant predators. Its waters are closed to angling.

The following are considered the province's best brook trout waters: the Bonaparte River system; Beaver Creek; Whitetail (Canal Flats) and Fortress (Hamber Provincial Park) lakes; Big Sheep Creek; Cameron and Plaid lakes; Hill Creek; Spectacle Lake; Lens Creek; and lower parts of Elk and Kootenay streams. Also included are Dugan, Edna, Edith, Lemieux, Yellow, Klinger, Echo, and Gantahaz lakes. While British Columbia has no trophy brook trout program, some of its lakes do produce large fish. The biggest is an 11-pounder (28 inches) that came from an unidentified lake in the southern interior of the province.

THE NORTHWEST TERRITORIES

Recent stocking of brook trout in several lakes around Fort Smith have been successful, but little information is available about this fishery. In 1987, the Department of Fisheries and Oceans began a five-year program of stocking brook trout in several small lakes along the NWT road system. The limit is three fish per day.

SASKATCHEWAN

In their colonization of the land after the last glacial period, brook trout never made it as far west as Saskatchewan, even though glacial Lake Agassiz, which was loaded with brook trout and other salmonids, covered most of the province for a long period. In fact, they never expanded their range into western Manitoba, just east of Saskatchewan. Some biologists believe that the mean annual rainfall, which is reduced west of a line from central Manitoba south to the head of the Mississippi River in Minnesota, plays some role in defining the fish's natural western limit. It may not have had an effect during early postglacial times, but it does seem to play a role today. Despite this phenomenon, in recent times humans have expanded the brook trout's range into Saskatchewan.

Saskatchewan was the last of the Canadian provinces to get caught up the wave of fish stocking that swept North America in the late 1800s and early 1900s. The earliest stockings of the province's waters were with smallmouth black bass, in 1887, and muskellunge in 1889. By the end of the first quarter of the 20th century, fisheries managers had begun to recognize some of the damage done by stocking nonindigenous species that competed with native fish.

Thereafter, exotic species were stocked only after an investigation of their likely effect on local fish. In 1924, rainbow trout, then brown trout, were stocked into watersheds that were suitable and without predator native species. Brook trout were stocked as early as 1928 in waters in Cypress Hills, but the first serious planting took place in 1933, when 13,600 brook trout from Alberta were planted in Cold Lake and four streams in Cypress Hills. Saskatchewan continued to go to Alberta, Montana, Washington, and Oregon for brook trout. However, by 1953 the province had established its own hatchery brood stock and has since domesticated its own brook trout.

Brook trout took readily to many streams, and today are the most successful naturalized exotic species in the province, but at best only offer limited fishing. They're found in 122 waters, but natural reproduction occurs in about 10 percent of them. Most others must have their populations supported by annual stockings. In addition to streams, where brook trout stocking is the most successful, the province annually stocks more than 127,000 fingerlings in 27 lakes, ponds, and reservoirs.

Waters in five separate areas within the province support fishable populations of brook trout. One area includes Cold Lake, on the Alberta/Saskatchewan border, and waters in adjacent Meadow Lake Provincial Park. The second area is just northeast of here and includes waters that feed Keeley and Macullum lakes, near Cole Bay. The third is in watersheds draining the Club Hills and Nipawan Provincial Park, in the very center of the province. The largest area is a collection of drainages centered on the town of Hudson Bay, near the Manitoba border. The fifth is the Cypress Hills, in the extreme southwestern corner of the province south of the town of Maple Creek and west of the town of Eastend.

Better brook trout streams include Mc-Dougal, Lost Echo, Sucker, White Gull, and Pine Tree creeks and the Fir and Swan rivers. Brook trout are stocked in Besant, Broad, Connell, English, Hay Meadow, Jackfish, Nipekamew, Sands, Scissors, and Steep creeks and the Mossy and Pasquia rivers. The better brook trout lakes are Lussier, Sealy, and Sedge lakes. Other lakes and reservoirs stocked include Atchison, Dorthy, Junction, Maistre, Negan, Nipawan, Noeth, Poplar Ridge, Ridge, Sand, Sands, Shannon, Snell, and Twin lakes; Baumann, Cadillac, Lightning Creek, and Wapella reservoirs; and Biggar, David Laird, and Redberry ponds.

Saskatchewan's biggest brook trout was a 6-pound, 2-ounce fish caught from Lake Amyot, inside Prince Albert National Park, in 1973. However, a 7-pound, 10-ounce brook trout was caught in May 1993 by Richard Meyers from Round Lake, near Perigord.

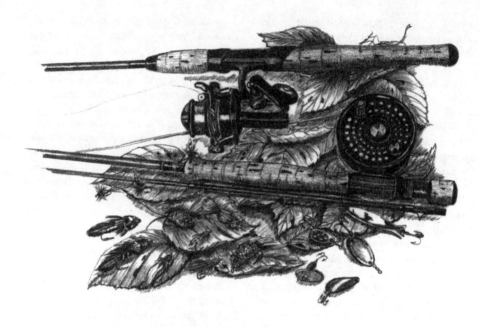

D FOREIGN DISTRIBUTION OF BROOK TROUT

Brook trout are the original worldwide travelers. Easily raised in hatcheries, hardy passengers whether by train, ship, wagon, or mule, brook trout arrive ready to colonize with a minimum of precautions. Their fast initial growth rate and great fecundity make them ideal settlers where the environment is clear, cool, and clean—and the competition not too stiff. Not all brook trout sent abroad were destined for sportfishing, however. Several foreign importers were commercial fish hatcheries with plans for the fish no more grandiose than the table.

MEXICO

Moving brook trout south of the border got a late start. The first fish weren't introduced until 1947, when they were planted in several streams near El Zarco and Mexico City. Brook trout adapted well to many high-level streams, usually at elevations near 6,000 feet. However, a few streams and lakes at these elevations must be stocked periodically to bolster self-sustaining

populations. Rainbow trout can sustain themselves over a wider range of waters, and most hatchery efforts today are directed toward this species.

GREAT BRITAIN

The first brook trout were shipped to Europe in 1869 as a consignment of fertilized eggs to Frank Buckland, commissioner of fish in England. Livingston Stone (who also sent Hudson River striped bass to San Francisco Bay) sent them from the federal Cold Spring Trout Hatchery in New Hampshire (MacCrimmon). A second shipment of 10,000 eggs was shipped in 1871 to John Parnably, owner of the Troutdale Fishery near Keswick. His was the first of several commercial hatcheries to supply brook trout as table fare; today, only one of these remains, in North Wales. Brook trout were widely distributed in waters throughout England, Wales, and Scotland, but became established in only a half-dozen small lakes.

Figure D.1   Naturalized distribution of *Salvelinus fontinalis* in Europe.

They were never introduced to Ireland.

NORWAY

Norway was the next country to receive brook trout eggs. From 1870 to 1919 fry were introduced to several streams, but none developed self-sustaining populations. In 1918, 1,000 fry were introduced to a small lake about 3,000 feet above sea level, in the far-northern Telemark district. Some fish moved out of the lake and into the stream and its tributaries to establish self-sustaining populations. Brook trout gradually worked their way to lower elevations of the river, where they coexist today with brown trout.

GERMANY

Biologists and fish culturists in Germany kept pace with their American counterparts during the latter half of the 19th century and developed their own hatcheries concurrently. It was only natural that Livingston Stone should ship brook trout eggs to Baron Lucius von Behr, an active angler as well as a fish culturist and president of the German Fisherman's Society. The eggs arrived in 1879. Six years later, the association sent their progeny to Boitzenburg Hatchery in Mecklenburg. From here they were stocked in Black Forest streams and lakes and also in several watersheds in Austria. Today the federal government doesn't stock brook trout, but several private hatcheries in Germany produce them for stocking or the table.

AUSTRIA

Brook trout were introduced to Austria almost as soon as they arrived in Germany in 1897. The species has since become established throughout most of Austria, especially in the provinces of Vorarlberg, Tirol, Salzburg, Upper and Lower Austria, Styria, and Carinthia.

OTHER EUROPEAN COUNTRIES

From 1880 on, brook trout spread throughout many nations in Europe, through direct shipments from the United States or from European hatcheries established on the Continent. These nations included Bulgaria (1930), Czechoslovakia (pre-1890), Denmark (circa 1900), Finland (1898, 1967), France (circa 1883), Hungary (pre-1917), Italy (1891, 1946), the Netherlands (pre-1883), Poland (after 1879), Rumania (pre-1900), Spain (1934, 1946), Sweden (1891), Switzerland (1883), and Russia (before 1914 and again after 1930). Brook trout didn't always adapt successfully and failed to establish populations in Finland, Hungary, the Netherlands, and Russia. Russia has substantial waters with several species of charr, so the likely problem there was the selection of an unsuitable habitat. Brook trout currently are raised on two fish farms in Ukraine and Russia.

ASIA

Even though Japan has an indigenous population of salmonids, including Pacific salmon and at least two species of charr, attempts were made before 1900 to introduce more salmonids. The first try with brook trout occurred in 1901, with eggs shipped from the United States to the Nikko Hatchery. The fry were stocked in the Yugawa River near Nikko City. Brook trout are now established in three rivers and a pond. In 1963, the U.S. shipped eggs to Harwan Trout Farm in India. In 1966 this stock was made available to other trout farms in the Kashmir Valley, primarily as food fish.

AFRICA

Fry from United States–supplied brook trout eggs were distributed in 1955 in several rivers and a reservoir but failed to establish a population. Another shipment was made in 1961 but it failed as well. Male brook trout are now maintained at the Jonkershoek Hatchery, South Africa, to hybridize with brown trout, producing the sterile tiger trout.

In 1949, a small shipment of English eggs went to Kenya; the fry were stocked into high-altitude waters, above 6,000 feet, but failed to establish a fishery. In 1961, the Paradise Brook Trout Company, of Henryville, Pennsylvania, shipped eggs, and fry were again planted into high-altitude streams and a reservoir. Very few survived, although they did reproduce successfully in one stream.

Stocking attempts were made in Rhodesia (Zimbabwe), Nyasaland (Malawi), and Tanzania, all at high altitudes to ensure cool summer waters, but they too failed. Brook trout were also stocked prior to 1958 in several small lakes on the Kerguélen Islands in the South Indian Ocean. These small islands, south of the equator, are equivalent in latitude to Anticosti Island in the Gulf of St. Lawrence. The fish are spawning successfully.

DOWN UNDER

Several brook trout stockings were attempted in Australia from 1908 to 1967, but they have not produced self-sustaining populations. Attempts in New Zealand began as early as 1877, but these, as well as attempts in 1880 and 1881, failed. However, an attempt in 1890 bore fruit. That year brook trout were stocked in the Horokoro River, which drains Rotorua Lake in the highlands of North Island. Several other North Island streams were stocked, as was Lake Emily on South Island, and all now have self-sustaining brook trout populations.

SOUTH AMERICA

No salmonids ever crossed the equator on their own. However, with human help they've rewritten Horatio Alger's success story, helped in part by the longest chain of mountains in the world. The Andes stretch from Central America to the tip of Chile at the edge of Antarctica. Even where the equator crosses Ecuador, one must climb above 10,000 feet to get to the other side.

Since 1928, brook trout have been stocked in seven South American countries and have succeeded in all but two, Ecuador and Colombia. United States–supplied brook trout were stocked in Venezuela from 1937 until 1942 in lakes and rivers draining the Andes. They became established in the Motatan, Chama, and Santo Domingo rivers in the state of Mérida and many small lakes in the western highlands. Brook trout and brown trout arrived in Peru in 1928 and quickly became established in several watersheds above 5,000 feet to the west of Lake Titicaca. Today, they're raised in several hatcheries, even though most populations are self-sustaining.

Stocks of brook trout of unknown source were shipped to Chile in 1935–36 and today are maintained in three federal hatcheries. The brook trout population is divided into three separate groups in the north, central, and south-central parts of this country, a narrow strip of land on the western side of the Andean cordillera. The bulk of established populations occur in the province of Aconcaqua and rivers of the high cordillera, which include the Rio Colorado and estuaries of the Ojos de Aqua, Piuquenes, Juncal, La Polvareda, and Los Leones. Brook trout have established themselves along the coast as sea-run populations and are pushing farther south, colonizing rivers whose headwaters weren't stocked. One of the more famous brook trout rivers in Chile is the Puelo, which rises in Argentina.

ARGENTINA

While there's good to excellent brook trout fishing in Chile, it doesn't compare with that of Argentina. Argentina seemingly was made for brook trout, except someone forgot to put them in the water. It wasn't until 1904 that this oversight was redressed. It may have been the American biologist John W. Titcomb who brought salmonids to Argentina, but it was the British enclave in Buenos Aires, and their love of trout fishing, that influenced Argentina's political leaders to stock salmon and trout.

Titcomb was invited to Argentina in 1903 to analyze Lago Nahuel Huapi and a collection of lakes surrounding the frontier town of Neuquén for water quality and potential for holding trout and salmon. After 19 days of traveling on horseback between lakes and their outlets and a month analyzing his samples, he pronounced these waters ideal for salmonids. He built a temporary hatchery on the eastern end of Lago Nahuel Huapi and ordered his associate, E. A. Tulian, to ship the first eggs. On March 4, 1904, the shipment arrived at the makeshift hatchery. It contained 1 million whitefish, 102,700 brook trout, 53,000 lake trout, and 50,000 landlocked salmon. After hatching, the fry were all put into the one lake. Fortunately, the whitefish disappeared but the others took hold.

Titcomb, aided by more American biologists, over the next decade established other hatcheries and introduced almost every salmonid on the list. In some lakes several species known to be compatible were stocked. In others, only one kind was planted. On the Patagonian plains there are a dozen lakes, some quite large, where brook trout are the only predator. Eight large shipments of salmonid eggs, mostly from the United States but some from Europe, were sent to Argentina between 1904 and 1910. In 1910, a shift in government personnel and policies stopped further shipments, and the American biologists returned to the U.S.

The Andes are relatively narrow, and most of the lakes are formed in valleys within the mountains or along the eastern foothills. However, many flow west through breaks in the chain into the Pacific Ocean. Some straddle the border, with part of a lake in Chile and the other in Argentina. Here, prime brook trout habitat covers an area more than 1,200 miles long and

Figure D.2 Naturalized distribution of *Salvelinus fontinalis* in South America.

about 10 miles wide.

Four species dominate sportfishing in Argentina's Patagonia—landlocked salmon and brown, rainbow, and brook trout—from Bariloche to the towns of Rio Gallegos and Rio Grande on the very southern tip of Tierra del Fuego. Sportfishing is centered on three hubs. The more northerly is around Bariloche and to the north, and includes the following rivers and lake: the Trocoman, Aluminem, Norquinco, Quillen, Malleo, Collon Cura, Chimehuin, Curruhue, Quilquihue, Caleuf, Meliquina, Filo Hau Hum, Traful, Correntoso, Limay, and Manso rivers; and Lago Nahuel Huapi, the

largest lake in the area. Lakes here are the most popular with traveling Americans, in part because they were the first to have fishing lodges and in part because of their proximity to Buenos Aires. While there are brook trout in many of these waters, it's the huge brown and rainbow trout that attract most anglers.

The second area is about 120 miles farther south. The town of Esquel is the jumping-off spot for fishermen. Lakes and rivers are to the north, west, and south of the town and include Lago Cholila and Puelo; Rio Carrileufu, Rivadavia, Arrayanes, Menendez, and Grande; and lakes Menendez, Futalaufquen, and

Amutui Quimei. These contain brook and rainbow trout, but many lakes south of Esquel were stocked primarily with brook trout. Rainbows are usually found in the outlet rivers, including the Palena, Vintter, LaPlatta, Fontana, Verde, and Blanco.

The third area, still farther to the south, is the realm of sea-run rainbow and brown trout; this includes the Rio Gallegos and its tributaries, and, on the island of Tierra del Fuego, the rivers Grande, Fuego, Ewab, and San Pablo.

Two hundred miles east of the Rio Gallegos, in the South Atlantic, are the Falkland (Malvinas) Islands. During World War II, brown, rainbow, and brook trout were stocked in several small streams, probably by British officers stationed there who missed their trout fishing. Only brook trout survived, and today are found in one stream, Moody Brook. This is the most southerly population of brook trout in the world—as far south of the equator as the Broadback River is north.

BIBLIOGRAPHY

Allerton, Rueben G., *Brook Trout Fishing: An Account of the Oquossoc Angling Association*, Perris & Brown, New York, 1869.

Balon, Eugene K., *Early Ontogeny of the Brook Charr*, Salvelinus (Baione) 631–666.

Bailey, Reeve M., & Gerald R. Smith, "Origin and geography of the fish fauna of the Laurentian Great Lakes basin," *Can. J. Fish . Aquat. Sci.*, Vol. 38, 1981.

Bates, Joseph D., Jr., *Streamer Fly Tying and Fishing*. Stackpole Co., Harrisburg, Pa., 1950.

Behnke, Robert J., "A systematic review of the genus *Salvelinus*" 441–481,1980 Charrs, Ed. E.K. Balon.

Behnke, Robert J., 1972. "The systematics of salmonid fishes of recently glaciated lakes." *J. Fish. Res. Board Can.*, 29: 639–671.

Bent, Mitch., "Can the coasters make a comeback?" *Trout*, Autumn 1994, 22–27.

Blake, W. H., *Brown Waters and Other Sketches*. The Macmillan Co., Toronto, 1915.

Blake, W. H., *In a Fishing Country*. The Macmillan Co., Toronto, 1922.

Bramble, Charles A., 1896–97. "The sportsmen's clubs of Long Island," *Sportsman's Magazine*, 1:216–228.

Bradford, Charles Barker, *The Brook Trout and the Determined Angler*, The E. P. Grow Pub. Co., Richmond Hill, L.I., New York, 1900.

Brown, John J., *American Angler's Guide, or Complete Fisher's Manual for the United States*. H. Long & Brother, New York, 1845.

Burroughs, John, *A Tramp in the Catskills, Afoot and Afloat*. The Riverside Literature Series, Riverside Press, Houghton Miffling Co., Boston, 1871.

Colvin, Verplanck, *Report on the Topographical Survey of the Adirondack Wilderness N. Y. for the Year 1873, Second Report. 1873–74*. Weed, Parsons and Co., Albany, 1874.

Connett, Eugene V, III, *Any Luck?* Garden City Publishing Co., Garden City, N.Y., 1933–37.

Crandall, Lathan A., *Days in the Open*, Fleming H. Revell, Co., New York, 1914.

Cunjack, Richard A., & Geoffry Powers, "Winter habitat utilization by stream resident brook and brown trout," *Can. J. Fish. Aquat. Sci.*, Vol. 43, 1986; 1970–80.

Cunjack, Richard A., & J. M. Green, "Habitat utilization by brook charr (*Salvelinus fontinalis*) and rainbow trout in Newfoundland streams," *Can. J. Zool.* Vol. 6, 1214–19, 1983.

Dawson, George, *Pleasure of Angling With Rod and Reel*, Sheldon & Co., New York, 1876.

Day, Walter Deforest, M.D. *The Fishicians: A Diary.* American Museum of Fly Fishing, Manchester, Vt., 1865.

DeKay, James E., *Zoology of New York*, 1842.

Dunham, Rex A. et al., 1994. "Biochemical genetics of brook trout *Salvelinus fontinalis* in Georgia," D-J Project F-42.

Elliot, Robert O.E., *All About Brook Trout.* Practical Science Pub. Co., Orange, Conn., 1950.

Embody, G.C., 1934. "Relation of temperature to the incubation period of eggs of four species of trout," *Trans. Am. Fish. Soc.* 64: 281–289.

Fadden, William. *A Chorographical Map of the Province of New York*, London, 1779.

Flick, William A., "Comparative first year survival and production in wild and domestic strains of brook trout *Salvelinus fontinalis*, 1964," *Trans. Amer. Fish. Soc.*, 93: 58–69.

Flick, W.A. & D.A. Webster, "Production of wild, domestic and interstrain hybrids of brook trout (*Salvelinus fontinalis*) in natural ponds," *J. Fish Res. Board Can.*, 33: 1525–1539, 1976.

Flick, William A., "Some observations, age, growth, food habits and vulnerability of large brook trout (*Salvelinus fontinalis*) from four canadian lakes, 1977," *Naturaliste Canadian*, 104: 353–359.

Forester, Frank (Henry William Herbert), 1849. *Frank Forester's Fish and Fishing of the United States, and the British Provinces of North America* (also 1850).

Ganz, Charlotte A., *Col. Verne La Salle Rockwell's Scrapbook*, Smithtown Historical Society, Smithtown, 1968.

Goode, G. Brown, & Theodore Gill, *American Fishes.* L.C. Page & Co., Boston (1887), 1903.

Goodspeed, Eliot, *Angling in America*, Houghton Mifflin Co., Boston, 1939.

Goodwin, Harry, "Brook trout—New Jersey's native trout," *N.J. Outdoors*, April 1967, 3–23.

Grady, Joseph F., *The Adirondacks Fulton Chain–Big Moose Region*, 1933.

Haig-Brown, Roderick, *Fisherman's Winter.* Wm. Morrow & Co., New York, 1954.

Hallock, Charles, *The Fishing Tourist: Angler's Guide and Reference Book.* Harper & Bros., New York, 1873.

Hallock, Charles, *The Sportsman's Gazetteer and General Guide.* Forest and Stream Pub. Co., New York, 1877.

Hammer, John, Swedish Institute of Freshwater Research, pers. communication, 1995.

Hammer, John, "Natural hybridization between Arctic charr (*Salvelinus alpinus*) and brook trout (*S. fontinalis*): Evidence from northern Labrador," *Can. J. Fish. Sci.*, Vol 48, 1991.

Hewitt, Edward R., *A Trout and Salmon Fisherman for Twenty-Five Years*. Charles Scribner's Sons, New York, 1950.

Jordon, David Starr, & Barton W. Evermann, *American Food and Game Fishes*, Doubleday, Page & Co., New York, 1902.

Karas, Nicholas, "The trout and Dan'l Webster," *Sports Illustrated Magazine*, April 4, 1966, E5–E8.

Karas, Nicholas, "Daniel Webster meets another kind of devil," *Rod & Gun Magazine*, Sports Afield Publications. Vol. I, No. II, 91–92, 161–162.

Kelly, Alan G., J.S. Griffith, & Ronald D. Jones, 1980. "Changes in distribution of trout in Great Smoky Mountains National Park, 1900–1977," U.S. Fish & Wild. Tech. Paper, 102.

Kendall, William Converse, "The fishes of New England," *Memoirs of the Boston Society of Natural History*, Vol. 8, No. 1, 1914 & Vol. 9, No. 1, 1935.

Kroll, Charles, *Squaretail*. Vantage Press, New York, 1972.

Krueger, Charles C., 1991. "Ecological and genetic effects of salmonid introductions to North America," *Can. J. Aquat. Sci.*, Vol. 48 (Suppl. 1).

Krueger, Charles C. et al., 1981. "Genetic aspects of fisheries rehabilitation programs," *Can. J. Fish and Aqua. Sci.*, 38:12, 1877–1881.

Lagler, Karl F., J. E. Bardach, & R .R. Miller, *Ichthyology*, John Wiley & Sons, New York, 1962.

Larsen, Gary L. & Stephen Moore, 1985. "Encroachment of exotic rainbow trout into stream populations of native brook trout in southern Appalachian mountains," *Trans. Am. Fish. Soc.* 1 14:2, 195–203, March 1985.

Longstreth, T. Morris, *The Catskills*. The Century Co., New York, 1918.

Longstreth, T. Morris, *The Adirondacks*. The Century Co., New York, 1920.

Longstreth, T. Morris, *The Laurentians*. The Century Co., New York, 1922.

Lose, Charles, "The vanishing trout," Times Tribune Co., Altoona, Pa., 1931.

Macdonough, A.R., *Nepigon River Fishing, Angling*. The Outdoor Library, Charles Scribner's Sons, New York, 1896.

Mallard, E. E., *Days on the Nepigon*. Foster & Reynolds Co., New York, 1917.

Marcinko, Martin, et al., 1988. "Changes in three brook trout populations after imposition of a 17.5 cm length limit," Penn. Fish Com. Report

Mayer, Alfred M., *Sport With Rod & Gun*, The Century Company, New York, 1883.

Mayle, Peter B., 1994, U. C., Davis. Personal communication.

MacCrimmon, H.R. & J.S. Campbell, 1969. "World distribution of brook trout *Salvelinus fontinalis*," *J. Fish Res. Bd. Canada* 26: 1699–1725.

MacKay, H.H., *Fishes of Ontario, 1963*. Ont. Dept. of Lands and Forests, Bryant Press, Ltd., Bryant Press Ltd., Toronto.

McCracken, Gary F., C.R. Parker, & S. Z. Guffey, 1993. "Genetic differentiation and hybridization between hatchery stocked native brook trout in Great Smoky Mountains National Park," *Trans. Am. Fish. Soc.*, 122: 533–542.

McGlade, Jacqueline M., "Genotypic and phenotypic variation in the brook trout *Salvelinus fontinalis* (Mitchill)," Ph.D. Thesis, Univ. Guelph, Guelph, Ont., 1981.

McGlade, Jacqueline M., "Taxonomic congruence of three populations of Québec brook trout *Salvelinus fontinalis* (Mitchill)," *Can. J. Zool.*, Vol. 57, 1979, 1998–2009.

McMcol, Richard E. et al., "Quantitative field investigations of feeding and fontinalis," *Envir. Bio. of Fishes*, Vol. 12, No. 3, 219–229, 1985.

Mills, Edwin, *Paddle, Pack and Speckled Trout*, circa 1935.

Mirror, N.Y., Dec. 1837, "Three days at Lif Sneidecker's, a deer hunt."

Mitchill, Samuel L., *Fishes of New York*, D. Carlise, 1814.

Mullan, James W., "The sea-run or 'salter' brook trout *Salvelinus Fontinalis* [sic] fishery of the coastal streams of Cape Cod," *Massachusetts Bul.* 17, May, 1958, 25 pp.

Murry, William H. H., *Adventures in the Wilderness, or, Camp-Life in the Adirondacks*, Fields, Osgood & Co., Boston, 1869.

Needham, Paul R., *Trout Streams*, Comstock Pub., Ithaca, N.Y., 1940. Revised, 1969, Winchester Press, New York.

Nelson J.S., *Fishes of the World*. 1976.

O' Callaghan, E. B., M.D., *The Documentary History of the State of New York*, Albany, 1849.

Norris, Thaddeus, *The American Angler's Book*, Porter & Coates, Phila., 1864.

Orvis, Charles F. & A. Nelson Cheney, *Fishing With the Fly*, Manchester, Vt., 1883.

Perkins, David L., Charles Krueger, & Bernie May, "Heritage brook trout project," Summary Report to NYSDEC, 24 pp., 1993.

Prime, W.C., *I Go A-Fishing*, Harper Brothers, New York, 1873.

Qadri, S.U. 1964, Doctoral Thesis.

Quackenbos, John D., M.D., *Geological Ancestors of the Brook Trout.*, Tobias A. Wright, N.Y. 1916.

Ricker, William E., "Trans. feeding habits of speckled trout in Ontario waters," *Am. Fish. Soc.*, 1930, 64–70.

Roosevelt, Robert Barnwell, *Game Fish of the Northern States of America and the British Provinces*, New York, 1862.

Roosevelt, Robert Barnwell, *Superior Fishing, or the Striped Bass, Trout, Black Bass, and Bluefish of the Northern States*, Orange Judd Co., New York, 1884.

Rhead, Louis, Ed., *The Speckled Brook Trout*, R. H. Russell, New York, 1902.

Rhead, Louis, Ed., *Bait Angling for Common Fishes*, The Outing Company, New York, 1907.

Rhead, Louis, Ed., *Fisherman's Lures and Game-Fish Food*, Charles Scribner's Sons, New York, 1920.

Sale, Peter F., 1967. "A re-examination of the taxonomic position of the aurora trout," *Can. J. Zoology*, 45:215–224.

Schullery, Paul, *American Fly Fishing, A History*, Lyons & Burford, New York, 1987.

Scott, Genio C., *Fishing in American Waters*, The American News Company, New York, 1875.

Scott, W.B. & E. J. Crossman, "Freshwater fishes of Canada," *Bul. 184*, Fisheries Research Board of Canada, Ottawa, 1973.

Scott, W.B. & E. J. Crossman, 1963, *Fishes Occurring in the Freshwater Fisheries of Insular Newfoundland*, Royal Ont. Mus., Univ. Toronto, 63–75.

Shewmaker, Kenneth, *American Fly Fisher*, Manchester, Vt.

Smith, Jerome V.C., M.D., *Natural History of Fishes of Massachusetts*, Allen & Ticknor, Boston, 1833.

Smith, Hugh M., 1907. "The fishes of North Carolina," 135–36.

Smith, Gerald R. & R. F. Stearly, 1989, "The classification and names of rainbow and cut-throat trouts," *Fisheries* 14 (1): 4–10.

Southside Sportsmen's Club, 1876, "Tenth annual report," 35.

Stoddard, S. R., *The Adirondacks*, Van Benthuysen & Sons, Albany, 1879.

Stoltz, Judith & Judith Schnell, Eds., *Trout*, Stackpole Books, Harrisburg, Pa., 1991.

Stoneking, Mark, D.J. Wagner, & A.C. Hildebrand, 1981, "Genetic evidence suggesting subspecific differences between northern and southern populations of brook trout (*Salvelinus fontinalis*), *Copei*, No. 4, 810–819, 1981.

Strange, Richard J., "Our native trout of the south: Will it survive?" *Trout*.

Trapnel, Edna V., "Daniel Webster and the big brook trout," *Field & Stream Magazine*, May 1933.

Van Offelen Henry K., Charles Krueger, & Carl. L. Schofield, 1993, "Survival, growth, movement and distribution in two brook trout strains stocked into small Adirondack streams," *N.A. J. Fish. Mgnt.*, 13: 86–95, 1993.

Venters, Vic, "In search of speckles," *Wildlife in North Carolina*, July 1993.

Wallace, E.R., *Descriptive guide to the Adirondacks*, Forest and Stream Pub. Co., New York, 1872.

Webster, Dwight A., 1962, "Artificial spawning facilities for brook trout *Salvelinus fontinalis*, *Trans. Am. Fish. Soc.*, 91 (2): 168–174.

Webster, D.A. & G. Eriksdottir, "Upwelling water as a factor in influencing choice of spawning sites in brook trout *Salvelinus fontinalis*, 1976, *Trans. Am. Fish. Soc.*, 105: 416–421.

Webster, D.A. & W.A. Flick, "Performance of indigenous, exotic and hybrid strains of brook trout (*Salvelinus fontinalis*) in waters of the Adirondack mountains, New York 1981," *Can. J. Fish. Aquat. Sci.*, 38: 1701–1707.

Wilder, D.G. "A comparative study of anadromous and freshwater populations of brook trout *Salvelinus fontinalis* (Mitchill)," *Fis. Res. Bd. Can.* 9 (4), 1952, 169–203.

White, H.C., 1928. "Some observations on the eastern brook trout (*S. Fontinalis*) of Prince Edward Island," *Am. Fish. Soc.*, 101–108.

White, H.C., 1940. "Life history of sea-running brook trout (*Salvelinus fontinalis*) of Moser River, N.S.," *J. Fish. Res. Bd. Can.* 5 (2), 176–186.

White, H.C., 1941. "Migrating behavior of sea-running *Salvelinus fontinalis*," *J. Fish Res. Bd. Can.*, 5 (3), 258–264.

White, H.C., 1942, "Sea life of the brook trout (*Salvelinus fontinalis*)," *J. Fis. Res. Bd. Can.* 5 (5), 471–73.

Willers, Bill, *Trout Biology: An Angler's Guide*, Lyons & Burford, New York, 1991.

Yuskavitch, James A., 1991. "Saved by the barriers," *Trout*, Summer 1991, 1827.

INDEX

Norway, 353
Nova Scotia, 344–45

Ohio, 322–23
Ojibway, 15–16
Old Brick House, 138
Old Stone House, 138
Ontario, 345–46
Oquossoc, 222
    Club (Angling Association), 68, *208*, 209, 218–19
    Indians, 203
    Lake. *See* Rangeley, Lakes
    Stream, 203
Orvis, Charles, F., 229–30
Osprey Charters, 243
Osprey Lake, 70, 278–80
otoliths, 270
Out of Door Library: Angling, The, 236
Outdoors Canada, 20
oxygen, 54

Pack, Paddle and Speckled Trout, 20
Page, George Shepard, 205–6, 208, 214–16
Palmer Family, The, 88–89
Paramachenee, 19
Paramachenee Belle, 20, 219, 297–98
    Lake, 297
parasites, 85
parr markings, 57
Patagonia, 282–83
Pennsylvania, 323–25
periods (epochs), geological, 35–36, *36*, 45
Perkins, David, 91–92
Peseco Lake, 184–85
pH, 59, 287–88, 291
phenotype, 37, 72–73
phylogeny, *36*, 36–39
Piedmont Plateau, 50
Plymouth (Mass.) 27–29
    Rock, 28, 100
pond trout, 20, 30, 101
Porter, William Trotter, 184
Post, New York (*Evening*), 206
Prime, N. S., 141
Prime, William Cowper, 199–200
Prince Edward Island, 346
provincialism, scientific, 93

Quadri, S. U., 44
Québec, 346–49

Rabbit Rapids (McDonald Rapids), 15, 26
Rangeley,
    James, 203–4
    Lakes, 202–22, *204*, 293
    (Oquossoc) Lake, 205
Rattlesnake Creek, 140, 145
records, 70–71, 241, 269–70
Red Rock, 225, 227, 234, 235

redds, 63, 242
Reed, Roland, 279
refugia,
    Atlantic, 94, 96
    first, 89, 125
    Mississippi (Great Lakes), 48, 98
regulations, 102, 156–57, 270, 285. See *also individual states*
reproduction, 61–64
Return a Gift to Wildlife, 79
Rhead, Louis, 43, 251
Rhode Island, 325
Richardson, C. T. 208–9, *211*
Richardson, John, 41
Rinkenbach, 84–86
"rivers" versus "brooks," 133
RNA, 111
Rockwell, Verne LaSalle, 153
Rod & Gun, 12
Roosevelt, Robert Barnwell, 144, 152, 173–74, 226
    Theodore, 150, 201, 222
Roscoe, NY, 179
Rowe, John, 132
Ruminski, Tom, 260

Sacandaga River (lake), 183–84
Saibling, 39
Sale, P. F., 86
Salmo fontinalis, 12, 42–44, 104
Salmo Fontinalis, 169
salmon (Atlantic), 35, 36, 61, 94, 102, 184, 218, 220, 239
    black, 115
    Sebago, 283
salmon (Pacific), 241
salmon trout, 12
Salmonidae, 35
salters, 30, 57, 100–19, 116–17, *132*
Salvelinus, 32, 38–39
Salvelinus fontinalis. See brook trout
Saskatchewan, 351
scales, cycloid, 56
Schullery, Paul, 135, 183
Schuylkill Club, 125
Scott, Genio C., 109, *135*, 137, 174
Scribner's Monthly, 210–11
sculpin, 16, 116, *297*, 243
sea trout, 27, 100–19, *113*, 146, 151. *See also* salters
    distribution, 101–2, *112*
    growth, 115
    map, 112
    migrations, 114–15
    waters, *112*
Sea-Trout Fishing, 110–11
Sears, George Washington (Nessmunk), 18
Seymour, Prof. Edward, 210–11
Shewmaker, Kenneth, 12–14
Shikellemus, vii